EPICUREAN DELIGHT

The Life and Times of

JAMES BEARD

Evan Jones

A Fireside Book
Published by Simon & Schuster
New York   London   Toronto   Sydney   Tokyo   Singapore

FIRESIDE
Simon & Schuster Building
Rockefeller Center
1230 Avenue of the Americas
New York, New York 10020

First Fireside edition, 1992
Published by arrangement with Alfred A. Knopf, Inc.
FIRESIDE and colophon are registered trademarks
of Simon & Schuster Inc.
Manufactured in the United States of America

1   3   5   7   9   10   8   6   4   2

Library of Congress Cataloging in Publication Data

Jones, Evan, date.
Epicurean delight: the life and times of James Beard/Evan
Jones.
p.   cm.
Originally published: New York: Knopf, 1990.
"A Fireside book."
Includes index.
1. Beard, James, 1903–   . 2. Cooks—United
States—Biography.   I. Title.
[TX649.B43J66   1992]
641.5′092—dc20
[B]   92-13946
CIP
ISBN: 0-671-75026-7

Front matter illustrations copyright © 1981, 1983
by Karl W. Stuecklen.
Photographic acknowledgments can be found on page 367.

For his friends,

and for his editor—mine, too

"What is patriotism but the love

of the good things we ate in our childhood."

— LIN YUTANG

Contents

Acknowledgments

Although I knew James Beard for eighteen years, my work on this book is the essence of all that has been contributed by others, some of whom knew him much longer and some of whom knew him much more intimately.

For sharing memories, and for original material, insights, information, and for practical help, I should like to thank the following:

Sam and Florence Aaron, Michael Aaron, Charlotte Adams, Jerry Alden, Beverly Allen, Len Allison, Albert Aschaffenburg, Gerald Asher, Grace B. Atkinson, Carl August, Mrs. S. Brooks Barron, Naomi Barry, Michael and Ariane Batterberry, Joseph and Ruth Baum, Janet Baumhover, Jean Beatty, Simone Beck, Jane Benet, John Bennett, Jerry Berns, Ruth Birnkrant, John Brady, Dale Brown, Pat Brown, Philip and Lois Brown, Cecily Brownstone, Neil Brunkhurst, R. S. Callvert, Angus Cameron, John Carroll, Harriet Cass, Narcisse Chamberlain, Mollie Chappellet, Isabella Chappell, Cecilia Chiang, Julia and Paul Child, Emmett D. Chisum, Craig Claiborne, Gino Cofacci, Keith Cohn, R. C. Cosgrove, Marion Cunningham, Julie Dannenbaum, John and Sally Darr, Elizabeth David, Susy Davidson, Jack and Jamie Davies, Jim Dodge, Sean Driscoll, Jane Ellis, Merle Ellis, Ella Elvin, Daphne Engstrom, Elizabeth Erman, John Ferrone, M.F.K. Fisher, Larry Forgione, Bill Fotiades, Pierre Franey, Cornelius French, Sr., Sarah Fritschner, Gwen Gaillard, Morris Galen, Eleanor Bretmeyer Gelbert, Ronnine Giacomini, Emily Gilder, Maggie Gin, Edward and Ellie Giobbi, Carl Gohs, Mary Goodbody, William and Martha Goolrick, Marion Gorman, Robert Gourdin, Tony Green, Gael Greene, Maryon Greenough, Francis Guth, Denise Hale, Mary Hamblet, Zack Hanle, Victor and Marcella Hazan, Nika Hazelton, Helen and Hank Hazen, Frank Hearne, Maida Heatter, Jean Henniger, Jean Hewitt, Janie Hibben, Grete

Hobbs, Catherine Laughton Hindley, William Hollingsworth, Ken Hom, Mary Homi, Norris Houghton, Madhur Jaffrey, William North Jayme, Margaret Jennings, Carl Jerome, Dorothy Johanson, J. Wilson Johnston, William Kaduson, Lea Kates Karp, David Keh, Martha Kelly, Michael Kinane, Malvina Kinard, Marion Kingery, Robin Klingberg, Alfred A. Knopf, Jr., Helen Knopf, Mayburn Koss, Paul Kovi, Otto Kraschauer, Irene Kuhn, Loni Kuhn, Albert Kumin, Peter Kump, Eric Ladd, Jerry Lamb, George and Jenifer Lang, Florence Layman, Fred Lazarus, Leon and Aphrodite Leonides, Leo Lerman, Mateo Lettunich, Alan Lewis, Alexis Lichine, Mary Lyons, Jean MacAusland, Elaine Mack, Jacqueline Mallorca, Stanley Marcus, Tom Margitai, Lydie Marshall, Jerry Mason, Bob Mayberry, E. Kimball MacColl, Alan McDermott, Glenna McGinnis, Bettina and Henry McNulty, Anne Mendelson, Susie Menefee, Janet Mercereau, Mrs. Robert Milch, Philip Miles, Jane Montant, Angelo Montuori, Edris Morrison, Charles Morris Mount, Francis Murphy, James and Helen Nassikas, Marshall Neale, Richard Nelson, Maureen Neuburger, Bill Newsom, Richard Nimmo, Anita Odeur, Cornelius O'Donnell, Don Osell, Denise Otis, Mary Jane Peel, Angelo Pellegrini, Jacques Pepin, Gail Perrin, Eleanor Peters, George and Sally Pillsbury, Anna Piper, Gene Poll, Toula Polygalaktos, A. L. (Bill) Powell, Alice Provensen, Geraldine Rhoads, Chet Rhodes, William Rice, Phyllis C. Richman, Edward C. Ritchell, Claudia Roden, Felipé Rojas-Lombardi, Yvonne Rothert, Frederick A. Rufe, Irene Sax, Mrs. John Schaffner, Jimmy Schmidt, Mrs. Frank Schoonmaker, Ann Seranne, Mimi Sheraton, Harmony Joy Slayton, André Soltner, Carl Sontheimer, Gwenyth Spitz, Lyn Stallworth, Harvey Steiman, Jane Nickerson Steinberg, Jack Stipe, Helen Stockli Stoll, Roger W. Straus, Julian Street, Jr., Caroline Stuart, Jean Sugg, André Surmain, Barbara Thornton, Raymond Thuilier, Jeremiah Tower, Clayton Triplette, Marian Tripp, Thomas and Sherry Vaughan, René Verdon, James Villas, Jeanne Voltz, Philip and Jocelyn Wagner, Maggie Waldron, Heidi Waleson, Betty Ward, Alice Waters, Harvey Welch, Ray Wemmlinger, Frederick Wildman, Jr., William F. Wilkinson, Chuck Williams, Helen S. Wilson, Burton Wolf, Clark Wolf, Mary Hunter Wolf, Paula Wolfert, Guy Wong, Jim Wood, Marjorie Dean Woodward, Helen Worth, Dan and Rita Wynn, Kathy Zuckerman. The handsome translation of the manuscript into type is the work of Anthea Lingeman.

Special thanks to Robert Lescher, valiant agent and friend—and to Judith Bailey Jones, last but always first.

Epicurean Delight

The Life and Times of

James Beard

1

"MUCH TO INFLUENCE MY PROFESSIONAL LIFE"

For a lot of people who knew him, the photograph of James Beard that remains most poignantly memorable shows him moving ponderously away from the camera, a giant hulking figure, his back to the lens, with rutted Pacific sands dominating the misty seascape. Again and again, for more years than not, Beard was drawn to the same Oregon coastline on which he spent the summers of his childhood. He came home repeatedly to Gearhart, to Seaside, to Cannon Beach, searching perhaps for portents that shaped his maverick life. Following his death, at age eighty-one, a few months after a sea trip to Alaska, his ashes were deposited at a nearby point of land he cherished, a place he had chosen very early for looking toward the ocean.

Gearhart, Oregon, was the focus of his childhood holidays—a tiny vacation village that appeased his mother's annual desire for country living, accented by foods fresh from the water, wild meadows, and woods. Elizabeth Beard's notion of life and its choices was the dominant influence on her child. Her husband John Beard tossed and turned in her wake. Their son drew in numerous ways from his mother's penchant for action and from his father's ability to deal with the best chances that came his way. Elizabeth Beard prevailed. "I grew up in the helter-skelter of her life," her son recalled.

Much of James Beard's writing (he was the author of twenty-two books on food as well as syndicated newspaper columns that reflected the larger story of an evolving analysis of American food) was autobiographical. "The kitchen, reasonably enough," he points out in his *Delights and Prejudices,* "was the scene of my first gastronomical adventure. I was on all fours. I crawled into the vegetable bin, settled on a giant onion and ate it, skin and all. It must have marked me for life." An insatiable acceptance of foods of all kinds, of every ethnic source, got him started on his remarkable lifetime pursuit, and his abnormally healthy appetites were exposed to the many new experiences that came along, from the first of his childhood summers at Gearhart, on the Oregon coast.

Food was also his mother's pleasure, as well as her livelihood. Elizabeth Jones was one of twelve children in a Welsh-English family of the midnineteenth century, and at the age of three she had been taken to live in the Irish countryside when her father was hired to manage property belonging to William E. Gladstone, England's four-time prime minister. As a British Liberal and party leader, Gladstone made repeated efforts to bring home rule to the Irish, and his policies often focused on agricultural progress to improve the lot of the average man. Reflecting his interest in food production, for example, he proposed that small firms be organized to transform fruits into jams and preserves.

There may be no reason to presume that young Elizabeth knew much of the ideals of her father's employer, however they affected Ireland. But her son believed that she had a deep affinity for the food as well as the people of all provincial precincts. "As a little girl," he said, "my mother would invite herself into the homes of rural families in that part of Ireland. She had a way with people, and even then apparently she so charmed these neighbors that they invited her to share their limited fare." Beard never lost his admiration for his mother's ease with neighbors and others she dealt with or for her accumulated knowledge of gastronomy gained in the various places where she later lived.

Few who knew Beard in his adult years heard him voice such open admiration of his father, but, earlier, his son had sketchily recorded memories of John Beard's influence on family life. In the 1860s the elder Beard, when only five, had traveled with his family by covered wagon from Iowa to Linn County, Oregon. On the infrequent occasions when he appeared at weekend gatherings on the coast,

Beard's father showed the skills, as mood dictated, learned on the cross-country trail in his boyhood. He taught his son knacks of campfire cooking he had picked up, and sometimes sprinkled in some appreciation of Indians he had observed.

At the same time, John Beard was urbane, and fond of city comforts. In his son's view he was a brilliant man, the only one in a family of sixteen children to go to college. He became a teacher, then a pharmacist, and eventually left Silverton, a farm town, for a political appointment as assistant appraiser of the port of Portland. The urban inclination, which included appreciation of fine meals, may have had much to do with his marriage to Elizabeth Beard.

In the burgeoning Portland of the 1890s, James Beard's parents found friends in common. By the turn of the century, Elizabeth had shown herself to be an enterprising and much-traveled adventurer; widowed after a year of marriage to a builder and sometime engineer named John Brennan, she later became the proprietress of a small residential hotel. Her life had taken her farther than across the plains by covered wagon—from Gladstone's Irish holdings to the other side of the Atlantic, and by circuitous routes to the Pacific West.

In her odyssey she had paused first in the Park Lane section of Victorian London when her parents, burdened by too many offspring and her mother's bad health, agreed to send her off to live with childless relatives. In a modest house of an aunt and uncle who might today be described as "born again" (her foster parents were followers of Dwight L. Moody, founder of modern evangelism, whose sermons in London drew great audiences), ten-year-old Elizabeth soon began to feel cooped up. She spent her adolescence under the pressure of these foster parents, who insisted that she study the Moody tracts, while she inwardly resisted. As her son put it, "The strictness of this religious environment was not pleasant for my mother." The two of them had much in common, some of it a restlessness drawn from their Welsh ancestors.

In her midteens she got to know several staff members of a steamship company who were friends, and sometimes guests, of her uncle. "At sixteen—unbeknownst of course to her aunt and uncle— she made a deal for a passage to America. Her thirst for life and her curiosity about all new things must have made a strong impression on her benefactors." Throughout Jim Beard's life there are plenty of indications that he and his mother had similar instincts. Perhaps with her encouragement, he suspected that she hadn't been charged for her trip—just as during his own adventurous times there were occasions when he was not required to pay as ordinary mortals do.

Though he admired his mother as a statuesque, attractive young woman with flashing eyes and beautiful skin, he remembered particularly her sense of humor. As to setting forth alone—he told friends wryly, "I believe it's called 'running away from home.'" The transatlantic journey that finally ended for Elizabeth in Oregon was interrupted first in Toronto. Here lived a relative sufficiently hospitable to shelter her briefly. Young Elizabeth, for her part, was bent on independence, her son believed; she was eager to make her own way, and to see the country.

Through a classified ad in a Toronto newspaper, Elizabeth obtained the kind of position affluent post–World War II British households would later come to think of as an au pair—employment in middle-class families for girls of similar social standing. In Toronto, she signed on as a serendipitous babysitter with a family about to emigrate to the United States. The trip west was to convince her that the booming Pacific coast was the place to settle down, and she was much taken with Portland, even then becoming known as the City of Roses. It was a salubrious place that some travelers described as comparable to San Francisco. A vital Pacific port, harboring scores of lean four-masted windjammers, Portland was dominated by residential hills looking down on the Willamette River, where ferries laced their way back and forth until the Morrison Street bridge was built in 1887.

Arriving in Portland in this period, Beard's mother was to establish herself socially through the family for whose children she was governess. Confidently, when her employers were called back to Canada, Beard recalled, she decided to travel, earning her way by teaching and cooking. He was clearly impressed with her ability, even as a young woman in strange circumstances, to somehow land on her feet, and he saw it as an inherited attribute.

He admired his mother for deciding to live in Portland, and he told of how she had saved her money until she could afford a trip to

London for what was to be a final visit with her aunt and uncle. Beard said they had been aghast at the news that their ward had decided to become an American. "So she, without really knowing how serious this was, decided she would make 'exhibit A' of her success in this country. She booked a room at the old Grand Hotel in Trafalgar Square, which was the Ritz of your grandmother's school days. She hired a carriage and drove out to Park Lane to visit her aunt and uncle in true style, with presents for each of them." When they coldly rejected her, she resolved never to come back. "As a matter of fact, she never again saw her mother and father, either," Beard once said in a conversation about his life. "I suppose it was something that started me on the same road—this disregard of family, but regard for tried and true friends."

His mother's leisurely journey back to Portland took her to San Francisco, then on a side trip to Panama when the early canal excavations were being made by the French. With her traveling companion, she came by way of the Caribbean. Of all this sightseeing, what appealed to her most, and would continue to be her own and her family's favorite mecca, was the city by the bay. She had discovered San Francisco during a boom period, when it was gaining renown for its splendid edifices such as the Palace Hotel and the ornate Taj Mahal–like hostelry that Lucky Baldwin (Elias J. Baldwin), whose immense wealth had come from the Comstock lode, had named for himself. With a population of more than 200,000, San Francisco was becoming cosmopolitan, and it attracted international celebrities. The soprano Adelina Patti brought her own three cooks to the Palace, where chef Ernest Arbogast's European kitchen staff was making the hotel dining room famous. Thus, Jim Beard's mother, with her interest in food, was more than superficially impressed with San Francisco's de luxe hotels, and she had already set her heart on a career in the "hospitality business" when she met Frances Curtis. This new acquaintance, the proprietress of several small residential hotels, was looking for someone to manage a new establishment in Portland.

In growing up, Beard heard a lot about Elizabeth's footloose days, and he seemed to relish the idea of a young woman of her generation skittering about, as adventure tempted her. He savored her stories of San Francisco visits and vacations in New York, where she was enthralled by the theater and got to know some actors. He came to understand that his mother's knowledge of Panama and the Caribbean was uncommon, and that not only was she singularly aware of unusual cooking but also devoted to high kitchen standards. From the start of her management of the Curtis Hotel in Portland, she emphasized culinary style, and people who thought they knew something about good food were drawn to the residential hotel on the slope of Morrison at the corner of Southwest Twelfth Avenue. Four years later, in 1896, she bought her own residential hotel and named it the Gladstone, a tribute to her father's employer who had recently retired from British public life. To maintain her reputation for serving good food, she developed a scheme to hire several European chefs, master their specific skills, then let them move on. She learned that she could teach some of the techniques to a new Chinese staff, and in the process she discovered a Cantonese named Jue Let, who for years was to dominate her kitchens because of his ability to cook as well as his employer.

With Let at her side when she needed him, Jim's mother, her son believed, established a reputation for "spectacular professional entertaining." She was adept at social graces, and she had become well known locally, while running the Curtis, for food that some considered as good as the best meals served in San Francisco, or even the fare of New York. Her talk of travel, and her instincts about others, proved to be the sort of attributes that impressed people of a Western city eager to consider themselves "cultivated."

By the end of the century, Portland was moving into its fifth decade and gathering newcomers from various points of the compass. In its boom years, its population had zoomed past the hundred-thousand mark, and some affluent Portlanders were pushed by the muggy summers to oceanside homes at such places as Gearhart and Seaside. For Beard's mother there were also evidences of entrenched civilization in the damp winters enlivened by trips to San Francisco concerts and enjoyment of its flourishing theater season. Touring companies from New York, led by such headliners as Helena Modjeska and E. H. Sothern, the best Shakespearean of his generation, made regular appearances. In addition, the sense of style and hospitality which Beard attributed to his mother had brought her friends of some sophistication, including the impressive General Owen Summers, a retired army officer who became Beard's godfather and was extravagantly remembered by him as "one of the great *bon vivants* of his time."

In later years, Beard thought his mother might have been content to maintain her establishment with great flair and energy for the rest of her days had it not been for matchmaking friends. General Summers and his wife, Clara, thought she should marry and share her zest with their friend John Beard, a widower with an eighteen-year-old daughter. The Gladstone's chatelaine was described by her son as a woman with "a good figure for those days, and she carried her pounds with grace and aplomb. Her complexion was the pink and white of the British Isles, and her black hair was extremely fine, worn in a French roll from the top of her head to her neck, where curly wisps called 'scolders' were arranged." That James Beard should sketch such details so many years later reflects something of the impression she made on his father, a man of considerable distinction himself. The son believed that his mother, however, chose to marry simply on the strength of her desire to have a baby.

Elizabeth Beard never lost the flair. Discovering soon after the ceremony in 1899 that her bridegroom was in debt, she paid off his creditors by selling the Gladstone Hotel, then built a house at Salmon and Twenty-third streets. Wanting nothing of her husband but a child, as her son saw things, she gave birth in 1903—at the age of forty-two and at a time when a first pregnancy so late in a woman's life was a risk not often taken—to a 14-pound son. He inherited her soft British complexion and her tendency to carry excess pounds easily, but his hair proved to be golden and thin.

From Portland's Chinatown, a community as thriving as any ethnic neighborhood on the Pacific coast, the new mother recruited an amah to watch over her blond progeny, and from the Gladstone she brought Let, who remained as a family fixture, freely coming and going until later in Beard's youth he returned to his home in China. As long as Let was on the scene, the boy was watched over by the cook. "When I was three years old and recovering from a long siege of malaria," Beard wrote, "our old Jue Let used to make small pots of chicken jelly for me almost every day."

Elizabeth Beard needed Let to help in catering meals for party givers, as well as in feeding the boarders in her new house. And Let's relationship with the youngest family member wasn't forgotten by the little boy. "I'm certain those little pots of true essence of chicken established a flavor sense for me I've never lost," Beard wrote. It was clear to him that his infant world was centered more often than not in the kitchen, either in the Portland house or during the summers spent in the Beard family cottage in Gearhart.

Jim grew up with enthusiasm for Gearhart and its coastal surroundings, for the lure of the ocean, in his mother's mind, was as important as any part of her life in Portland. Jim professed not to know when she had discovered, and then become smitten by, the Northwest coast and its bounty, but from the first he looked on it as his own territorial imperative as well. His mother, maintaining her connections with Frances Curtis in San Francisco and her general interest in hotels, certainly knew of the Holiday House in Seaside—it was a resort built by the pioneer promoter Ben Holiday as a way to draw passengers for his steamship line that followed the coast north from the Golden Gate. In contrast, she had chosen sparsely populated Gearhart, just above Seaside, because of its vacation appeal.

Beard remembered that he was five years old at the beginning of the first summer in Gearhart; in 1910, when he was seven, the family built a small beach house in what was then considered a remote part of a coastal meadow. About seventy-five miles west and somewhat north of Portland, their oceanside community was on the old Spokane, Portland and Seattle Railroad line. In a sense, it was a world away, and preparations for each summer seemed unforgettable to Beard: "I have gone to Europe for a year's stay with less packing and far less strain."

For the annual three-to-four-month stay, plus weekends in early spring and even winter, Mrs. Beard made sure she was prepared for any contingency. Convinced in the years before World War I that the Seaside markets carried inadequate merchandise, she made advance trips to Portland suppliers to insure a summer's quota of wax paper, wrapping paper, and bathroom tissue. She ordered such staples as dried beans, rice, spices, and other seasonings, and an emergency supply of canned goods. Because she hated the musty smell that linens took on when they were stored in the beach house, her son recalled, she bought new stock each year.

Two or three days before leaving Portland, the household was in tumult. There was likely to be a ham simmering, and bread in the oven along with hot dishes to see the Beards through the arrival period at the beach. The food went into wicker hampers, linens and clothes into an outsized trunk, kitchen supplies and miscellaneous items into huge packing cases. Everything was picked up by a horse-drawn hack that carried the family to the station, where they piled into the same passenger cars year after year with the help of familiar porters. For Jim, the annual Gearhart exodus was a series of rehearsals for a future of almost constant travel.

"We had to arrive at the station early," he wrote, "or I made a frightful scene." He made sure he was in his best traveling togs, and he saw himself as "a little dandy" much concerned with his wardrobe. He made enough fuss to insure that a certain chair on the observation platform was his alone. "I have never enjoyed trains as much as I did then, sitting in the open air, having a little box of marmalade sandwiches, and a hard boiled egg, and some fruit and cookies to while away the hours till lunch." It didn't matter to him if smoke and coal dust billowed around him—he saw the trip "as if I were touring the countryside on my back porch."

Inside the cars the ride was noisy with children running up and down the aisles to see who else was aboard, and to see who could recognize familiar landmarks first. The stop on the Columbia River at the village of Rainier was significant because people who knew Mrs. Beard came to the platform to exchange greetings through the train windows. At Astoria, on the river's vast mouth, there was a layover and the unpacking of food that Jim's mother had prepared for all the youngsters. "Then on we went over an endless trestle spanning Young's Bay, which thrilled me beyond words, for it was like going to sea."

A Reed College historian who grew up in Seaside described the stretch of the resort coast from Seaside to Cannon Beach as comparable to a small-scale Newport, Rhode Island. While there were modest houses, like that of the Beards', with shingled siding, or constructed of slats and boards, the appearance of grandeur was due to the number of affluent "houses with piazzas" with perhaps a Pierce Arrow sedan parked in a driveway, and to the Seaside stretch of hard sand and Sunday promenading—by much of the population in fine array, with parasols here and there. Beard thought Seaside, population 5,193, quite the opposite of Gearhart, population 961. It lacked the latter's isolation, and attracted "outsiders" because of its dance halls, restaurants, and places to shop.

Only three miles away by train, Seaside had one abiding temptation for youngsters that Beard never forgot. It was West's Dairy, an ice cream hangout, home of five-cent milkshakes whose twenty-eight flavors included tutti-frutti, of course, along with cherry, wild blackberry, and blue huckleberry. "I can see the soda jerks now, scraping the ice from a tremendous block, putting it in a mixing glass, adding the fruit, and then the whole milk," Beard once told me. "It was probably the best five cents' worth of anything I ever had." In fact there were times when he would walk the three miles to Seaside in order to save the nickel fare of the train ride for spending when he got to the ice cream stand.

In general for the Beard family, sweet tooths were more often satisfied by several kinds of berries that could be gathered in such abundance along back stretches of the coast, or by the Bing cherries his father picked from the big trees in the family's backyard in Portland and sent in large splitwood baskets to Gearhart. On the occasions when he was at the beach house, the elder Beard would join his wife and son and the Hamblet family, who were their close friends, and he earned his son's applause for finding wild food that everyone else might overlook, including the huckleberries that grew in hidden swales, as well as wild strawberries and bramble bushes laden with blackberries that were too tart to eat from the vine. These were the stuff of which jams and jellies were made by Elizabeth Beard to take back to Portland, and they also were dried in the sun for winter use in sauces and pies. Huckleberries became a special treat when they were cooked in a much-loved four-egg cake.

Five decades or more after the childhood summers that presaged Beard's urge to cross oceans, he dedicated his book of memoirs to Mary Patricia Hamblet, the child of Harry and Polly Hamblet, who, three years younger, was one of his Gearhart playmates and remained a part of his life until he died. Her mother, Polly (known as Grammie to young Portlanders), was Elizabeth Beard's closest companion at the beach; Harry Hamblet was one of the first Oregonians to ship oysters from Maryland and established the oyster beds on nearby Shoalwater Bay.

Jim remembered early mornings in the Gearhart kitchen when his mother and Harry Hamblet opened dozens of oysters fresh from the beds, then cooked them in pounds of butter. They weren't deep-fried oysters, he tried to make clear, but instead they were dipped in egg and cracker crumbs, sautéed briskly enough to heat them through, then seasoned with lemon juice, freshly ground pepper, and garnished with bacon and crisp toast.

The Hamblets had 100-pound sacks of the Shoalwater oysters delivered to their beach house every week—which guaranteed a variety of treats for the two families. But the high point, Jim recalled, would come after an early-morning adventure of clamming and crabbing followed by a dip in the surf. Then the children would climb the sand dunes with ravenous appetites as they found their way home and were met by the aroma of breakfast—"a mixture of melting butter and coffee gently simmering." He could envision the kitchen years later, the sight of crusted oysters waiting while butter bubbled in two huge iron skillets in which the oysters were cooked and turned out on plates as soon as all were seated at the table.

Apt to wake early, he spent scores of dawns as a boy sneaking up on Pacific razor clams, described by somebody as "the world's fastest burrowers." Sometimes accompanied by a dozen playmates, Beard mastered the damp art of following receding waves near Tillamook Head, scanning the smooth sand as the water slid outward, and immediately spotting the dimples or squirts as clam necks began to retreat downward. The trick was to be so swift that he could grab the shiny brown clams before they disappeared. Razor clams can be out of sight in seven seconds, and they shoot down under the beach surface at nine inches a minute. On a good day, he might have a couple of bucketfuls to bring home so that his mother could turn them into clam fritters.

His friend Mary and others remembered just that flavor of a Gearhart summer and its great variety of shellfish. Marion Kingery, a playmate who is still summering in a house of much glass and superlative views of the tide and Tillamook Head, described her recollections of tubby towheaded Jamie (as she and others chose to call him) walking from his family's cottage through wild sweet peas and primrose blossoms toward the ocean. She shared her friend's nostalgia for that "idyllic existence" of beach life, swimming, and crabbing. The ocean was a challenge.

"I was considered a daredevil swimmer," Jim said. "I'd swim out beyond the breakers. People used to tear their hair out because I was willful—but I knew my own strength." On some Saturday nights in summer a swimming teacher supervised races. "There was a girl almost as fat as I was," Jim remembered. "We would have to race each other, and I always beat her and made her horribly mad."

He was a youngster who wanted everything, wanted never to lose. And his mother wanted her son to be a winner, too—by seeing to it that he always arrived at the beach bearing food. "We all wanted to be with Jamie because he brought the best sandwiches," Mrs. Kingery recalled. His showing off as a swimmer was no problem for most of the beach gang, because he also came armed with a long-handled garden tool to join the raking in of crabs, Mrs. Kingery remembered vividly. "We just picked them up, and we sold some of them for twenty-five cents apiece. And afterwards we'd usually meet at the old coastal hotel where Mrs. Beard often supervised the preparation of dinner."

"The Hotel Gearhart and Natatorium"

Elizabeth Beard liked to think she was on vacation, simply because she was out of the city. She was a workaholic by nature, however, never one to miss the opportunity to reinforce her independence from her husband. She was known to vacationing Oregonians for her willingness to prepare meals at her cottage. "She would only take as many reservations as she chose to handle—no overbooking," Helen Knopf testified. Years after she had become the wife of Alfred A. Knopf, who was Jim's last publisher, Mrs. Knopf wrote to a friend of an earlier encounter at Gearhart. "She was a marvelous cook—everything from scratch," Mrs. Knopf remembered. "I got reservations for myself and six *ravenous* teenagers—they and I had been up and down the beach all day and we arrived before she was ready. She met us at the door and suggested to the teeners they go down on the beach and 'play,' and she would ring a bell. Instead they stood outside like a pack of drooling wolves. When she came out, they stampeded in. She was more than equal—in such good humor. They went through the delicious food like Grant took Richmond. I paid her double and felt guilty at that."

Mrs. Knopf remembered Elizabeth Beard as a hostess so vividly that she forgot the specifics of the menu. Others forgot that Jim's mother could admit that her best friend, Polly Hamblet, topped her at cooking Dungeness crabmeat in a baked dish. Jim was given to saying it was his favorite way with crab, and, with his mother's indulgence of her friend, called it Grammie Hamblet's Deviled Crab. He gives Mrs. Hamblet's recipe in a couple of his books.

Remembering the food of his past was a way to accent the glimpses Jim so easily brought to mind of the shared life of the two families. The articles he wrote for magazines were full of nostalgia, as are the few letters that remain. A half-century later, in writing to his friend Isabel Callvert, he said, "I think my first picnic memory was a thriller. We were invited by the Hamblets to go out in a great touring car—which opened at the rear. Everyone had their dusters on, and the ladies had their veils, and we were a gay group that chugged off to the countryside around Vancouver [Washington]. We had a great hamper of club sandwiches especially made for Harry Hamblet by the Royal Bakery. . . . What a whirl this first automobile ride seemed to me! It was as if I had suddenly been thrust into another age."

His future travel, in every sort of vehicle, was to shape his life as much as any single factor. But then, more than is true of most lives, his boyhood surroundings seasoned his career. The small cottage in a meadow was not far from the end of the Lewis and Clark Trail, where, two centuries earlier, the explorers had found Indians trading pounded salmon stored in pyramidal piles of rush baskets. For Beard's family, he liked to say, there seemed to be an endless flow of salmon through the house. Recalling his inherited appetite for all fish of the Northwest, he told how his father often talked of the way the Chinooks smoked and cured salmon as their winter food; John Beard would take his son to Astoria, which had been a fishing ground long before the first white traders arrived, for the Chinooks were an important Columbia

River tribe distinguished by their ability to catch salmon by the hundreds in kettle-shaped baskets.

John Beard had seen the Indians spearing and smoking salmon as a child, and he was admiring of Chinook skills. He kept his memories of the way they contrived their primitive grilling equipment by bending branches of spiraea, or sometimes alder, and tying the twigs together to form what Jim called "cages," to be suspended over slow-burning fires. He had been impressed to see an Indian woman slip a split fish between thin branches and hold the contraption in front of a mound of embers, adjusting the upright slant as necessary to cook the salmon without charring.

Jim savored as well the short trips with his father from Gearhart to Astoria, "a city on piers," as he described it, "with canneries and nets and fishing boats strung along the waterfront as far as the eye could see." On Astoria's hills in his youth, the streets were crowded with pigtailed Chinese who, along with increasing numbers of Swedes and Finns, cut up the fish for canning. He would go to the cannery and ask a worker for fifty cents' worth of salmon cheeks. Some of the Chinese who had been around for years knew the Beards and their feeling that the cheeks were a great delicacy, and the workers would go through a pile of heads to extract the small rounds so that they could be taken home and sautéed in butter. But more commonly, he and his mates, he said, would spend many days fishing at the mouth of the Necanicum River, where they caught crayfish and pogy, a flat fish resembling a sole. These were split open, cleaned, and cooked Indian style at a beach fire.

Polly Hamblet and Elizabeth Beard, both British by birth if not both professionals, were similarly enthusiastic about cooking. Mrs. Beard turned down invitations to dinner at other houses, telling her son that there was no sense in giving up the pleasures of eating well just because she was at the beach. "Our mothers would alternate Saturdays, having each other's family for dinner," Mary Hamblet remembered. "And they always had tea together—they served the best scones. But our fathers didn't have much in common. As a matter of fact, my father, whose family were in the hotel business in Massachusetts, was always talking food with Mrs. Beard."

John Beard was sometimes perceived by his son as a romantic, if for no other reason than his firsthand knowledge of the Oregon Trail. As Jim reported it in 1983, generations of the Beard family, over a period of sixty years, had trekked from the Carolinas through Kentucky and the Middle West to the Cascade Mountains. To be just one generation removed from the covered wagon, he said to me once, made him feel "allied to this country's gastronomic treasures." John Beard's family held some old Southern tastes with Scottish overtones. While the others talked more sophisticatedly of cooking details (they rejected his idea that spinach or other greens should cook four hours with hog jowl), the elder Beard retained a few unchallenged skills. He was a gourmet when it came to mushrooms. When spring arrived, Jim saw his father prove again and again that he was his family's most dependable finder of morels. And when he took time to catch trout for a family meal, Jim was sometimes at his side as they moseyed along streams and talked frontier history.*

His mother's palate had developed from the exposure her travels had given her to a variety of cooking styles. His father's tastes were closer to the earth, less sophisticated, but at least as appreciative of the fundamental pleasures of eating—and savoring. Jim divined from his father's conversation a perception of family menus which in a historical sense reflected the regional distinctions of the land. New waves of immigration brought new ways of preparing all kinds of food, but his father himself was proof of how tastes in America were carried by generations of a single family on a slow journey from one coast to another. Throughout the rest of his life, Jim was attuned to the importance of food in understanding the American way of life.

He left various observations of his mother's influence. "More and more I think about Mother's small woodstove at Gearhart," he wrote, "and the dishes that issued from that tiny kitchen. I still wonder at her technique. She could even do popovers in that stove, and without iron forms. Her hand was her infallible gauge." In those times there wasn't a lot of difference between cooking in the kitchen or out of it. John Beard's wagon-train know-how was refined by Elizabeth Beard as she perfected her own campfire methods. Both parents,

---

*Jim thought his father cooked trout better than anyone else, by frying it with bacon bits and then dressing it with cream gravy.

however, were models for Jim in his own mastery of outdoor skills, and he adapted many of his mother's techniques and shared them in the several cookbooks he wrote that made him the first nationally known exponent of backyard barbecuing.

Beard's mother was as intense in her approach to cooking-in-the-open as a White House chef preparing for a state dinner. To feed as many as two dozen diners, she assigned fireside duty to guests, her son remembered, and sometimes ordered them to arrive with food to extend the menu. Even for a breakfast party, they would go to the beach an hour or so before anyone else, laden with baskets, equipment, and a checklist of what others were to bring.

With the wood collected and the racks for the skillets and griddles set up, the makings of coffee (the kettle boiling, and the egg shells and cheesecloth for straining on the side) were set in motion. As guests began to turn up, it was time to start the bacon, toast the buns, arrange the fruit, and lay knives and forks and spoons on tablecloths smoothed out on the sand. Many times, guests were lucky enough to be in sight of the great perpendicular knob of ground called Tillamook Head and the high ridge with sweeping views. Or they could see Tillamook Lighthouse, with its rock base rising ninety-one feet above the water, and gulls wheeling over foamy waves.

It was then that Beard learned his mother's knack of grilling salmon over glowing coals, brushing the fish with bacon fat or butter; and her patience in broiling a steak to perfection. He judged his mother had a foolproof sense of timing, and he subscribed to her theory—people could wait for a steak, but she'd be damned, she said, if the steak would wait for people. The meat had to be a thick, aged porterhouse from her own butcher in Portland, and she cooked it slowly so that it developed a good crust yet was rare and juicy. As accompaniments, Beard remembered the crisp-bottomed sliced potatoes fried in skillets, and Grammie Hamblet's salad of boiled potatoes mixed with mayonnaise, grated onion, chopped parsley, and boiled eggs. His mother's version was made with oil and vinegar poured over hot potatoes, with a sprinkling of chopped onion and parsley when the salad had cooled.

In sentimental moments he told friends that summer at the beach seemed to have been one continuous picnic. In his seventies he described those parties on the sand as unforgettable moments "when the salty tang of a sea breeze or the fresh sharp scent of the pines seemed like nature's spice for the food we were eating." In like fashion, among friends he talked expansively, with projective thrusts that an actor might use, of small incidents in the Oregon outback. After establishing his annual return to Gearhart as a way to conduct cooking classes and vacation at the same time, he took his Peruvian protégé and fellow teacher, Felipé Rojas-Lombardi, to follow an ebbing tide at Gearhart so his companion could learn to spot the air holes left by razor clams just below the surface of the heavily dampened sand. He didn't want friends or readers to ignore the rudimentary ways that Oregon had shaped him. He'd been born a member of a Western tribe and that fact distinguished him wherever in the world he went.

"Those busy days on the Oregon coast," he would write, "left their mark on me, and no place on earth, with the exception of Paris, has done as much to influence my professional life."

RECIPES

Chicken Jelly

When he was three years old and recovering from a long siege of malaria, Jim said the Chinese cook, Let, used to make small pots of chicken jelly that seemed to line his throat with "a cool palate-tickling film." Jim credited the little pots of chicken essence for his early flavor sense.

2 pounds chicken gizzards	*2 cloves garlic, peeled*
2 pounds chicken necks	*1 bay leaf*
and backs	*1 sprig parsley*
1 onion, peeled and stuck	*1 teaspoon dried thyme*
with 3 cloves	*6 peppercorns*
1 leek, well washed	*3 quarts water*
and trimmed	*1 tablespoon salt*
1 carrot, scraped	*1 egg white plus 1 egg shell*

Put the chicken parts, vegetables, garlic, herbs, peppercorns, and water into an 8-quart pot, and bring to a boil. After 5 minutes skim off the surface scum. Continue to boil rapidly, skimming, then reduce the heat; cover the pot and simmer 2 to 2½ hours. Add salt and taste. Line a sieve with layers of cheesecloth and strain the stock into a large bowl. Chill. Skim the fat. When absolutely free of fat, put the chilled broth into a clean pot and boil slowly to reduce to one-half to one-third of its original volume. Strain through cheesecloth. To clarify, add 1 egg white, beaten to a froth, plus 1 crushed egg shell. Over medium heat, beat well until the stock comes to a boil and the egg white rises to the surface. Cool the consommé, then refrigerate it until it is jellied. MAKES ABOUT 2½ QUARTS.

Beach Potato Salad

"I can remember picnics at the beach or in the woods when the salty tang of the sea breezes or the fresh sharp scent of the pines seemed like nature's spice for what we were eating."

4–6 potatoes (preferably	*1 tablespoon vinegar*
waxy type)	*1/2 cup finely*
salt	*chopped parsley*
freshly ground pepper	*1/4 cup finely*
1/2 cup olive oil	*chopped scallions*
1/4 cup dry white wine	

Boil the potatoes in their jackets until just pierceable. Peel while hot and slice them into a bowl. Season lightly with salt and pepper. While still hot, pour the oil and wine over the potatoes and set aside to cool. Just before leaving for your picnic, toss the potatoes with vinegar and the parsley and scallions. SERVES 4 TO 6.

Barbecued Salmon Steaks

In a booklet he wrote called *Gourmet Adventures for Men on the Move,* Jim said, "If you are traveling in the Northwest or in Canada, you will no doubt find great pike, pickerel, halibut, bass, Ling cod, and numerous other excellent fish. You will also discover tantalizing shellfish in the markets—sandshell clams, razor clams, tiny shrimp, and Dungeness crab, all thoroughly delicious. But nothing, perhaps, will taste as good over coals as the famous Pacific Northwest salmon (as the Indians used to do it)."

4 salmon steaks	*1 teaspoon chopped dill*
3 1/2 tablespoons oil	*1/2 teaspoon Tabasco sauce*
salt	*2 tablespoons lemon juice*
freshly ground pepper	*1 cup canned tomatoes or*
1 medium onion, chopped	*2/3 cup chili sauce*
1 clove garlic, chopped fine	*Garnish: chopped parsley or*
2 tablespoons butter	*sliced lemon*

Oil a hinged wire grill. Rub the salmon with 1/2 tablespoon of the oil and sprinkle with salt and pepper. Arrange steaks in the oiled grill. To make the sauce, sauté the onion and garlic in 3 tablespoons oil and the butter. Add the dill, Tabasco, lemon juice, and the tomatoes or chili sauce. Simmer for 10 minutes. Meanwhile grill the salmon, turning once; allow 10 minutes' cooking time per inch of thickness. Remove to a hot platter and spoon the sauce around. Garnish with chopped parsley or sliced lemon. SERVES 4.

Father's Anchovy Mayonnaise

▼

In 1915, during the Panama-Pacific International Exposition in San Francisco, the Beard family sailed south from Portland on overnight trips to the fair on ships offering "food that was memorable...I still remember the whole Chinook salmon of enormous proportions in a wine aspic, served with anchovy mayonnaise. My father loved it, got the recipe, and it became an occasional treat, especially at the beach."

2 cups freshly	*¼ cup chopped parsley*
made mayonnaise	*¼ cup chopped fresh basil*
12 anchovy fillets,	*1 tablespoon chopped capers*
coarsely chopped	*1 tablespoon Dijon mustard*
2 cloves garlic, chopped fine	

Mix the mayonnaise with all the ingredients until thoroughly blended.

MAKES ABOUT 2½ CUPS.

Fried Oysters

▼

Admirer of Elizabeth Beard though he was, Harry Hamblet trusted no woman when it came to frying oysters; in his view it was man's work. And he seemed to prove it by handling two big skillets at once while he rushed the finished oysters to the table in relays. They were eaten piping hot with lemon juice sprinkled over them; buttered toast on the side. Jim believed to the end that there is no better breakfast dish, and the recipe turned up in most of his books. This version appears in *The New James Beard,* published a few years before his death.

1 quart oysters	*freshly ground pepper*
3 eggs	*1½ cups freshly*
3 tablespoons heavy cream	*crushed crackers*
salt	*butter*

Pat the oysters dry on paper towels. Beat the eggs with the cream, and season lightly with salt and pepper. Dip each oyster in the egg batter, shaking off excess, then dredge in crumbs. In a heavy skillet melt enough butter to cover the bottom 1 inch deep. When the butter is hot enough to brown a bread cube in 30 seconds, put in the oysters, being careful to see that they don't touch. Sauté just long enough to turn the crumbs a light brown. Drain on paper towels and serve immediately.   SERVES 4.

Broiled Porterhouse

Elizabeth Beard didn't cook over charcoal but rather over a fire of bark and driftwood gathered on the beach. She used a thick, well-aged porterhouse and cooked it slowly, according to her son, because she wanted a good crust and a center as rare as possible—but also heated through and juicy. For her there was nothing more important than getting the steak cooked to perfection.

1 aged porterhouse, 2 or   *freshly ground pepper*
    more inches thick   *butter*
salt

Bring the steak to room temperature. Trim off excess fat (and chop the fat fine to use for frying potatoes). Grill the steak over glowing coals, allowing 7 to 20 minutes per side for rare. If you want a charred crust, let the fire flame up after the meat has been browned and is well on its way to being done. Salt and pepper the steak to taste, top with a generous piece of butter, and keep hot. Carve the bone completely out of the steak with a sharp knife and hide it for yourself, then cut the meat in diagonal slices. Serve with sliced potatoes sautéed in beef fat and a huge bowl of watercress. A bottle of burgundy, French bread, and some cheese make this a pretty remarkable meal.

                                                            SERVES 6–8.

Polly Hamblet's Huckleberry Cake

High-bush huckleberries of the mountain forests were "fantastically good," Beard wrote, adding that "the famous Hamblet huckle-berry cake" resulted from seasonal berry jaunts outside Portland.

1 cup butter | 2 teaspoons baking powder
1 cup sugar | pinch of salt
3 eggs | 1/4 teaspoon vanilla
2 cups flour | whipped cream
1 cup huckleberries

Cream the butter and sugar together until very light. Add one egg at a time, beating after each addition. Sift the flour, and use 1/4 cup to coat the berries. Mix the remaining flour with the baking powder and salt, then fold it into the egg mixture. Stir in the vanilla and fold in the floured berries. Pour the batter into a buttered and floured 8-inch-square baking pan. Bake in a preheated 375 degree oven for 35 to 40 minutes, until the cake is lightly browned, or when a tester comes out clean. Serve hot with whipped cream.

SERVES 8.

Julie's Pineapple Soufflé

▼

Julie, a Frenchwoman who cooked for well-to-do neighbors of the Beard family in Gearhart, shared culinary secrets with Mrs. Beard. It was she, in collaboration with Jim's mother, who first produced a highly successful clam soufflé, and she made a pineapple soufflé "such as I have never eaten since." Beard said that if his mother had had the courage, she might have set her friend up in the restaurant business.

3 tablespoons flour | 2/3 cup well-drained
3 tablespoons melted butter | crushed pineapple
3/4 cup milk | 1 teaspoon vanilla
6 egg yolks | salt
1/3 cup Grand Marnier | 8 egg whites
1/2 cup sugar | butter and sugar

Blend the flour with the melted butter and cook 3 to 4 minutes over medium heat. Stir in the milk, blending until the sauce thickens. Cool slightly and stir in the egg yolks, continuing to stir for 2 to 3 minutes over medium heat. Add the Grand Marnier and sugar and cook until the mixture thickens. Add the pineapple, the vanilla, and a pinch of salt. Beat the egg whites until they are stiff but not dry. Fold them in with a spatula or with your hands. Butter a 2-quart soufflé dish and sugar it well. Pour the mixture in and bake in a preheated 400 degree oven for 35 minutes, or until the soufflé is firm enough for your taste. Serve it with a sauce of melted vanilla ice cream—an easy and perfectly delicious sauce for soufflés.   SERVES 6.

Summer Berry Pudding

▼

Beard's friend Elizabeth David once wrote that recipes for summer pudding seldom appeared in books, and she gave her own formula. Jim's way with this seasonal dessert derived from his British mother and from the abundance of berries on the Oregon coast. It was still in his repertory when we visited him at his Seaside classes. Here is the way we have made it for many years in our family.

> *1 quart berries (wild blueberries, currants, raspberries, blackberries— combination of 2 types best)*
> *1/2–3/4 cup sugar*
>
> *1/4 cup water*
> *9 slices good homemade-type white bread*
> *1 teaspoon soft unsalted butter, approximately*
> *heavy cream*

Pick over the berries, stem them, and rinse them. Put them in a heavy saucepan with 1/2 cup sugar and the water, bring to a boil, and cook, stirring often, until the berries are soft but have not burst. Taste and add more sugar if needed. Remove the crusts from the bread and very lightly butter one side of all but 2 slices. Line the sides and bottom of a 1 1/2-to-2-quart bowl with the bread, buttered side out, and pour the hot berries over. Top with what is needed of the 2 remaining slices to enclose the berries and put a plate on top with a small weight. Refrigerate overnight. Serve with heavy cream.

SERVES 6.

2

"THE MOST VARIED GASTRONOMICAL EXPERIENCE"

When Beard was born, just after the turn of the century, Portland had the appearance of unbridled energy, and was still drawing newcomers from the East along with European immigrants. On the Western edge of the continent, it was still a man's town, as frontier cities always are. And, in spite of the dominating personality of Elizabeth Beard, it was Jim's father's town.

John Beard was a man of characteristic habits who walked from the house near Hawthorne Park across the bridge to his office in the customs building. On working days he loved to get up early and get breakfast for himself; according to his son, he generally got little recognition for this, even though he often prepared a tray for his son, and sometimes one for his wife, "before putting the final touches on his toilet."

John Beard has been remembered as tall and stockily attractive, sporting a thick mustache and pomaded hair that had begun early to recede on the front of his head. As his son indulgently described him, "He was a very vain man and always well groomed." In a family snapshot he appears in a dark business suit, white shirt with wing collar, and a four-in-hand tie. A man not really comfortable on a country weekend. "His wardrobe, while not enormous, was very handsome," said his clothes-conscious son, "and he never set out on his morning walk without a red carnation in his lapel." The private office which impressed Mary Hamblet in her youth was in an Italian

Renaissance structure not unlike the city hall and post office at the edge of the business center and not far from Chinatown. As a city assessor of imported goods, John Beard was known to most Oriental residents, for Portland's harbor was the anchorage of hundreds of merchant vessels in the Asia trade.

In its heyday, Portland's China-town sprawled from Washington to West Burnside between Second and Fourth avenues. On circular mats laid out on sidewalks, unusual foods dried, and show windows were filled with other odd provisions. Jim re-membered his first look at hen's  eggs coated to preserve their contents, which were priced, like wine, with respect to age. He learned about dried shark fins, small devil-fish, dehydrated oysters, shrimp, and Oriental mussels. In the Chi-nese Drug Store on Second, there were usually dried turtles bound at the tail in the form of a fan which were used to make a soup that was considered an antidote for rheumatism. Among the stores he knew the tong halls, gambling dens, and the second-story eating places unfamiliar to most of Portland's Occidental citizens. All the Beards felt at home here.

Not surprisingly, perhaps, the family house at 2322 Salmon Street had a Chinese air about its interior, in contrast to its clapboard look on the outside. It was a narrow building with wooden columns framing the front door, but inside was a generous hall heavy with big pieces of furniture, some originating in China; Mrs. Beard and her friend Polly Hamblet collected Canton porcelain. A frequent visitor was Jim's Chinese godfather, a friend of Jim's father. Jim doesn't record his godfather's name, but he describes him as an aristocrat. "He was also a tyrant, and he could afford to be. He loved to eat. If his chef served him a dish that he didn't like, he dropped it on the floor and ordered the kitchen to send him something else. I was told by his son that in China the family often dined on a barge, with a kitchen barge in attendance." Jim added that this autocratic chum of his father's then simply overturned the plate into the water.

The fact that the senior Beard had a Chinese family (which

included a half-brother about whom Jim came to know) was a relationship he was not encouraged to speak of. But he did have a playmate
named John Kan, who spent much time in the household of an uncle
in Chinatown while his parents, as Christian missionaries, were trek-
king through eastern Oregon. Jim and the Kan boy found similar
careers—the latter was the founder of Kan's restaurant on San Francisco's
Grant Street and his mother was also a talented cook.

"No matter where the Kan family lived," Jim recalled, "even in
such a remote village as Grass Valley, Oregon, John's mother could
turn out delectable Chinese dishes with whatever she could find in
those lonesome places. I remember one dinner at the restaurant
when John brought me a dish made with steamed clams—a magnificent Chinese variation of an Oregon specialty that his mother invented.
It was simply razor clams in their shells, cooked by tossing in sizzling
oil seasoned with a couple of teaspoons of minced garlic and an
equal amount of dried onion."

With his exposure to Jue Let, the Chinese cook his mother had
trained in the classic French style at the Gladstone Hotel, Jim learned
even more about Oriental finesse in the kitchen. Let had become so
much a member of the family that Elizabeth Beard, her son said,
made him the first to know when she had found a buyer for the
Gladstone. In Beard's version of the event, Let came to his mother
and asked, "Missy, do you have all your money?" Elizabeth replied
tartly, "Let, I have every damned cent. Why?" That seems to have
given Let the opening he wanted. He told Mrs. Beard that he had lost
his enthusiasm for working in hotels and would prefer to come along
with her, if she had received full payment for the hotel. If not, Let
said, he would hang on at the hotel just long enough for Mrs. Beard
to collect all that was coming to her.

Always a shrewd businesswoman, Elizabeth Beard had made
certain that the hotel sale was a cash deal, everything up front; Let
quit the hotel kitchen, leaving behind Poy and Gin, who had been
assistant chefs at the Gladstone under Mrs. Beard. She now was
determined to see that her child was brought up in a family residence.
For a woman of enterprise, it was a logical move to do some catering
for Portland hostesses who had come to admire the food at the
Gladstone, and she told Let that she wanted him on call.

Taking in boarders was a natural enough follow-up to her successful career managing a residential hotel. The house was not large and certainly she took in no one who couldn't be treated as a member of the family. Some of Jim's friends who knew him in high school and his early theater days in Portland felt that he was reluctant to bring them home because of his uneasiness about the boarders. In his memoirs he seems to fudge the issue, referring proudly to his mother as the proprietor of the Gladstone Hotel but never as the chatelaine of a small boardinghouse, although the practice of taking in compatible paying guests was common enough in those days. Still, one of his oldest friends challenges the fact, despite the listing in the city directory for many years of 2322 Salmon Street as a residence for boarders.* (With the Beard family interest in the theater, Jim might have found reason for pride, had he known at the time that his contemporary Noel Coward was a wishful actor then growing up in London, in *his* mother's Ebury Street boardinghouse.)

As Elizabeth Beard had seen things, the house and its paying guests provided an extended family, but in Jim's mind there persisted the thought that he'd had too much sophisticated talk thrown at him and not enough time with companions of his own generation. He was precocious, he recalled, and developed snobbish ideas. "I expressed myself on almost any subject. I could toss a remark into mixed company that unnerved the entire gathering." His confidence pleased his mother, he wrote in *Delights and Prejudices,* but he admitted that he became "as nasty a child as any in Portland." At home everyone spoiled him, and in the kitchen he was Let's pet. Even Mary Hamblet said, looking back, that she often demanded of her mother why she had to play with "that awful fat boy." The sometimes obnoxious Master Beard, she remembered with fondness during their long adult friendship, was given to throwing himself on the floor and screaming while he kicked in the air.

Elizabeth Beard found it easy to indulge her son because she was no longer distracted by her step-daughter; Lucille Beard had gone off to normal school, and was later employed as a teacher in a

---

*Late in life, a confidant, the photographer William Fotiades, listened while Beard brooded over the subject in a park near a German hotel. Jim was still troubled, he told his friend, that he couldn't talk easily of the time when boarders were accommodated by his mother.

small Oregon town. As an only child in fact, Jim was integrated into the adult family social life. His mother's London background enhanced her standing among class-conscious neighbors in both Portland and Gearhart. Afternoon tea was de rigueur in her household and was served in style, with scones and muffins fresh from the oven. "Many Oregon families," Beard once said to me, "maintained British social patterns. There was usually enough money for a servant or two. I knew families with four or five children who were brought up in the nursery. Some of these kids were my friends, so I was sometimes at their houses for lunch. The idea of being waited on at those tables made my life different, believe me."

At home, as often as not, young Jim and his mother ate alone. The relaxed mood was not different from that of the dinners for guests at the Beard table, so for Jim there was memorable novelty in eating in the formal atmosphere of such contemporaries. Some of these meals made specific impressions. He noted, for instance, the simplicity of bite-sized pieces of poached chicken that had been heated in broth enriched only by fresh cream. No matter that he was in his eighties, his "taste memory," as he called his ability to recapture thousands of moments of eating, carried him right back in time.

His memory also saluted his father's cooking. He thought John Beard had reason to maintain that he could sauté chicken better than either his wife or Let; in fact, better than anyone else he had ever known. To make sure his dish was served for Sunday breakfast, John Beard was wont to don an apron and take over the kitchen while others slept. As his son told it, no one dared set foot in John Beard's "domestic offices," until the chicken was in the pan, "wafting its glorious aroma throughout the lower floor of the house. He would never keep the door closed ... "

His routine started with the hand-slicing of bacon which he cut in thin strips; "don't think for one minute that sliced bacon was ever allowed in his house." He cooked the bacon strips over a slow fire, so that they became crackly, and left the pan with almost a quarter inch of hot fat. Into the fat he put the chicken pieces dusted in flour, searing them quickly and turning them to make sure each was equally browned. After the pieces had simmered about 15 minutes, his son reported, John Beard would remove the pan's cover and let his work of art acquire just the right crispness and color. The making of perfect chicken gravy was the final rite. The early morning cook poured off excess grease, blending in a tablespoon of flour while scraping up bits left in the pan. He stirred in two cups of milk and ground in enough black pepper to suit his taste. His son thought he seemed to have a magic touch, for no one else Jim knew could match the "individuality" of his father's chicken.*

Beard believed that his mother, with the help of Let, endowed him with the "most varied gastronomic experiences any child ever had." His word to describe his mother's Sunday afternoon teas was "monumental." He remembered an assortment of muffin and crumpet rings that Elizabeth had bought in England for use at the Gladstone, and he liked to tell his culinary friends that Let used them to perfection in the Beard kitchen across from the park. And he savored the competition between Elizabeth Beard and her Chinese assistant. Let's teacakes, he thought critically, were consistently better, adding that after his childhood he sought in vain for a currant-dotted cake as rich in texture and flavor as those Let cut in squares for the afternoon ritual.

After Beard's death, the loyal Mary Hamblet continued to cherish the thought of tea with her friend's mother, and in her mind the scones took first place among the tea breads she defined as great delicacies. On weekends the Hamblets would frequently go across town to the Beards', "and sometimes Mrs. Beard would come to the door with flour up to her elbows"; she added that Jim and his mother were the same physical types, with "exactly the same arms and hands." The fact that Beard had so much in common with his parent, in talent and temperament, caused Elizabeth to be at least as competitive with her son as she was with Let. When it came to sharing a cooking project, her offspring chose to stay out of her way as often as he could. Let chose to spar, and often exploded in righteous indignation. Once

---

*With breakfast the one family mealtime when he was apt to have the kitchen to himself, John Beard (as he did in Gearhart) sometimes would wake up early to be the first to gather mushrooms that appeared about dawn on a nearby vacant lot in Portland. It was half a city block of well-tended grass to which Jim's father brought a pail, to fill with dewy meadow mushrooms that he brought home to sauté with bacon. This memory lingered throughout Jim's life, so much so that he wove the story of his father's breakfast skills into a speech he gave at a national conference of botanists and mycologists in 1977.

Let even threatened his mother with a knife, and another time she went after Let with a split log from the kitchen woodpile.

Sure of his place in the kitchen, Let knew better than to make his home with the Beards, and he refused to say where he lived. When he was out of sorts, or in a mood to retaliate against Elizabeth Beard, he made sure he couldn't be found, responding to messages left with neighbors only if he saw fit. Generally, he would arrive at the Beard house before breakfast, and feed the fire in the cookstove. Proud of his baking, he filled the kitchen with oven smells that Beard never forgot. When Jim first came upon *brioches mousselines* in France, he was reminded of the breakfast roll Let baked for his father in a one-pound baking powder can in which the pastry ballooned over the top.

The kitchen was the room in which everyone gathered. The house had small front and back parlors accented by Chinese objets d'art and brass candlesticks that were always polished. There was a sewing machine on a kitchen table, Mary Hamblet told me with renewed surprise, adding, "I don't know how Mrs. Beard whipped up such food in that kitchen." But clearly the limitations didn't bother Jim's mother. The preparation of all kinds of food was her challenge, just as she was determined to keep the storerooms overflowing in every season. Her son concluded that once she had the larder full all of Portland could have dropped by for a meal. He added that the neighbors "thought we spent all our money on our stomachs, and I guess they were right."

There was little tolerance for anyone who didn't understand that food was worth creative effort from cooks. Jim, even as a small boy, learned to recognize the cooks in the family who didn't care. One was an aunt with all the bounty of a large sheep ranch, but whose treatment of lamb and mutton was deplorable. His mother sought every excuse to get out of having a meal at Aunt Mary's; the leg of lamb she invariably served for dinner was wretched, virtually inedible. It would be simmered to death—covered with boiling water in a roasting pan and cooked until the meat turned gray and fell off the bones. For Jim, only breakfast made up for the disasters of dinner. In the morning there were great platters of hashed browns to go with ham and eggs, chops, or steaks, all cooked to order. The potatoes had been tenderly browned with a golden crust, and the memory of them lived on.

Jim developed the conviction that potatoes, cooked with love and respect, could save any meal, and he wrote frequently on the subject. Behind the Salmon Street house, his mother planted potatoes in her own small garden along with chives, shallots, onions, squashes, and several kinds of aromatic herbs, and she encouraged her six-year-old child to experiment in growing his own radishes. She nurtured her friendships with vegetable growers who drove their horse-drawn wagons—then a typical sight in American towns—through Portland neighborhoods two or three times a week, delivering garden produce. Much of what they sold Mrs. Beard was to be preserved, with the help of Let, in jars for the cellar shelves, as well as served fresh as often as possible throughout the year.

His mother had a friend, named Joe Galluzzo, who had a truck garden, and from him she got several kinds of vegetables that were generally unknown. Joe grew broccoli, cardoons, fava beans, garlic, leeks (reminders of Jim's mother's Celtic childhood), and zucchini, which had been introduced to the United States by Italian gardeners. She would also demand the season's earliest white asparagus, her son said, and she had alligator pears before other Oregonians knew them. Another truck gardener, Delfinio Antrozzo, would tie up his wagon in front of the house, then sit down and talk with Elizabeth Beard just as Joe did; they became members of the family circle. Sometimes Delfinio talked recipes, stopping long enough one day to make polenta, a dish not known by many non-Italians, the first Jim had ever tasted. Delfinio's recipe combined the cooked cornmeal with codfish, and his mother, Jim noted, collected other Delfinio dishes which taught her how much the Italian way with seasoning could do to enliven her repertoire of British recipes.

There was in Portland, as well as throughout the country in those days, a scarcely veiled scorn for immigrants whose eating habits betrayed their appreciation of garlic; but Elizabeth Beard nonetheless added Delfinio's recipe for pesto to her collection of sauces, and her son introduced it to his readers long before the average American knew the word "pasta." The significance of garlic as a social influence in Portland was demonstrated about this time when some boys in a grade school across town were accused by classmates of deliberately polluting the air by eating enough garlic to make their presence obnoxious. To chasten them, the principal of the school located a Middle Eastern store and sent the culprits there to buy so much garlic that its full consumption made the boys sick. They renounced the prank, if not their appetite for the ethnic accent that would take a couple more generations to be found in American kitchens in every region.*

Among the Beard neighbors on Portland's mixed-nationality east side, the ethnic cooking styles were mostly European. Some newly arrived households were French, and one next-door family was German. "They had a couple of boys with whom we played," a woman who had grown up across the street wrote to Jim in his old age. Her letter reminded him that she had heard their two mothers call each other so often that "I can still remember your phone number, East 6129." Jim's mother was indeed a wonderful cook, her letter said. "My most vivid memory is of her baking powder biscuits and those elegant tea cakes which she taught me to make. They were basically rich baking powder dough to which she added raisins or currants. She cut

---

*Part of his lifetime bag of opera jokes was Jim's story of the diva who so loved garlic that she constantly reeked of it—so much so that the leading baritone complained repeatedly. When the manager of the opera company put his soprano on notice, she retired to her suite for one last wallowing in her favorite seasoning. "Unconsciously," Beard said, "she proved a secret about the beauty of loving garlic. If you eat enough at a time, the odor is cancelled out." He brought his arm to his nose and frivolously sniffed from wrist to elbow, and laughed with delight. "Not a whiff!" he chortled.

the rolled dough in triangles and brushed the tops with cream. They were a toothsome delicacy especially enjoyed with some of your mother's perfectly blended tea."

In addition to the neighbors in town, there were Germans who were nearby farmers, including a family with whom Jim's stepsister, Lucille, lived when she taught school. Near the village of Aloha was a small farm operated by a family named Ruley but owned by John Beard, and it was here that two pigs were slaughtered in the fall to be cut up in Elizabeth Beard's kitchen. "We had what seems now a fairly primitive smokehouse in the garden, tucked way from the house," Jim told me. The hams from the Ruley farm were smoked in the backyard, along with jowl to be used sometimes in place of bacon or salt pork. The fresh pork included shoulders, tenderloins, and spareribs; pork breast was combined with goose fat, thin ham slices, carrots, and juniper berries to make the casserole that Elizabeth Beard contrived with the sauerkraut brought in by her German friend Ruley.

Sometimes the Beards would stay overnight at Aloha and many years later the aroma of fresh raw mushrooms would take Jim back to what he called "a special field." There, great patches of meadow mushrooms were reason enough for him to pile out of bed "to harvest the night's crop" in a five-pound lard pail. "Walking home with the rising sun warming the back of my neck and the cold dewy grass brushing my ankles, I always sampled a few." All the Beards had ready appetites for wild food. Jim also savored the look of brilliantly colored ducks and long-tailed pheasants hanging in the family larder, along with blue-winged teal that were also offerings of friends who hunted. "When we had teal, it was always reserved for the household, never served to guests."

On Salmon Street, Jim often sat with his mother when she urged her farmer friends and other droppers-by to stay for an impromptu lunch with conversation running from rural gossip to talk of far places that especially intrigued him. Grace Harris, who brought stories of her difficult husband and her rich, demanding mother, almost always stayed for pot luck when she made her weekly rounds with butter and eggs. Mrs. Beard had trained Grace to provide two kinds of butter. Long before American cooks took to the idea, Jim's mother served sweet butter with meals, sometimes using salted butter in cooking—

both supplied by Mrs. Harris's fawn-colored Jersey cows, esteemed for the high butterfat content of their milk.

In the Gladstone days, to insure her hotel dining room's reputation, Elizabeth Beard had started her days at 5 a.m.; and it became a lifelong habit. She dressed herself smartly, often in a divided skirt, well-starched blouse, fedora hat with a pheasant's feather, gloves, and fashionable shoes, and rode her bicycle more than three miles to do the marketing. What Jim gleaned from her about shopping, he said, was worth a college education.

He remembered a day when he was taken by his nurse to a doctor's appointment, with a stop as part of the jaunt to pick up groceries that his mother needed. The market stretched along four or five blocks of Yamhill Street. Few if any of the vendors failed to recognize Elizabeth Beard as a valued customer who knew her onions. On this occasion, in accepting the purchase that had been requested by her employer, the young Oriental woman who held Jim by the hand asked that it be charged to Mrs. Beard. The clerk turned white. "For God's sake," the man muttered in dread, "give me that package back. If I sent that to her, she'd kill me."

Jim often accompanied his mother on her marketing sorties, and he learned her craftiness in getting the best of everything. He noted that she cut through bacon slabs in order to have the part most streaked with lean meat. She carefully selected a side of beef, leaving most of the ribs and the short loin to be set aside and hung for her by the butcher. For meals on days immediately ahead, she was wont to take home a large, marbled roast and a few steaks. For pot-au-feu, she would buy plate or brisket, and Let would simmer it in its own broth and serve it with a horseradish sauce. Or he would cut up lamb shoulder and transform it into a curry that melded tastes of both Orient and Occident.

From the Yamhill Street market, the LaGrande Creamery sent the family samples of cheeses not widely available in the United States. These included the Rouge et Noir versions of Brie and Camembert (the first in the United States and produced in Petaluma, California), along with Roquefort and Emmenthaler from Europe. The LaGrande also had excellent local Cheddars, some of them orange-colored wheels made in Tillamook on the coast, others from

Clatsop on the Columbia, and these were ripened to various degrees of sharpness. Whatever the choice of Elizabeth Beard might be, when Jim was in on the cheese shopping, he often managed to get a slice of Emmenthaler as a premium, and he walked happily homeward nibbling his prize.

His notion of between-meal snacks brought similar satisfaction when he dropped in on neighbors; he used a certain back-door charm to ask if by chance the cookie jar was full enough to offer samples and he was equally pleased with healthier bites. He loved the crunch and the peppery white interior of the radishes his mother had let him plant and nurture, and sometimes he longed to have sandwiches filled with walnut halves as a snack.

"Once on Arbor Day when I was very young, somebody had the bright idea of letting me plant an English walnut tree in a somewhat crowded spot in the garden behind our house. Filled with infant importance, I duly supervised the operations and patted down the dirt around the walnut seedling, near the two enormous Gravenstein apples, the Lambert cherry, the Royal Anne cherry, the May Dyke cherry, and the small plum trees already in the garden. Before too many years passed the new walnut tree began bearing beautifully, and we sometimes saved out some green nuts, serving them at teatime in thin slices on well-buttered bread with a sprinkle of salt. Another thing was ripe walnut halves on a baking sheet with a dribbling of oil or melted butter. Mother, or Let, put them in a 350 degree oven for a few minutes to serve with a drink or a glass of wine—port or old Madeira."

Elizabeth Beard's near-favorite offering was raisin bread. "It was modeled on one she had admired at the Palace Hotel in San Francisco. During World War I she used to do benefit teas for the local chapter of the British Red Cross, and there were always requests for this bread ... " But her everyday loaf was "a more stalwart bread" which Jim said sliced to perfection, back in the days when store-bought bread was unsliced and was—when it was produced by factories rather than neighborhood bakers—too often low in quality. The Beard family loved sweet breads, and the kitchen turned out many kinds.

However, because Elizabeth Beard could admit that more

complicated baked desserts were not her strong suit, she often turned
them over to Let, who taught her how to make ladyfingers "as light as
a ghost's footsteps." His Chinese version of charlotte russe, topped
with whipped cream, currant jelly, or black currant paste, was considered a triumph by all the Beards. He had helped Elizabeth Beard
when she made many of the kinds of fancy cakes that were typical of
the era, including, in addition to his white fruitcake, a mace-tinged
pound cake with bits of citron or sultanas soaked in sherry. When
finally he returned to China, however, he was missed most for himself.
Jim remembered Let for the force of his personality and his subtle
ability to instruct his mother, "never losing his integrity" in the face of
his employer's strength. "How I wish I had him around now," Beard
wrote after his cooking school was under way.

Let would have been remembered for a number of reasons, not
the least of them being his presence when Jim's birthday celebrations
required his mother to produce a spectacular cake, to her son's
satisfaction. At least once, when the big event in May came around,
she staged a memorable picnic for a score or so of his schoolmates for
which only a coconut cake would do because of Jim's "insatiable taste"
for it. "I felt that candles ruined the beauty of the cake and was firm
about dispensing with the blowing-out ritual." Instead he demanded
that white icing and coconut be piled high on what might be Let's
version of a sunshine cake made of egg yolks and flavored with
orange. In lieu of candles, Jim insisted that the plate was to be
ornamented with the hawthorn blossoms that came with the season.

A high mark in his mother's youth had been her visits to New
York, where she became friendly with people in the theater. Among
them, Stella Chase-Ainsworth turned out to be a lifelong confidante
who visited the Beard family at least once. Elizabeth had crossed the
country with her; the two had gone to Mexico and Panama. In San
Francisco, where they had met Lucky Baldwin, they had been impressed
by the fact that the Baldwin Hotel not only had a room set aside for
women who liked to sew but an exclusive women's billiard room as
well. Four-in-hand coaches drawn by high-stepping horses, groomed
and harnessed in gleaming style, rolled between the hotel and the
ferries and trains. San Francisco thus for many years continued to

attract all the Beards for its theater and its restaurants, and Mrs. Chase-Ainsworth provided a recurrent link.*

"She was very close to my mother, and this friendship went on for many years," Beard told me. He was regretful that his chance to know the actress had been limited "because she and my mother spent all their time together reminiscing." She seems to have been a woman of uncommonly good looks and forceful presence. "I remember her riding in a black satin tailor-made suit with beautiful shoes. She gave forth a personality that was enormous, and I only wish that I knew what her position in the theater had been." Although he never learned more about this family friend, he may have wondered, at a time when he was beginning to ponder his own sexuality, what defined his mother's deep attachment. "I wouldn't be surprised if it were true that no one else in the world meant so much to her as Mrs. Ainsworth," he said.†

Elizabeth Beard shared with her friend some acquaintanceship with New York actors, and the interest added something to Portland's theater season attractions, which included all the popular plays that toured the West Coast and the rest of the country. John Drew, as famous as any actor of the period, appeared in plays by Somerset Maugham, and Drew's nephew Lionel Barrymore brought *Peter Ibbetson* to Portland. Maude Adams, the Broadway star who had grown up in the West, was also a favorite of audiences on the road. Hollywood star William Powell got his start in Portland's stock company.

Mrs. Beard found distraction not only in evenings at the theater

---

*Julian Street, known to Jim later in New York's Wine and Food Society, described San Francisco of that period in his book *Abroad at Home:* "With her hills San Francisco is Rome; with her harbor she is Naples; with her hotels she is New York . . . " He listed the St. Francis Hotel, "which is one of the best run and most perfectly cosmopolitan hotels in the country," the Fairmont, "commanding the bay as Bertolini's commands the bay of Naples," and the Palace Hotel, "where drinks are twenty-five cents each, as in the old days, and where, over the bar, hangs Maxfield Parrish's 'Pied Piper' balancing the continent against his 'Old King Cole' on the Knickerbocker bar, in New York."

†Late in his life, he seemed to allude to Mrs. Ainsworth when he shared some of his memories with his friend Marion Cunningham. In their many moments of confidence, he talked of his mother having been an adventuress, " . . . going off on ship cruises with a woman friend," Marion recorded in a diary. "He was puzzled about his suspicion of her lesbianism." And Marion added that he left her with no doubts about his early realization of his own homosexuality.

but also in ladies' lunches and tea parties. Beard, in adulthood, thought of his mother's great ability to put at ease the people she entertained, speculating that it must have added to her success in business. Whether at the tea table in her home, or at a beach party, he recalled, she was a hostess comfortable in her role. "She was never very formal in her entertaining, and her uninhibited style may sometimes have been thought shocking. But no one left our house without feeling happier."

How to make his guests happy, when he himself was the host, was something he had learned well from his mother. "Put on a fine show!" he exclaimed in *Delights and Prejudices.* "Like theater, offering food to people is a matter of showmanship, and no matter how simple the performance, until you do it well, with love and originality, you have a flop on your hands." He inherited his parent's unselfconscious style. Hard taskmaster though she seems to have been, his mother thought that he was precocious and gifted, and was proud of the fact that he entertained himself by reading voraciously as well as by being more than commonly transfixed by all kinds of performances.

Beard's parents seem to have chosen to disagree, on principle, about their progeny. The son remembered continual discord at home. One parent wanted him to be more physically active, and he was taught to ride a horse. He learned to swim, but was rebuked if he went out in a canoe. If one parent refused to let him rollerskate, the other forbade something else for equally nonsensical reasons. Beard often felt caught in their crossfire, and there were times, he recalled, when he withdrew as much as possible, creating a world of his own as frequently as he could.

It was also a time when many families habitually read aloud to each other, and Jim's imagination was well stocked by vicarious pleasure. His parents had read all of Dickens to him, and he assured himself that he'd been exposed more than most of his contemporaries to good books. He remembered himself choosing *Swiss Family Robinson* for reading aloud when he was sick in bed. On his own, he said, by the time he was fifteen he'd gone through the Russians, including Tolstoy and Turgenev. He read some of the classic playwrights, and every theater biography he could easily find. The Rose City branch library, to encourage reading on school vacations, allowed twenty books to a borrower during the summer, and for many like Jim the habit was thereby established for the rest of the year.

His clearly better-than-average mind led his parents to want him exposed to the best education possible, so he was sent to a boarding school in Vancouver, British Columbia. For whatever reasons, this did not work for Jim. He hesitantly mentioned the experience to his childhood friend Catherine Carter when (as Catherine Hindley) she worked with him in his cooking classes forty years later, but immediately regretted having done so. "It quite apparently was a bad time for him," she told me. It was one of a number of uncomfortable episodes that Jim chose to keep hidden in adulthood, in this case leaving the impression that all of his early schooling had been in Portland. Yet as other recollections have it, he was thought to have been in those years an outwardly self-confident, if overweight, youngster who could be counted on to bring enthusiasm to what juvenile roles there might be in the town's various amateur productions. Reflecting her own interest in the theater, his mother had arranged to have him join the drama classes taught by Estelle Marias, and she thought he could sing as well. (The daughter of the rector of Trinity Church off Burnside Street remembered him as one of a dozen choir boys recruited to sing at services throughout the winter months.)

About this time he began to think seriously of a career on the musical stage. When he was "a mere stripling," he recalled, he saw a song-filled spoof called *Chu Chin Chow,* and he reveled in it. One of its tunes, appropriately for him, was entitled "The Market Place," and after hearing it he was moved to sing the opening lines at the drop of a spoon. "Here be oysters stewed in honey," went the verse, "and conger eels in snow." The memory stayed with him. "This awakened a mad idea in my head. . . . I tried stewing oysters in honey, with rather unhappy results." Little did he realize then that his gift of voice was to be superseded by his greater knack for creativity in the kitchen. The stripling was perceived by some as blessed by protean talent. He was a youth who not only knew what was going on in the theater, but whose wide reading enriched his conversation. If there were some schoolmates who thought he put on airs, there were also those who admired his unusual abilities. Edris Morrison, a professional photographer and Portland actress who became a friend when he was eighteen, never forgot his speaking voice and his ability to make himself heard.

Janet Baumhover (still active in her nineties as an actress) was then the high school correspondent for the *Oregon Journal* and frequently cited him in her reports on student activities. "There was that something about him you couldn't overlook. I sensed what was special in him and my editor must have seen it, too, for they never cut out what I wrote about him." As was true all his life, Jim was outwardly friendly, but few who knew him were able to understand all his facets at the same time.

When the Beard family settled down, more or less, after each Gearhart summer, and after the school year was in progress, Jim was often his mother's companion on Saturday afternoons to see matinees of some touring musical comedy or such hit plays as R. C. Sherriff's *Journey's End*. Or they went to the art deco movie palace, where a Wurlitzer organ rose out of the floor (vibrating with fanfare and with the organist firmly seated aboard) to accompany the afternoon's silent film. At least as often, he was his parent's table mate at restaurant meals, and this heightened his social precocity while at the same time keeping his palate in training. Not that he didn't have a yen for hot dogs and hamburgers, but it didn't diminish his zest for new and uncommon tastes, a proclivity that began soon after the age when most children are still refusing to have anything to do with spinach.

When Jim was five, friends of his mother had come to Portland on a visit and invited Elizabeth Beard to have dinner with them at the establishment known as the Louvre. In spite of its reputation as a place of high living, Mrs. Beard "for some capricious reason," her son said, "took me along." There was dancing at the Louvre, and the food was French. There were private rooms for dining *à deux* upstairs, where the waiter peeked through the curtain before entering to serve succeeding courses.

For a chubby youngster with a mischievous sense about his mother's notions of child guidance, there were oysters in the shell on silver trays and the sight and sound of effervescing champagne, as well as a menu of choices he'd been taught by his parents to think of as tempting. "My mother was out of her mind to take me there," he

recalled with unabashed glee. But he maintained years later that even at five he had understood the Louvre's lure for an adult clientele and began to feel proud to be able to say he knew its charms.

More prosaically, in those years his mother would take her son to restaurants that served food aimed at pleasing the average Oregon palate. One of these was the Bohemian, a commendable dining place that Beard remembered particularly for a dish called Crab Louis. Writing about this chili-tinged way of serving Dungeness crab, he wanted to believe it had been first served at the Bohemian and later he sparred with his friend Helen Evans Brown, who credited San Francisco's Solari Restaurant for its origin. With his partiality for opera stars, Jim wasn't chagrined to discover that Crab Louis had been served in 1904 by the chef of Seattle's Olympic Club to Enrico Caruso. The tenor, an eater to be admired by the Beards, liked the sauce that distinguished the dish so much that he sent back for plate after plate until the Olympic Club supply was exhausted.

Jim managed, willy-nilly, to learn how to duplicate recipes of numerous restaurant kitchens he knew in childhood or youth. One other favorite of the family was House's restaurant, to which he was often taken by his mother to join his father, who habitually lunched there. The proprietor himself had been apprenticed in a French kitchen, and the chef at House's was probably Let's best friend, known to all as Billy. The Beards went to House's for Billy's coleslaw, his sautéed smelts, and for New Year's dinner, when Billy's version of goose stuffed with apples and chestnuts was considered a great treat.

In the first half of the twentieth century, Chinese cooks like Billy and Let, and Poy and Gin at the old Gladstone Hotel, were not sought after for their skills in the various regional cooking styles of their homeland. Few Americans, even on the West Coast where the Chinese population provided kitchen workers of high accomplishment, had learned to cook any Oriental dishes more sophisticated than chop suey and chow mein, or eggs foo yung, sweet and sour pork, fried shrimp, and fried rice. The successful Chinese immigrant who became chef of a professional American kitchen had been schooled in European classic techniques, methods that Let had been encouraged to use by Elizabeth Beard.

But Mrs. Beard would often allow Let to prepare Chinese dishes for a quick meal, or as a special treat for Jim or his father—such as Let's version of green beans fried separately and served with hog jowl. Let also liked imaginative cooking, and he developed a recipe for a special curry sauce that he said was originally Chinese. Its smooth texture was achieved by grinding onions, garlic, Chinese parsley, unpeeled tart apples, and dry-smoked ham, and the mixture was seasoned with curry powder, turmeric, various peppers, stock, and tomato paste. When Beard's reputation was established, he concluded that this country's enthusiasm for Oriental food might have surfaced earlier had Americans in Let's time been generally more open-minded about ordering in Chinese restaurants.

Beard believed that Orientals generally develop a much greater accuracy of palate than Occidentals, and, further, that he had something of the same flavor sensitivity himself. While most children who begin to learn by rote retain the memory of sounds and images through repetition, Beard perfected the ability to register subtle flavors indelibly, perhaps in an Oriental way, and to call back specific tastes after the passage of decades. He described the talent as "akin to perfect pitch." His taste memory was, in its way, an extension of his gift for retaining an enormous variety of facts, a talent that stayed with him until his death.

The Portland restaurant scene offered as broad an education as could have been found. The restaurant of Meier and Frank's department store was the domain of a chef named Don Daniels, who had a knack for emphasizing a variety of Oregon's bounty. Daniels's chief premise was simplicity. He might merely sauté the clams that had been shipped down from Seaside only hours before. Beard found Don's curry of crab unique and he never forgot the richly sauced veal birds, duckling salmi, salmon soufflé, or Don's boned squab. Sometimes he said his favorite memory was of the restaurant's unusual frozen desserts, variously flavored by maple syrup, cognac, lemon, or fresh strawberries from the village of Banks in Columbia County.

Beard's restaurant education continued at Portland's de luxe Benson Hotel, in the kitchen of Henry Thiele, whose best work Beard said was "sensational." Classically trained in France, Thiele had developed a reputation in the haute cuisine milieu of such San Francisco eating places as the Poodle Dog restaurant, the Palace Court, and Chef Victor Hirtzler's kitchen in the St. Francis Hotel. Because Simon Benson wanted his hostelry to be as highly rated, Benson brought Thiele north to Portland, and soon his salmon fillets, stuffed with salmon mousse, and such other French dishes as wild mushrooms Bordelaise were much talked about among ordinary restaurant-goers as well as the Beards.

Simon Benson had divorced his wife, who was a good cook, and she lived with her two sons not far from the Beards. With common interests, she and Elizabeth Beard became friends, as did James Beard and Chester Benson, who were high school classmates, equally fond of theater and music. Jim went to lavish parties for the Benson children, which were especially notable because their mother displayed her cake-baking skills, and he was often invited to lunch (the sons had charge accounts at their father's hotel, where Jim welcomed chances to see Henry Thiele's kitchen in action).

For a time, the Benson family and the Beards were frequently involved with each other's lives, and Mrs. Benson added to Jim's lifelong sentiment about Christmas. He remembered the sugar cookies she turned out in holiday seasons—long before the postwar franchising of cookie stores across the fifty states—when a dozen or more children and several mothers were invited by her to join in learning about cookie design. She gave her pupils choices of colored icings, which set off bursts of creativity. "Some should have been preserved for the currently popular shows of children's art," was Jim's assessment, "although others were better eaten on the spot." His image of cookie binges in the Summers family kitchen was equally vivid. There, stored in great tins he pictured as nineteen inches high and twelve to fourteen inches in diameter, were bar cookies, ginger cookies, fruit cookies, sugar cookies, and mock macaroons that remained, he asserted, his all-time favorites.

Cookies were more than the understandable sweet bites that bring passing comfort to most children—they remained one of Jim's mild passions. When he thought of his early years, he often was nostalgic about the intuitive neighbors who believed in a child's need for sugary satisfaction. Late in life, he described one as a sturdy pioneer in whose kitchen he felt free to head immediately for the ten-pound lard pails which were always full of cookies flavored with lemon or nutmeg—or with sugar cookies, four inches in diameter, which provided the model for the monster cookies he himself later kept on hand for visiting youngsters.

In a family for which the idea of food seemed perpetually urgent, Christmas had its resolute side. Mincemeat symbolized the holiday for his mother. Once when hospitalized during the season, she showed how much she could take things to heart. She had been left without even the smell of a mincemeat pie, so she contrived to leave her bed, sneak away from the nurse, and to go for a walk. "She covered her head with a voluminous traveling cape," Jim told friends, "and searched every bakeshop until she found the pie she hungered for. She smuggled two of them back into her room under the cape, and she ate one whole pie before dinner and the other before lunch the next day."

On her home ground Elizabeth Beard habitually made mince-meat, fruitcakes, and holiday puddings a year in advance. Periodic and generous lubrication with brandy throughout the year was the key to her success with mincemeat, whether she used a combination of beef rump, brisket, and tongue, or substituted venison that was brought to the Beards each fall by hunters.

Jim was to compose at least a dozen descriptions of his family

Christmases in memos, articles for magazines, and newspaper columns because the holiday was for him a small piece of theater in which he felt he had a special part. The last week before Christmas Day would bring wonderful surprises from friends of each of his parents—ducks, pheasants, sometimes wild geese and turkeys. Boxes of orchard fruit arrived from Oregon, mandarin oranges came from China by ship in "magic boxes" in which they had been packed for the voyage.

About four days before Christmas, there arrived from the family farm mistletoe, pine branches, and plumes of cedar boughs. The Beard holly boughs provided leaves for wreaths and arrangements, Jim remembered in old age, citing the huge Christmas tree he was allowed by his mother to help adorn with "enchanting old German decorations" and intricately designed baroque pieces.

For the annual "grand open house," on Christmas Eve, Jim remembered himself running last-minute errands while his mother fixed food and his father beat dozens of egg yolks and whites with sugar for the frothy drink called Tom and Jerry. "We had a light supper, usually a dish of salt codfish made with a flavorful sauce of garlic, onion, tomato, ripe olives, and olive oil." The hot drinks were served as the early guests arrived. For them the buffet table was often laden with suckling pig, salad, sandwiches, and crayfish in wine. There were homemade sausages—goose liver, blutwurst, cervelat, *weisswurst*—for the buffet. Sometimes there were cups of oyster stew made with Olympia oysters and cream, and crabmeat fritters or chicken patties.

His mother might invite strangers who would otherwise be alone for Christmas and the evening was characterized by the arrival of close family friends, and of young carolers with whom Jim—always ready to exercise his voice—would join. He wrote that Santa Claus had entered his life in the person of his second godfather, General Summers, habitually dressed in a red suit for the holiday. With his silvery hair and long white mustache, he seemed to a child rather like Santa Claus any time of the year. For Let, General Summers was the equal of a fabled white god, and the Chinese cook, said Beard, often stroked the General's tummy as if he were a giant dog.

Let loved Christmas; he had created especially for the Beard family holiday his white fruitcake flavored with preserved ginger. It was a work of art, mellowed by dosages of white rum—a cake that brought oohs and aahs from all the guests, including many from Chinatown. Let himself brought a more specific Chinese effect to Christmas Eve by climbing to the upstairs porch during the opening of presents and setting off a string of giant firecrackers he had tied to the railing. He provided a sort of Oriental overture, perhaps to draw attention to the gifts that "poured in" from members of the Chinese colony who idolized Elizabeth and whose respect for John Beard was great.

The cast of A Christmas Carol, *1933*

Breakfast on Christmas morning often meant porterhouse steak carved dexterously by Elizabeth. Just as frequently, John Beard had his friends come in for drinks on Christmas Day. And a prevailing recollection of Christmas was of Jim, as he grew older, joining his parents in the family's idea of personal celebration—each one doing separate things as opportunities arose. "We managed to see a lot of people that way, and if any one of us was invited out alone for Christmas dinner, and wanted to go, we did."

Independence was the family characteristic that enlarged the

Christmas spirit, at least in the minds of parents and son. As an inveterate reader, Jim had almost memorized *A Christmas Carol.* Scrooge might have disdained holiday kindness, generosity, and tenderness as he turned his back on sentiment, but for the Beards, Jim was wont to say, it was anything but. His was a family of go-it-aloners, even on Christmas, he sometimes said. As young Jim approached manhood, he sensed more and more his differences from others. Increasingly, he recognized his individuality. He thought he was seriously interested in theater—in finding escape, and a career, he hoped. His immediate challenge was participation in local productions, and in the course of things he was cast both as Bob Cratchit and as Mr. Fezziwig in separate performances of the Dickens Christmas story.

RECIPES

Chicken Giblet Salad

Portland's LaGrande Creamery supplied the Beard family with chickens and young Jim with the gizzards and hearts for which he developed a youthful passion. When his father came to the beach for a weekend he would bring Jim "my quota." One of the ways Jim liked them as an adult was in a salad.

> *2 cups cooked giblets, cut
>   in pieces*
> *1 head romaine lettuce,
>   washed, dried, and torn
>   in pieces*
> *6–8 small potatoes,
>   cooked in jackets, peeled,
>   and sliced*
> *18–20 cherry
>   tomatoes, halved*
>
> *3 tablespoons sliced scallions*
> *1 tablespoon capers*
> *salt and pepper to taste*
> *2 tablespoons
>   chopped parsley*
> *3/4 cup vinaigrette flavored
>   with thyme and garlic*

Arrange the giblets on a bed of lettuce, adding the potatoes, tomato halves, scallions, and capers. Season with salt and pepper. Sprinkle on the chopped parsley. Just before serving, add the vinaigrette and toss.   SERVES 4 TO 6.

Let's Ginger-Accented Codfish Cakes

This is a recipe used by Jim's mother's chef to make both codfish cakes and codfish balls. The codfish balls he made with it were always in demand, Jim recalled. Let added plenty of butter to the mashed potatoes, and then sautéed the codfish balls, spiked with ginger, in additional butter.

> *1 cup shredded cooked
>   salt cod*
> *1 cup mashed potatoes*
>
> *1 large egg, beaten*
> *1 teaspoon grated
>   fresh ginger*

freshly ground pepper	*flour or crumbs,*
to taste	*for dredging*
salt, if needed	*4 tablespoons butter*

Mix the fish, potatoes, beaten egg, ginger, pepper, and salt if needed. Form into cakes about 1 inch thick and 3 inches in diameter. Dredge and sauté in hot butter until crisp and lightly browned on both sides.　　　SERVES 4.

Chef Billy's Goose

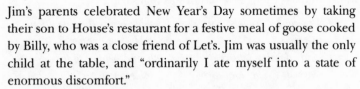

Jim's parents celebrated New Year's Day sometimes by taking their son to House's restaurant for a festive meal of goose cooked by Billy, who was a close friend of Let's. Jim was usually the only child at the table, and "ordinarily I ate myself into a state of enormous discomfort."

8–10-pound goose	*2 cups peeled,*
1/2 cup chopped onion	*chopped apples*
6 tablespoons butter	*1 cup coarsely chopped*
5–6 cups breadcrumbs	*prunes, steeped*
2 teaspoons salt	*in Madeira*
1 cup cooked peeled	*1/2 teaspoon nutmeg*
chestnuts or	*1 teaspoon thyme*
canned chestnuts	

Remove excess fat from the cavity of the goose and render it to use for cooking. Sauté the chopped onion in the butter, add the crumbs, moistening them with butter, and blend with the salt and chestnuts. Stir in the apples and prunes. Season with nutmeg and thyme, blending well. Stuff the goose with this mixture, truss, sew up, or skewer the cavity, and tie the legs together. Place the goose breast side up in a roasting pan. Roast 1 hour at 400 degrees, then reduce the temperature to 350 and roast for another hour, without basting. As the fat renders from the goose remove it to a jar for future use. After the second hour, reduce the heat to 325 degrees and continue roasting until nicely browned and done. The leg meat should be soft when pressed, and when the thigh is pricked the juices should run beigey-pink.

SERVES 6 TO 8.

Stuffed Squab Chicken

▼

His father's parents had learned to live off the fields, forests, and waters as they crossed to the Northwest in a wagon train, and Jim was pleased that he had learned from them many ways of using game, wild berries, greens, corn, and cornmeal. Here is his last version of the way to cook small birds that may be stuffed with fresh herbs and autumn nuts, such as butternuts or black walnuts.

*3/4 cup finely
    chopped shallots
1/4 pound or more
    unsalted butter
giblets and livers from
    the birds
1 tablespoon chopped fresh
    tarragon or 1 1/2 teaspoons
    dried, crushed
2 cups cooked rice*

*salt
freshly ground pepper
3 tablespoons
    chopped parsley
1/4 cup chopped walnuts,
    butternuts, or
    black walnuts
6 squab chickens
1 lemon, halved
watercress, for garnish*

Prepare the stuffing: sauté the shallots in 6 tablespoons of the butter until they are just limp. Chop the giblets and livers rather fine and toss them in the butter with the shallots. Add the tarragon, rice, 1 teaspoon salt, 1/2 teaspoon pepper, parsley, and nuts. Toss lightly to blend. If the mixture seems too dry, melt 3 or 4 more tablespoons of butter and blend in lightly to moisten.

Wipe the squab chickens inside and out with a damp cloth. Rub the cavities with the cut lemon. Stuff the birds lightly, skewer the vents, and truss the squabs. Arrange them on their sides on a rack in a very shallow roasting pan and rub the top sides well with butter. Roast in a preheated 400 degree oven for 20 to 25 minutes, then turn them onto the other side. Rub the top sides well with butter and roast 20 minutes more. Turn them breast side up, baste with the pan juices, sprinkle on salt and pepper, and roast 10 to 12 minutes. Be careful not to overcook them. Transfer the birds to a hot platter, remove and discard the string, and garnish with watercress.   SERVES 6.

Mother's Seedcake

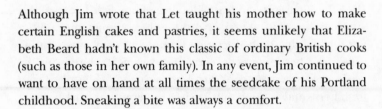

Although Jim wrote that Let taught his mother how to make certain English cakes and pastries, it seems unlikely that Elizabeth Beard hadn't known this classic of ordinary British cooks (such as those in her own family). In any event, Jim continued to want to have on hand at all times the seedcake of his Portland childhood. Sneaking a bite was always a comfort.

1/2 pound unsalted butter	*1 teaspoon baking powder*
1 cup sugar	*1 teaspoon vanilla*
5 eggs	*1–11/2 tablespoons caraway*
2 cups flour	*seeds*
1/2 teaspoon salt	

Cream the butter and the sugar, then add the eggs one at a time, beating thoroughly after each addition. Sift the flour, salt, and baking powder together and stir into the batter. Add the vanilla and caraway seeds, and beat by hand 4 to 5 minutes, or for 2 minutes in an electric mixer. Butter and flour a 9-inch tube or Bundt pan, and pour the batter into it. Bake in a preheated 325 degree oven for 45 to 50 minutes, until done. Cool 5 minutes in the pan before unmolding. MAKES 1 CAKE.

Elizabeth Beard's Mincemeat

"This Mincemeat recipe has been in my family forever and a day, and I consider it just about the best I've ever tasted. First, take 3 pounds brisket or lean rump of beef and 1 fresh beef tongue weighing about 3 pounds. Boil them in water until they are very tender, cool them in the broth, and skim off the fat. Remove all the fat from the meat, and either grind coarsely or chop very fine, and prepare 2 pounds seeded raisins, 2 pounds sultana raisins, 2 pounds currants, 1/2 pound citron, shredded and diced, 1/4 pound orange peel, shredded, 1/4 pound lemon peel, shredded, and 1/2 pound dried figs and dates, cut into small pieces. Chop 11/2 pounds beef suet very, very fine. Put the meats, fruits, suet and peels in a deep crock. Add 2 cups sugar, 1 pint strawberry or raspberry preserves, 1 tablespoon salt, 2 teaspoons nutmeg or

2¹/₂ teaspoons cinnamon, 1 teaspoon allspice, 1 teaspoon mace, and a dash of ground cloves.

"Add a fifth of good sherry and enough cognac to make a rather loose mixture of the meats and fruits—it will take two bottles. If you don't want to use cognac you can substitute Irish or Bourbon Whiskey, or even vodka or gin. Mix very well, cover the crock, and let it stand for a month before you use it. Check each week and add more liquor if it has all been absorbed. Then put it in sterilized jars and seal. This makes a most wonderful Christmas gift."

Mincemeat Tart

With no notice at all, Jim could always evoke the way things were in his boyhood. One December day in 1982 when he and Julia Child sat chatting in his New York greenhouse for the benefit of a television camera, he told her how his mother made the mincemeat that was a regular part of the Beard family Christmases in Portland.

rich tart pastry	1¹/₂ cups mincemeat filling
1 whole egg mixed with	(preceding recipe)
1 tablespoon milk	1¹/₄ cups peeled,
2 tablespoons	chopped apple
cinnamon sugar	¹/₂ cup apricot glaze

Line a 9-inch flan ring with pastry, saving the trimmings. Chill in the freezer for about 1 hour. Roll the trimmings into a 10-inch strip ¹/₄ inch thick. Brush with the egg mixture and sprinkle the cinnamon sugar on top. Cut into strips ¹/₄ inch wide. Preheat the oven to 350 degrees. Combine the mincemeat with the chopped apple. Pour into unbaked tart shell. Use the pastry strips to make a lattice over the mincemeat filling. Put the tart on the lowest rack in the oven, and bake for 1¹/₄ hours, or until the filling bubbles. If the lattice is not lightly brown, raise the tart to a higher rack and continue baking about 15 minutes. While still hot, brush the apricot glaze over the mincemeat through the lattice grill.   SERVES 8.

John Beard's Christmas Egg Nog

▼

Jim once said that as a child he believed that ham and egg nog belonged to Thanksgiving. Maturity ultimately revealed that the family's bountiful sideboard on Christmas Eve was peculiarly American, particularly small-town West Coast American. It seemed to Jim that there are only two requisites for holiday feasting. There must be enormous quantities of food and drink and there must be a few unusual and exciting dishes. "My father's egg nog is decidedly special; the best I've ever encountered," he wrote in a magazine article.

12 egg yolks	*3 cups milk*
4 tablespoons sugar	*4 cups heavy cream*
salt	*1 quart cognac*
nutmeg	*12 egg whites, beaten stiff*

Beat the egg yolks with the sugar until thick, then add a dash of salt, a dash of nutmeg, and gradually beat in the milk. Stir in the heavy cream and the cognac. Fold in the egg whites. Chill thoroughly. To serve, pour the egg nog into a punch bowl set in crushed ice. Dust each cup with freshly grated nutmeg.   SERVES 12 OR MORE.

3

YEARS OF WONDER

While Beard was exploring adolescence as a restless, overweight six-footer with an unmanageable dream, the world around him was just beginning to transform everybody's schemes for the future. Henry Ford's assembly line had changed things—ownership of a brand-new automobile was possible for anyone with $400 to spend. A by-product was the almost immediate mushrooming of roadside "drive-in" markets and hot dog stands. Portland's provision-jammed Yamhill Street wasn't affected, but neighborhood grocers, ma-and-pa confectionery shops, were threatened by the beginning of chain stores as the Great Atlantic and Pacific Tea Company, between 1912 and 1915, opened a new A&P branch every three days somewhere in the country. In the same period, the Piggly Wiggly food stores introduced the concept that became pervasively known as "self service." One of the first supermarkets, San Francisco's Crystal Palace, opened in 1923 with a parking lot big enough to take in 4,000 cars. The first home refrigerators were beginning to be marketed, and Clarence Birdseye's development of packaged frozen fish was in the works.

But immersed as he was in his own small world of plenty, Jim Beard was more interested in his dreams of stardom than in gastronomical progress. For him, good eating was one of life's just desserts, but good performances—onstage rather than in a kitchen—meant the possibility of future roles and appreciative audiences. Although Jim's opportunities to act in school plays were not greater at Washington

High than for the average American teenager of the day, some of his friends knew his ambition, and his yearning for a career in the theater was supported by his mother, who wanted to believe that her son had a voice worth training. She would see to it that he had the education he needed, and in 1921 he enrolled in Reed College. It was a liberal campus by reputation, but not enough to encompass homosexuality. When he was thrown out, and for years afterward, Jim maintained an understandable bitterness.

The present college attitude seems to be that the incident was not important, that Jim was asked to leave because of poor schoolwork.* Highly unlikely. Jim may not have been an organized straight-arrow student, but he had pride enough in his intelligence to avoid flunking out. None of his classmates in Portland survives, but there are other friends who refuse to hear of the possibility of Reed expelling a student for homosexuality, overt or otherwise. Still others remain sure in their memories of the gossip that circulated. Some of them, unwilling to be specific, remember efforts to reassure Jim, to help him restore his self-respect. The best tonic was his mother's encouragement to go to London to study opera, and she staked him to a time there.

"I had heard many of the 'greats' when I was very young, thanks to my mother," Beard told *Opera News* in 1983. When he was not yet six, he added, he had been taken to see *Madama Butterfly*, and on the family's habitual visits to San Francisco's theater district he and his mother had gone to the best-known operas. He was fascinated by the sets and the costumes; he memorized songs. He had a crush on Luisa Tetrazzini, "the Tuscan Thrush," who boasted of never dieting, and he himself boasted later on of having seen Mary Garden in "practically everything she ever did."

At nineteen he set sail for England, following his mother's route through the Canal Zone and the Caribbean. He found the freighter trip achingly boring and threatening to his health. When the boat docked at St. Thomas he set out to counter the miserable ship's fare by foraging in the island's open market. He brought back basketfuls of

---

*In his seventies he told Marion Cunningham that he always got good marks at Reed College, and "he left me with no doubts he was expelled because of homosexuality."

fresh greens, tomatoes, cucumbers, pineapples, and tart cashew melons—the only way, he said later, to stave off malnutrition or beriberi. And in his first long jaunt away from home by himself, he began to see food shopping as one way to learn more about the culture of other places.

Clearly, he was desperate for a good meal when the *Highland Heather* disembarked passengers at Southampton. Years later he wrote that were he asked to remember one meal above all others, he might have to cite the luncheon he had when he walked over to the harbor railroad station restaurant and settled hungrily for pea soup, lamb cutlets, cauliflower polonaise—hardly a meal for a bon vivant but the kind of honest, simple food that he loved and a banquet compared to the meals served at sea.

Jim went on to London to meet Gaetano Loria, a voice coach whose boast was that he had worked for Caruso.* He found Tano (as the coach was called) to be "short, round and jovial" and almost as knowledgeable about food as he was about opera and London's concert scene. The two had common interests in the Royal Opera House and for browsing in the adjacent Covent Garden food market, and their friendship thrived.

Jim found himself spiritually at home in Soho, where "few of its restaurants had succumbed to British influence." Tano introduced him to the Italian eating places that then dominated the neighborhood, including Gennaro's, the restaurant of a recently retired dancer who had brought the cooking style of Milan to London. Gennaro's was famous for decades as a gathering place for the arts. "He had lost his

---

*Caruso and Tetrazzini, who were best friends, shared a passion for pasta. As one of his practical jokes, the tenor offered to make homemade pasta for the lady. "He laughed gleefully when she discovered that he had used her face powder in place of flour." Jim told this story several times when putting together his book *Beard on Pasta*.

figure but not his grace," according to Jim, "and I shall never forget the sight of him tiptoeing, as if on *pointe,* over to a table to present a rose to a lady he wished to welcome."

Gennaro not only served up authentically Italian dishes such as *osso buco alla gremolata* but was regularly host to Beniameno Gigli, and the bel canto baritone Matia Battistini, along with other renowned singers to whom Jim was introduced by his voice coach. Tano's teaching was at least as gastronomical as it was musical, and he was sympathetic to his pupil's limited budget. Another of Loria's favored eating places in Soho was Bertorelli's, where a hungry man could satisfy himself on a one-dish meal (*risotto con funghi,* say) for ninepence. Tano and his wife took Jim on trips into the English countryside to dine with affluent friends, or to harvest wild greens which Tano brought home for salads accented by *pancetta* and fresh mint. For a summer lunch that Jim remembered, the coach sent his protégé to the Ristorante del Commercio, an obscure trattoria where Jim learned to eat uncooked artichokes enhanced by a peppery vinaigrette, and was taught a good deal about other Milanese dishes by the proprietor's daughter.

Tano also encouraged Jim to hoard his allowance for excursions into richer parts of London, perhaps divining that the son of an American hotelkeeper might do well in a secondary career in the world of food—risks being what they were for opera singers. In addition to sampling the first-rate Italian menu at Oddenino's in the West End, Jim foraged at the Savoy Grill, a stopping place for opera's most renowned singers, and at Claridges; and his favorite pastime, as reported in *Delights and Prejudices,* was Sunday afternoon tea at the Ritz in Piccadilly.

He was only heeding his mother: "A sandwich at the Ritz," he once heard her say, "is worth three meals in any other restaurant, no matter how poor you may be, or how hungry." As a student, he couldn't afford to invite friends to dinner, so tea parties became a way of repaying the hospitality of people who had been nice to him. He would invite two or three at a time to join him of an afternoon at the Ritz, and sometimes at Brown's Hotel, or the Grosvenor. With the soothing musical background on which London hotel tearooms prided themselves, Jim found that new English friends appreciated his modest hospitality.

Theatricality revved up London's tempo in the 1920s, and Jim was ready to shift gears with the times. The Savoy Hotel opened its American Bar, and the Savoy Orpheans and the Savoy Havana Band brought the Jazz Age to England. From New York came Paul Whiteman and his orchestra, first of the big bands that were to prevail in the next decades. With the new American downbeat so influential, Beard, who loved all kinds of entertainment, had a chauvinist's pride. But he didn't backslide on his more serious purpose—he went as eagerly to variety shows at the Palladium as he did to concerts in Albert Hall, and he made a lasting friendship with the Palladium's publicist, daughter of a newspaper drama critic. Helen Dircks saw to it that he met opera headliners and other stars of the day. Squiring Mrs. Dircks at the de luxe Pagani restaurant, he took care to add up the check before he paid it, and this won him her approval. "If you had paid the bill without examining it," his guest told him, "I would never have gone out with you again." Not long afterward Jim extended his stylish deportment by having his "first dry Martini" with Mrs. Dircks and her husband at another West End watering hole.

A New York gastronomic critic, describing the London of the twenties, wrote: "People who say that English cooking is poor are inaccurate. The great joints of roast meats at Simpson's! The beautiful grilled soles, whitebait, crabs, lobsters, to be found in London restaurants! The steak and kidney pies at bars!" Jim Beard would have applauded with equal enthusiasm. He hadn't left his confidence at restaurant reviewing back in Portland, and he would continue to champion British food at its best throughout his career. Yet his youthful palate was equally struck by the temptations offered by London's French-born chefs, and he was about to finish his first year in Britain when he began to make plans for his initial stay in Paris.

Meanwhile, in the summer of 1923, friends and acquaintances got the first published news of his activities abroad. On July 22 his picture appeared in the *Oregon Sunday Journal* alongside a story headed, "London Hears Portland Boy in Concert." The event took place in Wigmore Hall, not far from Oxford Circus, where Horowitz and Rubinstein and other virtuosos appeared, and the impresario was Gaetano Loria, described by the *Journal* as "one of the world's foremost teachers of the art of singing, and by many esteemed as the greatest living teacher of diction." Loria, in fact, was retained by the British royal family to work with the stuttering problem of the Duke of York, who later became George VI.

The Portland paper's report quoted extensively from Jim's most recent letter home. He wrote that Melba had just given her farewell concert in London, adding in the tone of a seasoned reviewer, "Her voice shows that it is worn, but her technique is perfect." In the 1923 season, the twenty-year-old Beard said, London had a "wealth of recitals." Paderewski was such a favorite that he was forced by radiant audiences "to play another full program at the end of his concert. They began at 3 and continued to almost 7 o'clock." Listing some of the stars he had heard, he said that Chaliapin, Dinh Gilly, Frieda Hempel, and the American Mario Chamlee "have done their bit to make London brighter." For himself, he reported he had sung three numbers in Italian at the Wigmore Hall debut, followed by one in French, plus "When I Was Twenty" by Tom Dobson. He wasn't the only Oregon singer studying abroad; he reported that Erwyn Mutch's operatic debut in Nice would be of interest to Portland, which was Mutch's hometown as well.

When he arrived in Paris soon after mailing the letter, he stayed at a pension on the rue Jacob, near the Hotel Angleterre at which Ernest and Hadley Hemingway were living and not far from the home of Gertrude Stein and Alice Toklas, who was later to be his friend. Paris in 1923 was a magnet for American expatriates and Jim was ready to take it all in; he was intent upon discovering as much good eating as possible, and to get to the Opéra Comique as often as he could afford.

At his pension he ate the kind of peasant food he savored—calf's feet *poulette*, pot-au-feu, and *blanquette de veau*, and he sometimes had a small spree at another boardinghouse in the rue Bonaparte, where the hors d'oeuvres—a subject that was to come in handy in the next decade—were particularly interesting. With his sporadic correspondence, Portland was still on his mind, however, and the arrival of a hometown visitor, "someone I wished to impress," provided a chance to check out the Au Caneton Restaurant, run by recently arrived Russian émigrés—"more talked about than any other and reputed to be elegant and blessed with a good chef."

To be sure of making a good impression, he called for the visiting Portland lady in a carriage with a convertible top for the drive across the Seine to the rue de la Bourse. As a student not only of food but of all its appurtenances, he was struck both by the decor and the effusive welcome from the maître d'hôtel. "We started the meal with caviar and blinis—my first public adventure with blinis—served with a great crock of cream." He ordered champagne, and it was poured freely, "through shashlik and kasha, vegetables and an elaborate dessert. It was a dinner I have never forgotten, nor have I forgotten the bill. It was a hundred francs—the largest restaurant bill that ever was, I thought at that time." He was consoled when he began to be taken by French acquaintances to such meccas as Boeuf à la Mode (notable because it occupied the house of Cardinal Richelieu near the Palais Royale) and Rumpelmayer's, where the pastries were so tempting "I went on eating for hours." For a special occasion he saved enough to treat himself to Maxim's—as much because he knew by heart the score of Lehár's *Merry Widow* as for the much-touted food.

Through ignorance, Jim confessed later, he missed the restaurant of Prosper Montagne, a chef described by a critic of the period as "distinguished above all others," but when his mentor, Tano, came for a visit in Paris, he took his young singer to Tour d'Argent—"this was before it moved up to the roof of the building it was in." Thirty years later, as co-author with Alexander Watt of a guidebook titled *Paris Cuisine,* he found that the fabled restaurant still served not only its pressed duck but had maintained its notable wine cellar under *chef-caviste* Joseph, and Jim described his experience there as a "supreme pleasure." *Paris Cuisine* also had praise for Maxim's owner, Louis Vaudable, who had become Jim's friend.

Back in London with Tano, Jim went on singing. In all, he learned about fourteen baritone roles—including Emilio in *Carmen,* Ford in *Falstaff* (a role recently sung by the American Lawrence Tibbett, a baritone much admired by Jim). Others included Germont in *La Traviata,* Schaunard in *La Bohème,* Tonio in *I Pagliacci;* and he began working on Wolffram in *Tannhäuser* because, as he said expansively, "they thought I'd develop into a Wagnerian tenor, the way Melchior did." Talking about his musical career, Jim confessed that his hunger for audiences prevented him from turning down chances to perform, no matter how obscure the setting. And when he failed at last to continue, he blamed the fact on nodes which he said had developed on his vocal cords. Friends seem to think that he took the blow in stride, and that the condition of his throat, however serious, provided an excuse. He gave up singing. "It was just foolish to go on," he told *Opera News* in 1983.

Yet he wasn't ready to abandon the nonmusical stage when he made a visit to New York in 1924. He felt some anguish at leaving Europe and reported later that he had "no particular joy" in his first Manhattan exposures. In that moody phase he was permitting himself to forget the simple pleasures of city life. Deep into old age he remained an urban explorer; he had an anthropological curiosity about people and places. In 1924 in New York, while most of the city slept—Jim continued to be an early riser—he canvassed the spreading Washington Market, from north of Fulton Street to Greenwich and East streets. His affection for the old buildings erected early in the nineteenth century remained with him until the great produce head-quarters was moved to Hunt's Point. His curious eye catalogued the array of cheese from Gorgonzola, hams from Flanders, sardines from Norway, native quail, English partridge, freshly landed swordfish, pompano, codfish tongues and cheeks (among his favorite morsels). And he learned his way among the Washington Market eating places.*

In 1924, also, he discovered Schrafft's. He would talk years later with nostalgic appreciation of the restrained Irish waitresses (he would imitate their brogues for those around him as he remembered the precisely trimmed egg salad sandwiches); and he described with boyish approval the ice cream sodas snowcapped with frothy whipped

---

*As described in *From My Mother's Kitchen,* by his friend Mimi Sheraton, whose father was a commission merchant at Washington Market: "I remember...the huge golden brown Western omelets, flecked with green peppers, glassy onions, and dicings of pink ham, accompanied by crisp, yet tender home fries. There was London broil in thick, bloody slices nestled under beefy brown gravy full of fresh mushrooms and served with mashed potatoes; or pink, gently saline corned beef and cabbage with gray, floury boiled potatoes; Yankee pot roast or sauerbraten with potato pancakes, applesauce, and a ruby mound of winy-red cabbage...." He and Mimi liked the same kind of eating.

cream. In that first attempt to take on Manhattan he accepted a job that for all its short run provided an opportunity to combine a little of his hunger for theater with gastronomy. He was hired as master of ceremonies at a coming-out party for junior misses at the Plaza Hotel, where he served cider and doughnuts instead of champagne and caviar.

He took a break in the countryside to visit friends, and returned to find himself struck by an affection for the city that he was to maintain henceforward. On Broadway, a sensation had been created by the opening of *What Price Glory?*, by Lawrence Stallings and Maxwell Anderson; the Theatre Guild had begun to persuade the money people that the old clichés of playwrights were outmoded. Current productions were reflected in the May 10 issue of *The Judge*, a humor magazine, by Ralph Barton's satirical centerfold of drawings showing caricatures of Minnie Maddern Fiske, a fragile Eva Le Gallienne in Molnár's *The Swan,* and Ethel Barrymore in *Romeo and Juliet.*

In spite of, or because of, Prohibition, New York for Jim was "wild and gay," and he made a point of getting a taste of things—as, for example, at a speakeasy where "the ambience was elegant as the Plaza's." He sipped oyster stew one day after a visit to a dentist, while people-watching from a window of the old Waldorf Hotel dining room, and he listened to Lüchow's four-piece orchestra play tunes from *Rigoletto* and sometimes *Madama Butterfly.* "In those impoverished days as an actor in New York in the twenties, I still ate well," he remembered with self-satisfaction. Soon he was being frequently invited to private homes of new friends. For a bachelor-about-town, he said, much depends upon "your agility in the kitchen and how many times you get invited out. I smiled prettily back then, and wore my dinner jacket nearly every night." He maintained an affectionate memory for the Algonquin Hotel, "which was frequented by theatergoers and actors—as well as would-be actors." Like himself.

The midtwenties was a time of national ferment among young Americans interested in theater. Some were old enough to have reacted to the advice of Ireland's Lady Gregory while on tour in the United States: "Start your own theatres. Train amateurs as we have done. Make your theatres in your own images." Reports of the work of George Pierce Baker at Harvard's 47 Workshop also had influenced stagestruck young people in most regions. In Portland, the impact of

John Reed's life was underscored after his death in Moscow and sub-sequent burial in the Kremlin wall.* More than his renown as an early Communist, it was his youth in Portland and his work as a young play-wright and as one of the founders of the Provincetown Theater that made Reed a local celebrity and hero to Jim Beard's friends. While Jim was in New York, another experimental group, the Washington Square Players, got under way. Jim, however, had no luck at casting calls. There was plenty of activity with the works of new playwrights opening and closing, but Jim (at three hundred pounds or thereabouts, and tall enough to dwarf most other aspirants) remained at liberty.

As one last stab in the thespian dark, he tried a direct approach. "I was living in Chelsea," he told an interviewer years later, "and I wrote a very self-assured note to the actor-manager Walter Hampden, because I heard he was casting *Cyrano*—and someone told me he liked tall people, large people. So I remember saying, 'I'm large but not colossal.' Sent the letter, waited, and I didn't hear anything. And then it was Labor Day, nineteen twenty-four, and, lo and behold, there was a special delivery letter from Mr. Hampden." Jim had been eloquent enough to get a walk-on role in the Broadway revival of *Cyrano de Bergerac.* "We rehearsed at Greenwich House, right here in Greenwich Village. We went on the road with practically a special train, because we had horses, children, stage mothers, an enormous cast, and a hell of a lot of scenery."

The experience gave him a realistic sample of the food of the hinterland, and the play itself, night after night, reminded him of food, for the entire second act takes place in a seventeenth-century kitchen.† In a program of the Schubert Pitt Theater in Pittsburgh, his name appears among the cast, and he was in the company when Hampden brought it to New York's Broad Street Theater in December.

---

*In 1981, four years before Beard died, the movie *Reds* was released. This was the story of John Reed, the Communist sympathizer who was in Petrograd with his lover Louise Bryant during the Russian Revolution of 1917. Reed wrote the bestseller *Ten Days That Shook the World* about his experiences. Reed's role was played by Warren Beatty.
†Beard had the chance to learn about mutations in recipes: "A passage in *Cyrano de Bergerac* reveals that lamb stew, *haricot de mouton,* in the days of the Durante-nosed Gascon, was made exclusively of red beans, chopped lamb, and garlic; the original red beans in this primitive ragout were replaced by the upstart turnip . . . then, white beans in the place of red beans." (From *On the Tip of My Tongue,* by Iles Brody, Greenberg, New York, 1944.)

The tour was a chance for Jim to see something of provincial America as well as to gather insights about the acting life. Discreetly naming no names, he wrote that "in my theatrical days I traveled with one of the greatest actresses I have ever known. She should have been very famous, but for her slavery to drink." From her he may have learned very little stage technique he could use himself, but he did pick up a tip about getting sober in a hurry when he noted his inebriated friend "rush-ing into a restaurant or hotel din-

ing room and ordering a large soup plate of canned tomatoes, cold." Invariably, he said, the leading lady's hangover was sufficiently appeased to let the show go on. It was later, after he himself had become a celebrity as a consultant on food and drink, that he could add, "I'm sure that if she'd thrown in a dash of vodka the remedy might have been even better."

At home the Beards did their drinking as connoisseurs. Prohibi-tion failed to stop Elizabeth Beard's use of liqueurs in a recipe which called for them, and on the right occasions wine was served at mealtimes. When Jim returned after the Hampden road tour, moon-shine was part of the social life. "I spent much of my time in my youth helping concoct such stuff. The mother of two pretty girls, very good friends of mine," he wrote in a magazine article, "believed it was wiser for her daughter to entertain at home than to traipse off to local spas where the quality of the liquor and the character of the customers were doubtful. So she gave Sunday evening parties for our young crowd for which preparations began early—when she combined alco-hol and flavorings in a small keg. I spent many Sunday afternoons at their home, rolling about on their floor to blend the ingredients." Jim's father customarily presented a flask of bootleg gin before his son left the house on a party night.

Friendship was Jim's real need, perhaps more so than for most insecure youths. Perhaps, also, because of his mother's inclinations toward people of some consequence, he sought firm connections with his classmate Chester Benson of the hotel Bensons, with David Piper of the *Oregonian* publishing family, and with a number of affluent young women. In those circles he made a place for himself. He was remembered for years as an entertaining party guest. At gatherings in the Piper house, where the whole family was known to be musical, Jim was more than once prevailed upon to sing Gilbert and Sullivan tunes along with current popular songs; and there were taffy pulls, according to another schoolmate, which were also song-filled occasions. On one such merry evening he got himself stuck in the taffy as part of an improvised comedy routine.

His professional experience in a road company was to make him welcome especially among Portlanders who were smitten by the pervasive enthusiasm for the stage. With their mutual yearnings for acting careers, his lifelong admirer Janet Baumhover shared with him a deep admiration for Bess Whitcomb. This teacher and voice coach affected many Portland young people during the heyday of little theater, when active amateur groups included the Liberal College acting company, the Art Theater, the Red Lantern Players, the Portland Civic Theater, and the Beth Whitcomb Players.

There were also professional companies doing repertoire. In this period a neophyte named Billy Gable turned up in Portland with so little money that he and some friends were forced to sleep on the beach at Gearhart. In town, Billy solicited want ads for the *Oregonian*, worked for the telephone company, and sold ties at Meier and Frank's department store, where he met Earl Larrimore, an actor who was well connected in the theater world and the moving spirit of the Red Lantern Players, the company Beard was to join. By the time Billy left for Hollywood, where he became Clark Gable, he had been a pupil of the Portland acting teacher Josephine Dillon, who became his first wife. Gable, Jim said, "would eat at the old Millionaires Club Cafeteria down on Fourth Street. He would eat oatmeal mush and milk twice a day because it was cheap and sustaining."

Fifty years later, Jim's enthusiasm for Portland as a jumping-off place for actors was still high. He talked admiringly of Mayo Methot, the daughter of a Columbia River steamboat captain who grew up as a member of the local stock company and was also a featured actress in Hollywood, where she married Humphrey Bogart. "Then there was Ona Munson, who became an outstanding musical comedy star and went to Hollywood," Jim said. "She did a brilliant job in *Gone With the Wind* as the tart, Belle Watling, who was in love with Gable."

Jim was impatient on the sidelines. He simply loved the theater and wanted parts. Although he had an assortment of jobs for the next few years—he taught at the Gabel Country Day School, worked in the decorating department at Meier and Frank's, and listed himself as a voice coach—he was also a dedicated little theater participant, sometimes as an actor, sometimes as energetic and creative production staffer. He developed a knack for costume design and stage sets.

In 1926–27, the winter season of the Portland Art Players, he played the part of Father Hyacinth in Molnár's *The Swan*. His biggest role of the twenties was as Baron Reghard in Andreyev's *He Who Gets Slapped,* a play that in 1925 was made into a hit movie with Lon Chaney and John Gilbert, who had played juveniles in Portland. Jim was tempted by Hollywood just as his predecessors, and he took the advent of talking pictures as an incentive to head south.

Palm trees lined the streets into Hollywood, orange groves had their beginnings in backyards. Across Mount Lee stretched the thirteen four-story-high letters that spelled out HOLLYWOODLAND as the designation of a new real estate development. The town's boulevard seemed alive with bathing beauties, extras in Indian warpaint and feathers, others at high noon in black-and-white evening attire. Tile-roofed stucco houses dominated the low skyline, and the scent of eucalyptus trees was pervasive. In the wake of his introduction to John Gilbert, son of the Portland theater director, Jim Beard surveyed the scene with insatiable curiosity about everything that contributed to this nouveau-riche style of life.

Burgeoning Hollywood was the magnet for what was known in the era as "flaming youth." Elinor Glyn, creator of the "It" girl, author of novels replete with tiger skins and voluptuous passion, titillated a public still too unsophisticated to accept fiction that dealt with homosexuality. Her *Three Weeks* was only whispered about in places like Portland. In Hollywood, the dream factory, Glyn held sway as a writer and sometime director, and the kind of iconoclasm she represented appealed to young Americans who felt fettered by provincial inhibitions. Hollywood must have seemed to Jim, as it did to many Americans and Europeans as well, a place where anything goes, where sexual preference didn't have to be covert.

One of the friends Jim made was Paul Fielding, an effete young Englishman who had been brought up in India and who shared Jim's fascination for a place that had so much effect on everyday life. The way Hollywood behaved was changing—women redid their hairstyles to look like the stars; they read gossip columns to learn how to entertain. Unattached men were increasingly the delight of fledgling hostesses, and Fielding had international connections more imposing than Jim's.

Together they noted the Hollywood homes in which menu books were kept for guests and their favorite cocktails listed. Through Fielding Beard met the family of William de Mille, whose daughter, the choreographer Agnes de Mille, remained a lifelong friend. Here there was none of the excess of the more ambitious Hollywood crowd. In contrast to his brother Cecil B. De Mille, William was a scholarly Broadway director and playwright whose only film to be preserved, *Miss Lulu Betts,* is in the Museum of Modern Art collection. In a tree-shaded house more fitting for upstate New York than southern California, the two de Mille girls and their parents lived unpretentiously, and Beard and Fielding were among frequent guests.

Through the cordial relationship, Jim met Cecil B. De Mille and was cast as an extra in the 1927 movie *The King of Kings,* in which he is to be recognized among bit players at the base of the cross. He landed a role that year as a German officer in an Erich von Stroheim film called *Queen Kelly* that was never to be distributed in spite of having as its star the youthful Gloria Swanson. There were also some "dress extra" jobs and other walk-on bits, but he came closest to being singled out as a singer when he appeared in prologues at Grauman's Chinese Theater (once he was cast as Buddha), where stage pageantry with an orchestra was part of the big movie house presentations of the period. "I was in one for *Noah's Ark* [a De Mille movie]," he reported.

He was back in Portland to play a minor role in Elmer Rice's *The Adding Machine,* an expressionist drama that had helped to shake up Broadway while Jim had been in Europe; and the same year, again as a member of the Taylor Street Players, he was in the cast of *A Christmas Carol,* a dramatization by a local writer, for which he also, as he recalled years later, had a hand in doing all the costumes. Onstage, Beard proved to be well cast as J. B. Fezziwig, the self-important businessman satirized by Charles Dickens for his own amusement as much as for that of readers. Dickens wrote that Fezziwig's ankles "winked as he danced," an image that brings a smile to the remembrance of Jim as a young actor the size and shape of Oliver Hardy.

In his brief professional acting career, the whimsy in Rostand's *Cyrano* highlights another trope suggestive of Jim. In the play, the baker cries, when questioned about his love of theater, *"I adore it!"* He's willing to pay for his art in bread or in tarts, pies, and cakes. *"Well,"* rejoins his interlocutor, *"pastry pays for all."* Back in Portland, little theater friends were similarly cheered by the backstage meals Jim often organized as a kind of trade-off for the conviviality of opening night.

In addition to the amateur productions, he found chances to add to his teaching income by working for Portland radio stations. For a while he was a round-the-clock utility announcer, and in company with Janet Baumhover, a stock company veteran named Lawrence Keating, and Isabel Errington (who was to be an important part of his future), he acted in radio serials—one called *Covered Wagon Days,* and *Homicide Squad,* turned out weekly with local police cooperation. Among other things, every Sunday they did a dramatization of the funny papers. Jim played Daddy Warbucks in a piece of adroit casting, as well as the comic strip caricature "The Little King." (It was a lifelong habit of his to turn first to the comics when picking up a newspaper.) He remembered the broadcasts from KOIN with jaded humor. "To see this group of fairly worldly people arriving at 8:30 a.m. to get ready...all looking a little bit bleary from the night before and then being utterly funny-paper on the air was quite an experience."

Always restless, Jim took some time off to go south to San Francisco, where he worked in other radio plays. He spent part of one summer in Seattle at the University of Washington, studying with Ben Iden Payne, a distinguished teacher who had directed the Abbey Players and had staged Shakespeare in England and for Walter Hampden in the United States. In 1932 Jim entered the Drama Department at Carnegie Institute of Technology in Pittsburgh for more work with Iden Payne, and there he met Franklin Heller, who was to have a long career in the theater and television and who remembered Beard as a college actor.

Jim and Franklin Heller were both cast to play the leading role in *Kismet*, a part created by Otis Skinner on Broadway and performed in a movie by Ronald Colman. Beard and Heller were scheduled to appear in alternate performances when *Kismet* was produced on campus. A half century afterward, Heller realized that Jim "had the stature and voice that fit the flamboyant role. Neither of us was very accomplished but I think it is fair to say that Jim was a terrible actor and I was not very good. But I was neither as awkward nor as artificially declamatory as Jim was.... The comparison between us became not only obvious but laughable...." Beard confessed to Heller that his inadequacy made him drop out of Carnegie. He was back in Portland in the early thirties, when there were yearly productions of an adaptation of *Alice in Wonderland* performed on platforms as part of the city's annual Rose Festival. With an almost equally corpulent theater buff named John Emmel, Jim helped to create a stir in vivid performances as Tweedledum and Tweedledee. Several lifelong comrades—Harvey Welch, Janet Baumhover, the White Queen, and a third close confidante, Harriet Hawkins, as the Red Queen—were in the cast.

Bob Mayberry, a young newcomer, also found a role in *Alice*, after which Jim introduced him to a Seattle friend who helped Mayberry get settled at the University of Washington, and thus began another lasting friendship. Still under twenty, Mayberry was found equally appealing by Elizabeth Beard and her son. He was a welcome overnight guest at the Beard house on Salmon Street, and Mrs. Beard was sufficiently taken with him to prepare his breakfast in her ample kitchen with its "flaked oatmeal wallpaper." Mayberry thought of Jim as a helpful big brother, and felt at home in the Beard ménage. Fifty years late, he pictured the steps that led from the kitchen door to the backyard that was shaded by the walnut tree planted by Jim as a boy. He remembered vividly sitting down to Mrs. Beard's fried chicken at a big table near the stove. He had Jim's filial support away from the family, and Jim's friend Bess Whitcomb took him on as a pupil during the time that he was also studying musical composition.

When a Whitcomb production of Chekov's *The Three Sisters* was underway, Mayberry did the background music, Jim was cast as the moody uncertain Andrei Prosorov, and Isabel M. Errington was the inconstant Masha. The play was staged in the expansive living room of one of Portland's richest families—it was the kind of comfortable atmosphere that Jim Beard found most appealing.

He found his way into other such homes when he took up catering. Among his friends was Agnes Crowther, who had begun a career as an interior decorator in Portland before moving on to New York, and she had clients among the affluent sections of their hometown. "As an adjunct to Agnes's decorating services," Jim wrote in *Delights and Prejudices*, "I went to clients' houses to teach them how to cook complete dinners, usually international in flavor." He was something new in Portland—a young man of the world who could make a catered party an entertaining evening by his gift of conversation.

Some of his Portland friends, looking back, remembered Jim as always having had social talents. Yet in the view of Hattie Cass (who had been Hattie Hawkins before her marriage), when he was in school Jim had had "a fat boy complex" that wasn't easily overcome. His insecurities began to disappear only after "he began to click in the theater." He was considered by his mates, she thought, as "a father confessor." He seemed to know New York and he'd made his pass at Hollywood. His spirit had been bashed but he was sure that New York was where he belonged. Hattie remained convinced that the sense of being an outsider haunted him, and he and she would take long walks together and talk of the allure of New York.

dreams and of the allure of New York.

As it turned out, in those Depression years, some of his friends were ready to leave Portland before Jim could manage it. When Hattie announced her departure, Jim shared his New York impressions by composing for his friend his own subjective guide to Manhattan, and dedicated the effort to "My Well Beloved Countess to be used by her as a guide to the Baron's New York." It was a compilation of Jim's recommendations for shopping, eating out, going to museums, and other cultural amusements available night and day. His identity as the "Baron" was a joke instilled by the admiration of his friends for his style as a well-dressed man about Portland.

Another facet of Jim's style showed itself in a breakfast farewell which he arranged as a surprise for Hattie and a friend who were to drive the distance to New York. "He lured us to meet for a farewell parting at a favorite spot just outside of town," Hattie told me. "When we showed up at 6:30 a.m. as it had been arranged, we caught the aroma of coffee from an enamelled pot on the fire he had built. Eggs and bacon were sizzling, and he'd brought a red-checked tablecloth for the table on trestles. The center of the table was piled with fruit, and then other friends showed up and there were farewell speeches, all arranged by Jim." He presented the New York guidebook to Hattie with a flourish, and a flowery inscription:

Old Lady Gotham is a stern, gay, fascinating, lecherous old wench—learn to love her and forgive her faults—cherish her gifts and moods.

The scrawled paean to cosmopolitan attractions was still treasured by Hattie after Jim died. In it she had found the essence of a young romantic's New York. There is straightforward advice on how to get settled, names of Beard friends who would be helpful, the recommendation that restaurants like Childs and the Automat "are always clean and good." However, much of Jim's guide extols the attractions of the Metropolitan and other museums, the convenience of the streetcars, the charm of a bus ride uptown to Riverside Drive, the lure of the piers where ocean liners could be boarded by visitors, and the Brevoort Hotel, which he praises as representing "Old New York"—where a girl like Hattie can imagine herself a real star of the stage like "the great Lina Cavalieri, or some other such person."

Hattie took this guidance to heart as Jim, figuratively spinning his wheels in Portland, played the part of Burbage in *Elizabeth the Queen* in 1935. He was a costume designer for Bess Whitcomb's production of *Much Ado About Nothing*, and had the title role in Frederick Jackson's comedy *The Bishop Misbehaves*. Local newspaper reviewers were warm. "Mr. Beard," said the *Oregonian*, "gave every indication of just being poured into the part." *The News Telegram* on the same day cited the suaveness and gentle charm of the leading

Scene from The Bishop Misbehaves

player. His friends were pleased because they understood his chronic need for appreciation.

Perhaps the greatest positive influence was that of Bess Whitcomb, who loved Jim, Janet Baumhover said, "above the others in the group and wanted him to succeed." Bess Whitcomb fueled Jim's will to think well of himself. She cast him in two Chekov plays, and their friendship continued until her death at ninety-one in California. She had more talent as a director, he said, than anyone else he knew. The town, however, had another gifted director and actor named Earl Larrimore, who had hired Billy Gable to join the Red Lantern Players. Larrimore later signed Jim Beard to travel with his company as it brought *Hedda Gabler* to serious audiences in towns along the Columbia River and, as lighter entertainment, presented *Nothing But the Truth*—sometimes to backwoods Oregon lumber camps. Larrimore and Jim became close friends, and Jim followed Larrimore's success with yearning as the latter went to Broadway to be cast in Theatre Guild productions of Eugene O'Neill plays.

Soon Jim faced some facts. He was ready to settle in New York, and still hoped to make it in the theater world. "I know I had a lot of talent," he said from the rosy perspective of old age, "I was convinced of it. But I was so definitely typed ... because I was large. I was scarcely beautiful. I had ability but if I got something it would be a little bit thing. ... So I thought it would be wiser to look first for something that was financially more agreeable." At last he put enough money together to go East. "There was doubt that I would ever be the greatest star that ever trod Broadway," he said decades later, "so I began to think of what I would have fun doing."

RECIPES

Watercress Tea Sandwiches

Elizabeth Beard considered herself a connoisseur of London's hotel tearooms and a specialist in tea sandwiches. Her son learned to gather watercress along local streams, and when he himself got to London he soon became addicted to watercress sandwiches served along with scones and tea breads much like those he had first had from his mother's kitchen.

4 thin slices brown bread *coarse salt*
(whole wheat, oatmeal, or *1/3 cup chopped*
barley grain) *fresh watercress*
4 tablespoons unsalted butter *2 tablespoons mayonnaise*

Cut the crusts from the bread and spread generously with butter. Add a light sprinkle of the coarse salt to the watercress and mix with the mayonnaise. Spread on two slices of bread and cover each with a second slice. Cut the sandwiches in quarters and arrange on a plate to serve with tea or other drinks.   MAKES 8 SMALL SANDWICHES.

The Savoy's Famous Omelet

When studying music in London, the young Beard saved his farthings for splurges at such restaurants as Simpson's on the Strand and the Savoy Grill. At the latter, he noted how often the haddock omelet, named for the critic and novelist Arnold Bennett, was served, and he took some pains in *Theory & Practice of Good Cooking* to explain the technique for the filling.

1/2 pound cooked finnan *freshly ground pepper*
haddie, flaked (11/4 cups) *6 eggs*
2 tablespoons grated *1 tablespoon unsalted butter*
Parmesan cheese *3 tablespoons heavy cream*
salt

Mix the finnan haddie with the grated cheese and add a sprinkling of salt and pepper. Break the eggs into a bowl. Heat the butter in an omelet pan until the butter foams. Beat the eggs lightly and pour into the hot butter. Cook briskly over high heat until the edges become firm and the center is runny. Spread the flaked fish in the center and pour on the cream. Place the omelet under a hot grill until it begins to brown and is bubbly. Slide onto a hot serving plate without folding the omelet over. SERVES 2 OR 3.

Waldorf Salad à la Beard

▼

The Waldorf Hotel was for Jim the epitome of New York style, a place he would not have missed on his first brief Manhattan stay. Later, he became a colleague of Oscar Tshirky, who invented this salad ("originally merely equal parts of diced tart apple and celery with mayonnaise") on a night when Walter Damrosch conducted the New York Symphony Orchestra for a benefit held in the hotel.

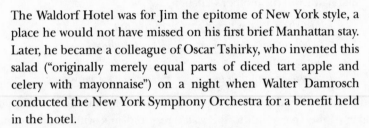

1½ cups diced tart apple	*mustard*
1½ cups thinly sliced celery	*salad greens*
⅔ cup mayonnaise	*walnuts*

If the apples are beautifully colored, you might keep some of the brilliant red or green skin on. Combine the apple dice with the celery and bind with good mayonnaise (preferably homemade) flavored with mustard. Arrange on a bed of greens, sprinkle with chopped walnuts, and put a perfect whole walnut half in the center. SERVES 4.

Continental Sauce à la Palace Court

▼

As a boy, Beard thought of San Francisco as "my dream city" and the court of the Palace Hotel as the ideal place for elegant dining. This sauce was created by Alfred J. Bohn, the Palace's chef in the years before World War II, to serve with chicken or steak.

4 large mushroom caps	1/2 pound beef marrow
1 onion	1/4 cup red wine
2 shallots	1/4 pound unsalted butter
1 clove garlic	1 tablespoon chopped parsley
2 tablespoons olive oil	1 tablespoon crushed black
2 tomatoes, chopped	peppercorns
1 cup beef stock	salt
3 tablespoons glace	
de viande	

Clean and chop the mushrooms. Peel the onion, shallots, and garlic, chop, and add to the mushrooms, then sauté in olive oil for about 5 minutes. Add the tomatoes, stock, and meat glace, bring to the boil, and cook 10 minutes. Off heat, stir in the marrow. Stir in the wine and the butter. Add the parsley and the pepper. Salt only if necessary.   MAKES ABOUT 1 QUART.

Crisp-Bottomed Pan-Fried Potatoes

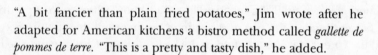

"A bit fancier than plain fried potatoes," Jim wrote after he adapted for American kitchens a bistro method called *gallette de pommes de terre*. "This is a pretty and tasty dish," he added.

3–4 large baking potatoes	salt
1/4 cup butter or beef fat	freshly ground pepper

Peel and slice the potatoes. Melt the butter or beef fat in a heavy skillet, reserving about half of the butter or fat. Arrange the sliced potatoes in a spiral layer in the bottom of the pan, starting from the center and building out around the edges, so the potatoes overlap slightly. Repeat in layers, dotting each with one with fat and seasoning to taste with salt and pepper. Cover the pan and cook slowly until the potatoes are soft and the bottom and sides crisply brown. Invert onto a heated plate.   SERVES 3 TO 4.

Poire Maxim's

In *Paris Cuisine*, the rue Royale restaurant so loved by Jim is called probably the most famous in the world. "No other restaurant with the possible exception of Jack and Charlie's 21 in New York has become so much a household word," he wrote. This recipe came to him from the owners, Louis Vaudable and his wife, Maggie.

2 cups sugar　　　　　　　　*1 inch vanilla bean*
2 cups water　　　　　　　　*6 pears*

Mousse:
9 egg yolks　　　　　　　　*1 pint heavy cream, beaten*
1½ cups sugar　　　　　　　*very stiff*
½ cup Grand Marnier

Garnish: vanilla ice cream
　　and whipped cream

To poach the pears, boil 2 cups of sugar, 2 cups of water, and the vanilla bean for 5 minutes. Meanwhile, peel the pears, cut them in half, carefully remove the seeds, and core. Cook them in the syrup until tender but still firm. Lift them from the pan to a towel on a plate and chill. For the mousse, beat the egg yolks with 1½ cups of sugar in the upper part of a double boiler, over simmering water, until the mixture "forms a ribbon" when you drop it from the beater. Remove the pan and continue beating until the mixture is cool. Add the Grand Marnier and fold in the beaten cream. Chill the mousse in a serving dish. To serve, arrange the pear halves in a circle on top of the mousse. Fill the center with vanilla ice cream and decorate with sweetened whipped cream piped through a pastry bag.　　　　SERVES 8 TO 10.

French Tile Biscuits

Commonly called *tuiles,* Jim recognized this specialty of his mother's friend Julie on his first trip to Paris. As a French cook in Oregon, Julie shared many recipes with the Beards, and Jim was an admirer of her talent all his life. Shaped like terracotta roof tiles, Julie's cookies, Jim said, became a permanent part of the family repertoire.

6 tablespoons soft butter　　　*2 egg whites*
½ cup sugar

| *¹/₃ cup sifted* | *salt* |
| *all-purpose flour* | *1 cup sliced almonds* |

Cream the butter and sugar together until well blended. Stir in the egg whites, flour, a pinch of salt, and the nuts. Butter a heavy cookie sheet and drop the batter by teaspoonfuls 1½ inches apart, leaving enough room to allow them to spread. Bake in a 400 degree oven for about 8 minutes, or until golden brown around the edges and slightly yellow in the center. Remove the cookies from the sheet with a spatula and press them onto a rolling pin while still hot. Leave them for a few minutes and remove to a cake rack to cool completely.   MAKES ABOUT 2 DOZEN.

Bananas Caribbean

During his long freighter voyage through the Caribbean and on to London by way of the Azores, the youthful Jim developed an affection for bananas which he put to good use when he began to polish his party skills.

| *1 banana per person* | *vanilla ice cream* |
| *grated coconut* | *banana liqueur* |

Select large unblemished bananas. Use a sharp knife to split the skin lengthwise. Carefully pull it away from the fruit so that it remains intact in one piece. Spread the coconut out on a smooth surface and roll each peeled banana in it. Arrange the skins on plates. Fill the skins with a layer of ice cream. Cut the coconut-coated bananas in thick slices and insert into the ice cream so they will stand upright. Spoon over each serving a little banana liqueur and sprinkle with more coconut.

Schrafft's Oatmeal Cookies

Jim's admiration for Schrafft's began when he first sampled the good things of New York, and it continued until Schrafft's influence on cookie-lovers ended in the seventies. He suggested the research that turned up this recipe. The original formula produced ten-pound batches, so with Beard an interested overseer, we reduced the amounts to produce a family-sized supply. Jim would have preferred the original quantity.

1/4 pound butter	1/2 teaspoon baking soda
1 cup sugar	1/2 teaspoon salt
2 eggs	1 teaspoon cinnamon
1 teaspoon vanilla	1/2 teaspoon allspice
1 1/2 cups oatmeal	1/4 cup milk
1 1/2 cups flour	1 cup raisins
1/2 teaspoon baking powder	1 cup chopped walnuts

Cream the butter and sugar together. Add the eggs and vanilla and beat until light and fluffy. Stir in the oats. Mix and toss the flour, baking powder, baking soda, salt, cinnamon, and allspice, then add the butter-sugar-egg mixture and the milk. Beat until well blended. Stir in the raisins and nuts. Drop by tablespoonfuls onto greased baking sheets, about 1 1/2 inches apart. Bake in a preheated 350 degree oven for 12 minutes. Remove and cool on racks.

MAKES ABOUT 40 COOKIES.

4

NEW YORK, ACT ONE

The welcome by a handful of his closest Portland friends was, in its way, affirmation of Jim's lifetime loyalty to his childhood milieu. He was peripatetic by nature, but he always clung to his roots. He came east this time as a migrant who already knew New York as well as Great Britain and France, and Hattie Cass, as one who came to greet him, had not forgotten that it was he who had written the guidebook that had helped her settle in four years earlier. Now he was in Manhattan to stay, come what may.

The welcomers included Harvey Welch who, with Jim and Hattie, was affectionately remembered by the latter as one of "the three steps," so called because of their relative height. The hometowners already living in New York were rounded out by the interior decorator Agnes Crowther, who had moved her career east and whose real estate savvy provided, near the theater district, a minimal West Side apartment into which Jim moved.

It was an easy walk to any of the ninety playhouses then scattered through the Times Square area, or to Shubert Alley, which was thronged with supplicants when a production was being cast. Nearby also were the radio stages of CBS, and of NBC with its Red and Blue Networks. Shocking the entire complacent nation, the Mercury Theater led by Orson Welles had broadcast in 1938 the fictional news of a Martian invasion, and Clifford Odets's *Golden Boy* was still a big hit, along with Thornton Wilder's *Our Town*. But it was also the year that recession interrupted economic recovery from the Great Depression and it proved to be a bleak one for out-of-work actors as well as the country generally.

Identifying sometimes with the "haves" instead of the "have nots" may have been one of Jim's significant characteristics—he'd been polishing his mastery of social amenities most of his life. In New York he had used the same techniques as he had in London and Hollywood. He had developed for himself the air of a gentleman conqueror. At six-feet-three or -four with his weight varying from two hundred to three hundred pounds, he carried himself as if to the manor born. To Hattie in the guide that he'd written, he had expressed himself clearly: "The one with the grim determination to battle through in New York wins—always let it be known you think you are the best."

Soon after unpacking in his walk-up flat, he began his New York battle in a manner true to the advice he had given. As he renewed old acquaintanceships in the city, his circle widened, even as he and his Oregon friends explored the reality of living frugally. Jim's capacity to enjoy his friends, and the good (not necessarily costly) things of life, was at least as developed as his fixation on the future. He retained his ability to live for the moment when he had the security of friendship. He found pleasure in showing his concern for others, and was, as Hattie emphasized, "a father figure who cared." Before he had joined them, she and the other Portlanders had sometimes splurged by meeting at one or another of Childs's white-tiled restaurants, where a six-course meal could be had in those unaffluent times for seventy-five cents. (In the Benson Hotel in Portland a meal of considerable panache cost $1.50.) Childs was all right for Jim, but there were eating places he considered more interesting.

"Jim introduced us to food we didn't know anything about—in Little Italy. All over town," Hattie recalled. For Jim, in the twenties and thirties, when there were pushcart markets everywhere, New York was a street show of sight as well as sound. He had been excited to find the French, the Greeks, and the Irish selling "old country" provisions

on Ninth Avenue, with Bleecker Street almost exclusively Italian.*
Along Second Avenue he found Hungarians, Germans, and Czechs,
and on Delancey there were Jews and Italians, intermingling with
Chinese on Mulberry Street. The Portlanders tagged along with Jim
in the discovery, as well, of unaccustomed tastes in the restaurants of
cooks from all over the Mediterranean, and he used them as willing
guinea pigs when he tried to emulate ethnic meals.

Sometimes, Hattie said, the friends would pool their money, and
Jim would do the cooking. One night, she remembered, as they
turned the corner under the Sixth Avenue El and started up his
brownstone steps, Beard saw a big basket of field mushrooms outside
the basement grocery that spilled out onto the sidewalk. "Jim transformed them into enormous plates of mushrooms and toast—oceans
of both." In addition, there were those times, as his social circle
expanded, when Jim "sang for his supper." As he had in his first
New York stint, he concocted feasts for affluent new acquaintances,
who, taken by his companionship, began to include him on their
guest lists.

According to Lucius Beebe, the *Herald Tribune* café society
columnist, the Depression was a time when any sophisticated young
man or woman, with good manners and a stylish wardrobe, could live
"like J. P. Morgan" for next to nothing. For Jim, the later years of
success never dimmed the romantic view he had of himself as a
youthful New Yorker. "I worked that gambit pretty well for a couple of
years. I'd play theater often, I guess. I'd go and buy one beautiful rose
and send it to a hostess with thanks, which probably meant more than
if I had sent a dozen."

He could no longer deny to himself that his size precluded him
from casting calls for most Broadway productions. He was trying to
hang on in the theater world; while he made his bread-and-butter at
parties, he tried to make use of the backstage crafts acquired at
Carnegie Tech. Even so, while he was more interested in designing
the sets for new plays, he found more attention paid to his ideas for

*Among Americans in general, an ethnic uneasiness was prevalent, even in the sports
arenas. In 1939, *Life* magazine, in an article full of praise for Joe DiMaggio, the Yankee

costumes. Making the rounds—he "had a good portfolio," a friend said—he met Cheryl Crawford, a producer with the Theatre Guild who had been one of the founders with Harold Clurman and Lee Strasberg of the Group Theatre.

Cheryl Crawford didn't get him any closer to the footlights, but she did recognize his gifts of style and presentation. When she gave a cocktail party crowded with actors and others of the stage—and William Carlos Williams as well—she hired Jim as the caterer. "The crowd came away from the party saying he did such marvellous things—everything looked so marvellous on the table!" His flair for design made his presentation of buffet meals the talk of parties that might otherwise have been dull. Moreover, he was accepted as one of the guests. But clever as Cheryl believed Jim to be as a designer, there were few jobs that she could line up for him.

He needed a steady stipend, and something of the sort came his way when a friend named Mary Houston Davis helped to get him hired by a New Jersey private girls' school. There his assignment was not to a domestic science kitchen but to a classroom where he taught

---

superstar, pointed out what made him different from most who were not of Wasp origins. "Instead of olive oil or smelly bear grease, he keeps his hair slick with water. He never reeks of garlic and prefers chicken chow mein to spaghetti."

English, conversational French, and civics. By this time in his rounds of parties, Hattie Cass's housemate Peggy Martin, a dashing redhead who worked in a bookstore, had entered his life. She was the girlfriend of James B. Cullum, Jr. Cullum was a graduate of West Point (where Cullum Hall is named for his family), and he had an elegant Washington Square apartment with an extra bedroom in which Beard lived while commuting daily to his classes. As his friendship with Jim Cullum developed, he was a frequent guest at the Cullum family's Riveredge Farm near Reading, Pennsylvania, and between the farm and the apartment he was able to demonstrate the abilities he had shown for getting a party off the ground with good food. His conversation was always exuberant, full of travel talk and gossip about the kind of people most friends at home in Portland would have liked to meet. Portlander Margaret Jennings thought Cullum "just plain dull. He courted Jim," she said, "because Jim added an exciting dimension to life."

The Cullums lived in a style to which Jim wanted to become accustomed. Riveredge Farm was a country setting with topiary effects which Jim once described as "a garden for displaying the art of the gardener." The family owned a place in France, which they called the White Farm, where everything was white, including flowers and buildings; symbolic of peace, it had been established in memory of a son lost in World War I. Jim Cullum had a career as a Wall Street statistician and he was a wine connoisseur—his Washington Square apartment had a large closet full of good vintages. Beard considered him a master of gracious living. He drove an apple-green Rolls-Royce with a canvas convertible top and isinglass curtains.[*]

In such company he met Irma Rhode and her brother Bill, who were friends of Lucius Beebe and Richardson Wright, editor of *House & Garden*. Beard said later he'd never met anyone so disarmingly likable or who "so flourished in the limelight" as Bill Rhode. The two shared stories of high times in Hollywood and in continental watering holes, and Bill knew how to make "good copy wherever he went," as

---

[*]On a visit to the Cullums' White Farm, Jim borrowed another vehicle to go for a drive only to be baffled by the intricacies of the foreign-made machine. He found himself unable to prevent the car from going in one continuous circle, and when he was rescued he swore never again to get behind the wheel. He never drove again.

Beard put it. Equally to the point, the two Rhodes had as much passion for food as Jim, and after a talk that lasted into the early morning hours they all—with the encouragement of the influential Beebe and others, plus financial help from Jim Cullum—decided to open a food shop in the heart of New York's upper east side. Prohibition's era of speakeasies was over and Americans were becoming persuaded that hospitality could be assessed by means of the quality, or its lack, of the snacks that were served with drinks.

"We developed plans that would astonish the bellies of New York," Jim wrote in *Delights and Prejudices.* It may well have been the moment for such surprise, for at the Stork Club Sherman Billingsley was being applauded for serving with cocktails a mere bowl of celery, olives, radishes, and scallions buried in crushed ice. The idea of tidbits to temper the effect of drinks was a carryover from the free lunch served at saloons. Seasoned imbibers were just beginning to accept that thought, while distinguished men-about-town like the critic and humorist Robert Benchley still worried more over the contents of the glass (a martini, Benchley has been quoted as saying, required three parts gin and just enough vermouth to take away that ghastly watery look). A sustaining bite of finger food, hostesses now began to believe, could bring some elegance to the serving of drinks, as well as provide a sop for the alcohol.

Of an estimated two hundred fifty cocktail parties held daily in the affluent neighborhood between Fifth Avenue and the East River, and between Ninety-sixth Street and the Fifties, Beard and his new partners calculated that at least half were catered affairs. They took note of the fact that in those prewar times many pecuniary New Yorkers had full-time help, with a majority of such household staffs categorized as "Irish maids" who were willing enough but sketchily trained in the amenities of the American living room. What was needed in Manhattan "society" was provocative, attractively served food to accompany the party-time drinks. A cool glass in hand was not enough to insure a hostess the success she yearned for in those days of post-Prohibition relaxation. The challenge for Jim as a young entrepreneur—who never lost his distaste for the cocktail hour, which he described as "this bastard form of entertainment"—was to replace the prevalent tiny, soggy canapés of the hors d'oeuvre tray (his word was "doots") with elegant morsels that showed care and creativity.

Next door to the sorority for accomplished women called the Cosmopolitan Club, Jim and the Rhodes found a carriage house with a kitchen. Jim had the sure knowledge of his mother's catering days, and Irma Rhode had been tutored in cooking by the Grand Duchess of Baden. The appreciation of New York immigrant neighborhoods had made Jim a canny shopper for ethnic foods and this kind of provender sparked the imaginations of all three. When, for instance, a steady source of tiny artichokes was found, they devised ways to stuff them with foie gras, pâté, and caviar. A sudden recollection of his freighter voyage through the Caribbean once caused Jim to search Ninth Avenue for hours, until he found enough bananas the size of his little finger with which to decorate a silver service platter.

"We were revolutionaries," Jim told one friend in jest. "We were determined to do things that were different. We used tiny tomatoes which were a novelty in those days, and I'm sure we were the first to stuff them." Decades later, when he went to a party in a huge Florentine villa with his friend Bill Veach, he found that Veach had adapted the idea and passed it on to their friend the Marchesa Esther Maurigi. The cherry tomatoes that were being served had been scooped out and stuffed with jellied tomato aspic that was dusted with eggs mimosa under a swirl of mayonnaise. The dish, set in cracked ice, looked very elegant, he remembered, and he wasn't displeased to find a remnant of their catering establishment Hors d'Oeuvre Inc. on the banks of the Arno.

Cornucopias of smoked salmon filled with horseradish cream were another specialty of the hors d'oeuvres makers that Jim saw frequently at other people's parties. "We created an hors d'oeuvre," he recalled, "that has been a world beater ever since—it was simply rounds of brioche spread with good mayonnaise and slices of brisk onion. The edges were rolled in mayonnaise and again, in chopped parsley, to make as beautiful an hors d'oeuvre as one can think of. It has been copied by every caterer in the country and by housewives everywhere. We started them in 1938 and they have been going forty years and have grown in popularity. So I suppose that if the Rhodes and I did nothing else in our lives, we pleased the palates of probably millions of people by this simple onion ring."

Decades later Jim received a letter from Maida Heatter, by then a well-known restaurateur and cookbook author whose father, Gabriel Heatter, had been a highly regarded newscaster: "Your onion sandwiches," she wrote, "were famous at my mother's and father's home. During World War 2 there were many important people in government from both London and Washington in and out of their home constantly. The onion sandwiches were always ready. I wish you could have heard the raves..." Unrestrained praise never disconcerted Beard; he reveled in the closing paragraph of the letter: "I could go on and on...as far back as Poulet Paul Gauguin. You've provided us with so much happiness. We all love you." The recognition was like caviar and champagne, which he could consume, separately or together, without ever having enough. He was willing to accept a great deal of credit for the success earned by the three partners.

While sliced bread was still revered as a labor-saving gift to the average kitchen, they searched out immigrant bread bakers in every borough and used the often rustic flavorsome loaves to make elegant cartwheel sandwiches of puréed ham, or herb-seasoned veal or chicken paste. Like the world-beater brioche rounds, the hand-formed ethnic loaves called for a sharp and steady device, and Beard therefore found himself performing with a crank-operated slicer that turned out delicate, even collops half the thickness of factory-sliced bread.

In most of America, the Depression had eliminated many local bakeries which had supplied old-fashioned bread full of nutrients. For those consumers who still cared there was not much that they could do about the situation. But there was one newcomer from Europe who hoped to make his protest in dramatic terms. He was the playwright Bertolt Brecht, author of *The Threepenny Opera,* a great theatrical hit in 1928, and he was in Hollywood. As a refugee writer, free to express himself with ideas no matter how offbeat, Brecht saw in the subject of bread the possibility of a movie. The tastelessness of the loaves produced on assembly lines seemed to him to symbolize what was wrong in America.

In his workbook he described a scenario to be titled "The Bread King Learns Bread Baking." Brecht, whose habitual nightly meal was bread with butter, asserted that because of corporate greed no real bread was available in the States. For the story, he created a villainous millionaire who would find happiness in munching bread baked by a poor farmer's wife; he would try to buy her recipe only to be told to put away his checkbook and leave the honest loaves to honest people. Good bread and the good life, Brecht wrote, required "one day of good work; one world of good neighbors; a heart of good will; and a good appetite." Alas, the moral tale did not interest Hollywood's merchants of dreams.

Nevertheless, the assembly lines of the real world had not eroded all the traditions of the good life. Jim noted that everybody could get freshly killed chickens and turkeys in those days. The skin crisped as the poultry cooked, and the meat, moist and delicate, made beautiful sandwiches; it was an era when the best turkeys were milk fed for ten days before killing. He also used good tongue, sliced country ham, sometimes cheese mixtures, and a potted meat called Strathborough paste—something of his mother's repertoire which he said he'd never encountered anywhere else. Putting up puréed beef as Strathborough paste may well have been an idea brought from England by Elizabeth Beard, for the recipe is similar in many details to other British methods of potting viands. There was no doubt, however, about other recipes from home such as that for the white fruitcake that Let had perfected in the Hawthorne Park kitchen. "Aunt Lizzie's Bacon Tart" came from Gearhart, where it was made by a Scotswoman who had been so fond of Jim that she often handed out treats to the pudgy young summer neighbor.

As his partner in the Hors d'Oeuvre Inc. kitchen, Irma Rhode baked for Easter her own version of *kulich* and *pashka,* the Russian rich bread and cheesecake that celebrate the end of Lent, and it was she who created the sandwiches of brioche and sliced onions. The kitchen had no nationalistic bounds. In addition to French hors d'oeuvres, there were various *antipasti,* and the Russian *zakuski,* defined by Jim as prepared "probably with caviar and perhaps with more violent kinds of fish and much black bread and vodka." Red caviar was mixed with cream cheese and mounded on small wheels of toast (presumably served with a momentarily favorite cocktail known as the vodkatini). But apparently their customers were not introduced to Peasant Caviar, an eggplant pastiche of fish roe then turning up at Hollywood shindigs. Variations of smorgasbords, however, provided challenges that Jim and Irma took to with enthusiasm.

"On one occasion," Jim remembered long afterward, they created a buffet centerpiece that he thought particularly theatrical. "We had to provide a holiday dish with roast goose. For contrasting flavor and garnish we were able to find some tiny little Puerto Rican pineapples that were beautifully ripe and very sweet, so we incorporated an old German custom—we scooped out those tiny pineapples, cut the fruit into small bits that we mixed into simmering sauerkraut. With the goose, we served them forth, one to a person, and it created a sensation, just what the goose needed."

Even more popular was the Crème Vichyssoise prepared in vats by Jim and Irma from the recipe they had borrowed from Chef Louis Diat of the Ritz-Carlton. This triumph of potato soup wasn't new. Diat had smoothed out his French mother's country recipe and served it first to a rich New Yorker named Charles Schwab in 1910. When the Vichy government took over in the Nazi occupation of France, soon after Beard and the Rhodes were established, Diat dropped the name temporarily until the onus of the Vichy government was forgotten.

Beard, no doubt, was happiest when busy in the Hors d'Oeuvre kitchen, but nobody in the shop seems to have been above delivery chores. Portland friends would volunteer to help, sometimes just to have his company. Peg Jennings said, "Doing the deliveries made him feel like a servant, so I asked him if I could come along one day when I was in town. I helped him tote a tray of canapés to a fashionable east side address and held the precious hors d'oeuvres while Jim went to the doorman to gain access. Seven years later, things were different for him. I was in New York again and he had concert tickets—and he picked me up—in tails and a cape—and we walked arm in arm to Carnegie Hall."

Bill Rhode's more elevated chore was to serve as promotion man. He could dress for the occasion, too, and as a pal of Lucius Beebe he got publicity through the latter's column. Hors d'Oeuvre Inc. also won the interest of Clementine Paddleford of the *Herald Tribune,* whose writing was splashed with color and enthusiasm. ("Pick a tomato fresh from the vine," Miss Paddleford wrote. "It lies warm in the hand, a vermillion globe subtly charged with properties of life-giving sun.") Her enthusiastic reference to the new caterers had what Jim called an "extraordinary" effect. And in a more calmly worded way, so did the space given in *The New Yorker* by Sheila Hibben, who in the early 1930s had rounded up recipes from every corner of the land and told readers of her cookbook, "our palates must be awakened to old and simple pleasures."

As Beard and Hibben (and Paddleford as well) became friends,

Jim began to consolidate his own ideas about food. Well-traveled Americans in New York and elsewhere were reacting to a new interest in how things taste—a tentative revival of interest in the act of cooking was taking place. "At its best," the city editor of the *Herald Tribune,* Stanley Walker, wrote in a book about New York, "the cooking of the United States is marvellous." But he added: "It ranges from Maryland fried chicken [for which Escoffier had his own recipe] down to corn pone and fried pork swimming in grease . . . and even worse, the diet of bananas and skim milk with which Hollywood actresses seek to reduce."

Jim had also noted the uneven quality of American cooking. Only three years before he and his partners started Hors d'Oeuvre Inc., the New York chapter of the International Wine and Food Society had been formed under the aegis of André L. Simon, a London wine importer and author of *The French Cook Book,* among other informed writings. The critic and playwright Julian Street, who had recently published an authoritative book called simply *Wines,* was the first member; Frank Schoonmaker, a rising expert on California and European vineyards, was secretary; and Richardson Wright, the *House & Garden* editor, became the New York group's president. Other members, a small number of affluent Americans interested in getting together to dine well, began to develop wine cellars as discriminately as some of them collected books in fine bindings. Followers of Monsieur Simon, internationally known for his palate and vintage erudition, organized their own groups in Chicago, San Francisco, Los Angeles, and other cities in between. Some New Yorkers, like Jim, already were members of the Gourmet Society, Bachelor Brotherhood of Cooks, Le Club des Arts Gastronomiques in Boston, or Princeton's Gun Club, whose president, Dr. Charles Browne, had published a successful cookbook in which he assured readers that "To love and to Dine are man's chief ends . . . "

Restaurant dining in Manhattan, in its myriad temptations, was a subject few people knew as well as Jim—from Renganeschi's Old Place on West Tenth Street to the Southern cuisine of Therese Worthington Grant to the noted Riverside Drive landmark, Claremont Inn, which he had marked "must" for his friend Hattie. He knew the old Greenwich Village French-Italian restaurant called The Golden Eagle, and he could recommend places to which he'd been introduced, such as Voisin and the Marguery (two restaurants then still reaching for the excellence achieved by their Paris namesakes), Sweets on Fulton Street, Keen's English Chop House, and the Brevoort and Lafayette dining rooms. The hotel that had epitomized New York for him on his first visit as a twenty-year-old was the old Waldorf Hotel, where, at the window table looking out on Thirty-fourth Street, he had treated himself after an emergency trip to a dentist.

With its original site occupied by the 102-story Empire State Building, the new Waldorf-Astoria, fifteen blocks north, was a focal point of Manhattan's emphasis on good living. Its Men's Bar was a rendezvous which often drew members of the Wine and Food Society, including a producer named Crosby Gaige. A close associate of André Simon, Gaige lived up the Hudson on his Watch Hill Farm, where as one of many extracurricular pursuits he raised shallots— then a rarity—to supply the Waldorf kitchens.

A sometimes erudite writer on food and a singular authority on herbs and spices, Crosby Gaige seemed to Jim someone for whom life was a constant reward. He was original enough at the time to rent an air-conditioned apartment for the sole purpose of keeping his wines at controlled temperatures. A cosmopolite of many talents, Gaige also had a gift, similar to Jim's, for cooking over open fires. His Watch Hill house, built in 1760, was a frequent gathering place for guests from Manhattan who sat on his flagstone patio bordered by a step-terrace of aromatic herbs, to watch him cook al fresco. Jim saw him as "a man of delicious wit, somewhat of a charlatan, but brilliant and gay, and always someone that would be amusing to know." His theatrical office in midtown served for a time as headquarters for Wine and Food Society business, which was then run by the executive secretary, Jeanne Owen.

For Jim, not yet quite sure whether he was more interested in food than in the theater, the stylish, Paris-groomed Jeanne Owen was to become the substitute maternal guide in New York and, after his mother's death, a successor to Elizabeth Beard. But comforting as she was toward the young man so recently from Oregon, Jeanne Owen was a personality who had enormous effect on many who called themselves food specialists. Crosby Gaige believed that had she lived in another age she "would probably have been Mrs. Lucullus, Mme. Grimode de la Reynière, or Mme. Brillat-Savarin."*

A man who knew her as well as any other New Yorker, Jerry Berns of the "21" Club, described her bobbed white hair as "neatly trimmed, and she was impeccably made up. She sailed into a room, took a deep breath and never stopped talking. She had an unusual, full-toned voice, absolutely perfect diction. Her French was as good as any French person's. When with her, you didn't have to open your mouth—everything reminded her of something in her past." And her past had the illuminations of a way of life that the young Mr. Beard envied.

Mrs. Owen, having lived in France after growing up in California, knew a great deal more about wines than Jim had been able to glean from his mother, but he admitted that different as they might be in other ways, each was opinionated about oysters. "One of the great things Jeanne did for the Wine and Food Society," he told me, "was a Long Island oyster tasting she put on in the Waldorf kitchen. She

---

*Much tuned into gastronomical history, Crosby Gaige was ahead of trends as well. He wrote a syndicated column called "Meals for Males," had a five-day-a-week radio show, and long before the word "pasta" was familiar in the United States, he published an encyclopedia of spaghetti, macaroni, and noodles. "Probably the most complete book ever published on Italian pastas was by the late Crosby Gaige," Morrison Wood wrote in 1949.

plied the members with blue points, Cape Cods, Robbins Islands, even some from Gardiner's Island, and for each kind she had exactly the right wine to give the tasting its point."* He remained somewhat in awe of her throughout his career, just as his regard for his mother stayed with him in spite of his parent's imperious possessiveness. In fact, as the camaraderie between Jeanne Owen and Jim developed, it often had the love-hate dimension of life under his parent's dominance.

They hit it off from the start—when Jim took Jeanne's telephone call to Hors d'Oeuvre Inc. The fact that she had so offended Bill Rhode that he rejected the call served Jim well in various ways. "She delved into my past—the fact that I'd been on the stage and knew the theater, and we had some friends in common. We found we both loved opera and loved to go to restaurants." Mrs. Owen was as keen about food shopping as Jim, and they went together to Tingaud's, the best meat market in town, and at the best fish market she introduced him to the proprietor, Lucien Prince, her intimate friend.

Her great influence on Beard's life makes it easy to exaggerate their comradeship, as Jim himself seems to have done years after they had parted ways—and at a time late in life when his conscience may have troubled him. He didn't want to be guilty of short-changing his debt to her, and he talked to me about her at length, with a tape recorder going:

> Yes, it was fun. . . . The drawback was that Jeanne was a very possessive female, and she was curious about the other things I might do. When I left her house in the evening to go home I would call as soon as I reached home because she felt that I should not go wandering, but be there, at her beck and call, when she wanted to phone me. I soon found out that if I did want to go elsewhere I could go home first, and then go out. . . . If she ever called me a second time, she probably thought I was asleep or in the bathtub—it was almost automatic that I would get the call the minute I got in. She would be on the phone the first thing in the morning, and sometimes five or six times during the day telling me the gossip,

---

*It may be noted that M.F.K. Fisher, in *Consider the Oyster,* asserts: "Oysters, being almost universal, can be and have been eaten with perhaps a wider variety of beverages than almost any other dish I can think of . . . and less disastrously. They lend themselves to the whims of every cool and temperate climate, so that one man can drink wine with them, another beer, and another fermented buttermilk, and no man will be wrong."

sometimes reading letters she thought amusing. She had a system of armed barbs for people who were against her in any way or who interfered with her way of living. Her great faults were her possessiveness and her jealousy. She could be oozing with charm one moment and bring forth blistering accounts the next one.

She once, wandering past the cardinal's residence on Madison Avenue, felt that he was taking up too much of the sidewalk—so she plowed through pushing the cardinal to the side, saying, "You don't own all the sidewalk!" She was actively a bold speaker for women's rights, or anybody's rights, for that matter, and she could cut people low with a remark. I well remember her ordering at one of the great New York restaurants, and when it was put before her, looking at it through her lorgnette and turning to the waiter, saying, "What is this little turd of misery?"

She adored trying new restaurants. She admired going to new plays. She hated late-night life because she liked to go to bed early and get up frightfully early and work. She loved plowing through the shops, chatting with the people, getting all the gossip. She was an unpredictable female—a great person. I can't begin to tell you the things I learned from her, gastronomically speaking.

The rapport between Beard and Mme. Owen resulted in an agreement that Hors d'Oeuvre Inc. would show off its cocktail party wares at a Wine and Food Society gathering at the Waldorf's Starlight Roof. Beard and his partners, along with several importers of epicurean products, would supply food for milling guests as they sampled the wines introduced by the society. In a period when wine drinking had not become common, such tasting parties gave Jeanne Owen the chance to cajole importers and producers into providing the necessary bottles to demonstrate the affinity of wine and food.

The Starlight Roof tasting put his friendship with Jeanne Owen into high gear. Not only was she for years virtually his closest New York friend, but she was the one "who taught me most about cooking." At a time when highway versions of fried chicken had damaged the image of poultry in general, Jeanne Owen turned Jim into a master of the technique of sautéing. He said she had thirty different chicken sautés in her repertoire. "She'd do one with white wine, salt and pepper, and then add perhaps a dash of tarragon or a little thyme; or do a red wine sauté with shallots and onion and garlic, tomato, rosemary, each one taking no more than 25 to 30 minutes and producing a magnificent meal for two or four with practically no effort at all."

Jeanne had grown up in San Francisco in the period when Jim was being taken there frequently by his family, and they had a mutual appreciation for the then not-so-common flavors of Mexico. As a main course, for instance, she served chicken Calandria often enough for the recipe to become one of Jim's favorites. It was a dish that in those days required a cook to deal with America's limited food shopping. Jeanne's friend Calandria, for whom the dish was named, had to locate a pharmacy that sold sesame seeds, and had to grind her own peppers, whole spices and nuts in a *metate* because such packaged condiments were not generally available.

Jim cheerfully recognized how much he had absorbed from Jeanne of cooking ideas that were new to him. "A lot of things surprised me from the home standpoint—you might have these unfamiliar things in a good restaurant, but not at home. She reminded me—as I traveled more and more in France—of certain French women who love to cook for the fun to be found in experimenting."

Beard and his strong-minded mentor usually agreed on restaurants. Jeanne's knowledge of wines gave her a keen interest in the cellars developed by the "21" Club, and this restaurant's hearty menu pleased her as it did her sturdy friend—the tall, fat young man and the stylishly stout divorcée often went together for the roast beef, the deviled beef bones, and the grouse that arrived in August. With her connections, she also introduced Jim to the Parisian cuisine of the French Pavilion that opened in May 1939 on the World's Fair grounds at Flushing. This seminal restaurant was an immediate success with New Yorkers and with visitors who came from around the world, but Jeanne Owen, in her perversity, was reserved. Although Henri Soulé, the *directeur,* catered to her, according to Jim, she said she found him self-important, "nothing but a maître d'."

Soulé's menu was more than enough to impress Jim: *Supreme de Barbue Mornay, $1.50; Homard Monte Carlo, $1.75; Coq au Vin de Bordeaux, $1.60; Gigot D'Agneau Boulangère, $1.60; Soufflé Palmyre, $0.90; Crêpes Suzette, $1.25;* and *tous les fromages, $0.50;* a bottle of

1929 Château Margaux cost $4.50. At such prices, 131,261 authentically French meals were served to fair-goers during the summer. As one of the satisfied clients, Jim remained an admirer and often a guest of Henri Soulé until after the latter's death in 1966, when Le Pavillon closed its doors on Manhattan's Fifty-seventh Street, still rated as America's best French kitchen.*

Although Jeanne Owen never surrendered to the persistent New York enthusiasm for Soulé, she maintained what Jim described as an armed truce. He and she became frequent diners at the Brussels, an exemplary Belgian restaurant which had been opened at the 1939 World's Fair by their friend André Pagani and which, with the Swiss and Italian Pavilions, hung on for decades in Manhattan as much-appreciated gastronomic souvenirs of Flushing Meadow. Nineteen thirty-nine was a good year for the American food scene, as it turned out. Not only did numerous young French cooks—who had come to work at the fair—begin to find their place in New York professional kitchens, but prospective writers and editors (who became Beard cronies) got hints of their own futures—for instance, Glenna McGinnis, later food editor of *Woman's Day,* was hired to promote dairy products in the streamlined rotunda built to call attention to Elsie the Cow.

There was a beguiling buoyancy about the Fair and its theme, "The World of Tomorrow"; the word "futurama" had been coined by the designer Norman Bel Geddes, whose streamlined exhibit seemed a reasonable augury of things to come in spite of the imminence of World War II. With the Great Depression perceived to be over, and with Europeans pouring into the States, the Fair represented optimism.† For many of Jim's generation, New York was more than ever the one place to eat, drink, and be merry. For friends from Portland, Jim's cheerful personality added to the general magnetic force. Among those who found Jim a willing Flushing Meadow guide was Bob Mayberry, who nourished his impression of the Fair's soaring foun-

---

*"Because of his preeminence in his field, Henri Soulé, the proprietor, has probably had the greatest influence on other French restaurants in America of any restaurateur of this age." *The New York Times Guide to Dining Out,* 1964.

†When the abstract painter Piet Mondrian arrived as a refugee he found New York liberating. He recognized in New World tempos "the great difference between modern times and the past." It was time to discard the old, he said—fresh winds were blowing.

tains and the multicolored flood of light that drenched the sky as, in
the company of Beard and his friend Jim Cullum, he took things in.
"We had a whole routine," he said. "First the Swiss Pavilion for cheese
that we took over to the Russian Pavilion to eat with vodka, then
dinner at the French Pavilion."

In return, he added, he was host to the two Jims and Peggy
Martin when they all had dinner in the Rainbow Room, New York's
newest and most elite nightclub, with its revolving dance floor on
Rockefeller Center's sixty-fifth floor. There were two orchestras, one
of which satisfied the current rage for rhumbas. Carmen Miranda, the
Argentine entertainer, was in New York for the first time, along with
the Jack Cole Dancers; and Betty Comden, Judy Holliday, and Adolph
Greene were making their reputations as an act called The Reviewers.
"Jim Cullum picked a white Meursault I'll never forget," Mayberry
recalled, "and for the works—breast of guinea hen with black cherries,
a *pièce montée* dessert in the shape of the Eiffel Tower—the total tab
was $25."

For Beard and his friends there was welcome change in New
York's night life. Benny Goodman had brought his swing band to
Carnegie Hall, and Café Society Downtown, in Greenwich Village,
was becoming home base for jazz singers such as the trend-breaking
Sarah Vaughan. In the square below Cullum's apartment there was an
annual outdoor folk festival alive with dancers and singers, and the
restaurant scene got a new emphasis when, one sunny day, an antique
horse-drawn coach arrived. With a postilion blowing his brass horn,
the rig drove through the Washington Square arch to announce to
Village restaurant-goers that the White Turkey Inn was bringing real
New England country food to Manhattan. The new restaurant's menu
offered such colonial specialties as chicken pie and chicken Maryland
with corn fritters—"which always characterize the American table."
That was Beard's judgment when he later reviewed the restaurant,
expressing his approval of its white painted woodwork and furniture
with accents of flowery chintz fabrics.

His emerging reputation as an informed restaurant-goer must
have persuaded Jim that he had the makings of a new kind of calling.
The most respected chefs and restaurateurs in the United States had

always been those who had come from France or, as in the case of the famous Delmonico family, from Switzerland. Now, there were plenty of New World opportunities for restaurant cooks and other personnel who had been brought to New York for the World's Fair. But with thousands of Fair visitors exposed for the first time to sophisticated dining there was a demand for experts on food and wine that was increasing too swiftly to be met by newcomers. Jim saw himself as one American—knowledgeable about the best restaurants in Europe and with a lifetime interest in food—who could fill that need.

His charm had always been persuasive, especially with people less traveled than he, and he was getting good at selling himself. In 1940 his persuasiveness resulted in his being hired as consultant to a country inn. He was taken on as adviser to the new owners of the Bird & Bottle Inn, a wayside stop that had been built in 1760 on the post road near Garrison, New York. To celebrate the new menu, which featured baked chicken stuffed with breadcrumbs, chopped oysters and sweet butter, and celery and green pepper from the garden, Jim invited his friend Mary Hamblet, in town on a visit, to make the drive north along the Hudson. As Mary remembered the evening, she was piled into one of three limousines hired to transport a gastronomic group that included Jeanne Owen and two magazine writers—one named Mary Frost Mabon, the other Iles Brody, a recent European refugee of *boulevardier* inclinations who had become gastronomic editor for *Esquire*. In addition, there were Lucius Beebe, whom Mary Hamblet found ingratiating, and Richardson Wright, "who was my disappointment—a terrible snob."

Wright may have offended Mary, but it was Beebe who was then building a career on his mastery of social put-downs. "No one ever has been such a wonderful snob as Lucius," Jim recalled much later, in a generous moment. And he added, "Iles tried to be as elegant as Lucius but didn't have the brains—or the background." As always, Jim was intrigued by social ploys, and instinctive as he was in judging his acquaintances, he was not always confident of first impressions. He put up with Beebe's haughty act until the latter died, but he also relished any chance to find the café society specialist embarrassing himself. In a period of saturation cocktail parties and admiration for excessive drinking in general, Beard relished the memory of Beebe sliding under the table at a banquet as he was being introduced by Jim.

Mary Hamblet remembered the trip up the Hudson for its interludes at every bar along the way. As a nonchalant drinker herself, she conjectured that the writers were in real need of food by the time they arrived at the Bird & Bottle, and was convinced that the dinner Jim had arranged—although she had forgotten the menu—persuaded the writers to turn in glowing accounts of Beard's talents for innkeeping.

It was his mother's death in 1940 which defined the watershed in Jim's not yet steady course. When Elizabeth Beard died in Portland of cancer of the breast, her son was at her side. Both knew that their relationship hadn't been resolved, and he let her final sentiment linger with him through his own last years. "She looked at me from her pillow," Jim recounted to me, "and she said, 'You know, if we weren't related we might have been friends.'" He saw it as a truth he should have recognized earlier. When he had settled her estate, and given mementos to the friends who had known her best, he brought Hattie Cass as keepsakes a silver buttonhook which his mother had used in putting on her gloves and a small cloisonné box.

Jim was back on track when, once more in Manhattan, he and Jeanne Owen made another pilgrimage to the World's Fair. Among the many restaurants serving food in so much variety, they came upon one with some of the style of an American country inn. At lunch in the women's building, "where some of the best meals on all the grounds were served," the two found themselves caught up in intense conversation with a man named Hubbard Olson. "He had been instrumental in bringing Irma Rombauer's *Joy of Cooking* into the hands of Bobbs-Merrill and had built up a name in publishing." As the energetic force at M. Barrows & Co., Hub Olson plied Beard and Owen with questions and, "before dessert," Jim recalled, "he had asked each one of us to present him with a book."

Olson stipulated that Jim, if he were to write a cookbook devoted to recipes for cocktail food, would have to deliver his manuscript in six weeks in order to serve the prewar social appetite for the high life. Later Jim said he thought that the challenge made his life more hectic than it would ever be again. He was still working at Hors d'Oeuvre Inc., so producing a book meant moonlighting—spending weekends writing and testing recipes in the country house of Jeanne Owen's son and daughter-in-law near Ridgefield, Connecticut. Yet work on his first book proved to be invigorating as well as demanding— "learning to read galleys for the first time, talking about illustrations, gathering new information, eating dishes with wine and analyzing them." Recipes and research covered everything from steak tartare (he called it raw meat paste) to *zakuska,* the Russian-style buffet.

Beard's book *Hors d'Oeuvre and Canapés,* published in 1940, was a pioneer effort at teaching the hows and whys of food to serve with drinks. In the weeks allotted by Hub Olson for timely publication, Jim compiled a hundred recipes, including three supplied by Mrs. Owen, whom he described in his text as "one of America's truly great cooks." Yet in discussing the onion trifle he called Brioche en Surprise he didn't doff his *toque* to Irma Rhode for a contribution that was hers, choosing to cite "some famous French hostess who supposedly started the fashion" for sandwiching slices of onion and brioche. More, he failed to mention Bill Rhode in any connection with his hors d'oeuvre career, and the eventual result was a bitter end to the partnership. Irma Rhode forgave Jim in later years, but her brother did not. *Hors d'Oeuvre and Canapés,* nevertheless, was a success for decades.

Jeanne Owen's *The Wine Lover's Cook Book,* which she wrote at the same time as Jim was learning about bookmaking, was equally unique and another demonstration of Hub Olson's prescience about a new American interest in books about food. The foreword to the Owen book was written by Richardson Wright. He emphasized the fact that most food writers had been avoiding the subject of alcohol in cooking because they were "Daughters of the Dark Ages of Prohibition" and their lack of knowledge of wines was "so profound as to make the angels weep."

In 1937 the singular writer M.F.K. Fisher (who in later years was to form a close bond with Beard) had made a case against the plethora of boring books about food, and her *Serve It Forth* seems in retrospect to have ushered in a period in which food nostalgia became a welcome subject. At the same time a Michigan farm woman named Della Lutes wrote two memoirs with recipes—*The Country*

Kitchen and *Home Grown*—that caused at least one reviewer to remind readers that the nation might have reached an age when it could look back appreciatively on its traditions. Marjorie Mosser, niece of the historian Kenneth Roberts, at his instigation published the retrospective *Good Maine Food,* in the same season that the volumes by Beard and Owen were getting their first attention. And joining Mrs. Owen's own thesis that cooking could be a proud boast of men and women alike, the designer Merle Armitage turned out a gastronomic collection titled *Fit for a King,* in which such stars of the theater as Alfred Lunt, Angna Enters, Feodor Chaliapin, and John Charles Thomas, artists Rockwell Kent and Raymond Loewy, and writers Crosby Gaige and James M. Cain were among the contributors. Their assorted recipes seemed to indicate that public insistence on good food was gaining over a hitherto chronic state of mind that all too often settled for uninspired menus at home as well as in public eating places.

Beard's success with *Hors d'Oeuvre and Canapés* was reassuring, as it turned out. Twenty years after its publication, his treatise on cocktail food was reissued, and in 1980 his editor at Morrow, Narcisse Chamberlain, saw to it that the same book was republished as the "definitive" work on the matter—"better the original than any spurious new contraption on the subject," she said in a letter.

Soon after that new printing, Jim was interviewed about his debut in the hors d'oeuvre business—had it given him a sense of rebirth? "Were you happy in a way that was different from the 'acting' kind of happy?" he was asked. "Well, it *was* acting," he told the interviewer for *Gastronome* magazine. "Designing hors d'oeuvre is not different from designing sets and costumes. And," he added, "being nice to people. Food is very much theater. Especially cocktail parties *per se.*"

RECIPES

Spiced Waffles with Maple Butter
▼

Beard's breakfast waffles are enhanced by his friend Crosby Gaige's seasonings and by Jeanne Owen's maple butter.

1³/4 cups sifted flour	¹/2 teaspoon salt
2 teaspoons baking powder	2 tablespoons sugar
1 scant teaspoon cinnamon	3 eggs, separated
¹/3 teaspoon allspice	1³/4 cups milk
dash of nutmeg	6 tablespoons melted butter

Maple Butter:

1¹/2 cups maple syrup	6 tablespoons melted butter

Sift together the flour, baking powder, spices, salt, and sugar. In a mixing bowl beat the egg yolks, then add the milk and butter. Stir in the seasoning flour4808il just moistened; do not beat. Beat the egg whites until they hold firm peaks, then fold them into the batter. Use immediately, spooning the necessary amount of batter into a preheated waffle iron. Bake until steam has stopped coming around the edges, usually 5 minutes. Meanwhile prepare the maple butter by boiling the maple syrup with the butter until syrupy.

MAKES 6 WAFFLES.

Lucien's Oyster Canapé
▼

The Manhattan fish shop owner Lucien Prince was a friend of Jim's as well as the intimate companion of Jeanne Owen. He catered to the best restaurants and to the kitchens of New York society, and he was a fine cook who passed along this recipe.

8 rounds stale bread	salt
¹/4 pound butter	paprika
16 large oysters	8 lemon wedges
1 cup breadcrumbs	chopped parsley

Fry the bread rounds in 2 tablespoons of the butter. Set aside on a hot platter. Pin 2 oysters together with a toothpick, one at each end. Repeat for the remaining oysters. Mix the breadcrumbs with a little salt and paprika and dip each coupling of oysters in the crumbs. Fry quickly in the remaining butter, turning, until browned but leaving the centers juicy. Place each "double oyster" on a piece of fried bread. Garnish with a lemon wedge sprinkled on one side with chopped parsley. SERVES 8.

Peg Jennings's Whisky-Flavored Crab Soup

No good cook is above profiting by another's mistakes. When his friend Mrs. Jennings added a splash of Scotch instead of using sherry in the crab soup she made for him, Beard didn't object to the flavor but did add her recipe to his lifetime collection.

1 pound crabmeat	2 tablespoons butter
1/2 cup milk	

Cream Sauce:

3 tablespoons butter	1–1 1/2 cups heavy cream
3 tablespoons flour	4–5 tablespoons
2 cups milk	Scotch whisky
salt and pepper	chopped parsley

Heat the crabmeat in the milk and butter. Make the cream sauce by cooking the butter and flour together slowly for 2 minutes, then whisking in the milk, and salt and pepper to taste. Bring to the boil and whisk until smooth. Add the heavy cream, and when simmering immediately add the crabmeat. When it is just at the boiling point stir in the whisky. Serve in heated cups with a sprinkling of parsley. SERVES 4 TO 6.

Corn Bread and Ham Sandwiches

"For people who have large appetites," Beard wrote in an *Argosy* magazine column in the early fifties, "corn bread and ham make the ideal snack. . . . Serve these by the dozen to your guests and you won't need any other food for your party."

3 eggs	*¹/₄ teaspoon salt*
2 cups cornmeal	*1 cup light cream*
1 cup flour	*¹/₂ cup melted butter*
1 tablespoon baking powder	

Filling:

6 tablespoons soft butter	*sliced ham*

Beat the eggs until they are light and lemon colored. Mix the cornmeal with the flour and stir into the beaten eggs, blending thoroughly. Add the baking powder, salt, cream, and lastly the melted butter. Butter a 9 × 14-inch pan and pour in the batter. Bake in a preheated 400 degree oven for about 20 minutes, or until lightly browned and crisp at the edges. Remove from the pan and cut the corn bread into squares. Split the squares and butter well. Put a slice of richly flavored ham into each split square of corn bread.

MAKES ABOUT 28 SANDWICHES.

Chicken Sauté Passy

As a restaurant reviewer, Jim was much given to going home to his Twelfth Street walk-up to replicate a dish he had just eaten. In those days chicken in various guises was always on the menu of the elegant Passy Restaurant on Sixty-third and Madison.

One 2¹/₂-pound broiler	*3 tablespoons butter*
chicken, cut in 8 pieces	*8 shallots, chopped*
salt	*¹/₄ cup white wine*
freshly ground pepper	*1 cup heavy cream*
flour	*1 cup puréed spinach*

Sprinkle the chicken pieces lightly with salt and pepper and dredge them in flour. Heat the butter in a large skillet and sauté the chicken, turning the pieces, until very tender and all the pieces are lightly browned. Add the chopped shallots to the wine, pour over the chicken, and simmer until the wine is reduced by half. Mix the heavy cream with the puréed spinach and stir into the chicken juices. Spoon the sauce over the chicken and simmer slowly, covered, for 15 minutes.

SERVES 3 OR 4.

Sweetbreads with Braised Celery

▼

"You really *dine* at the Brussels," was the verdict when Beard reviewed the long-remembered Brussels Restaurant for his first column on New York dining in *Gourmet* magazine. His version of André Pagani's sweetbreads maison is as follows.

1–1 1/2 pounds celery	2 eggs, lightly beaten
10 tablespoons butter	1 1/2 cups dry breadcrumbs
3/4 cup chicken broth	3 tablespoons oil
salt	lemon wedges
freshly ground pepper	chopped parsley
2 pairs sweetbreads,	1 1/2 tablespoons flour
blanched and trimmed	1 cup heavy cream
flour	sherry

Cut the root end off the celery and separate the ribs. Trim off all the leaves. Cut the ribs into uniform lengths, 6 to 8 inches long. Cut the thickest ribs in strips. Melt 4 tablespoons butter in a large skillet and place the celery flat in the pan. Brown lightly in the butter, turning once. When lightly colored, add the broth and heat. Cover the skillet and cook 15 minutes, until the celery is just tender. Sprinkle lightly with salt and pepper and keep in a warm place. Cut the blanched sweetbreads into serving-sized pieces. Dip first in flour, then in beaten eggs, and lastly in breadcrumbs. Sauté gently in 6 tablespoons butter and 3 tablespoons oil until delicately brown on both sides. Season to taste with salt and pepper. Arrange the hot braised celery on a warm platter with lemon wedges, spoon the sweetbreads over the celery and sprinkle chopped parsley over; set aside and keep warm. Drain all but 2 tablespoons of fat from the skillet, stir in the flour until smooth, cooking until slightly colored. Stir in the cream and a liberal sprinkling of the sherry. Whisk and cook until the sauce is well blended and thickened. Season to taste with salt and pepper, and serve with the platter of celery and sweetbreads.   SERVES 4.

White Turkey Inn "Stickies"

▼

Beard, as a restaurant reviewer in New York, saw the White Turkey Inn as a font of traditional American specialties, and he particularly liked these sweet baking powder biscuits, known as "stickies," which are similar to Pennsylvania pecan rolls.

2 cups sifted flour	1 egg, beaten
1 scant teaspoon salt	1 cup seedless raisins
2 teaspoons baking powder	1/2 cup granulated sugar
41/2–5 tablespoons	1/4 cup maple syrup
unsalted butter	11/2 cups brown sugar
21/2 tablespoons shortening	1 cup chopped nuts
3/4 cup milk	

Mix the flour, salt, and baking powder, and lightly work in 2 1/2 tablespoons of the butter and the shortening. Mix in the milk and the beaten egg in alternate amounts. Roll the dough out to 1/2-inch thickness and sprinkle with half the raisins, the granulated sugar, and small dots of butter. Roll up the dough and cut in 1-inch slices. Spread the bottom of a large greased pan with the maple syrup. Sprinkle with brown sugar, the remaining raisins, and the chopped nuts. Press the sliced rolls into the pan, cut side down. Bake in a preheated 450 degree oven for about 15 minutes.

MAKES 10 TO 12 BISCUITS.

Squid San Pedro Style

▼

Jim's research in 1953 took him to San Pedro, California, for a day with an Italian family of fishermen which he described in *Argosy* magazine.

6 small squid	juice of 1 lemon
2 cloves garlic	1 cup red wine
1/2 cup olive oil	salt
1/2 teaspoon fennel	freshly ground pepper
seeds, crushed	

Wash the squid well, split, and remove the ink sac and cartilage or bone. Put them in a baking dish with the garlic, oil, crushed fennel, lemon juice, wine, and salt and pepper to taste. Cover and steam on top of the stove or in a 350 degree oven for about 45 minutes or until tender. You will be surprised at the delicious result. SERVES 3 OR 4.

Chicken Paprikash

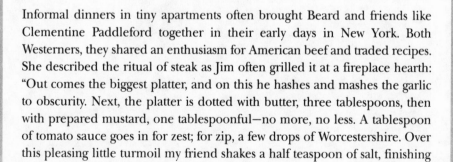

Jim's guests in his first Greenwich Village apartment included fellow cook and columnist Iles Brody, among whose specialties was chicken in the style of his Hungarian relatives.

two 2¹/2-pound chickens, each cut in 8 pieces	*1 tomato, peeled, seeded, and chopped*
2 large onions, chopped fine	*1 clove garlic, chopped fine*
1 tablespoon butter or lard	*salt*
1 tablespoon imported sweet paprika	*1 tablespoon flour*
2 green peppers, cut in strips	*1 cup sour cream*

Wipe the chicken pieces with a damp cloth. Put the chopped onions in a skillet with the butter or lard and simmer over very low heat for about 30 minutes, covered, until almost jellylike. Watch to prevent burning, stirring occasionally. Stir in the paprika and simmer 10 minutes more. Put in the chicken pieces, turning them in the paprika mixture, then cover the skillet and simmer 20 minutes. Add the pepper strips, tomato, and garlic, and a light sprinkling of salt. Continue simmering for about 10 minutes. Mix the flour with the sour cream to make a smooth paste, then stir into the liquid in the skillet, allowing the sauce to thicken. Serve with dumplings or steamed rice.   SERVES 6 TO 8.

Hearthside Steak

Informal dinners in tiny apartments often brought Beard and friends like Clementine Paddleford together in their early days in New York. Both Westerners, they shared an enthusiasm for American beef and traded recipes. She described the ritual of steak as Jim often grilled it at a fireplace hearth: "Out comes the biggest platter, and on this he hashes and mashes the garlic to obscurity. Next, the platter is dotted with butter, three tablespoons, then with prepared mustard, one tablespoonful—no more, no less. A tablespoon of tomato sauce goes in for zest; for zip, a few drops of Worcestershire. Over this pleasing little turmoil my friend shakes a half teaspoon of salt, finishing with a flourish of pepper and a crimson halo of paprika. The platter and its contents are moved to the blazing hearth. While the steak sputters in the long-handled grill our cook gives his sauce an occasional stir. He says young and extravagant things, hailing all the world with superlatives, the steak in particular. Then it is done. Flop, it goes onto the platter; he wallows it in the sauce so every little shred of fat or lean has a coating of the smooth, buttery heavenly stuff that lingers in memory for many a long, long day."

5

NEW YORK, BETWEEN ENGAGEMENTS

It's hard to cite a more pervasive effect on everyday life than the change brought about by food rationing. Beard's days were transformed dramatically along with everyone else's. With sugar and butter among the earliest provisions to be regulated, Hors d'Oeuvre Inc. was hit hard. Ration books—thin light-tan cardboard covers stapled over pages of tiny stamps about half the size of those required for postage—became the bane of everyone's existence.

The allotted amounts of sugar were curtailed enough to cause average law-abiding citizens to steal lumps from restaurant sugar bowls. Caterers had to minimize their offerings of lavish desserts—Schrafft's restaurants reintroduced the honey-molasses-coconut kisses that had first been offered to appease World War I limitations. Rationing during World War II caused cooks at home to cut down on their baking and to use saccharin and corn syrup as sugar substitutes. The meat situation became so acute that when a New York butcher had some smoked meat for sale a line formed immediately around the block, and the ensuing threat of violence caused the police to be called. Jim Beard and his partners, for their part, were inevitably forced to abandon their service of cocktail parties.

"By government decree," Michael and Ariane Batterberry wrote in *On the Town,* "sugar, coffee, meat, butter, and canned goods were to be strictly rationed, ice cream flavors reduced to ten, and all the production banned on metal asparagus tongs, beer steins, spittoons, popcorn poppers, and lobster forks. In their windows, housewives were urged to post an Office of Price Administration sticker portraying a gallant young matron in ruffled apron, her right hand held aloft to voice the Home Front Pledge: 'I Pay No More Than Top Legal Prices. I Accept No Rationed Goods Without Giving Up Ration Stamps.' "

With men being drafted, many hostesses were discommoded because there were now new jobs in industry that attracted women away from domestic service. As Richard R. Lingeman reports in *Don't You Know There's a War On?*, "Suddenly, the 'servant shortage' became a cliché topic at ladies' luncheons all over the country."* It was hard for some to maintain a semblance of gaiety. In spite of a *New Yorker* report that shortages of imported spirits could be countered by the availability of Australian and South African champagne and Portuguese brandy, a pall had been thrown over the elegant hospitality scene in which Jim had been finding sustenance.

At the same time, the government's encouragement of Victory gardens was affecting Jim's world, and while it echoed Elizabeth Beard's commitment to homegrown vegetables it had historic importance because the wartime program involved 20 million amateur plots that accounted for more than 40 percent of all the vegetables produced in this country. Growing food in the backyard was properly patriotic. There were nationwide competitions for gardeners, with prizes for grade school youngsters, adult clubs, and for industry employees. At Bennington College, for instance, the campus Victory garden embraced students who nurtured plants in fertile soil by pulling up weeds while such faculty members as the philosopher Kenneth Burke sprinkled seeds in the minds of the same undergraduates, including one who years later became Jim's editor.

As Americans became more conscious of the war in Europe, the publisher Hub Olson not only got Beard to write *Cook It Outdoors* but also issued Jeanne Owen's *Book of Sauces*. Mme. Owen had affirmed her maternal interest in Jim after the death of Elizabeth Beard the year before, and had given him a temporary bed in her apartment. Jeanne let her affection show between the lines of her sauce cookbook.

---

*New York's state employment agency got 667 requests for sleep-in maids in one month and only 118 takers. One hostess offered "room, radio, good salary and nice home" plus the privilege of wearing her fur coat on days off.

She added a note to the recipe entitled "Jimmy's Sour Cream Dressing" that emphasized his gastronomic promise: "We owe this excellent dressing," she wrote, "to James Beard, whose culinary imagination and knowledge are worthy of the highest honors, and whose experiments lean to success with astonishing regularity."

Her book also included a simple green mayonnaise from *Hors d'Oeuvre and Canapés,* and from his *Cook It Outdoors* she borrowed a barbecue sauce recipe that Jim had devised for basting meat. He had suggested: "It's also a good idea to dip the muffin on which the hamburger is to be served into this sauce, instead of buttering the muffin." This Beard campfire guide was the first of several that in future years he devoted to the subject of cooking outside the kitchen, and each increased his reputation as the most influential mess sergeant among America's backyard barbecuers.

Jim recognized that many amateur cooks, though removed from the countryside, never lost their love for the taste of food grilled outdoors. In his introduction he appealed to such readers, "whether you have a small electric grill on a stamp-size terrace on the ninety-second floor of a New York apartment, or an outdoor stove in the heart of Wyoming," adding, "Of course I don't expect you to dig up your lawn for a New England clambake or a Polynesian barbecue."

He made it clear that he was pleased to find that a number of his friends among New York's culinary professionals were what he called "rabid supporters of the C I O [cook it outdoors] group." As contributors to his book there were his new colleagues Charlotte Adams, food editor of the newspaper *PM,* and Nancy Dorris, food editor of the New York *Daily News,* as well as Jeanne Owen, who made authentic chili and whose Chippino "has recaptured some of the true character of the Spanish Southwest." The recipes included Wild Blackberry Flummery with Custard Sauce and a fried salt pork dinner, both from Nancy Dorris, "a real Westerner." And there was Camper's Bouillabaisse from his New York friend Ruth Norman.

In 1941, a generation before fast food was to conquer America, *Cook It Outdoors* was a notable contribution to kitchen libraries if only for Beard's essay on hamburgers, a basic American food which he had embraced early in his eating career and about which he would still be theorizing at the age of seventy-eight, in his final cookbook. In 1941, with rationing of meat a threat to national complacency, he wrote: "In these days of Hamburger Heavens, Hamburger Bars, Hamburger Houses and all the roadside Hamburger stands, which if stood end to end would probably fence the Lincoln Highway, I suppose the word is a bugaboo for everyone."

Nevertheless, he mustered a dozen variations on the ground-meat theme. He cited the "Gay Nineties Variety—lots of slop and slurp," the "Gourmet's Hamburger" nested in an English muffin, the "Baghdad" made with eggplant, the "Hamburger with a Cluck" that used ground chicken and onion instead of beef, and the Irish version based on chopped corned beef, onions, and chopped potatoes seasoned with nutmeg; there was also the Pig Hamburger composed of ground pork mixed with basil, ginger, garlic, and thyme, and the Streamlined Hamburger for sophisticates, which required minced sirloin, garlic, and Escoffier sauce. Beard's most original, perhaps, was the Pascal, which called for the soaking in milk for two hours of lamb kidneys which were then surrounded by chopped lamb and rings of bacon and grilled. The Pascal Burger was served with grilled tomatoes and onions.

If there was mischief in some of these ideas, it was evidence of Jim's lifelong determination to show that cooking need not be boring. His developing reputation at this stage did not erase his debt to Jeanne Owen, but that was tabled when Jim was moved to serve the country after Pearl Harbor. Jeanne described him in her *Book of Sauces* as a disciple of Comus, a character in Milton's *Paradise Lost* who was the mischievous fun-making son of Bacchus and Circe; "he lives up to all the requirements," she wrote, "including 250-plus pounds of all too, too solid flesh and genial nature." Jim remained good-humored after vainly trying to enlist in various branches of the armed services, only to be drafted. He was sent to Fort Dix, New Jersey, and soon he was given reason to think he was in line for the hotel management division of the quartermaster corps, instead of tending cookfires on bivouacs.

The army, of course, knew better than to make use of his culinary experience, and he was enrolled in the air corps for basic training in Florida. The closest he came to dealing with the feeding of hungry soldiers was when he was pulled out of line as one of a dozen who were ordered to carve several thousand pounds of Christmas turkey. "I thought I would never get the odor of turkey off my hands or out of my head," he wrote. "While the rest of the Air Corps feasted on a traditional dinner that Christmas Day, I was in Miami eating steak tartare."

A few days later he was in Paw-ling, New York, to be trained as a cryptographer, expert on codes. His six-week course in secret ciphers came to an end, however, when he was informed that servicemen who had reached their thirty-eighth birthday were considered bad risks for overseas duty. "I remember viv-idly," he said, "being told that I had my choice of going to Washington, D.C., or Presque Isle, Maine, for the remainder of the war. So I went to see Colonel Pickering, the head  of the school. He told me I could get out of the service because of my age, if I got a job that was necessary to the war effort."

Few things were more necessary than maintaining food supplies, which were increasingly regulated by the Office of Price Administration —it dealt out ration points and indirectly encouraged such patriotic efforts as Victory gardens. Because the draft eroded the manpower that made farms productive, agricultural employment was specified as civilian war work. Through the intercession of the Cullum family, Beard was taken on, his two hundred fifty pounds notwithstanding, as a hand on Riveredge Farm, which had "a prize Guernsey herd and a shortage of labor," Jim recalled. "I settled in, worked on the records, made butter, checked the milkings, and [as an Oregon-trained ama-teur] cultivated a thriving vegetable garden."

He had weekends on which to maintain his claim to being a New Yorker by visiting Jeanne Owen and other friends. On one of them, "I had come in from the farm to see the second performance of *Oklahoma!* which had opened the night before." The triumph of his friend Agnes de Mille, whose choreography for the Rodgers and

Hammerstein hit revolutionized Broadway musicals, might in itself have been sufficient reward for the Comus of Pennsylvania dairy country. What changed his life was a chance meeting with an old friend who was with the United Seamen's Service and had been hoping to take on Beard as a possible addition to the staff that was opening canteens for merchant marine sailors.

On West Forty-fourth Street, with such plays as *One Touch of Venus* and Ray Folger's *By Jupiter!* cheering things up, Broadway stars had opened the Stage Door Canteen, where coffee was poured sometimes by Katherine Cornell and dishes were washed by Alfred Lunt (an amateur cook). Bette Davis presided over the opening of the Hollywood Canteen, and USO clubs had opened in conjunction with armed services bases all over the country, as well as overseas. Not only were young soldiers, sailors, Wacs, and Waves invited to come and dance with stars and starlets and to be otherwise entertained; they were offered the comfort of food away from a chow line.

For the merchant marines, on hazardous duty outside the reach of USO, the United Seamen's Service was a part of the War Shipping Administration and designed to give nonuniformed sailors "a home away from home" when they were lucky enough to have shore leave. Jim Beard seemed an ideal choice to see that such aid and comfort were available for men in need. "It had started as a national, but became an international, organization, following the fleet, as it were," Jim recalled. He went through special training in New York, and thought he was to be assigned to manage a domestic club. A few days before he was slated to take it over, however, he was shipped off to Puerto Rico.

"All we had there initially was an office and a place to interview seamen," Beard wrote. Torpedoings off the island were frequent at the time, and on his arrival he found himself having to pull survivors out of the water. In record time, he said, a club had to be opened, and one was established in an abandoned bowling alley which was fitted up with dormitories, recreational rooms, and a small kitchen, where the overweight former air corps code-breaker supervised the preparation of meals based on local pork, enormous shrimp called *camarones grandes,* fried green plantains, and yams.

"Fortunately we had available *lechón asado,* the traditional barbecued pig with its crisp skin and deliciously tender meat," he wrote in *Delights and Prejudices,* and thus he added some *jíbaro* finesse to his outdoor cooking skills. He remembered the cooking of a forty-five-pound pig with the juices dropping on a bed of plantains—the crackling skin served first as a kind of hors d'oeuvre with the drinks, followed by plates of meat chopped in thumb-sized pieces, along with a bowl of greens.

From the Caribbean he brought back a love for roast pork sandwiches, often based on barbecued meat: "You take a long sort of hero-shaped soft roll, split it and butter it, and put on the lower half a good portion of nicely seasoned cold roast pork. On top of that you place an equally healthy portion of cheese that melts well, such as Emmenthaler or Gruyère or Monterey Jack or even what is known as American Munster, if that is all you can get. Slap on the top of the roll, and put the whole thing in the oven or on a griddle, with a weight on top, so the cheese melts all over the pork. This takes its place alongside the 'poor boy' and the 'hero' and all those other honest, hearty sandwiches that are so satisfying."

His United Seamen's tour of duty was an unguided round of cuisines unlike those he'd begun to understand in his tutelage by Jeanne Owen. He was transferred from San Juan to Rio de Janeiro, where the club was housed in a beautiful old mansion within a coconut's throw of one of the city's beaches. There his first move was to find a cook named Manuela, who told him she had cooked for the Argentine and Italian ambassadors but was even more inspired to be feeding American sailors on leave. He reported that Manuela made a dessert with bananas which was so popular with the men it had to be on the menu every day.

The cook, whom he described as a sort of Mrs. Five-by-five, also cheered Jim and his charges with desserts made with avocados, as well as bananas baked with rum. He discovered through Manuela that South American liquors had other uses. He recalled that he first discovered *cachaca,* white rum, literally upon his arrival. "I had just settled into my new living quarters when I heard wild shrieks in the kitchen," he wrote in *House & Garden,* in 1959. "I rushed in and found a plump turkey reeling drunkenly around the room while the kitchen help roared with laughter. In a few minutes the bird became stupefied and was shortly thereafter dispatched. Then it was explained to me that this was an old custom. When turkeys are to be killed for the table, they are always fed large doses of *cachaca* in the belief that if a bird were relaxed when slaughtered its meat would be tenderer."

With less hilarity, Manuela showed him a number of variations of barbecued meats, including her delicate chicken hearts, skewered and dipped in a green pepper marinade. She divined his weakness for picnics, and he learned of a fisherman's harbor where the ingredients for a shrimp dish, *vatapa de camarao,* could be purchased and chicken hearts could be grilled for an outdoor meal.

Manuela introduced him also to variations of bean dishes his mother in Portland had never known. The famous national dish of black beans called *feijoada completa* held enormous appeal because of its use of many neglected parts of pigs, for which Jim already had a lifelong partiality. She added to Jim's file of recipes, and Rio—its Atlantic beaches swirling into the downtown area—continued to be a tempting place to live out the war in cosmopolitan comfort. He wanted to be assigned to Europe when the American traffic in the Brazilian harbor thinned out, but U.S.S. headquarters in New York thought their man in Rio was the one to improve things along the Panama Canal. The result was that Manuela was replaced in Beard's life when he moved to Cristobal, the canal's terminus on Limon Bay. There he found Margaret Tingling, "a jewel of a cook," who came from the Cayman Islands and had a deep-seated preference for feeding men—after having cooked at a women's jail.

Cooking at the Cristobal Seamen's Club, Jim wrote later, was a job made to order for Margaret. When the Christmas season of 1944 approached, he said, "Margaret and I decided on an open house to be held Christmas afternoon. For days the kitchen was awhirl with activity as we made mince tarts, fruit cakes, and Christmas cookies by the gross, and wonderful spicey smells permeated the whole club."

At last Jim Beard was cast in a role for which he was superbly gifted, perhaps the best of all the parts he played with enthusiasm throughout his life. It was Christmas (even more his favorite holiday than the Fourth of July). He was the host. He had a house, and a kitchen stuffed with food. He cooked a half-dozen turkeys, along with crackling beef roasts, while Margaret made dozens of hot rolls. Lined up on the buffet also were relishes, jellies, cold meats, salads, and cheese. A table was loaded with Christmas sweets, and Margaret had made two of her holiday specialties—a chocolate cake for which he failed to get the recipe, and a coconut cake made with two dozen eggs and slathered in a cream icing. Finally, there were egg nogs, beer, coffee, and tea.

In January, Jim wrote a thank-you letter to a friend for the gift of some books, and here we get a vivid glimpse of Elizabeth Beard's son at the age of forty-one:

I thought of you all fondly on Christmas when I had a chance to think. I am very short of trained staff and have to keep myself going about sixteen hours a day and Christmas was an eighteen hour one. It was a strange day for I worked all day to give a party for two hundred and twenty fellows after having hung out a shoulder for about twenty young kids to weep on the night before. I shall never forget that Christmas as long as I live. I wanted to go to bed and cry myself, after all the homesick kids I had talked to, before the night was over. However we got through the party the next day without any serious mishaps and I spiked the egg nog so that everyone would get themselves into a glow and really have a gay time. . . . There were turkeys and ham and homemade rolls and plum puddings and salad and all sort of things and nothing ran short. I have the most wonderful cook you have ever seen—her cakes and pies and rolls fly away like puffballs and she is a real genius at managing, as well.

I'm frightfully tired and looking forward to the time when we are properly staffed and ready to let me go, for I am supposed to go to Europe before long, but only after I have had a little time in New York. . . .

I think I shall go back to Brazil after the war for I have never found a place I loved so well. It is truly the golden land of opportunity and expansion. The future of that country is unbelievable. But more of that when I get a chance to sit down and talk and talk and talk for a long time. I'm pretty enthusiastic over Peru as well, and feel that all of South America can be made to count a great deal in our lives if we handle things right.

. . . This is the first day of winter, I believe. We have a brilliant sun and the trade winds are blowing everything off my desk. I have a large fat turkey in the oven and there is enough

noise to make a stab at New Year's Eve in Times Square. It is all
something I wish you could see. People playing pool, in one
corner, ping pong in another, the phonograph flooding the place
with music, cards, chess, beer being consumed by the bottle and
hamburgers forming an endless chain from the kitchen through
the front door. A whale of a coconut cake disappeared like magic
when Margaret brought it out—topped with tons of freshly grated
coconut. It is a lovely club, this one, full of light and screened on
three sides so that we get all the air in the world and there is a lot
of color and gayety about it that seems to make a hit with all the
fellows. I have found that breaking the place up into pleasant conversational groups and letting things run casually and with a mini-
mum of snooping makes a happy place that goes over with a bang.

I mustn't keep this up the rest of the day or you'll be bored
reading and never want to answer . . .

From Rio de Janeiro, Jim had flown over the vineyards of Chile
on his way to Cristobal. In the Canal Zone he faced the reality of war
in the knowledge that nearby jungles hid enormous 16-inch guns
behind tropical foliage. Now he still had his promise of transfer to the
European theater of operations, and when his Panama resort for
sea-weary merchant sailors was finally going strong, he headed for
New York.

Manhattan was even more the romantic destination that he had
first found it to be two decades earlier. The city then was for people
with Jim's sensibilities the unchallenged center of the planet, "the
supreme metropolis of the present," as Cyril Connolly described it for
British readers. The wartime Broadway theater was vibrant with hits.
Oklahoma! with its Agnes de Mille dancers was still a big success; one
of its new stars, Celeste Holm (moonlighting in the intimate club La
Vie Parisienne) nightly sang "They're Either Too Young or Too Old."
Nevertheless the several weeks of liberty failed to dampen his interest
in the European front. During a torrential rain in May, the United
Seamen's Service put Jim aboard a C-47 bound for Casablanca. It was
a place, he was to find, that did not remotely bring to mind the
folkloric Bogart film that became, for another generation, symbolic of
the time.

Eggs—fried, hard-boiled, and in soggy sandwiches—were all there
was to eat as he flew over the Atlantic by way of the Azores en route to

Casablanca. Described by another traveler then as Morocco's New York, the African city proved to be a place of neon-lighted bars where snails in green sauce could be downed by the score and where, among Berbers, Jim learned for the first time to eat all hot food with his fingers. Moving on toward France after several days, he was held over in Naples, where he discovered an uncommon Neapolitan pasta sauce distinguished by the use of pine nuts (then hardly known to Americans) and pork, the one meat he savored above all.

He was to be stationed in Marseille. By the time he came to know it, Marseille had been bombed by the Germans in an effort to clean out Resistance fighters holed up in the Old Port. Close to the harbor filled with damaged ships was the Hotel Continental, about to become jammed with United Seamen's Service charges lingering in Marseille, the port of embarkation for the United States and for the Pacific, where the war continued. Beard reported that his arrival put an end to the black marketing of the French hotel manager and that he found a good chef on duty along with an efficient housekeeping staff. Soon the kitchen was known, as Jim remembered things, among army officers as well as sailors, for its ability to embellish GI food supplies and turn out elegant meals.

Marseille was also a port of entry and it was Jim's city of welcome as he began his discovery of the south of France. Its quays, teeming with vendors of seafood, appealed to him as the coast of Oregon had and would throughout his life. He thrived on the street life of the Cours Belsunce, a wide thoroughfare, tree-shaded on the east side in summer, its west side blown away in the bombardment of May 27 the year before. Here were food stands that supplied the local shoppers; on the other side of the *canebière* was the open market from which women with heavy string bags of provisions hurried onto the narrow streets toward their kitchens, and here in June was held the annual Garlic Fair.

Small eggplants, fragrant rosemary, and a plethora of garlic from the open market were transformed in the Hotel Continental kitchen into a memorable luncheon dish which caught Americans off guard. Jim's hotel chef would scoop the pulp out of eggplants roughly the size of an ear of corn, then set aside the boat-shaped skins. He chopped the pulp and sautéed it with the garlic and fresh rosemary, then mixed it with chopped meat—sometimes the remains of a roast or a pot-au-feu—and colored it with fresh tomato paste. Beating in an egg as a binder, the chef spooned the mixture into the dry-docked eggplant shells, spread them liberally with breadcrumbs and dots of butter, and baked them.

Early in Jim's life, he'd stowed away a number of Mediterranean recipes, including one for braised lamb Provençal, "a cooking method Mother and Let had brought me up on." It required a boned shoulder of lamb, a couple of garlic cloves, an anchovy fillet, onions, zucchini, a green pepper, tomatoes, olives, and eggplant. He'd even included an encouraging paragraph about garlic butter in his book *Hors d'Oeuvre and Canapés*.

Yet it was the reality of Provence, with garlic as its essence, that lured him as nothing else ever would. His taste memory catalogued the obvious—bouillabaisse and the Marseille version of *brandade*—as well as a vision of "a magnificent carp I saw fished out of a pond," which was filleted, sprinkled with garlic and a dusting of parsley and thyme, and baked under a little olive-studded tomato sauce. He was confronted with the fabled, garlicky *poulet aux senteurs de Provence* when he took a jeep and a driver to travel through Côtes-du-Rhône country in search of wine. He discovered a "cache of Châteauneuf-du-Pape [which had a great year in 1943] where I could get a limited amount each month" and he took the time to wander in the vicinity of Cassis, where he also found good wines for his hotel, along with memorable lobster salads.

In the months that remained before his return to New York, he managed to save up leave time and made forays as far as an Alpine village near Grenoble where his driver took him to visit his mother-in-law and his children, whom she had taken care of throughout the war. Their hostess prepared a treat that transported Jim back to childhood summers when he and friends had dangled baited lines in the Necanicum River. The rustic dish was a great bowl of *écrevisses* that had been cooked in a courtbouillon flavored with wild thyme. He thought all the food had something in common with the frontier fare he'd known while growing up. He was in Dauphine country, where the mountain herbs that lambs nibbled on delicately flavored the meat, and where local cooks disdain sophisticated recipes and take pride in such rural family standbys as rabbit in milk that is seasoned with thyme.

Although the fighting in France was over, there was still wartime rationing that fall and therefore good things to be learned about cooking by a culinary journeyman. Jim took to heart the French penchant for making even the most meager food into "something appetizing." In traveling north toward Paris with an acquaintance who had brought along eggs from his farm, Jim had an idea. "We thought we could have a meal by stopping at a tiny auberge to ask them to make us an omelet and give us whatever they could spare. It turned out they had a catch of young partridge and were delighted to feed us the partridge in exchange for the eggs!"

The episode seems to have been a sustaining thought through the thirty-six-day crossing—eating GI food—that brought him into New York Harbor on December 23, 1945. Ocean liners were parked like wheeled vehicles at the piers that studded the Hudson shore of Manhattan. Some passenger ships were refurbished with red and yellow paint banding their smokestacks, others in camouflage or scruffy with the marks of war. The skyline was not yet boxed in and the streets running inward from the quays let in the river light, as it had bathed the West Side when he had first seen New York and the city had first dazzled him. Coming or going, booked on a luxury vessel or prowling the quayside like a tourist, Jim had always been fascinated when he walked west under the Sixth Avenue elevated. He had made it a point to get to know all kinds of eating places, including the Anchor Café, a Forty-ninth Street bistro that was a sailor's haunt (pictures of transatlantic liners on its walls). Serving hearty meals, it was not without reminders of his life with seamen in Europe and Latin America.

His third cookbook, *Fowl and Game Cookery,* had been published during his lengthy service with the United Seamen's organization, but the book was causing little stir, except among his most loyal acquaintances. Jeanne Owen, of course, was on hand, her reputation as the energetic executive secretary of the Wine and Food Society enhanced by articles that she wrote for *Vogue, House Beautiful,* and *House & Garden* magazines. Among her coterie was Earle R. MacAusland, founding publisher of *Gourmet,* who had hired Bill Rhode as editor (the rift that existed between Beard and Rhode had not healed when the latter died in 1945). The friendship between Jeanne and Jim went  on as if without interruption by Jim's overseas service, and they often went to new plays together. He liked the fact that his friend "could upset a theater magnificently. She'd sit down and tap the person ahead of her and say, 'Tell the woman two rows in front to take her hat off. She is ruining the sight line of everybody!'" And he remembered wickedly, when they left the theater, "her stepping into a cab and someone getting into it from the other side at the same moment, and she merely pushed him out with all her strength and slammed the door in his face and then made a few very vulgar remarks to him as we drove off." He added, "We both had a sense of the ridiculous that gave us many chances to laugh—sometimes at other people's expense."

The two friends preferred not to burden their digestions with big dinners before the curtain, but afterward to have a light supper. Often they would drop in at "21," where the mood was gay and where that year another townhouse had been added to the hallowed restaurant's space. The food here was deliberately bland, a cuisine defined by director Jerry Berns as "luxury dining, not gourmet dining." Hamburger at a fancy price and with a hint of nutmeg and minced celery was then the most popular item on the impressive "21" menu.

The fact that the proprietors of "21," like many other restaurateurs, took Mrs. Owen seriously helped Jim Beard a lot in his campaign to find a place in gastronomic New York. Through her good offices, his friendships with many who were preeminent in the wine business began.

RECIPES

Marseille Garlic Soup

Jim learned in Marseille that old-timers in Provence call garlic the truffles of Provence. He also learned to make this traditional soup. The true regional flavor comes from using chicken, goose, or pork fat. In the days when the aberration known as garlic powder was more apt to be on supermarket shelves than fresh heads of garlic, Jim had this word of warning: "The robust and beautiful flavor of this soup is something that could never, ever be achieved with garlic powder. So leave those substitutes on the shelf, look at them once with distaste—and then forget about them."

3 tablespoons chicken, goose, or pork fat
30 peeled garlic cloves (more or less)
6–8 cups chicken stock
salt

freshly ground pepper
nutmeg
4–5 egg yolks
3–4 tablespoons olive oil
6–8 slices toast

Melt the fat in a heavy saucepan over low heat. Add the garlic cloves and shake, keeping the heat gentle so that the garlic cooks without browning. It should just melt in the fat; letting it brown is fatal as the flavor turns bitter. Add 6 to 8 cups of chicken stock and season to taste with a little salt and pepper. (Jim adds that he likes to grate in a tiny bit of nutmeg. He also adds that in other recipes you may drop in a sprig of thyme, another of sage, or a clove.) Simmer for 15 to 20 minutes and then force through a sieve or a food mill to purée the garlic. Reheat the soup. Beat 4 or 5 egg yolks into the olive oil. Stir some of the hot soup into the yolk and oil mixture, then stir this very gently into the soup and heat. Do not under any circumstances let the soup come to a boil, or the yolks will curdle. Serve in large soup plates, ladling the soup over crisp toast, one piece to a serving.   SERVES 6 TO 8.

Nancy Dorris's Sea Squab

▼

As he did with a number of professional friends, Jim exchanged recipes with Nancy Dorris, who succeeded Alice Peterson as food editor of the New York *Daily News*. Sea squab, or blowfish, was not a familiar fish in the forties or fifties but it could be found in Italian fish markets in New York. Jim had a way of simply sautéing it but Nancy Dorris's method gives the little sea squab a crunchy coating while the flesh remains moist.

1¹/₄ pounds sea squab
1 teaspoon salt
freshly ground pepper

1 egg
1 cup cracker crumbs
3–4 tablespoons oil

Wipe the sea squab with a damp cloth and season with salt and a few grinds of pepper. Beat the egg with 2 tablespoons of cold water. Dip the sea squab, one at a time, into the beaten egg, then into the crumbs; set apart from each other on wax paper. Heat enough oil to cover the bottom of a pan ¼ inch deep. When hot but not smoking, put enough of the sea squab in so they are not touching and can be turned easily. Pan-fry to a delicate brown on all sides, cover, reduce the heat, and cook slowly until the flesh comes easily away from the bone—about 5 minutes. Keep warm on a heated platter while cooking the remainder. Serve with lime or lemon wedges. SERVES 4.

Baked Spareribs with Sauerkraut and Apples

▼

In Portland Jim's mother habitually made her own sauerkraut and served it in many ways—giving her son a lifelong appetite for it so that he often would turn out sauerkraut feasts as one of his favorite ways of entertaining his guests in New York. His mother's sauerkraut casserole was something he had particularly loved as a boy.

2 sides (4 pounds) country-
style spareribs
3–4 pounds sauerkraut, well
rinsed and drained

2 tart apples, peeled, cored,
and sliced
3 medium potatoes, peeled
and sliced thin

1–2 teaspoons caraway seeds
1 teaspoon freshly ground
  black pepper

Place one side of spareribs in a lightly buttered baking pan, fat side down. Layer sauerkraut, apples, and potatoes on top, sprinkling the layers with caraway seeds. Season with pepper. Top with the second side of ribs and press down into the sauerkraut mixture. Cover pan with aluminum foil and bake in a 350 degree oven for 1 hour, then remove foil and bake 1 hour more or until brown and tender.   SERVES 4 TO 6.

Cassis Beef Stew

▼

After his first visit to Cassis, Beard came to know many kinds of Provençal stews and, with his inborn yen for trotters and innards, he savored the characteristic Provençal *pieds et paquets* (feet and packages, literally) as served at a one-star restaurant on the Quai Baux. The dish is sheep's tripe cooked with pig's feet, salt pork, white wine, and tomatoes. Here is a variation which substitutes beef shin for tripe.

3 pounds beef shin (in
  1 piece)
2 pig's feet
coarse salt
6 cloves garlic
1 onion, sliced
rosemary
thyme

basil
peppercorns
1 bottle red wine
3–4 ripe tomatoes, peeled,
  seeded, and chopped
1 cup pitted black olives
1/2 cup chopped parsley

Rub the beef shin and the pig's feet in salt. Put the garlic, onion, a good pinch of each of the herbs, a few peppercorns, and the wine in a saucepan and bring to a boil. Cook 10 minutes. Cool slightly and pour over the meat; let stand 12 to 14 hours in the refrigerator. In a heavy braising pan, bring the meat and its marinade to a boil, reduce the heat, and simmer very gently (or cook, covered, in a 275 degree oven) for 3½ hours, until almost tender. Add the tomatoes (you may substitute 2 cups canned Italian tomatoes) and cook 45 minutes. Remove the beef and slice it thick. Skim excess fat from the sauce. Remove the meat from the trotters and add to the sauce. Add the beef slices and cook 15 minutes. Stir in the olives and the parsley. SERVES 6 TO 8.

Lamb in Chili and Vinegar Sauce

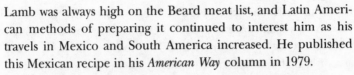

Lamb was always high on the Beard meat list, and Latin American methods of preparing it continued to interest him as his travels in Mexico and South America increased. He published this Mexican recipe in his *American Way* column in 1979.

*3 pounds boneless lamb
(shoulder or leg), cut in
1½-inch pieces
2 medium onions, chopped
2 cloves garlic, chopped
3–4 sprigs fresh coriander
salt
3 ancho and 3
mulato chilies*

*⅛ teaspoon ground cumin
½ teaspoon oregano
2 tablespoons red
wine vinegar
3 tablespoons lard or
vegetable oil*

Put the lamb into a heavy saucepan or casserole with 1 onion, 1 clove garlic, the coriander sprigs, about ½ teaspoon salt, and water barely to cover. Bring to a boil, lower the heat, and simmer, covered, until the meat is tender—about 1½ hours. Drain the lamb, strain the stock, and set aside. Rinse out and dry the casserole and return the lamb to it.

Prepare the chilies. Rinse in cold water, tear off the stem ends, and shake out the seeds. Tear the chilies roughly into pieces and soak in 1 cup warm water for 30 minutes. If they are still dry soak them a little longer. Purée them with their soaking water in a blender or food processor. Add the remaining onion and garlic, the cumin, oregano, vinegar, and a pinch of salt, and blend until fairly smooth. The mixture should be more of a paste than a purée. Heat the lard or oil in a skillet and cook the chili paste over moderate heat, stirring constantly with a wooden spoon, for about 5 minutes. Thin with 1½ cups of the reserved lamb stock. The sauce should be the consistency of a medium cream sauce; add more stock if necessary. Pour over the lamb and simmer over very low heat for 20 minutes. Serve with rice, beans, and a green vegetable. Tortillas are good with this, too.   SERVES 6.

Chicken with Forty Cloves of Garlic

▼

Fellow professionals gave Beard credit for introducing to Americans many regional French specialties, including this one, which was singled out by wine writer Bob Thompson of the Napa Valley as a dish "that destroys any wine that vacillates," but is companionable with whites made from the Sauvignon grapes. "A Provençal recipe that I taught for years in my classes," Jim said, "and one that never failed to astonish the students because the garlic becomes so mild and buttery when it's cooked through."

2/3 cup oil
8 chicken drumsticks and
* thighs (or 16 of either)*
4 ribs celery, cut in
* long strips*
2 medium onions, chopped
6 sprigs parsley
1 tablespoon chopped
fresh tarragon, or
1 teaspoon dried

1/2 cup dry vermouth
2 1/2 teaspoons salt
1/4 teaspoon freshly ground
* black pepper*
nutmeg
40 cloves garlic, unpeeled

Put the oil in a shallow dish, add the chicken pieces, and turn them to coat all sides evenly with the oil. Cover the bottom of a heavy 6-quart casserole with a mixture of the celery and onions, add the parsley and tarragon, and lay the chicken pieces on top. Pour the vermouth over them, sprinkle with salt and pepper, add a dash or two of nutmeg, and tuck the garlic cloves around and between the chicken pieces. Cover the top of the casserole tight with aluminum foil and then the lid (this creates an air-tight seal so the steam won't escape). Bake in a 375 degree oven for 1 1/2 hours, without removing the cover. Serve the chicken, pan juices, and whole garlic cloves with thin slices of heated French bread or toast. The garlic should be squeezed from the root end of its papery husk onto the bread or toast, spread like butter, and eaten with the chicken.   SERVES 8.

Puerto Rican Chicken-and-Rice Stew

▼

"Because it is built on ingredients native to the New World," Beard said, "I think Latin American food is the purest American food of all." He and Elisabeth Lambert Ortiz, author of the *Book of Latin American Cooking*, frequently collaborated, with this recipe as one of the results.

1 large clove garlic, chopped very fine	*freshly ground pepper*
1/2 teaspoon oregano	*4 cups chicken stock, or more*
1 teaspoon salt	*1/8 teaspoon saffron, crumbled*
3–31/2-pound chicken, cut in 8 pieces	*2 cups long-grain rice*
2 tablespoons oil	*1 cup frozen peas*
1 onion, chopped fine	*1 tablespoon capers*
1 green or red bell pepper, chopped	*1/4 cup stuffed green olives, sliced*
2 ounces diced ham	*1 whole canned tomato, cut in strips*
3 tomatoes, peeled and chopped	

Mull the garlic, oregano, and salt to a paste. Rub it into the chicken pieces. Heat the oil in a heavy skillet and sauté the chicken pieces until golden. Transfer the chicken to an earthenware or enameled iron casserole. In the oil remaining in the skillet sauté the onion and pepper until they are soft. Add them to the casserole with the diced ham, chopped tomatoes, a few grinds of pepper, 4 cups of stock, and the saffron. Simmer, covered, over low heat for 30 minutes. Lift out the chicken pieces onto a warm dish and set aside. Pour the liquid through a sieve, reserving the solids. Measure the liquid and add enough chicken stock to make 6 cups. Pour into the casserole, add the rice and the reserved solids, stir to mix, and bring to a boil. Arrange the chicken pieces on top of the rice, cover, and cook over very low heat about 20 minutes, until the rice is tender. Blanch the peas for 1 minute in boiling water, drain, then stir them along with the capers and olives into the dish. Scatter the tomato strips on top and return to the heat just long enough to warm through. Serve from the casserole.   SERVES 6 TO 8.

Cassis Ice Cream

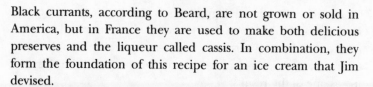

Black currants, according to Beard, are not grown or sold in America, but in France they are used to make both delicious preserves and the liqueur called cassis. In combination, they form the foundation of this recipe for an ice cream that Jim devised.

*2 cups black
    currant preserves
1 cup crème de cassis
juice of 1 lemon
1/2 teaspoon vanilla*

*2 cups light cream
2 cups heavy cream
1/8 teaspoon salt
Garnish: currant preserves
    mixed with cassis*

Purée the preserves in a blender or food processor, adding a little cassis as the mixture spins. Add the lemon juice, the remaining cassis, and the vanilla. Mix the light and heavy cream with the salt and stir into the currant mixture. Pour into an ice cream freezer and freeze according to the manufacturer's instructions. Serve with currant preserves mixed with cassis as a topping. SERVES 8.

6

ENTRÉES AND HOUSE SPECIALTIES

In the year of his death, Beard jauntily reviewed a book called *Good Food from a Small Kitchen,* written by Moira Hodgson, who was one of his Greenwich Village neighbors. The author boasts of cooking everything—from couscous, using a three-pound lamb shoulder and six pounds of vegetables, to a suckling pig—in what she describes as "a disused closet" measuring four and a half by six and a half feet. "When the oven heats up, the refrigerator buckles," she wrote.

On the same street of front-stooped brownstones, Jim had pioneered the art of cooking-in-confinement following his return to New York at war's end. "My first New York apartment had a kitchen that was roughly the size of the inside of a fountain pen," he confided in his seventy-fifth year, to readers of his newspaper column. With ingenuity, he had contrived to make the limitations fit his needs. "What made it bearable was the fact that it was right next to a very large, two-level bathroom that had a magnificent bathtub. After I washed the dishes, I would put them in the tub, pull the shower curtain closed and turn on the shower full force. It was the most accommodating dishwasher I've ever owned because in it I could do untold piles of dishes."

For Jim the inadequacy of his kitchen was a minor threat to his determination that he could find a livelihood in the food world. At last he'd faced the reality of his minimal chances on the stage. His wartime tour of duty had rekindled his ardor for feeding and entertaining—the more expansive the hospitality the better. With the help of his friend Agnes Crowther, the Portland designer who was one of those hometowners who had settled in New York before Jim, he made his cooking space a bit more accommodating with ingenious racks and cupboards fitted into his flat's narrow hall. He needed space for the *batterie de cuisine* he'd acquired.

While in France, as the war was ending, he had managed to locate Paris shops with large stocks of copper pots and pans that had been retrieved from bombed-out buildings "or had been sold by refugees evacuating the city." The worn condition was not enough to fuss over. He said that he staggered away with as much as he could carry or afford. Retinned inside and warmly glowing outside, the hand-hammered copper cookware offset the otherwise modest tone of the brownstone walk-up and, as a friend said, certified his reputation as a culinary authority. He knew what he wanted when it came to having a well-equipped kitchen, for he'd been brought up, as he liked to say, in the Iron Age of American cookery.

His mother had cooked on cast-iron wood stoves in both Portland and Gearhart, and had used iron skillets and Dutch ovens, as well as an iron stew pot. There had been "ghastly enameled pots known as granite-ware," and Jim had dealt with sturdy cast aluminum. But he believed that lined copper was the best foundation for the superior cooking he championed in his three books then for sale in the stores; his *Hors d'Oeuvre and Canapés,* in fact, was in its fifth printing, and there would be new editions in the years ahead.

He was beginning to attract more attention in the press. In her first interview with him, in 1945, Jane Nickerson of *The New York Times* came to talk to him in his Twelfth Street flat. She remembered peering up to see him looming at the top of the stairs. "He looked enormous," she said, "like a giant baby. He called to me to come up, and welcomed me to his simple room beside the kitchen—I remember the box spring and mattress for a bed. He offered me instant coffee, giving that engaging smile of his, and I plied him with questions about hors d'oeuvres and appetizers. Everything about him was unpretentious."

In his book titled *On the Tip of My Tongue,* in 1945 in its second printing, Iles Brody also called attention to the prowess that could be demonstrated in a small flat. "Mr. James Beard, well-known culinary writer and expert of outdoor cooking," Brody wrote, "weighs 250 pounds and is six feet three inches tall; he barely fits into his very small kitchenette, and still he prepares the most delicious meals." As food editor of *Esquire,* Brody knew whereof he wrote: "What's more, the menus are complete from soup to nuts—an additional score for Mr. Beard, since most men are afraid to attempt cooking more than one dish, even in a perfectly appointed kitchen."

As one of the group with whom Mary Hamblet had driven north to look in on the Bird & Bottle Inn before the war, Iles Brody knew the New York scene as well as a restaurant reviewer needed to. The confrérie to which he belonged included Lucius Beebe, the *Herald Tribune* columnist, and Danton Walker of the *Daily News,* who had been a champion of Hors d'Oeuvre Inc. Brody was one of a growing number of wine enthusiasts who hailed American vintages. He reported that H. G. Wells, the British historian and novelist, "had fairly saturated himself with native wines during his last visit to this country, saying that the best wines in the world are American, and that he simply can't understand why the lucky natives don't drink more of this liquid sunshine." Brody added, "A war had to occur before Americans really discovered what treasure they have in their own country."

World War II, like every other, changed lives, caused service men and women to stay in New York instead of going home, caused others to turn a hundred and eighty degrees in their careers. Jim had taken his turn from theater to food and, having made his way in foreign countries honing his palate by adventurous eating and drinking, it was natural for him to seek out others with the same inclinations. He had been introduced to the Sherry wine shop on Madison Avenue by Jeanne Owen, and, as one who had lived abroad, in uniform and out, Jim found much in common with Jack and Sam Aaron, the brothers who ran the store. Sam's change of career had been from psychologist of an army neurological center to wine entrepreneur, and he and Jim became immediate friends. Jim soon joined the Sherry staff as a retail salesman, a convenient way for him to round out his meager income as a freelance writer.

Like Iles Brody, Beard and the Aarons were prudent enough to smile at the extravagance of wine amateurs like H. G. Wells, but there

Jim with Sam Aaron

was no doubt that a new appreciation was developing, for California wines in particular; their friends Frank Schoonmaker and Alexis Lichine had been promoting the new vintages under their varietal names before the war, and had sold their stocks of American wines for distribution by "21" Brands before going into the service. Sherry's, through Jack Aaron's marriage, was closely associated with "21" enterprises and, with Jeanne Owen's friendships at the "21" Club, it was a small world in which Jim found himself.

"He went back to France with my brother on a buying trip," Sam Aaron recalled one day at lunch. "There was a lot of on-the-job training, and Jim's palate was damned good. He liked a lot of the simple wines—he translated everything into American, he understood the average American nervousness about wine. And he had a lot to say about food—but it was a desert when he started writing—who the hell else was writing about food?" There was Julian Street, and he worked for Bellows and Company. In this period, when Bloomingdale's was beginning to develop a food department aimed at the growing popular interest in epicurean eating and the Maison Glass was thriving as a specialty food store, the Aarons set Jim up in a similar emporium called Allen Berry. They filled its shelves with high-quality canned goods from S. S. Pierce in Boston that included preserved fruitcakes and puddings, some regional cheeses, as well as imported chocolates, foie gras, and caviar. It was a brief experiment, brought to a halt by the expiration of the building's lease, and Jim then took on the writing of notes for the Sherry wine catalogues.

In addition he became Sherry's most sought-out adviser to wine novices. (His success in gaining the confidence of women remained unimpaired.) He thrived at taking telephone calls from such hostesses as Mrs. George Pillsbury, who wanted help in selecting wines that would complement the food at the New York dinners she gave when her husband's company entertained guests from abroad. "Jim knew the palates of Europeans and South Americans, and helped me decide on menus," Sally Pillsbury recalled with lasting appreciation.

Well past his fortieth birthday, he was buoyed by another sign of changing times. He was stopped on the street in the spring of 1946 by a friend who told him that people at NBC were looking for James Beard because of his experience as an actor as well as a cook. Television was in its infancy, with a big need for unusual talents and new ideas for attracting home audiences. One such effort was a show, called "For You and Yours," getting under way at WNBT, the New York station of the National Broadcasting Company, and home cooking was one of its subjects.

Coast-to-coast broadcasting was yet to come, but the weekly show (sponsored by the Borden Company, which had introduced Elsie the Cow at the World's Fair) found an unexpected audience. Generally, there were more attentive TV watchers in saloons than in private homes, and the Borden program's time slot—leading into the weekly broadcast of Friday night fights—attracted some male viewers who found the cookstove proceedings fascinating. Billed as "Elsie Presents James Beard in 'I Love to Eat,'" Jim's TV experiment was a precursor of many future cooking shows, including those of Dione Lucas, Julia Child, and a man who calls himself "the frugal gourmet." Jim's act, coming before the introduction of videotape, was photographed in black-and-white and was given to such effects as the use of ink to bring out the mold in Roquefort cheese and the brandishing of a blowtorch to highlight cooking *en flamme*.

Twenty-six men in Peekskill were intrigued enough, according to Jim, to write a letter to the program's star to say that they had become aficionados of the range as well as the ring, and there was a good-natured caller from the management of "21"; Jim's televised barbecuing of spareribs was described there as such a smash act that "everyone at '21' was in the bar watching, and refused to go into the dining room and eat."

The idea of a TV cooking show brought almost immediate competition from several directions, including the feisty Columbia Broadcasting System (which hired Lucas, as a graduate of Paris's Cordon Bleu Cooking School). In the wake, the Borden Company relinquished its sponsorship of "Elsie Presents" in 1947, as did the succeeding underwriter, Birdseye Frozen Foods, in the following spring. Television's early programming was capricious, with producers trying various formats as they began to build shows around nationally known personalities. Although Dione Lucas's telecast cooking classes prevailed for a couple of seasons, no food show would become a dominant force in television until a dozen or more years later, when Julia Child demonstrated her gift of straightforward naturalness; she used the video lens to enter hundreds of thousands of kitchens. In the 1940s, it soon was clear, Jim didn't have the easy knack of speaking directly through the camera.

However, he had begun to reach the audience he would keep for the rest of his life through the printed word. Again his ability to get to know new people and nurture new friendships was shaping his career. For *House & Garden*'s December 1942 issue he had written the first of many pieces he was to do for various editors on celebrating Christmas and he turned out another article called "Caribbean Cookery," for publication in April 1948 in the same magazine. In 1949, he joined the staff of *Gourmet,* where his erstwhile friend Bill Rhode had worked before he died. But his rapport with *Gourmet* was uneasy.

The first issue, subtitled the Magazine of Good Living, had raised eyebrows on Madison Avenue, and led a reader to protest the signal thus given off, that "we may again be in the dark ages of food worship." *Gourmet*'s publisher, Earle R. MacAusland, and his partner, Mrs. Roger W. Straus, Sr., believed "that more thought should be given [as was said in a *Gourmet* editorial] both to the preparation of foods and to the manner of eating them [rather than] eating merely to satisfy one's hunger.... The cultivation of taste should be encouraged in all lines..."

Three decades later, Jim nodded positively when he read MacAusland's accounting in the *National Observer.* "When I started

Gourmet," the founder was quoted as saying, "the average person's conception of flavor was the salt and pepper shakers and a bottle of catsup." MacAusland was also expressing the Beard contention that Americans could eat at home cheaper, and with more style, subtlety, and appreciation by making use of the kind of recipes offered by *Gourmet* than those in newspapers or women's magazines. What MacAusland realized, Jim reflected, was that his magazine's problem was the average conception that good meals meant steak, chops, and fried chicken. *Gourmet* in those days, he pointed out, was the only stimulus to persuade you to let go on your imagination in cooking.

For Jim as a fledgling magazine writer, *Gourmet* was a temporary haven. His knowledge of European cuisines was as good or better than that of the few other people writing about food. Most were entrenched home economists who were taught that they must have a scientific approach to food, that food wasn't supposed to be fun. That word "fun" came as close as any to defining Jim's notions about dealing with food. His strength was that he was both well informed and amusing in person. He could cheer up *PM*'s Charlotte Adams when she groused about the home ec newspaper writer who told her, "What you and Clementine ought to do is take your degree in domestic science." He praised Adams for her writing in the newspaper *PM,* and he was a sought-after pal of others among his new colleagues, including Clementine Paddleford, who in addition to her seven-day-a-week work for the *Herald Tribune* for a time turned out a monthly news roundup, "Food Flashes," for *Gourmet*.*

"Now in this month of sundaes," Clementine once told July readers, "the sauces parade. One new arrival is Gold Brick Topping . . . a chocolate syrup thick and nobbly with chopped pecans, every bite crisp as crunch." She added, "Spoon it over ice cream. Taste! Isn't that different? This sauce isn't gooey and gummy like most of its kind." Not an easy, polished stylist himself, Jim could laugh naughtily at his friend Clementine. Her articles, he told an interviewer, were "like nothing else that has happened before or since. They were the most exhaustive collection of flowery prose . . . " Certainly, the Paddleford verve in food writing was jauntier than the style he himself was able to muster when he began writing "Specialités de la Maison," as the editors of *Gourmet* called the section on restaurants. At *Gourmet,* he was now not only in the company of the well-established Paddleford but of Lucius Beebe, who gave Jim glimpses of the vanished world known as high society and whose contribution was called "Along the Boulevards." There were also Frank Schoonmaker, often writing of his knowledge of European vineyards without neglecting his enthusiasm for the future of American wines, and Samuel Chamberlain, whose etchings illustrated his stories of gastronomic travels in a series that MacAusland later published in book form as *Bouquet de France, British Bouquet,* and *Italian Bouquet.*† Louis Diat, a handsome Frenchman famous as the Ritz-Carlton's chef, shared with the magazine's readers recollections of his early career. Interspersed with recipes and tips on how to cook, his articles were written by Helen Ridley, his constant companion, who worked at a Madison Avenue advertising agency.

---

*Clementine Paddleford's oddness was summed up by Craig Claiborne, who reported that her pet cat Pussy Willow slept in her "in basket" until the cat's death. Clem ordained that the pet must be buried in her own office bed, and so she was. When the funeral was over there was a horrifying discovery, Claiborne said. "My God," cried Clem, "my book manuscript was in that basket!"

†In his introduction to *Bouquet de France,* MacAusland wrote of Chamberlain that "friends told me about an architect and etcher who . . . had lived in France for most of the years between the wars, was a scholar, an artist, and a gourmet of the first order. . . . I found him in Boston, in the basement of one of the old buildings of the Massachusetts Institute of Technology. He was pulling etchings, in a badly stained smock that made him look rather more like a genial automobile mechanic than a fine artist. But when we talked of food and drink, and of France, we were on common ground."

"Mr. Mac," as MacAusland was called by his staff, established himself at what may literally have been the summit of epicurean New York. *Gourmet's* offices were in the penthouse of the Plaza Hotel and the publisher's desk was under the rotunda, with a dining room at the top of an interior flight of steps. "He had a three-course lunch every day that began with two martinis," Ann Seranne told me at her New Jersey country house. "Often his guests were Clementine Paddleford and Lucius Beebe, although he really wanted advertisers to join him," she said. Getting the magazine off the ground was difficult until ad men unbedazzled by lunch and a bottle of wine perceived its possibilities.

When at MacAusland's behest Jim took time off from the Sherry wine shop to try out as an editor, his friend Ann Seranne became his assistant, and together they would shop and cook for themselves on weekends. One day when Ann saw an ad for fresh truffles—imported from France by Bloomingdale's, three in a basket for $10 a pound—she bought them and rushed down to Jim's small kitchen. "He practically said so what," she told me on an afternoon many years afterward. "He heated some goose fat in a big sauté pan, sliced in some potatoes, then threw in my truffles. I couldn't believe what he was doing to my truffles—my very first! It turned out to be the best dish ever. He was very creative—always knew just what to do with ingredients, how to give things their best flavors."* Yet when it came to writing Jim was a different person. "It took one article to find that Jim really couldn't put a story together," Seranne recalled. MacAusland cut him loose, and "three months later, I became editor." In addition to her past work as cook and secretary for Crosby Gaige, Jim's friend Ann had studied with Dione Lucas, and her sense of culinary fare continued to keep their rapport in good condition in spite of his failure at *Gourmet*.

Facing reality, Jim was beginning to understand that his career as a magazine contributor could succeed only with the collaboration of

*"My own way of coping with unforeseen situations," Beard wrote in a syndicated column, "is to keep a special shelf stocked with things I can reach for when I have to make a meal in a hurry or feed unexpected guests." Canned white truffles were among the minced clams, salmon, corned beef, sardines, pimientos, broths, and olives.

trained writers. The thing that made his articles singularly interesting
was their personal quality—he could get across the feeling of pleasure
that he himself drew from cooking, and was at his best when spilling
out ideas and enthusiasm confident that an editor could provide the
needed shaping. He had the far-ranging intellect that had made him
a constant reader and he wanted his pieces to be supported by
historical background when such material could be enlightening.
Most of all, he thought food and people should be brought together
to enrich the writing by emphasizing the importance of food in the
art of living.

In his Greenwich Village flat he practiced what he preached. He
entertained several times a month. His spirit of fun transformed the
minimal accommodations of the floor-through flat into attributes. He
had brought home from Europe two life-sized statues of Greek
goddesses, and these classic plaster sculptures—he called them "the
girls"—dominated the small room, somewhat the way his copper pots
seemed to expand his kitchenette. The group he often brought
together was a mix of Portland friends and Manhattan food people.
The perception of one of the former, "in those crowded days," was of
drinking parties so jammed that the shuffling bodies were threatened
by "many interfering elbows. But the food was lavish and the companionship exuberant."

The host, always beaming in his delight at bringing together odd
assortments, often served dishes with spectacular effects—a favorite
was hot sauerkraut and sausages into which he plunged splits of
chilled champagne that spurted as he made his entrance and titillated sophisticates no less than the out-of-towners. He left no doubt
that he knew, more than most of the food fraternity, how to make food
interesting. What some Portlanders may have thought to be "interfering
elbows" frequently belonged to New York editors.

In this period he was asked to write a book to be called *The
Fireside Cook Book,* and it was, as Jim said later, "a very large project,
heavily advertised and promoted. But the publisher told me that I
would not have the standard royalties, just an outright fee. So, all my
friends said, 'You're crazy to do it.' I thought about it very carefully,
and I reasoned: if it's going to be this big a thing, it's going to do me

more good than the royalty payments could. So I took it." As it happened, Jim seemed to believe throughout his life that he'd made the wisest move of his career.

In the fall of 1949 *The Fireside Cook Book,* by James Beard, was published with much success by Simon and Schuster, bearing an acknowledgment notice that cited the help of: "Jeanne Owen [to whom the book was dedicated]; Jack and Sam Aaron of Sherry Wine and Spirits; Marjorie Dean of General Foods; and Earle R. MacAusland of *Gourmet* Magazine." The contents were illustrated by Alice and Martin Provensen in splashes of color to make the volume the most lavishly produced American cookbook to date.

The immediate recognition that came with *The Fireside Cook Book* established Beard's name across the country, which, Jim recalled, "would have taken me years to do otherwise." And for all who participated in the enterprise there was what Mrs. Provensen remembered as a celebrity lunch at the "21" Club "with what must have been seven or eight wine glasses at each place." The party's bounty persuaded the Provensens (who were on the verge of vegetarianism) that they wouldn't be able to eat for a week; but as the celebrating came to an end, the illustrator recalled, "Jim and his friends were already talking about where they would go that night for dinner."

Beard's introduction to the *Fireside* book, composed with editorial assistance from Simon and Schuster, stated his career-long thesis that "America has the opportunity, as well as the resources, to create for herself a truly national cuisine that will incorporate all that is best in the traditions of the many people who have crossed the seas to form our new, still-young nation." At its best, the text continues, "American cookery is as straightforward, honest, and delicious as the fish that swim off its shores or the cornmeal dishes that were the mainstays of its earliest settlers. At its worst, it is a careless imitation, not merely of what is least good in the tradition of other countries, but, what is still worse, of its own traditions."

The book was a one-volume omnibus, its flap copy boasting of 1,217 recipes, along with sections on seasonings, frozen foods, and wines: "Do not insist on drinking only imported wines. Do not be a chauvinist who insists that only American wines are really good. Let each wine, regardless of origin, stand on its own." As a guide for uninitiated buyers, he listed thirteen varieties of grapes by whose names California wines are categorized.

The *Fireside* book was even more up-to-date in the section titled "Frozen Foods and Pick-up Meals." It pointed out, "Modern living is coming increasingly to mean informal living; but informality in cooking and entertaining should not by any means signify thrown-together meals." The text emphasized that Americans should treat unexpected guests as handsomely as those invited some time ahead. Convenience foods could make the servantless life easier, but that did not excuse slapdash cooking or serving. Jim was circumspect about frozen foods, vetoing precooked meat pies. "I am obliged to withhold my enthusiasm for the great majority of prepared dishes," the book tells its readers. But he wrote forthrightly that freezing as a means of preserving one's own cooked foods had merit.

After leaving his editor's job to Ann Seranne, a couple of Beard contributions appeared in *Gourmet* as the *Fireside* volume was being published. In the first piece in the magazine to bear his byline, he compared restaurant reviewing to theater criticism, and regretted that there was no "Restaurant Reviewers Circle."* He may have seemed to some a trifle stiff-necked as he let his readers in on his current dismay at the popular acceptance of the word "brunch." And he bolstered his credentials by pointing out that he had first dined at one of his recommended restaurants twenty years before (unlike Brody, he was an old New York hand, he suggested slyly). In the column a few months later there was another reminder of the rapport he was establishing with restaurateurs. He told of the trip via Air France to Paris and his friendship with Louis Vaudable, the proprietor of Maxim's, while he also saluted the pig's feet served at La Mediterranée on the Left Bank and the *pissaladière* at the Restaurant de la Boule d'Or.

In a subsequent article he inadvertently described himself to a degree: "His chest distends, ever-widening, to well below his waistline.

---

*Leo Lerman, the editor and social chronicler, remembered the "real kindness" showed by Jim. "When I began reviewing restaurants, Jim took notice of me. He'd come and stand at my table, and that helped restaurateurs to take me seriously," Lerman said after Beard's death.

There is a rotundity about the man which is mindful of perpetual good living. As is usual with people who live exceedingly well, there is a benign and comfortable expression on his face and a general aura of well-being. You are at once aware that here is a man who knows living and all its embellishments..." The irony is that Jim was not trying to offer a writer's self-portrait—the subject, indeed, was Fernand Point, proprietor of the Restaurant de la Pyramide in Vienne, who was respected by France's most famous chefs as "the King." Of course, Point was one of Jim's heroes as well and remained so throughout his life. (Whatever else the two men may have had in common, they were both addicted to colorfully made bow ties—Point, especially, as Joseph Wechsberg observed, chose flowery untailored designs, "like those Italian tenors wore in the old days.")

Beard's visits in France with its gastronomic luminaries became a habit. He helped organize a tour of vineyards that included forty food professionals and was sponsored by the San Francisco chapter of André Simon's Wine and Food Society. The Associated Press food editor Cecily Brownstone and another of Jim's friends, Ruth Norman, were in Paris at the same time, and the former "had the most marvellous time of my life," as Cecily remembered. "I was blue with food. Jim was in a small homey hotel just off the rue Castiglione, and went with us everywhere. He loved both haute cuisine and bistro food." He introduced the young women to lark pâté, and showed them markets that were open twenty-four hours a day in Les Halles. "I remember the little quails—it was a wonderful education," Cecily said. "I was an apt pupil and an appreciative one, and he loved that."

The game birds remembered by Jim, as the tour continued south of Lyon toward the vineyards of Condrieu and the Côte Rôtie, were partridges served at the Pyramide in Vienne. "We had an unforgettable dinner chez Fernand Point," he recalled in a letter, "partridges wrapped in a blanket of pastry—light as a sigh and tender as a lover's caress. The little heads were still on and they were made up before arriving at table to look alive and uncooked—and the crust was molded into wings and tail—a pretty and delicate sight if I ever had one set before me." An even more poignant pleasure was the beginning of his long friendship with M. Point and his wife, Mado.

The lush images aside, Jim was eloquent in his appreciations, and during the junket with the posse of food and wine writers he exchanged enthusiasms with most of the group. Thus he met Alexander Watt, a London journalist who was living and working in Paris, and they formed a partnership that produced a restaurant guide, called *Paris Cuisine,* published in 1952. Their book was to be the first postwar assessment in English of eating places in the French capital, and it was the happy result of many meals, in expensive dining rooms as well as modestly priced bistros, that Jim shared with Sandy Watt and his wife, Grete. The couple lived on the Quai des Orfèvres in an apartment with a sweeping view of the city in which the Watts entertained maybe once a year. Sandy's Scottish background was the excuse, among Parisian surroundings, for an afternoon of haggis and malt liquor. Jim (his credentials underscored by his Scottish middle name, Andrews) was among the guests, including a few French and Americans, who always met the challenge. In Portland, indeed, where Scots composed a good portion of the population, haggis was far from unknown, and Jim consistently welcomed any offbeat ethnic dish as a "conversation piece" if nothing more.

Among Europeans, he found bigoted notions about food as common as those among Americans—few people abroad, he once said, really liked corn on the cob. But he and Watt became fans of one typical bistro, in an unlikely spot off the Champs-Elysées, which made a specialty of *maïs frais, poché*. L'Escargot, as the place was called, was conveniently located for fashion buyers, especially, and the fresh ears of corn delivered from the farm of a former GI were often served as an hors d'oeuvre by Chef Perrot. "His secret," as later described by Jim in a syndicated column, "was to cook it in a mixture of two-thirds water and one-third milk . . . it gives a quality to corn that mere water cannot. Just let it come to a boil and simmer about one minute. I serve the cobs forth with plenty of melted butter." He put himself on record as against cold pats of butter that slipped around, preferred instead to quickly saturate the corn kernels with hot liquid butter.

On his return from Paris, it was clear that the impact of *The Fireside Cook Book* had made him something of a celebrity, especially among food professionals. Jane Nickerson told *New York Times* readers that he was "a titan of the table art, a leading personality in contemporary cookery on this side of the Atlantic and a man whose vast culinary talents match his heroic proportions." Alice Petersen of the *Daily News* was also impressed. His new reputation brought brief assignments that stemmed from his good-naturedness and his gift for communication with all kinds of people. One chore that amused him was his role as "famous author" escorting a busload of high school home economics students on a tour of New York City's Fulton Street fish market, the Fourteenth Street abattoirs, and the wholesale provisioners of the Washington market. Leading excitable teenagers through the basics of the culinary life brought forth both his gift for teaching and his instinct for transforming such a job into a traveling show.

He was gathering stories of occasions like this one with which to regale his successful friends, who felt singled out when he invited them as guests at dinner, including some who had also experienced the struggle for acceptance in New York and sometimes worried about him. At an evening party at which Ron and Isabel Callvert were

among the guests, Cheryl Crawford admitted that she was so exasper-
ated at Jim's laissez-faire attitude that she jumped up with her fists
clenched in passion. "Jim," she cried, "when are you going to get an
agent!"

The agent was to come later, for at this point Jim had to
recognize that he had no exploitable reputation as a writer for
national magazines. This fact was what persuaded Jim to ask Isabel
Callvert to be his collaborator, and, as Ron testified, it led to "their
success in placing articles in *Harper's Bazaar* immediately, and to an
unabated demand from other national publications." Ron recalled
that his wife had been attached to Jim "since he was the neighborhood fat boy cadging cookies from housewives on the block." She had
written some of the Portland radio scripts they had performed together
and, in following her husband's career, had begun to write professionally for an educational network.

Isabel and Jim collaborated for eighteen years. "Financial arrangements between them," according to Ron, "were originally informal.
Then, as the literary agent John Schaffner took over Jim's relations
with publishers, Jim and Isabel worked with a fixed percentage that
divided the proceeds from magazines. Among his major books she

was the editor of *James Beard's Fish Cookery, How to Eat Better for Less Money* (with Sam Aaron), and his acknowledged collaborator in *The James Beard Cookbook*. She shared in advance payments, but not in book royalties."

About this time Jerry Mason, who had just been made editor of *Argosy* magazine, was introduced to Beard in the Sherry wine shop by Sam Aaron. Mason remembered clearly that although Jim was there as a salesman who provided comment for the wine catalogues, his encyclopedic knowledge of food was obvious from their first conversations. "He'd just done the *Fireside,* and I was converting *Argosy* from a pulp magazine to a slick. I was sure it would be smart to have a food column because I knew a lot of men who loved to cook." He got Jim started immediately. "They were wonderful pieces," ranging from evocations of breakfast, about which Jim "knew everything," to one titled "Good Grits from the Galley," in which the collaborators included a recipe for a variation of rarebit that could be made with canned ingredients to facilitate cooking onboard. This was a cheese dish that combined condensed tomato soup with condensed milk, dry mustard, and grated sharp cheese in the upper part of a double boiler. The heated mixture was to be poured over poached or fried eggs on crisp toast. He noted that a slice of fried or cold ham could be added, covered by the eggs and the cheese mixture.

The success Jim was now having at *Argosy, Apartment Life, House & Garden,* and other periodicals, the publicity he was getting, the friendships he established with such theater people as Cheryl Crawford, who had conquered Broadway with her production of *Brigadoon,* all combined to turn Jeanne Owen against him, he later said. "She decided I was getting too famous. So she decided to cut me off. After that I was everything from a SOB to a thief, to just about everything else. And yet—all those years that she hated my guts, and spent time spreading around what she thought, she would call up a friend of mine and say, 'Now, I don't think that Jim looks very well. You'd better tell him to be careful. Tell him to see the doctor, if he hasn't.'"

Both had come to realize that their need for each other was over. It was not a lovers' quarrel—it was more that Jim had outgrown his surrogate mother. As Ron Callvert put it, he had learned to stand up to her.

RECIPES

Mushrooms Stuffed with Snails
▼

In 1977, an international gathering of mycologists in Lebanon, Oregon, was given this recipe for snails, developed after experiments that Beard had conducted long before with Jeanne Owen, whose favorite snail recipe combined escargots with frog's legs. America's black walnuts make this mushroom dish a singular one.

> *2 dozen good-sized*
> *mushroom caps*
> *4 dozen snails*
> *1/2 pound soft butter*
> *2–3 tablespoons*
> *chopped shallots*
> *2–3 cloves garlic,*
> *chopped fine*

> *1/4 cup chopped parsley*
> *salt*
> *freshly ground pepper*
> *1/4 cup chopped*
> *black walnuts*
> *24 toast rounds, fried*
> *in butter*

Wipe the mushroom caps with a damp cloth and drain the snails. Cream the butter with the chopped shallots, garlic, parsley, and a sprinkling 4808alt and pepper. Rub the mushroom caps lightly with the seasoned butter and put them, hollow side down, under a broiler for 1 minute. Remove, turn them over, and put 2 snails in each cap. Sprinkle with chopped nuts and divide the remaining seasoned butter among the mushrooms. Bake in a 450 degree oven for about 8 minutes. Remove from the oven and place each mushroom on a round of fried toast.   SERVES 6.

Cheryl Crawford's Tuna Fish Salad
▼

Jim's friend didn't pretend to be a cook; when she produced food for guests she was as much in earnest as in getting a play staged. Like Jim, she understood the virtues of canned tuna—he thought fresh tuna too often dried out and lacking in flavor by the time it was sold; she found canned tuna convenient as a complement to cut-up fruits.

two 7-ounce cans tuna
1 cup finely chopped celery
1/4 cup chopped scallions
1/2 teaspoon salt

1 ripe apple, diced fine
1/4 cup white seedless grapes
mayonnaise
lettuce

Drain and flake the tuna. Put it in a bowl and toss with the celery, scallions, salt, apple, grapes, and enough mayonnaise to make the ingredients cling together. Serve on lettuce leaves.　　　　　　　　　　SERVES 4.

Baked Bass for Ann Seranne

▼

When Ann Seranne was producing her long list of cookbooks, she included recipes from friends, among which there was one that had been given to her by Jim when they were young New Yorkers. "Save this dish for very special guests or when you want to impress someone with your culinary savvy," she wrote. "It's expensive but worth it." She might have added that it was a dish typical of the entertaining her friend Jim did in his walk-up apartment with its minuscule kitchen and bathroom-shower dishwasher.

3–4-pound striped bass
salt
freshly ground pepper
1 pound fresh
　lump crabmeat
1/4 cup chopped chives
　or scallions
1/4 cup chopped parsley
3 tablespoons chopped celery

1/4 cup melted butter
1/2 cup fresh breadcrumbs
1/4 cup heavy cream
cooking oil
1 recipe remoulade sauce
　(p. 194)
watercress or parsley and
　lemon wedges, for garnish

Wash the fish thoroughly under cold running water, making sure all scales are off and scraping out any blood clots along the backbone. Sprinkle lightly with salt and pepper. Pick over the crabmeat, discarding bits of shell or cartilage, and set aside 1/2 cup. Mix the remaining crabmeat with the chives or scallions, chopped parsley, celery, melted butter, breadcrumbs, heavy cream, and salt and pepper to taste. Stuff the fish with this mixture, then sew up the opening or close it with skewers. Line a baking pan large enough to hold the fish with a double fold of foil. Oil the fish and place it in the pan. Cover with additional foil and refrigerate while making the remoulade sauce. Preheat the oven to 400 degrees. Remove the covering foil and bake for 25 to 30 minutes. Fold the reserved 1/2 cup of crabmeat into the remoulade sauce and leave at room temperature until serving time. When the fish is baked, remove from the pan by grasping each end of the foil and transfer it to a warm serving platter. Garnish with watercress or parsley and the lemon wedges.   SERVES 6 TO 8.

Beef on a String

▼

Beard adapted this recipe for *boeuf à la ficelle* from one given him by the chef on the S.S. *France,* which he often called his favorite transatlantic liner. With Burt Wolf as his assistant, he appeared later in an enormous theater in Kansas City with the task of keeping a vast audience interested in cooking. "We're not here just to lecture," he cried. "We've got to entertain!" He ordered a fifty-foot rope to be made ready so that he could pull the rope and elevate his beef high in the air above the casserole, and like a performing magician he introduced the swinging roast: "Ladies and gentlemen—beef on a string!"

2 1/2-pound piece top sirloin, tied crosswise and lengthwise
3 pounds beef marrow bones
1 bay leaf
2 cloves garlic, crushed
1 tablespoon chopped fresh thyme
1 tablespoon black peppercorns
2 tablespoons salt

Leave enough string after tying the sirloin to suspend it in the stock without touching the bottom of the pan. In a deep stock pot cover the beef with water, then add the marrow bones and the seasonings. Remove the sirloin piece and set aside while you simmer the marrow bones for about 1 hour to make a rich stock. Remove the bones and skim off the fat. Now suspend the reserved sirloin in the broth (it should not touch the bottom of the pot) by tying the ends of the string to the handles of the stock pot (or if there are no handles, by looping the string over a large skewer long enough to bridge the rim of the pot). Cover the pot tightly with foil and then put on the lid so that no steam escapes. Simmer for approximately 15 minutes per pound (about 35 minutes total). After 25 minutes test with a meat thermometer: internal temperature should register 125 to 135 degrees, depending on how rare you like your beef. Serve with poached carrots, turnips, leeks, boiled potatoes, and horseradish sauce.   SERVES 6 TO 8.

Grilled Pig's Feet
▼

As a child, Jim learned to love all parts of the pig and pig's feet browned in crumbs, as he discovered them in Les Halles, the old Paris city market, remained among his favorite dishes. When hundreds of friends gathered in the Stanford Court Hotel to celebrate his eighty-first birthday, the tables were decorated by the talented Molly Chapellet of Pritchard Hill vineyards—her "bouquet" of pink and white frozen pig's trotters was the elegant centerpiece at the Beard table. In *Beard on Food* Jim offers his recipe for *pieds de porc* as one of "the splendors of charcuterie." Here's how he prepared them:

4 large meaty pig's feet	2–3 garlic cloves
8 cups water	2–3 sage leaves
1 onion, stuck with 2 cloves	1 teaspoon salt
1 carrot	12 peppercorns
1/2 rib celery	breadcrumbs
1 bay leaf	melted butter

Wrap each of the pig's feet in cheesecloth, muslin, or an old pillowcase, and tie them very firmly. Put the water in a largish pot and add all the seasonings. Bring to a simmer and add the pig's feet. Cook, covered, over low heat for 2 1/2 to 3 1/2 hours or until very tender. Cool in the broth, then remove the wrappings. Roll the meat in toasted breadcrumbs and dribble melted butter over them. Either brown them under the broiler or roast in a 475 degree oven, turning them several times until brown and crisp on the outside. Serve with a mustardy vinaigrette.   SERVES 4.

Orange-Lobster Omelets

Isabel Callvert kept the notes on this sunny idea of Jim's for a simple course to be served at lunch. When we tried making it, it worked out so well that the result is something that Jim would surely have passed on.

1 large juicy orange	*2 anchovy fillets*
4 tablespoons butter	*4 eggs*
1 teaspoon minced shallots	*2 tablespoons water*
1/2 pound cooked	*salt*
lobster meat	*freshly ground pepper*

Peel the orange and remove 4 segments from it. Set aside. Melt 2 tablespoons of the butter in a small skillet and sauté the shallots gently for 2 minutes. Add the lobster meat and squeeze the juice from what is left of the orange into the pan. Mash the anchovies and stir them into the juices. When the lobster is hot, add the orange segments, cover, and set over very low heat while you make the omelets. Mix 2 eggs together with about 1 tablespoon water and salt and pepper to taste. Heat 1 tablespoon butter in an omelet pan, and when sizzling pour in the eggs. As soon as they are set, spoon half the lobster into the center, quickly finish cooking the omelet, then fold it over and slide it onto a warm plate. Garnish with 2 of the orange segments and pour some of the pan juices over. Repeat to make the second omelet.

SERVES 2.

Hashed Brown Potatoes

In prewar days, Jim remembered, hash browns were often "incredibly good"—served up by steak houses, or small town cafés. As a child, he said, he was fascinated by short-order cooks "who were seldom trained chefs, but they were deft and had an innate sense of flavor." One he noted in a Western diner was a counter man who chopped potatoes with a one-pound can and then tossed them into a skillet with bacon fat. Beard recommended potatoes that are waxy and not too mealy.

8 medium or 10	salt
small potatoes	freshly ground pepper
6 tablespoons butter, beef	
drippings, or bacon fat	

Boil the potatoes in their jackets until just tender. Peel and cut coarse or fine, as you wish. Melt fat in a heavy skillet, swirling it so the bottom of the pan is covered generously. Press the potatoes down into the fat and let them cook fairly slowly to form a crust on the bottom. Shake the pan from time to time. Run a spatula around the edges to keep them loose, then fold over the potatoes so the unbrowned ones are exposed to the heat. Or invert the pan on a plate, add more fat to the pan, and slide the uncooked side into the pan. Salt them to taste and give them a few grinds of pepper. Slide them out onto a hot platter.   SERVES 3 OR 4.

Crêpes Soufflés

▼

Because Jim believed that the making of crêpes is one of the most basic cooking procedures, he always started off students with them. He himself once cooked a mammoth crêpe on the old Jack Parr television show that he claimed was the largest ever made. He found almost as much theater in this method of orange-and-lemon-scented crêpes soufflés.

Crêpes:

3 eggs	1 teaspoon grated
1/8 teaspoon salt	lemon rind
1–1 1/4 cups milk	Note: If you were to make
7/8 cup flour	crêpes for a savory dish
4 tablespoons melted butter	leave out the sugar,
3 tablespoons sugar	cognac, and lemon rind.
2 tablespoons cognac	

Soufflé Filling:

3 tablespoons butter	grated rind of 1/2 orange
3 tablespoons flour	1/4 cup Grand Marnier
1/2 cup milk, heated	5 egg whites, beaten to form
1/4 cup sugar	firm peaks
4 egg yolks	sugar for sprinkling

To make the crêpes: Mix all the ingredients together, using 1 cup of milk; beat vigorously or spin in a blender or food processor. Cover and let rest 2 hours or overnight, refrigerated. The batter should be the consistency of heavy cream; if thicker, stir in more milk. Heat a 5-inch crêpe pan and when good and hot, brush it with melted butter. Pour about 3 tablespoons batter into the pan, swirl it around to cover the bottom completely, and bake [Jim's precise word] over medium-high heat until the surface is set (1 to 1½ minutes). Flip the crêpe over, or use your hand to turn it, and bake the other side for ½ minute. Stack the finished crêpes on a plate. You'll need 12 for this recipe; freeze the extras.

To make the filling: Melt the butter over low heat, add the flour, and stir for 2 to 3 minutes. Remove from the heat, stir in the milk, and continue stirring until smooth. Add the sugar and egg yolks and blend well. Return to the heat just long enough for the mixture to thicken. Stir in the orange rind and Grand Marnier and cool slightly. Fold in well half of the egg whites, then fold in the second half more lightly. Butter a baking sheet. On it spoon 2 to 3 tablespoons of the soufflé mixture along one side of each crêpe and fold the other side over very lightly. Sprinkle sugar on top and bake in a 425 degree preheated oven for 5 to 8 minutes or until the soufflé filling is set. Serve very hot on hot plates. SERVES 6.

7

ON THE ROAD AND
AT THE STOVE

Some who look back at the 1950s remember them as a time of tremendous prosperity. As Russell Baker, the *New York Times* columnist, had it: "A typical American family then could afford three children, a house, two cars, three weeks at the seashore, a television set, and meat seven times a week," and he added, "all on a single wage earner's income."

Those were the Eisenhower years, when the country for the first time had a president who liked to cook. There were occasions when Ike let himself be photographed while turning sirloins on a charcoal grill, and he had, among others, his own recipe for a vegetable stew that simmered overnight. No need for him to consult Jim Beard.

Yet cookery in some quarters was being slighted by hundreds of thousands of women. Science was carrying the day—the first complete, lap-sized TV dinner appeared in 1953. Packages of bland meat dishes and equally uninteresting vegetables were popped into the heat and served up as jiffy meals. Magazines were beckoning readers by offering lessons in how to get dinner ready in the fastest possible way—why waste time? Many published recipes of the period dwelled on simple procedures such as cutting frozen fish fillets in half for broiling, or stuccoing canned pressed meat with crumbs and honey to pass for a roast.

Jim was firmly on record for his dubious view of such innovations as TV dinners, but he recognized that the technology of the food industry was a fact of life after World War II and that it was also advantageous under certain circumstances. As he began work on *James Beard's Fish Cookery,* he admitted that frozen fish could "solve problems" for cooks who live far from fresh supplies or who demand a specific fish not at the height of its season. He was a pragmatist by nature, and resourceful in finding ways to improve flavor and texture in convenience foods.

But in spite of his increasing renown among those housewives who bought cookbooks, he was continually struggling to meet his own self-imposed standard of living. His Greenwich Village apartment was still the walk-up at 36 West Twelfth Street, and he was even more the welcoming host who was sought out by old friends who wished him well. He wanted success so that he could live in greater style, but he was never to be a conformist. The Jim you saw was the Jim you got.

Not unlike the impression made on Jane Nickerson, one of the New York memories of Janet Baumhover, his Portland friend and fellow actor, was of an overgrown boy hiding his doubts under freshets of good humor. "I buzzed him from the vestibule, and suddenly there he was at the top of the stairs, in pink shorts and a polka dot shirt. There was a little curl on his forehead, and he looked like a cherub."

His light hair, in fact, was thinning fast, but there was still a layer that could be parted in the middle—the equal division perhaps a complement to the bow ties he wore—his guileless smile under almond-shaped eyes and an almost-invisible blond mustache caused various friends to think he had the look of a giant baby. His height and weight made his taste in clothes even more noticeable than it might otherwise have been. Tweeds—often loud tweeds—were his trademark. His wardrobe was tailormade (most often in Toronto), obviously because his figure made it impossible to buy suits off a rack and because his designer's instinct required special attention to detail. He bought the cloth himself for the shirts he had made in Barcelona, and his haberdashery left an unforgettable impression on his friend Bettina McNulty when they were together in Spain. "Jim's shirts were like billowing sails and his T-shirts were jibs," she wrote to me. "He was fastidious, and those made-to-order shirts, often in the most amazing stripes in the most beautiful Pima cotton, were part of the *mise-en-scène* across the table for ten days of beautiful lunches." With similar flair, he ordered a long wool topcoat in Ireland, with emerald checks and matching cape that was cut to fit his bulky shoulders.

Formally disposed or informally relaxed, Jim exuded style. His size added emphasis to his entrances, yet no two people agreed on why he managed to appear as a benevolent royalist when approached. Among those who knew him, friends of long standing agreed that he seemed to show various Jims (or Jameses or Jamies) to various people. "To see him standing there on his own two legs," Leo Lerman told me, "you knew he was a ham of quality—barefoot boy with cheek." He had a sense of himself for whatever occasion might arise—and he often saw himself with humor. There were points beyond which the defense of his inner privacy couldn't be penetrated, but he had few compunctions in exposing his skin.

He often lolled about in specially designed short kimonos that were inclined to fall open because the sash was untied. More, he was proud of what he described with delight to his readers as "cooking in the nude." In the heat of New York summers, before air conditioning was common, he had his own unusual way of solving the temperature problem. He was an inveterate early bird, "and when I'm preparing for a dinner party, I enjoy rising at 5:00 or 5:30 and going straight from the bath to the kitchen. . . . It is so cool and quiet in the early hours that before mid-morning one can have a whole dinner ready, except for the final bits of cooking and the garnishings." Dawn was also a time for personal calls, catching up on gossip with friends in his inner circle. Cecily Brownstone, who met Jim through Jeanne Owen and became a lifelong intimate, remembered one of the preworkday calls she got from him. He not only told her his breakfast menu, "he had to emphasize that he was frying his bacon and eggs in the nude. I could just see him standing there in his rolls of fat and I couldn't resist saying, 'Don't let the hot fat hit the hot fat!'"

Jim was not a heterosexual, but he was a ladies' man, and he earned deep affection from women of his own and other persuasions. Among the friends he kept for life more were women than men. Cecily Brownstone—a native of Toronto and thereby as frontier-oriented as he—was shattered when he died. She was among his first culinary cronies.

When Jim asked friends to a sitdown dinner in those days, they sat around a marble-topped table with unmatched chairs. Most of the people he gathered for parties were professionals on periodicals and in restaurants or belonged to the increasing coterie of wistful but affluent epicures for whom food gave sustenance in status, in addition to well-being.* Among New York editors and writers there were Cecily Brownstone, Ann Seranne, Alice Petersen of the *Daily News*, Glenna McGinnis at *Woman's Day*, Jane Nickerson of the *Times*, Helen McCully of *McCall's*, Alvin Kerr of *Gourmet*, Nika Hazelton, Zack Hanle, Jerry Mason of *Argosy*, Peggy Foster of Doubleday and her sculptor husband, and Ron and Isabel Callvert, as well as his old colleagues Sam and Florence Aaron.

No matter what cooking skills or encyclopedic knowledge of food he demonstrated, it was always Jim's personality that drew listeners to become friends. His awareness of his own magnetic quality never wore out, but he seldom admitted recognizing it. When he set out to

---

*Beard once spelled out his own dictum for making guests happy with an all-too-neat allusion to his early ambitions: "To entertain successfully one must create with the imagination of a playwright, plan with the skill of a director, and perform with the instincts of an actor. And as any showman will tell you, there is no greater reward than pleasing your audience."

write retrospectively, he was characteristically objective as he looked back. He was almost eighty when I found him one day editing a magazine piece that was about to be sent off. Its subject was the ever-changing American attitude toward food, and it contained a paragraph I was moved to copy:

> By the Fifties, well, there I was right in the midst of this burgeoning interest in food. People were taking the time to cook complex and international dishes. Don't get me wrong—people had always taken the time to cook good food, but it was only now that the general public began to realize the varieties and possibilities of food. With this sophistication came a quest for diversity; no longer was eating simply a necessity, it became a pleasure . . .

The pleasure of food. This was his creed, and it was often his nemesis at the same time. Friends remember that his weight went up and down, in the fifties particularly. "When he got too fat he wasn't attractive," a *House & Garden* editor told me, adding reluctantly, "he looked like a pig." Almost as often as not, he was contriving some way to fight off temptation. "One November day I remember finding him with his hands behind his back, in front of a candy store on Lexington. 'I wish I could buy something but I can't,' he said, his eyes on the store window. He wanted me to go inside and get something for myself. 'It would make me feel better,' he said. Sooner or later, surrounded by food as we always were at the magazine, he would break down. He felt guilty when he was carrying too much weight."

But he stuck to his conviction that good food always brought pleasure. And he held on to it, not in the simple necessity of earning a living but as a way of life for everyone. For him it was a style that brought him increasing numbers of admirers and increasing diversity in his social life. When he first knew Ruth Norman, she had been a stage manager, and through her and Cheryl Crawford he met many actors and others in the theater world. For years he had a close friendship with Freddy Schrallow, a young decorator from western Pennsylvania who had a friend who was a singer in the chorus of the Metropolitan Opera Company. At Felix's, a Seventh Avenue hangout for Villagers with artistic yearnings, he had met a young architect named Gino Cofacci, and their relationship evolved from inseparable companionship to a burdensome tie which in Jim's last years was akin to that of a father with a son who wouldn't leave home.*

"Jim was in a perpetual avuncular state," Leo Lerman said one day in his office as he looked back at the early years in New York which they had shared. "People were attracted to Jim because of his enormous charm. They trusted him. He led a perfectly normal life according to his tenets, and he had 'family' around him all the time."

And he joined the families of others. One day in 1952 the phone rang in the leaf-canopied home of Philip and Helen Evans Brown in the Pasadena hills, and the voice was that of James Beard, who had just read Helen's *West Coast Cook Book.*† "He wanted Helen to know he thought it was the best new work he'd seen," Philip Brown remembered. "He wanted to know if he might stop in to see us. He came out to the house immediately and we began to talk as if it were an unfinished conversation. We were so into it, he stayed all night." In the years before Helen's death, Jim spent scores of nights with the Browns, as his peripatetic life kept him touching base on the West Coast and touching the lives of other people wherever the subject of food led to stimulating rapport.

Helen Brown was bright, photogenic, vivacious, and younger than Jim, but she was also firm and opinionated (as were both his mother and Jeanne Owen) and her letters to him are punctuated with advice and concern. Theirs was a partnership of equals. She had been an editor and writer for a magazine called *The Californian,* a regular contributor to *Sunset,* and had been published in *McCall's, Glamour,* and *The Atlantic Monthly.* She was the author of *California Cooks, Some Oyster Recipes,* and the *Patio Cook Book.* Her most recent book had been published by Little, Brown, the house that put out Beard's *Paris*

---

*"We had a subscription at the old Met—for years," Gino told me one evening in the apartment Jim had given him when he bought his last house. "During intermission we'd get our shoes shined across the street. Or sometimes we'd go backstage to meet Freddy Schrallow—he knew Martinelli, and also lots of Italian singers that Freddy would have at his parties." They both loved the "yellow brewery," as the opera house was affectionately known, just as they shared a deep sentiment for Sherry's Restaurant, the last of the chain owned by Louis Sherry, with its faithful opera-goers crowded in among its red damask walls.

†In the updated edition of the book (Knopf, 1991), Philip Brown recounts his memory of the Beard-Brown meeting.

Cuisine and to which he was under contract for a fish book. It may have been inevitable, what with Philip Brown joining in the enthusiasm for al fresco meals, that Helen and Jim should begin work on *The Complete Book of Outdoor Cookery* not long after they became friends.

With his earlier volume, *Cook It Outdoors,* and articles for *Argosy* and *House & Garden* on the same subject, Jim had become recognized as a pioneer champion of campfire and barbecue cooking, and he and Helen shared their charcoal-grilling thesis in pre-sexual-revolution terms when they composed their preface:

"We believe it is primarily the man's job, and that a woman, if she's smart, will keep it that way. Men love it, for it gives them a chance to prove that they are, indeed, fine cooks. The ladies can do the planning and marketing, the preparation and the hostessing, but the man will do the actual cooking over the coals."

Looking at Jim's commitments in the fifties it seems hard to accept easily that one person—even with skilled (and affectionate) help from Isabel and others—could have juggled so many balls and hit so many bull's-eyes. Although averaging at least one round trip to Europe each year, he published six important books, a half-dozen lesser treatises, established a cooking school that continued through the rest of his life, represented brandy and wine producers, was a restaurant consultant in Philadelphia, New York, and elsewhere, all the while periodically serving as a judge of cooking contests and contributing to assorted magazines.

In 1952, the year that he made friends with the Browns in California, he signed on with the French National Association of Cognac Producers to show average American cooks for the first time what high spirits could add to home menus. His fellow worker was a young newsman-turned-flack named Bill Kaduson, who arranged appearances before women's groups, and on radio programs and television shows. With Kaduson as advance man, he exercised his penchant for early rising through his guest appearances to help rouse viewers of morning TV in cities like Los Angeles, Detroit, Boston, and others of various cosmopolitan inclinations.

"We did a dozen towns a year," Kaduson recalled. "The traveling act was called 'Cooking with Flair.' What made it so successful was the fact that all the food eds knew Jim and really loved him. He made

John Bennett shows off a James Beard sweatshirt

them feel good when he walked in—we took them to lunch, and they ate up his stuff about his last trip to London or France. I don't know how many halls we filled or how many times we showed off flaming duck recipes, or lobster with cognac, or steak au poivre." What held the two men together in good humor for seventeen years of sporadic sawdust trail performances may have been a common tolerance for corny lines. Bill the writer would plant a question in almost any audience: "What is a gourmet, Mr. Beard?," a stooge chosen by Bill would ask. The reply, as Kaduson's script went: "Anyone who eats broccoli," Jim grinning smoothly as he spoke. On a coast-to-coast talk show he blazed a crêpe suzette so enormous that it had required a cooperative tinsmith to construct a six-foot pan. Jim was a regular with Mike Roy's West Coast television program, lunched frequently with Stanley Marcus when he worked in Dallas with the Zodiac Room's Helen Corbitt, and was sponsored in Denver by the city's opera company.*

---

*In earlier, leaner times Jim arrived in a small Southern town to give a cooking demonstration. His hosts had scheduled him to prepare steak au poivre and crêpes flambées, but the only equipment he was provided with was a saucepan, an iron skillet, and an electric warming

In Detroit Beard was the emissary for *Holiday* in delivering the magazine's best-restaurant award to Les Gruber's London Chop House, and that was the start of a lasting friendship with Gruber and his wife, Cleo. Jim knew Detroit as the city of Hudson's department store, where he had given cooking demonstrations, and as the temporary home of the Callverts (keeping in touch with Isabel by letter and especially by phone calls was made easy by Ron's position as a vice president of Michigan Bell). Jim found Gruber a rare restaurateur in mid-America because he knew the cuisines of the world, sometimes, with his wife, joining Jim on his travels.

The London Chop House was a chosen gathering place for automobile kings and princelings who pretended to know more about good wines than Jim or Les, but dimmed their lights by belting down Scotch, bourbon, and Canadian whiskey. Cleo Gruber and Isabel became fast friends. Both were chic, and the C.E.O.s buzzed around Isabel when she was first introduced to them. With Ron and Jim and Les all silently cheering, she rejected one slurred invitation to dance "because you have tailfins growing out of your back."

Unlike Ernie Byfields's Pump Room at the Ambassador hotel in Chicago, where shish kebabs aflame heated up the Sunday brunch crowd, Gruber's London Chop House affirmed its name with unimpeachable beef and lamb and seafood. "The food was terrific," Ron Callvert said. In addition, Jim was appreciative of the Grubers' collection of modern art, in the restaurant and in their home too. They were the hosts of one Christmas Day dinner, given in honor of Jim. After the caviar, the oysters, the double turkey consommé, there was a saddle of venison *à la Bourguignonne* served with purée of chestnuts *à la crème* and braised romaine. The *fromage de Brie* and the *bûche de Noël* were flown in from Jim's friends at Fauchon in Paris. In addition to estate-bottled Montrachet, Malmsey 1868 with the consommé, Richebourg 1961 with the roast, there was Château Cheval-Blanc 1949 with the Brie, a magnum of Dom Pérignon with the dessert, and Hine's family reserve with the coffee.

---

plate. Resourceful as always, Jim rushed to the nearest all-night drugstore and bought a couple of usable pans and two electric irons. For his demonstration he braced the irons upside down to get enough heat for the job at hand. He told me afterward that he was tempted to add to his menu: "Well-ironed beef."

The feast was in marked distinction to the cognac trail Jim followed with Bill Kaduson in those years. Lighting up the place with flaming brandy transformed the promotion assignments into center-stage showmanship. But it was simpler cooking with cognac that pleased Jim and other friends when entertaining in privacy. He described for readers of *Apartment Life* a meal in Pasadena that he termed a perfect spring dinner, adding, "I am stealing the menu from Helen Evans Brown."* It began with a West Coast chicken liver appetizer known as rumaki, was centered on a flaming steak served with parsley, potatoes, and San Fernando–style asparagus. The dessert he described was pure American—a brandy-doused angel food cake with strawberries stuffing the hole. The sirloin was completely covered by the dried rosemary pressed into it before the liquor was added; accompanying the meal, the wine was a Château Lascomes 1950. ("It is a young claret with gay charm—delightful for this season," Jim told *Apartment Life* readers. And it came from Alexis Lichine's vineyard on the high ground of Margaux.)

Because he knew Lichine intimately (having spent hours with him in the small backrooms of the Sherry wine shop or climbing the stairway with him to the catwalk across the roof that led to the Aarons' office), he could describe entertainingly the gray stone château and the owners' pride in it. Its hexagonal-roofed three-story tower is a village landmark, and Jim liked to tell of the château's Sèvres coffee service, given in gratitude by Napoleon III, which was delicately decorated with portraits of the Sun King's mistresses. He had traveled with Lichine through Bordeaux and Burgundy before Lichine purchased the Lascombes vineyard in 1952. Jim loved history and treasured anecdotes that related food to the past.

In Provence he picked up the story of the Mediterranean's best-known fish stew. "I go along," he told friends, "with the idea that bouillabaisse is one of the oldest seafood dishes known to man." He was intrigued with the history of the port Les-Saintes-Maries-de-la-Mer in the Camargue. The town was named for the saints who are supposed to have set sail for Marseille in their escape from the Holy

---

*The friendship with Philip and Helen Brown had become as close as any he had in his long years. In May 1953 he wrote to Helen: "Never have two people been nicer to another person than the Browns have been to Beard."

Land after the Crucifixion. As Jim told the story, the saints' vessel hit a storm that left the women unconscious on the shore for almost two days—until they were revived by fishermen who fed them their first bouillabaisse.

Not above exaggeration in making a point—whether talking of wine or of food—he was a conversationalist who often had a serious thought embroidered in his tales. It was veritably a mission with him, this nudging of others to appreciate the bounty inherent in good living, and when he was an adviser to restaurateurs he wanted to be equally persuasive. He had this in mind while discussing food prejudices on one of his visits to New Orleans. "Recently I was asked by Ella Brennan," he reported, "to give a talk about food to members of her restaurant staff. One of them had a real prejudice against oysters; he said he couldn't like them, that he'd made a vow never to taste one. We somehow talked him into trying just one, and you could just see his misconception fading. The boy sipped some wine, ate a piece of rye bread—and then fell to, and before he was through he'd downed at least a dozen oysters." As years went by, Jim got better and better at his major talent: his enthusiasm for his knowledge of gastronomy.

In New York, Cecily Brownstone was one of those who helped to widen his contacts with cooks and writers. As a wire service columnist, she kept track of food people, often interviewing such authors as Irma S. Rombauer, whose *Joy of Cooking,* published earlier in Indianapolis, had been given a title that was brought to life on every page. The book was a collection of recipes written to anticipate questions of uneasy housewives, and it persuaded many readers that preparing meals *was* joyful. It reflected the zest of Middle Western kitchens, where cooking styles had been influenced (especially in St. Louis, Mrs. Rombauer's hometown) by early French and German immigrants who were unpretentiously creative. " 'Joy' has won the hearts and minds of cooks for forty years," Raymond Sokolov of *The New York Times* asserted, "because it is plain as well as fancy—and it works."

The author's comments enhanced the recipes with her personal brand of good cheer, and in 1951, after sales of the book had topped a million copies, a revised edition was published. Jim's friend Cecily introduced him to Mrs. Rombauer on one of her winter trips to Manhattan. In Cecily's Jane Street townhouse they sat at dinner talking of Europe and musical concerts; they had similar tastes.* And Jim had respect (perhaps even envy) for the Rombauer book as it was kept up to date.

In spite of some differences, his working philosophy was not unlike that of his new friend. Some years later he described it for publication. "I think some cookbooks are put together like paper dolls," he told Chris Chase, author of *The Great American Waistline,* "there's no feeling of humanness in them. I write about things I like, done the way I like them."

He emphasized his belief that a cookbook should reflect the personality of the author along with his or her kitchen techniques. Mrs. Rombauer, an enthusiastic lover of life as well as of good eating, scattered her pages with choice recipes from "Cockaigne" (her affectionate label for dishes she and her family cherished). She instilled confidence, and she believed the average cook profited by showing how she cared about cooking and the food she chose to serve. That there's joy to be found was her message. "Mrs. Rombauer realizes," a food industry historian wrote, "that present-day cooks will, for example, use frozen vegetables quickly cooked in a pressure pan. But let them take a few more minutes to season them in new ways with cheese, herbs, paprika, butter, curry powder and so on."

She and Jim Beard, with whom she found another joy in exchanging appreciations of opera, shared a deep understanding of flavor. With Cecily, Jane Nickerson and Alex Steinberg (whom she married), they probed New York's ethnic neighborhoods, titillating their palates and venting their curiosities about origins of recipes. Both understood that Americans again were thinking of eating as a pleasure, as prosperity took hold after the war. Service men and women had come home to their roots—they had been everywhere. "And they knew the real thing," Jim said. Wide-ranging as his reading was, he was alert to food as cultural history—ongoing as well as in the past—and he collected anecdotes along with recipes.

His story-telling friend Angus Cameron had worked with Irma

---

*In recalling her life, Mrs. Rombauer said once, "I was brought up to be a 'young lady.' As a family we traveled extensively, filled our hours with opera-going, gallery-visiting and letter writing—almost useless from a practical standpoint. So my camp-loving husband taught me to cook."

Rombauer in Indianapolis, and was
the Little, Brown editor of Beard's
Paris Cuisine. "Jim could wring the
neck of a chicken with one hand,"
Angus said, remembering their frequent meetings in restaurants. "He
seemed to feel reprieved to be able
to talk to a farm boy like me—he
liked all the farm stuff. He and I
had a kind of countrymen's conspir-
acy against the East."

Irma Rombauer might go back home to St. Louis, but more of
Jim's friends than not were former out-of-towners. Among them,
Cecily Brownstone was one who was always on deck for Jim. In spite
of her work load for a national news organization, she was consistently
generous in sharing her own research. With their common understanding of food as a reflection of the American past, she dug hard for
the origins of the curried chicken dish called "Country Captain" that
was often served in the Old South after the recipe had been published by Eliza Leslie a century earlier.*

The bitchery and backbiting that developed after the recognition of the money to be made in working with food was absent in the
fifties. It was "a kinder and gentler" society that then consisted of
Beard and his close colleagues. And Cecily was invariably among
those present when Jim cooked dinners for all of them in his improvised kitchen as a salute to Mrs. Rombauer's seasonal visits. His regard
for the Rombauer book caused him many years later to cite it
frequently in discussions with colleagues. "You know Irma disagrees,"
he might say about a point of reference. Talking about food seemed
as important as enjoying the meals he put before his friends. In a
column that Cecily wrote about Beard for Associated Press syndication,

---

*The Brownstone research established that Alessander Filippini, a renowned chef at
Delmonico's in the 1870s, put Country Captain on the restaurant's menu in his own
adaptation. The popularity of the dish is such that it became a perennial offering at
Huberts a century later. Recipes change, of course—the 1990 *Fannie Farmer* adds orange
juice as an accent. Both the Leslie and Filippini versions were published in *American
Cookery* by James Beard (Little, Brown, 1972).

she called him "the most relaxed host (and cook) I know, with a colossal curiosity about the infinite knowledge of food."

His historical knowledge derived from his collection of social annals and books on gastronomy gathered during his close friendship with Eleanor Lowenstein; she was the discerning proprietress of the Corner Book Store, on Fourth Avenue not far from Jim's walk-up. The shop was an organized disorder of almost every volume, pamphlet, brochure, or stapled treatise that touched upon American gastronomy— and because of the Lowenstein dedication to her subject and its pursuers, it was to be compared with Shakespeare & Company, Sylvia Beach's mecca for writers on the rue de l'Odéon in Paris. Eleanor knew Jim's shelves and their contents as well as he did. "She was always on the lookout for special items she thought I should know about."

As one whose spare time (fortunately, he needed little sleep) was devoted to reading and remembering everything about food that came his way, Beard made no pretense of being an original in taking a cooking show on the road; he knew about a Paris-trained chef named Pierre Blot who had organized a "tour of Lectures" through the Eastern states in the 1860s. Blot was the author of a book entitled *What to Eat . . . And How to Cook It,* and he trained Juliette Corson, who took over his New York Cooking Academy and taught in other parts of the country after the Civil War. In Jim's library there were various editions of books by Mrs. Rorer of Philadelphia and by Boston's Fannie Farmer, both of whom had traveled to conduct classes as far afield as the Middle West. Jim also had some admiration for an enterprising woman named Jessie Marie de Both, who in the 1930s established a traveling cooking school which she took from state to state. He told friends he respected her showmanship, and he was happy to take to the road himself; he felt that his teaching and acting background (plus the fact that he was a man in the kitchen) made him the ideal culinary performer.

He wasn't the only self-trained male cook after World War II to make a living through classroom sessions or writing about food. At the Chicago *Tribune,* for instance, there was Morrison Wood, whose column "For Men Only" was widely syndicated and whose collection of adventures-cum-recipes had been published in 1949. "I do not belong to the school which holds," Wood pontificated, "that only men are great cooks. I do believe it is true that most men approach cooking in an adventuresome spirit, simply because they are not obliged to cook day in and day out. It is first to them a game, then a pastime, and finally a hobby. . . . But to most women who have to cook three meals a day . . . cooking is likely to be a sorry bit of drudgery."

No drudge himself, Beard was putting together a career like that of none before him. "Jim created the post of food consultant," said his neighbor and colleague (and later restaurant critic of *The New York Times*) Mimi Sheraton. And the post was making him a slave to the seemingly incessant pattern of travel that never exhausted his curiosity about other places, other people. Mixed in with domestic flights to the West Coast, New Orleans, or Florida were the one-night stands that were the result of a kind of local fame. One New York women's club was boundlessly enthusiastic in sending out a mimeographed announcement in the Fall of 1952:

... On October 14, at 6:00 P.M. you are in
for a dramatic encounter. You are going to meet
in person one of the "greats" of our time.
You will hear—you will chat with:

James A. Beard

... renowned authority on food ...
radio performer ... TV artist ... the author of

The homey tome ... *The Fireside Cookbook*
The he-man tome ... *Fowl and Game Cookery*
The sunny tome ... *Cook It Outdoors*
The exotic tome ... *Hors d'Oeuvre and Canapés*
The (?) naughty (?) *PARIS CUISINE* (just off the press)

James A. Beard will answer your personal questions.
James A. Beard will demonstrate how-to-do-it.
James A. Beard will prepare a taste thrill for you to try!

(Yes, he will make enough to go around.)

As in many careers there were elements of chance in Jim's. All his life he had wanted—as he had confessed when he took long walks in Portland with his friend Hattie—to be famous, to be a star. He had hoped to be an opera singer, only to be frustrated, and the theater had not reached out and grabbed him. But also for decades he had nursed a yen to be his own man as a restaurateur. True, he had served as an adviser on menus and wine at the Bird & Bottle before the war. But his closest contacts with New York restaurants were his friendships with chef-proprietors. The owner of the Brittany on Ninth Avenue was one of these who served him well when Jim did a stint with a public relations firm and needed a place to demonstrate the advanced qualities of a new line of aluminum cookware.

Given that the object of such occasions was making money, Jim nevertheless persuaded himself that products he represented could justify all claims. Over the years he extended his income by various kinds of work for restaurants and food manufacturers, but now, in between public appearances with Bill Kaduson (and still writing for publication with Isabel's help), he bracketed the summer for what he hoped would be a fun-and-games stab at managing a short-order beach place on Nantucket Island, a New England resort where Yankee cooking dominated the scene.

Chez Lucky Pierre was the name given the breezy, tent-topped wharf-side hutch. It was hung with fishnets, furnished with barrel-shaped chairs, and it was owned by Claude and Kathie Sperling, who were among Jim's party guests in New York. They had managed to touch the nerve in Jim that was most likely to make him jump at a chance to preside over even a humble eating place. ("I have had one of the busiest weeks of my life—my first as skinker at Lucky Pierre's on this perfect island of Nantucket," he wrote to a friend.)*

Much of the time he was theatrically garbed in a Breton fisherman's striped sweatshirt and a French sailor's cap crowned with a red pompon; as usual his costumes won him friends rather than detractors among his neighbors, and he savored local recipes that some of the islanders offered. Later in one of his books he passed along a rustic formula that, as a pork lover, he couldn't ignore. It was titled Nantucket Fireman's Supper in the community's small cookbook and was little more than fried chops put in a casserole with sliced onions and potatoes layered on top and simmered in some water. If the firefighters' instructions were a little bleak, Jim knew that flavor-minded cooks could season the dish with fresh herbs or spices.

The casserole was no-nonsense food, characteristic of a fishing community in New England, but hardly the sort of chow for a roadside stopping place—or ferryside, as was true of Lucky Pierre. With hordes of trippers shuffling off the lugger, there were appetites for more frivolous dishes, and Jim had other notions about changing the Lucky Pierre image. "Just to be different," he jazzed up the menu with cold salmon and remoulade sauce, and gave his own touch to New England clam chowder. He added some green pepper to the onion, salt pork, clam juice, and chopped clams. Cream was incorporated when the chowder was served—"so there is no curdling as a result," he said.

Some of his letters of that summer recount his curiosity about

---

*"Skinker" is one of those neglected words that Jim loved. It derives from Old English, and is still used occasionally, especially among proprietors of Yankee inns who like to underline the traditional quality of their enterprises. The word means one who draws, pours out, or serves liquor, a tapster.

Nantucket's year-round rhythms, and show that he did pay close attention to the produce to be had from the island farmers. "There is something about the sandy soil and the sea breezes [that produces] spectacular vegetables and small fruits," he noted. He was able to buy "tender peas and tiny luscious beans which cook in no time at all with hardly any water. And the oak leaf and Boston lettuces are extraordinary," he continued. "How few people realize the utter deliciousness of good lettuce all by itself. And how few people realize how much joy you can get out of good vegetables properly cooked. The other night I bought some baby beets with the tops from local farms and cooked the baby beets with butter, lettuce leaves, and a bit of onion. Marvelous." And he took note of another gift of the sea: "The game caught here—they are like the lambs from the salt meadows of France—salted as they grow and with a flavor that is startling and wonderful."

He was trying to find some fun in managing Lucky Pierre and at the same time to perfect recipes for the fish book that he was doing for Little, Brown. "I have been delving into the sex life of the clam," he told Helen Brown in a midsummer letter. "I personally like to use soft shell clams for chowder, but that seems a revolutionary idea to New Englanders." Yankees and vacationers alike weren't enough taken by his changes in the bill of fare, however. Most customers wanted familiar roadside food. "We have something here called the Polynesienne—which is three small scoops of ice cream with raspberry and pineapple fruit dressing and marshmallows and a topping of nuts—and you should see young and old alike go for that sort of balderdash—it is sweeter than a saccharine pudding and gooey as a gluepot but they fall for it."

While the island and its meadows and beaches were baking in the sun he determined to turn Lucky Pierre (he called it not a restaurant but a joint) into a culinary theater. Jim had met Rudy Stanish in the course of his own tours of the United States and sensed that a man who could bring showmanship to the making of omelets might bring new customers to Lucky Pierre. "Turned out to be a thundering success," Jim told friends. "You could say I was the power behind the throne, because afterwards Rudy was known everywhere as 'the omelet King.' "

Dione Lucas, an artist with omelets herself, as well as the most admired woman, at the time, among New York restaurateurs, turned over to her friend Jim the recipe for the Lucky Pierre souffléed chocolate roll,* and Beard developed—the fish book ever on his mind—a house specialty tailored to wharfside tastes. It was a shellfish pizza made with brioche dough and lobster, the supply of which had improved since the establishment a couple of years earlier of the Martha's Vineyard Lobster Hatchery and Research Station. The pizza was a novelty but no more a success than his other efforts because, as Jim said, people prefer lobster in simplicity, either boiled or broiled. "Lobster itself is so good it doesn't need to be improved upon." That was a discovery he'd made when eating lobster for the first time in England, during his youth.

Weather permitting, outdoor food dominated the offerings at Lucky Pierre. Dan Wynn, a photographer on vacation, met Beard for the first time on Nantucket, not realizing that he and Jim were to become fellow travelers for many years as Wynn shot the photos for Jim's food articles. After Wynn and his wife stopped by Lucky Pierre one night and were introduced, they kept coming back. The Wynns noted that for six nights in a row Jim barbecued spareribs without repeating a recipe. Some were grilled in a simple coating of butter and salt and pepper, some with frequent brushings of honey and curry, or honey and lemon. Some had marinated overnight in a spicy bath of tomato and wine, others were laced on the spit and served with "fingers of pineapple." Wynn (who later ranked as "court photographer") said he was fascinated to watch Jim. "Standing outside there, he wasn't overly fat then, but his trousers were loose—as if he were preparing for the future."

As summer was waning, there was no Lucky Pierre in his future, even though the Sperlings had begun to talk about starting a chain, using the name, and signing up Jim to continue running things. But the season had been a baptism of fire for a man who for so long had thought he wanted his own restaurant. "I only know I have to get caught up and get away in September," he wrote to Ron and Isabel, "if

---

*Beard remembered Lucas, whose Cordon Bleu restaurant specialized in omelets, as both "sad and great," adding, "When people tried to help her she would go off on a tangent and ruin everything... but she was one of the most talented women I have ever known and she had the most wonderful cooking hands I have ever seen."

I am going to keep my sanity. Yesterday was the biggest day of the season—almost seven hundred dollars, and that with two men short who are ill. Well, you can imagine what it was—total bedlam for hours and hours." As chance would have it, however, Jim's prospects began to brighten when he began a lasting friendship with André Surmain, a young Paris entrepreneur, and his wife, Nancy, who were visiting Nancy's sister. This Nantucket encounter resulted in a partnership with Surmain and a couple of years later the founding of a cooking school in New York. Meanwhile, he'd had a letter from Helen Brown. How would he like to join the Browns on an extended drive through the mountain states come spring?

The summer at Nantucket ended in bitterness. When Isabel visited him she found him dejected. He had just been frying hamburgers. "These people want crap—they want no attention paid to details," he said, "and if you give them some pleasant little tidbit as a garnish or added dividend, they will merely leave it on the plate without enough curiosity ever to taste it." What's more, he said in a letter, the Sperlings had been insulting to him when they questioned the local dairy about a bill for milk, as if he had set out to cheat.

He looked to the Callverts for solace. Isabel's job with Jim was born of their long friendship and the satisfaction she took in being a part of his world rather than dependent on the little he sent to her as payment. The arrangement was informal but left no doubt who was boss; firm instructions came from Jim. His typewriter sometimes broke down, and when it worked the pages were littered with typos—he typed out ideas or sent unorganized, unfinished manuscripts which she skillfully finished with the necessary heavy editing, sending them on to magazines according to prearranged schedules. He mailed off requests and scrawled progress reports almost daily. The magazines paid low fees, and he was desperate to keep afloat. He shared his misgivings and resentments with her, sure that she and Ron understood him.

"I am all strapped up," he wrote toward the end of his Nantucket stay, "strained my back and it nearly killed me and am taking pills and sleeping on a board. Too much working over the kitchen table and too much on the feet says the doctor. I have nearly died from the pain these last three days." He was six months past his fiftieth birthday, and yet he passed over these signs of future health problems. Now he told Isabel that he and Gino Cofacci would spend a couple of days at Cheryl Crawford's Connecticut estate, after Lucky Pierre closed for the season. He wanted to tell Cheryl, who had begged him to get an agent, of his agreement with John Schaffner, the gentle, seemingly unaggressive man who already represented Helen Brown, and who had been vacationing on the island with his family.

In Connecticut, Cheryl's two seventeenth-century Cape Cod houses had been moved to New Canaan and joined to make one splendid bucolic retreat. ("They still even smelled of the sea," Ron Callvert told me.) The Crawford place had become Jim's second home; he had his own room—given to him as a birthday present—and when Cheryl was away he was often the house "sitter"—there to make sure that Cheryl's pet canine wasn't lonely. "That was the dog," Ron Callvert said, "that betrayed Jim. We'd pick up Jim in our blue Studebaker convertible, which he really loved because he had a thing about cars. He and the dog would sit with their heads in the air, loving the countryside. And the dog showed up Jim's sneaky habit of stopping on the road for snacks—every time we approached his favorite frankfurt stand on Route 7, the dog would start to drool."

Until the Crawford house caught fire and burned to the ground, it was a rural hideout for Cheryl and for Ruth Norman, who ruled over the vegetable garden, and it was one of the places where Beard feasts were produced (with help from Ruth) either indoors or out. He had been ensconced there when he had tested recipes for *Paris Cuisine.* Out of sight of the kitchen and the rest of the house, there was a strategically located swimming pool for nude bathing, and aside from Jim, the guests who came habitually included such Broadway luminaries as Thornton Wilder, Tennessee Williams, Tallulah Bankhead, Frederic Loewe, Kurt Weill, Mark Blitzstein, Mary Martin, Eli Wallach and his wife, Anne Jackson, and Arthur Miller and his wife, Marilyn Monroe.

Listing those names in her autobiography, Cheryl added glimpses that amused her. "One special afternoon one of Jim's friends, a monumental man [whom she failed to identify] with a Santa Claus belly, asked Marilyn to dance on the small back porch." With Jim there frequently as a part of the theater crowd, Cheryl continued,

"I ate very well." She also noted for her readers' benefit that Jim impressed the weekenders as "a storehouse" of musical-theater knowledge. "I would play recordings of operas, and he would guess who was singing. I seldom fooled him, even with Hugo Schmidt, Supervia, Muzio, Tetrazzini, and Ponselle."

Identifying the voices of divas and their partners was only the beginning—Beard loved to revive his stories of operatic foibles, some of which went back to his early London days with Gaetano Loria. Boulestin's restaurant near Covent Garden was a rendezvous for performing artists, the kind of center for gossip Jim loved. Conchita Supervia was often seen eating at Boulestin's, he told his fellow guests, while Chaliapin favored the Savoy Grill. Supervia's choice was renowned for its cloudy mirrors and its Dufy-designed silks, while the Savoy was a place to dazzle mistresses. Chaliapin, according to Jim, once told a blonde with whom he'd gone to bed, "I shall give you tickets so you can hear me sing tonight." But the lady, protesting hard times, said she wanted cash. "When you're hungry," she told the singer, "you need bread." To this, Jim said, "Chaliapin retorted, 'If you want bread, you should have slept with a baker.'"

Content to have shaken off the Nantucket sand, Jim was looking forward to another trip to London when he wrote to Isabel in the fall of 1953. He told her he wanted to stretch his planned stay in England, to do a piece on British sports fishing "or something on English breakfasts" for *Argosy*. He invariably felt at home in London, and continued to look more kindly on British food than most of his confreres. In the spring, before taking off for Nantucket, he had appeared at a "coronation clinic" for American travelers and had assured the New York gathering that Britain's prolonged wartime austerity did not prevent elegant dining out for those wanting to see the crowning of Queen Elizabeth.

"The famous English rib roast has not returned," Beard had reported. "A few other things are still limited. But many specialties, such as beef and kidney pie, and magnificent seafood, are in abundance." He yearned for a prosperous England as in the Victorian upper-class times of his mother's recollections. Ever since he first became interested in its history, he had tried to picture in his mind the roasting of a baron of beef. The thought of great banquets in the

Middle Ages stirred his twentieth-century relish of good meat. "I might as well stay an extra week in England," he told Isabel in a letter from Chez Lucky Pierre, "then on to Brussels and to Paris as planned."

During the fifties Frank Schoonmaker had an office in Paris where Jim would meet him, and together they would drive south in Frank's Porsche to Chablis, stopping to sit under trees as they picnicked en route. "Nobody knew as much about wine in those days as Frank," Beard told me one day in Greenwich Village. "Back before World War II, he'd bicycled as a young man all over the continent, staying with people who would take him in. One time he stayed with a winemaker who just about forced him to recognize the difference between two glasses of local wine. Frank developed as a result of that—sort of being thrown in the water to see if you can swim—the palate that made his reputation. He taught me more than Jeanne Owen. Many a time I was with him, visiting vineyards. After Lucky Pierre, I remember having to write a piece for *Apartment Life* to encourage Americans to realize they don't have to be pretentious about what they know about wine." Beard shook his head, looking sidewise at me. "It was full of what I'd learned from Schoonmaker. That was when we began to work together on a book about wine. It was in the works for half a dozen years."

During the same period, his monthly *House & Garden* contributions in a single year included pieces about the wines of Bordeaux, the Loire, Burgundy, the Rhône, Champagne, Sherry, as well as the wines of Italy; nor did he neglect domestic bottlings from California and New York. In addition, he was writing for the bulletins published by Julius Wile, wine importers, and maintaining his close rapport with Sam Aaron as well.

His writing about wine in popular magazines with "upward mobility" readership reached more Americans in those days than that of anyone else writing on wine. In *Paris Cuisine,* already in a third printing, the subject of ordering French wine in Paris with confidence is addressed in the introduction with some words about the sommelier: "His job is to guide you through . . . local wines, to be drunk young as a rule, from districts such as the Rhône, the Jura, the Loire, which are less known in America, and to Americans, than Bordeaux and Burgundy." There is advice, of course, about luxury places where "the cellar lists wines of great vintages," and where advice is even more important. And the introduction concludes that although "some of the dishes are expensive and elaborate, we have included nothing that cannot with a little ingenuity be prepared in an American kitchen."

From Maxim's there were four recipes given to Jim by Louis Vaudable. (The two had recently agreed that Jim would test some of the restaurant's sauces for possible sale on the American frozen food market.) And another recipe was one for Tarte Tatin—a dessert thus introduced to Stateside cooks a couple of decades before it was much heralded on United States restaurant menus. From the Plaza-Athénée, "where the cuisine is superlative and by far the finest of any of the hotels in Paris" (as *Paris Cuisine* put it), the contributions were similar, and gave evidence of Jim's familiarity with French chefs. Jim had renewed his rapport with Lucien Diat (brother of Louis Diat), who ran the Plaza-Athénée kitchens, and the book included Lucien Diat's recipe for kirsch-perfumed Crêpe Montaigne, which had become a favorite treat of Americans in Paris for the seasonal promotions of nearby fashion houses.*

Paris Cuisine, a collaboration, is a book that saluted in a handsome way the new wave of travel, but the pretensions of some of its recipes shouldn't be identified with Beard's growing understanding of what food in this country was. Soon enough he was back in the States and, in response to Helen Brown's proposal, was driving north in California on a trip ostensibly to survey the blossoming enthusiasm for backyard barbecuing.

In the Browns Jim had found a new fulfillment for his need to surround himself, wherever he was, with family. With them he was an avuncular third musketeer. He found in Philip a man of mixed interests who was at ease with life; in Helen he admired a peer, a

---

*"Fashion cannot play with our food and drink quite the same tricks that it plays with woman's dress," Jim's mentor André Simon wrote in "The Aesthetics of Eating." "A woman's head will wear any hat, but her stomach will turn if she takes the same liberties with it. Gastronomy is, of course, greatly influenced by social and economic changes, [yet] there is neither time nor money nowadays . . . to indulge in the type of gastronomy which gladdened the hearts and stretched the waistcoats of our fathers."

writer whose West Coast book energized him because of its verve, its appreciation of food as significant in defining American history, and because its pages were full of the author's personality. No doubt in his mind—he and Helen should collaborate on a book about outdoor cookery. This was the focus of the trip; and there were side interests, of course, as there always were with Jim on board.

With Jim packed into the Browns' convertible, they headed up 101 from San Francisco to Ukiah and the state's northern fruit country. He was saddened by what he observed. He could see the specter of thousands of acres of arable fruit lands being sacrificed, he wrote later, to build what he called "the slums of tomorrow." To him the prospect seemed all too clear in California—he thought the fertile Santa Clara Valley fruit production had been handed over without sufficient reason to real estate construction. "The sacrificing of quality food for inferior housing," as he saw it, was proof that stricter laws were needed to assure Americans of ample acreage on which to raise food.* From California Jim wrote to Isabel sardonically: "Political situation here enchanting. People still don't know that there are other states in the Union besides California. They consider that anyone who is not for isolation, high tariffs and the Southern Pacific is a communist plain and simple. Horrible to hear the reactionary fools carry on. There is one liberal democratic paper, however, but that is looked upon askance by most people—though not by the Browns and their friends."

He could talk to the Browns of such social concerns in good humor, and he found them amiable companions, whatever the mood of one personality or the other. Helen and Jim might be, in spells, dead serious about the growing problems of collaboration, but Philip kept them happy with his light touch. In Ukiah, Jim scouted around to find a smorgasbord restaurant. "He just wanted to prove it was there," Philip Brown recalled. "We went on up the coast to Langlois, in Oregon, where Hans Hanan for years had been making what everybody said was the best blue-mold cheese in the U.S.—then on to Tillamook for a look at the Cheddar plant. It was getting to be a real

*His concern for arable land influenced him throughout his life.

cheese tour, for before we were through Jim had us in Utah's Cache Valley where the Swiss cheese they make there, according to Jim, was the best copy yet of Emmenthaler."

Philip Brown was obviously no less a friend of Jim's than Helen. The three often took the investigation of food and related possibilities as opportunities for frivolity. He was a food consultant for Jurgenson's epicurean stores, and as an antiquarian book man as well, he kept 12,000 antiquarian books lining the walls of the Browns' Pasadena house. In addition, he was his wife's habitual collaborator as well as a writer of books and articles about food himself. A man who cooked for the love of eating, he was at his best when there was meat on the fire. When the Browns entertained they produced the meals together.

They shared the Beard predilection for roadside eating, and in place after place, during their ten days on the road, they stopped to stock up not only on local cheese but on country ham and other sliced meats, local sausage where it was still being made, and regional fruit. Jim was not to be trusted on his own, Philip Brown told me, because he shopped without regard for price.* But his instincts seemed with few exceptions to lead to unexpected good food. They drove through sheep country and found Basque dining rooms "where there was a wonderful spread every evening." All of them knew the Basque hotels of San Francisco—the small sheep-town hotels, however, where shepherds who came from the Pyrenees lived when they weren't in the High Sierras, seemed more real.

"Helen liked the pipérade—the heavy dark-smoked Basque ham really perked up all those eggs. And at dinner there were at least two kinds of meat, a lot of vegetables cooked with garlic, Basque bread, and good thick soups, of course, with a lot of red wine. Talk about food," Philip said, "there was this place in Idaho Falls that specialized in chicken. We had a Basque chicken dinner, and noticed they also had fried gizzards and hearts. There was a fridge in the hotel, so we took back five pounds and had them the next day for lunch, with cheese and wine."

*When Jim used to come to stay, Philip recalled, "he and Helen would go shopping. He would see goodies and slip them into the cart, letting Helen pay at the check-out. Helen finally fixed that by parking so close to the curb he couldn't get out of the car to follow her into the store."

In *Delights and Prejudices,* Jim reported that in those days, before the wines of Oregon and Washington had been developed, he and the Browns carried bottles from the Napa, Sonoma, and Santa Clara valleys, and they found a few shopping surprises. Among local food counter specialties, he said, there were "exceptionally good things—nothing to compare [however] with provincial France." And he also made the best of it as his almost-bald head started turning bright red, and, when pulling the canvas top down, he scraped his sunburned scalp. Seeking a handy medicament, he hit upon the liquor supply. "Gin was applied," Brown told me, adding, "Could be we were a little drunk."

Balancing one project against one of the others was a constant challenge. Keeping his interest in fish uppermost for a spell, Jim and his companions headed for Seattle, where he had studied theater arts twenty-odd years earlier. The city that then had had space and trees and gardens was no more. Eight-lane torrents of highway vehicles cut through where hills had been. Factories stretched where there had been country lanes rich with berries. But where the land ended, Jim could see the Pacific, his home ocean. In the old port of Seattle was Pike Place Market, and giant crabs and shrimp and fish lay on beds of sweating ice; tourists moved among the shoppers, consuming clam juice and plastic cups of crab cocktail above the waterfront.

"The trip is proving to be fascinating," he said in a letter to Isabel. "I can't begin to tell you all the things which have happened, there is so much work to be done. Tomorrow off to be flown over the oyster beds and taken on an oyster dredge and a few other things of equal wonder. I shall have to take a night and a day to figure them all out. . . .

"We leave Sunday for the trek across Idaho and into Salt Lake. By that time we shall have included about twenty-five hundred tons of cheese into the back of the car. To say nothing of a few assorted bits of fish and wild life and some wine and liquors. I hate to admit that I have a traitor been—not a bottle of French wine since I have been here. Awful. I have drunk California's best all the way like the brave lad I really am—and some of them are really very good. But I haven't really transferred my allegiance—need you be told."

In Jim's home country, they headed for the lodge of his old

friends Ralph and Mabelle Jeffcott, both of whom were talented home cooks. He had more than once taken over their kitchen overlooking the Tualatin River south of Portland and he had in those days cooked for fellow cast members who gathered there at theater parties. Ralph was an outdoor-cooking stalwart to be consulted on the matter of Helen's and Jim's book-in-progress, and Mabelle was considered by Jim to be an example of the best among American housewives, cooking indoors or out.

She had discovered the small turkeys, new on the market, that had been developed by the Department of Agriculture. The birds weighed four to seven pounds, and could be cut up and cooked much like chicken. Mabelle's way was to brown the turkey pieces before arranging them in a casserole along with sprinklings of chopped shallots, bacon cut in tiny strips, and a couple of cups of broth made from the neck and giblets.

Mabelle offered her recipe for graham bread, which Helen and Jim described to their readers as "wonderful when toasted over charcoal or simply heated in foil." And when they rolled on to Virginia City, Nevada, for a visit with Lucius Beebe (with whom Jim shared New York friends from café society), they turned up another bread recipe—and, fatigued as Jim had said, they celebrated enough to admit hangovers. The Virginia City bread, Jim wrote in a book on the subject, was one of "two or three favorites in this country," and the recipe belonged to Jinny Smedesrude, at whose inn they stayed. The celebration was as much, perhaps more, in honor of the Browns as Jim, because Helen was a regular contributor to the *Territorial Enterprise,* published by Beebe and his friend Charles Clegg.*

Jim wrote to Isabel that all three trekkers had vowed to go on diets as the result of putting on so much weight during the trip, and he confessed to drinking more in Virginia City "than I did at my grandmother's wake—and everyone knows that was record-breaking in its importance." He may have had an excuse: in addition to the *Outdoor Cookery* research, the fish book was in its final phase and he had a casserole book to write for Jerry Mason. He owed monthly contributions to *Argosy* and *House & Garden,* while *Vogue, Woman's Day,* and other magazines had claims on him as well.

The book project of the moment was a Jerry Mason production dedicated to the proposition that desperate women sometimes submit to desperate solutions. "Casserole" was a euphemism for a one-dish meal—a mixture of meat or fish and something starchy such as potatoes, rice, or macaroni. With the help of home economists in high school "domestic science courses" and state and county "home agents" in rural America, the combination of ingredients stuffed into oven-proof vessels had become a plague upon the land. In New York and other cities, services with names like Casserole Cookery could be called upon to provide a meal at the end of the day for working men and women too jaded to go out to dinner. These concoctions, pretending to be elegant, were really not much different from unsophisticated America's "hot dishes." (In one cookbook I know, the best of fifty under this rubric is a straightforward dish of wild rice and mushrooms.)

"Personally I am not a believer in one-dish meals," Jim asserted

---

*That summer the Callverts received a formal letter from Charles Clegg on an *Enterprise* letterhead to advise them that "Mr. James Beard has entered your name on our subscription list . . . as a gift from him for the next year." In the giving, Jim was tipping his hat to Beebe (Beard often referred to him as "Luscious"), who published the newspaper as an icon of the Old West. Beebe and Clegg were also railroad buffs, and they had their own opulent Southern Pacific parlor car.

in the paper-covered tome he wrote for Mason. "I find them too monotonous." Nevertheless, he added that the casserole "is a godsend to beginning cooks, harried housewives, and the millions of apartment-dwellers who are hampered by tiny modern kitchens." He composed a compendium that ranged from "pork chops with sweet potatoes" and the jambalaya of New Orleans to a Western casserole of pinto beans which was a primitive version of southern France's cassoulet. His casserole cookbook was an inexpensive handbook for the times.

Among those to whose attention it came was Sheila Hibben of *The New Yorker,* who turned to Jim in discussing ideas for Christmas giving. One suggestion he gave made reference to one of his students, John Clancy, who was running a catering service. "Our respect for Mr. Beard's knowledge of good food impelled us to order straightway the *cassoulet Castelnaudary* that, we are told, is one of the young man's most noteworthy successes," Mrs. Hibben wrote. "Whatever the robust dish contained to start with, it has by this time become incorporated into French *haute cuisine* as a mixture of white beans, fresh pork, salt pork, young goose, lamb, garlic sausage, and herbs. It is this formula that Beard sets down in his cookbook 'Paris Cuisine,' and it is this formula . . . that Mr. Clancy has followed scrupulously." She gave the price for this Beard-via-Clancy one-dish meal, or casserole, as $24.50, delivered, to feed a dinner party of six persons.

Jim's chores outside the world of publishing included a contract to help promote one of the flashy symbols of summer in the 1950s—a vibrantly red-and-yellow plaid bucket-shaped portable charcoal stove known as the Skotch grill. He and the Browns arranged a garden party behind the Pasadena house which "did a great deal in the way of good will," he wrote the manufacturer. "While we were on our trek through the West," he continued, "we mentioned the party to the heads of cheese factories we visited." As a result, there was all the free cheese they could use. And he described a row of Skotch grills on a large marble table which turned out three kinds of hot shrimp, skewers of chicken livers, water chestnuts, and bacon, and broiled Mexican pork cubes served with a pepper-haunted sauce. "With the hors d'oeuvres went a punch bowl of good martinis, a rum punch, and iced tea for the non-alcoholics." It's clear enough that Beard stimulated a lot of publicity for the Skotch grill (which he continued to represent for several years) but again, with all those punch bowls, he had "pinned one on for the cause," he wrote to Isabel, and "I am thinking seriously of becoming a member of the W.C.T.U. and stumping the country."

To the Callverts he didn't try to hide how tired he was, and at times how gloomy. Like many others in America that year, he was also disheartened by the radio broadcasts of the McCarthy hearings in Washington. Jim Beard had been an admirer of John Reed as well as of Franklin D. Roosevelt. In Portland in his youth he had turned away from the Federal Theater, not because he objected to the work of his friend Bess Whitcomb, but because, as his fellow actors saw things, false pride made him decide he was not needy enough to accept WPA money. He was a lifelong liberal when it came to voting, but, much as he was appalled at the tactics of McCarthy and his cohorts, he began to be more guarded in talking politics, except among a few trusted friends. He was an accommodator, but most of all he was caught up in juggling commitments, and too headily involved in the pursuit of ephemeral stardom.

RECIPES

Jane Nickerson's Frittata for Two

One of Jim's oldest professional friends, Jane Nickerson was among those he continued to see—in Florida, as it happened in this case, after her retirement from *The New York Times*. She was as much a champion of simple dishes brought to America by immigrants as he was.

4 tablespoons olive oil	*¹/₄ teaspoon salt*
2 tablespoons butter	*freshly ground pepper*
2 cups sliced or	*1 tablespoon grated*
chopped zucchini	*Parmesan cheese*
4 eggs	
3 tablespoons	
chopped parsley	

Heat 2 tablespoons of oil and 1 tablespoon of butter in an omelet pan. Add the zucchini and cook slowly, stirring, until limp and lightly browned—about 5 minutes. Cool. Beat the eggs until fluffy. Add the parsley, salt, a grind or two of pepper, the cheese, and the cooled zucchini. Heat the remaining butter and oil in the cleaned-out pan. Add the egg-zucchini mixture and cook over medium heat, lifting the eggs occasionally around the edges so that the uncooked part runs under, for about 3 minutes, until the frittata is quite firm but still somewhat uncooked in the center. Run under the broiler and cook until the center is firm. Turn out onto a large plate and cut in pie-shaped wedges to serve. SERVES 2.

Guacamole with Ham

Long before the notion called "California cuisine" became much publicized in the sixties, the avocado was a West Coast favorite and guacamole recipes were appearing in the work of both Beard and his friend Helen Brown. One of Jim's favorite variations calls for thin strips of Smithfield or smoky country ham.

1–2 canned, peeled green
   chilies, or 1 canned
   jalapeño or serrano chili
2 large ripe avocados

2 tablespoons lime juice
1/2 cup ham strips
salt

Open the canned chilies and scrape away the seeds, which are intensely hot, then chop very fine. Cut the avocados in half, remove the pits, and scoop the pulp into a bowl. Mash until smooth with a fork. Mix in the chili and lime juice, and the ham strips. Add a light sprinkling of salt only if needed. Serve as a dip with tortilla chips or as a salad on lettuce leaves.   SERVES 4.

Fish Pudding Rombauer

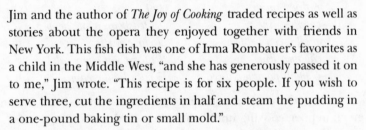

Jim and the author of *The Joy of Cooking* traded recipes as well as stories about the opera they enjoyed together with friends in New York. This fish dish was one of Irma Rombauer's favorites as a child in the Middle West, "and she has generously passed it on to me," Jim wrote. "This recipe is for six people. If you wish to serve three, cut the ingredients in half and steam the pudding in a one-pound baking tin or small mold."

2 cups flaked or grated
   cooked halibut or
   other fish*
3/4 cup fresh breadcrumbs
1/4 cup melted butter
3 eggs, separated

2 teaspoons lemon juice
   or 1 teaspoon
   Worcestershire sauce
salt
paprika

Combine the fish, crumbs, butter, egg yolks, and seasonings. Beat the egg whites stiff and fold them into the mixture. Pour it into a well-buttered timbale mold or pudding tin and steam for 1 hour. Unmold onto a hot platter and serve with cream sauce flavored with Worcestershire sauce, or a mustard or tomato sauce.   SERVES 6.

*We used bluefish and it was particularly good.

Lucky Pierre Clam Chowder

▼

Jim said he liked to use soft shell clams in chowder, but he would accept others, depending upon circumstances. In Nantucket, he said, "we are being a trifle unusual by adding a bit of green pepper to the onion and salt pork when we sauté them, then using clam juice and chopped clams. We add cream to the chowder when it is served—so that there is no curdling as a result. I am convinced that Pacific Coast Chowder is a specialty all its own."

3 slices salt pork, cut in shreds	2 cups chopped clams, with juice
2 medium onions, chopped fine	salt
1 small green pepper, chopped fine	1/4 teaspoon white pepper
	1 clove garlic
5–6 small potatoes, diced	1/4 teaspoon celery salt
	3 cups light cream

Cook the salt pork over medium heat until quite crisp and add the onions and green pepper, cooking until light brown. Add half of the potatoes and all of the clams and their liquid. Stir in salt to taste, then the white pepper, the garlic clove, and the celery salt. Simmer until the potatoes are soft, then remove the garlic and discard. Put the remaining potatoes into a blender with a little of the chowder broth and blend until creamy. Stir into the chowder, simmer 5 minutes, and add the cream. Serve hot.   SERVES 4 TO 6.

Philip Brown's Romaine Soufflé

▼

Jim helped Philip Brown get started as a cooking teacher. Observing at one of his friend's classes he discovered "one of the most delicious romaine dishes I've ever had. This is really a complete vegetable course in itself," Jim said. "With a roast of lamb or beef, or a chicken dish, you need no potato or green vegetable or salad to complete the meal."

1 large head romaine lettuce	4 tablespoons butter

3 scallions or green
  onions, chopped
3 tablespoons flour
1 cup milk, heated
4 eggs, separated
1 cup shredded
  Cheddar cheese

1 teaspoon salt
1/2 teaspoon
  Worcestershire sauce
Tabasco sauce
grated Parmesan cheese

Cut off the coarse bottom of the romaine. Wash the leaves thoroughly and coarsely chop. Put in a heavy pan with a little water and cook until wilted. Drain well and chop fine. Melt 1 tablespoon of butter in a skillet and cook the scallions or green onions, including green tops, until soft but not browned. Add the romaine and cook, stirring, until the moisture evaporates. Melt the remaining butter in a saucepan, blend in the flour, and cook for 2 to 3 minutes, stirring. Mix in the milk and cook, stirring, until thickened. Beat the egg yolks into the sauce, one at a time, then add the Cheddar, and cook until smooth. Stir in the romaine mixture until well blended. Season with salt, Worcestershire, and Tabasco. Lavishly butter a 1½-quart soufflé dish, and sprinkle with Parmesan, coating the bottom and sides; shake out excess. Beat the egg whites until stiff but not dry; fold one-third into the romaine mixture and blend thoroughly. Fold in the remaining whites lightly. Pour into the soufflé dish, sprinkle on a little grated Parmesan, and put in a preheated 450 degree oven. Immediately reduce the heat to 375 degrees and bake 25 to 30 minutes, according to how you like your soufflé. At 25 minutes it will still be runny in the center.   SERVES 4.

Asparagus San Fernando

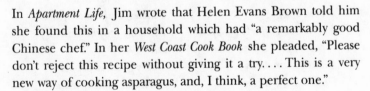

In *Apartment Life,* Jim wrote that Helen Evans Brown told him she found this in a household which had "a remarkably good Chinese chef." In her *West Coast Cook Book* she pleaded, "Please don't reject this recipe without giving it a try. . . . This is a very new way of cooking asparagus, and, I think, a perfect one."

2½ pounds asparagus
melted butter

salt
freshly ground pepper

Snap off the ends of the asparagus and remove the scales. Cut into very thin diagonal slices so that they are several times longer than the diameter of the stalk. Heat lightly salted water in the bottom of a deep pot. Place the asparagus slices in a frying basket or a large sieve. When the water is boiling rapidly, submerge the basket of asparagus and cook 2 minutes. Drain and transfer to a serving dish. Add melted butter to your taste, and salt and pepper. This asparagus has a delicate crispness and a garden fresh flavor.

SERVES 4.

Poached Salmon Lucky Pierre
with Remoulade Sauce

▼

During his summer on Nantucket, Jim took note of the July Fourth tradition of serving salmon and described this dish as "some really spectacular eating. The salmon was poached gently in a court bouillon with tarragon and white peppercorns. It was basted while poaching, and when the fish just flaked easily when teased with a fork, it was removed and cooled—not chilled. It was served with a sauce remoulade which had no one outstanding flavor but rather a composite of five or six wonderfully complementary flavors. This with some cucumber and oakleaf lettuce fresh from a farm made a memorable dinner."

6–8-pound salmon	1 onion
2–3 quarts water	1 branch fresh tarragon
2–3 cups white wine	1 tablespoon salt

Remoulade Sauce:

4 finely chopped scallions	1 tablespoon finely
1 finely chopped hard-boiled egg	chopped tarragon
	1 tablespoon lemon juice
2 tablespoons finely chopped capers	1 1/2 cups mayonnaise
1 mashed anchovy	salt
1 tablespoon finely chopped parsley	freshly ground pepper
	Garnish: oakleaf lettuce and sliced cucumber

Put the salmon in a fish boiler, lying flat, and add a mixture of water and wine to cover the fish. Remove the fish and set aside. Add the onion, tarragon, and salt to the poaching liquid and bring to a boil, then lower heat and simmer 20 minutes. Add the fish and poach gently for 10 minutes for each inch of thickness. Set aside to cool in its broth while you make the sauce. Mix the scallions, egg, capers, anchovy, parsley, tarragon, and lemon juice with the mayonnaise and season to taste with salt and pepper.

Arrange the salmon on a platter with lettuce leaves and thinly sliced cucumber around it and serve the remoulade on the side.

SERVES 12 TO 14.

Cecily Brownstone's Country Captain

▼

Jim wrote of his friend Cecily, from whom he got this recipe, that "she had made a thorough study of this dish, which has fascinated her over a period of time. She has reconstructed a version of it which was published in *Specialty of the House*, a cookbook compiled for the benefit of the Florence Crittenton League." Although it was thought to have originated with Britain's occupation troops in India, it was found to be a thoroughly established Southern colonial dish by Eliza Leslie in her nineteenth-century *New Cookery Book*.

2¹/2-pound chicken, cut in 8 pieces
¹/4 cup flour
1 teaspoon salt
¹/4 teaspoon freshly ground pepper
4 tablespoons butter
¹/3 cup finely diced onion
¹/3 cup finely diced green pepper

1 clove garlic, crushed
1¹/2 teaspoons curry powder
¹/2 teaspoon dried crushed thyme
1-pound can stewed tomatoes
3 tablespoons dried currants, washed and drained
blanched toasted almonds

Coat the chicken with a mixture of the flour, salt, and pepper. Heat the butter in a large skillet and brown the chicken all over. Remove the chicken and add the onion, green pepper, garlic, curry, and thyme to the skillet. Add the stewed tomatoes, including the liquid. Return the chicken to the skillet, skin side up. Cover and cook slowly until tender, 20 to 30 minutes. Stir the currants into the sauce. Serve accompanied by almonds. SERVES 4.

Roasted Spareribs

Whether in the Waldorf ballroom, at Lucky Pierre on Nantucket, or the garden of his townhouse, Beard was expert at cooking spareribs in a great variety of ways. "To be quite frank," he says in *Theory & Practice of Good Cooking,* "there is nothing as good as simple roasted spareribs seasoned merely with salt and pepper."

2 sides spareribs, about 4	*coarse salt*
pounds, heavy bone or	*freshly ground pepper*
gristle section removed	

Put the ribs on a rack in a shallow roasting pan and roast them in a 350 degree oven for 30 minutes, then season the ribs well with salt and pepper, turn, season the other side, and continue roasting for another 30 minutes. At the end of an hour they should be nicely browned and fairly crisp on the outside. Roast another 10 to 15 minutes if you like them very well done.

Remove the ribs to a carving board and cut between the ribs into smallish sections. Heap them on a hot platter and serve with sauerkraut cooked in chicken broth with a few juniper berries. Add perfectly boiled potatoes in their jackets and you will have a delightful feast. Drink the beer of your choice.

SERVES 4.

Roast Wild Duck

Everyone in Jim's family wanted roast duck timed differently. Jim liked rare, bloody duck that someone described as being held over a candle for three minutes. His mother preferred hers pink with one or two shallots and a sprig of thyme; his father wanted bread stuffing with celery and onions—he liked to have the duck barded with bacon and cooked in a medium oven for 45 minutes to an hour. Below is the James Beard way of spitting mallards outdoors.

4–6 mallard ducks (1 to 1½	*2 celery ribs*
ducks per person)	*1 apple, sliced*
lemon	*12 juniper berries (optional)*
1 onion, sliced	*brandy*

Clean 4 to 6 birds and singe off any remaining feathers. Rub with cut lemon. In each cavity put 1 slice of onion, 1 piece of celery rib, 1 slice of apple, and a few juniper berries, if you like them. Spit the birds firmly, alternating with 1 breast side up, 1 breast side down. Usually 5 or 6 ducks may be put on a spit when lined up crosswise through the center, just below the breasts. Using long skewers, fasten the ends of the birds together, then fix the holding forks firmly in the two end ducks. Roast over a medium fire for 20 to 25 minutes—12 to 15 minutes if you want them bloody rare. Basting is not necessary. To crisp the skin, pour brandy over the finished ducks and set it ablaze.   SERVES 4.

Jinny Smedesrude's Oatmeal Bread

▼

"I believe that Fannie Farmer was the first person to popularize oatmeal bread," Jim told *Gourmet* readers in his series on fundamental cooking. He was staying in a Virginia City country inn when he discovered this recipe and talked the innkeeper into sharing it.

1 cup coarse rolled oats	1 cup warm milk
1 cup boiling water	1 tablespoon salt
2 packages active dry yeast	1/4 cup dark brown sugar
1 teaspoon granulated sugar	4–5 cups all-purpose flour,
1/2 cup warm water	approximately
(100–115 degrees,	
approximately)	

Cook the oats in the boiling water until thickened, about 3 minutes. Pour into a large mixing bowl and allow to cool to lukewarm. Meanwhile, stir the yeast and teaspoon of sugar into the warm water until dissolved, and allow to proof. Add the warm milk, salt, brown sugar, and yeast mixture to the oats and stir well, then stir in 4 cups of flour, 1 cup at a time. Turn out onto a floured board. Knead into a smooth, pliable, elastic dough, if necessary using as much as 1/2 to 1 cup, or more, of additional flour to get the right feel. (This will take about 10 minutes.) Shape the dough into a ball, put into a well-buttered bowl, and turn to coat on all sides. Cover and let rise in a warm, draft-free place until doubled in bulk, 1 1/2 to 2 hours. Punch the dough down. Knead for 2 to 3 minutes and shape into two loaves. Thoroughly butter two 8 × 4 × 2-inch tins. Place the dough in the tins, cover, and let rise in a warm place until about even with the top of the tins, or almost doubled in bulk. Place the bread in the center of the lowest rack and bake for about 45 to 50 minutes in a preheated 375 degree oven or until the loaves sound hollow when tapped on top and bottom with the knuckles. Return the loaves, without the tins, to the oven rack and bake for about 5 minutes to acquire a firmer crust. Remove the loaves to a rack and cool.

MAKES 2 SMALL LOAVES.

Helen's Campfire Chili Beans

▼

A frequent visitor to Nevada, Jim's collaborator and traveling companion picked up this garlicky outdoor way of serving chili beans without fresh meat.

1 pound Mexican pink beans	*1/2 teaspoon oregano*
water	*ground cumin*
1/4 pound salt pork	*2 cups puréed tomatoes*
3 cloves garlic, chopped fine	*3 tablespoons chili powder*
2 cups chopped onions	*salt*
	freshly ground pepper

Cook the beans in water to cover until they are not quite cooked—just a bit bitey. Cut the salt pork into small pieces and fry until crisp in a large skillet or Dutch oven. Add the garlic and onions and brown well. When the onions are soft, add the oregano, a healthy pinch of cumin, the puréed tomatoes, and chili powder. Bring to a boil and add a little salt and pepper. Stir in the beans and simmer for 1 1/2 hours.

SERVES 6 TO 8.

8

CULINARY REVOLT

The signs of change were sometimes capricious, often on the lavish side. As the fifties kept Beard hopping—in great airplane jumps—from coast to coast, from New York to London, Paris, Nice, Rome, from one major airport to another—he was tuned in to seismic clues. The fast food era had begun, and the "theme" restaurants were about to be unveiled. No other traveler (and postwar travel was increasing by the hundreds of thousands of trips per year) was as cognizant of cooking and eating trends. In the Southwest he had come across drive-ins where a curb-service waitress in a cute uniform rushed out and placed a portable air conditioner around you as you ordered your hot dog. In New York one morning when the phone rang for Jim it signaled an offer of a helicopter ride (only the police had choppers in the fifties) to the Newarker restaurant across the Hudson.

Among savvy restaurateurs, Jim was a little like a doctor on call, and the patient this time was an airport dining room about to be given birth by the New York firm known as Restaurant Associates. Who then would not have chuckled at the idea of a three-star place to eat in a transportation terminal? A Frenchman might have cited the good old days of gastronomic triumph in the Restaurant du Gare de l'Est. In America no one would do anything much but groan at the thought of a rewarding meal while waiting for a train or plane to come in. But on this day, a copter had been warmed up to swing Jim Beard into the New Jersey flats to taste the new menu that Albert

Stockli, chef, had put together under the creative eye of Joseph H. Baum.

Baum had grown up in his family's small hotel in Saratoga Springs, where he had been surrounded, as he once said, by characters from Damon Runyon's wisecracking racetrack world. He was a Cornell Hotel School graduate, but his small stature—he's not much bigger than a jockey—and his darting energy give him the air of an inveterate bettor. What Jim found appealing in Joe Baum was his conviction, a drive similar to Jim's own urge, that eating out in itself should be made a form of fulfilling entertainment. Baum had worked as a youth for Norman Bel Geddes at the World's Fair, as well as backstage with Martha Graham's dance troupe. Like Jim, he believed in finding theater in everyday life. Restaurants should be havens that give pleasure—to the eye, to the mind, to one's sense of well-being, and to the stomach. Throughout their friendship of over thirty years, Jim Beard and Joe Baum each considered the other to be a genius.

At lunch in the unbaptized Newarker restaurant, having taken the helicopter jaunt with characteristic aplomb, Beard found another kindred spirit in Chef Albert Stockli, a man of his own heft and contours, who was singlemindedly dedicated to cooking. Stockli had won over Joe Baum when the latter traced him to a beach place near Atlantic City; the barley soup that the mountainous young Swiss-born chef served Baum had proved to be a persuasive collation. Stockli took over the kitchen of the Newarker and he and Baum began to devise a menu unlike any ever hinted at in Jersey.

Jim immediately applauded the presentation of oysters at the airport—there were giant Absecon Island mollusks, described as "knife and fork oysters," so large they had to be cut with a whetted blade, and there were ordinary oysters served seven to a diner instead of the customary six (the extra one was served on the side, on a small plate, to give the diner the feeling he'd been especially blessed). Not a dessert man in the usual sense, Jim never lost the boyhood memory of West's Dairy that caused him to break out a grin when he saw Joe Baum's "sparkler snowball"; it was a dazzling scoop of ice cream covered with syrup and shredded coconut and bristling quills from which sparks sprayed the immediate space. (Baum admitted that some of his early notions had been pretty flashy. "I wouldn't do that again," he said, but he was smiling.) Of the menu in general, Beard asserted that Albert Stockli had "invented what became known as nouvelle cuisine." Stockli, as a classically trained cook, believed absolute knowledge of culinary basics to be the initial, unavoidable step toward earning the title of "chef"; yet he was the first to bring lightness, to accent standard Western recipes with Oriental ideas. He had the open-mindedness to put together surprising combinations such as his chilled mussels in a tart sauce of celery root and curry. Stockli seemed to love everything American, especially its bounty, and he had the fresh idea of going himself to visit farmers in order to encourage the growing of new kinds of produce that would enliven cooking.

New concepts weren't common in those days. The New York restaurants accepted by sophisticated diners were led by Soulé's Le Pavillon, of course, and Café Chambord, where the cuisine was Parisian French, as was that of other reputed places like La Caravelle, the Brussels, Louis and Armand, Le Moal, and Chauveron. There was the fashionable Colony, and there were intimate rendezvous like Charles à la Pommes Soufflés, informal lunch places like A La Fourchette, and Le Bistro. Louisa, on the upper east side, and the Italian Pavilion were known for Italian food, but there was little on

Jim with Helen McCully, Albert Stockli, and Frederick Rufe

menus that had originated in Lombardy or Piedmont or even Tuscany. For Jim himself, the Piedmontese *bollito misto* of the posh Quo Vadis made Saturday lunch a salutary event. He called this Park Avenue restaurant a paragon, "a place of beauty, quiet and comfort." "I have known the owners, Gino and Bruno, for many years," he said in a syndicated column, "and when I eat there, or take friends from out of town, I feel almost as if I'm in my own home."

Beard, who in this period was reviewing restaurants routinely for *Apartment Life,* sometimes recommended such offbeat trattorias as Café Orsini, because "there has long been a need," he wrote, "for more places where one could sit in the evening with just a cup of coffee and pastry—places where one feels no compulsion to order drinks or a large amount of food." The word "ethnic" was not yet in use to describe restaurant food, and the word "American" had the down-to-earth connotations (dismissed by some as pedestrian) of chicken fricassee served with corn bread or sausage cakes with glazed apples, as featured at the Kirby-Allen on Madison Avenue. This homey place, where some New Yorkers might be found when there was no help in their own kitchens on Thursday nights, saw to it that the menu explained things: "Lasagna (a very interesting Italian dish)"; and "Quiche Lorraine (a very interesting French dish)."*

Restaurant reviewing did not conflict with Jim's newly begun career as culinary adviser and, at Joe Baum's behest, he became gastronomic counsel to Restaurant Associates, working with Stockli and Baum on the menus and wine lists. As RA developed, the small Beard flat became even more the hub of things. Fred Rufe would come over after work as manager of the Newarker; so would Alan Lewis, who joined the staff and recognized Jim at once as "my mentor." And there was Leon Leonides, the lean and handsome Greek proprietor of The Coach House, who had been counseled by Jim to go to Paris for lessons in French cooking at L'Ecole des Trois Gourmandes. New among women on his guest list was Kate Titus, a public relations tycoon who'd spotted Jim's own PR gifts.

More of his talents had now been recognized. He was still the leading contributor of articles on food and recipes to the general

---

*It was not until the sixties and seventies that the dish called "quiche," with all its corruptions, became a kitchen cliché, at home and in take-out shops.

interest magazines of the day. In the same period he was the author of
The Complete Book of Barbecue and Rotisserie Cooking and *The Complete
Cookbook for Entertaining* (both published by Jerry Mason in hardcover
and paperback), and in 1954 Little, Brown published *James Beard's Fish
Cookery,* written with the help of Isabel Callvert (and some moonlight-
ing assistance from Ron Callvert). That year, also, Appleton-Century-
Crofts issued *How to Eat Better for Less Money,* with Sam Aaron as
co-author. Within twelve months Jerry Mason had published *Jim
Beard's Casserole Cookery,* and Doubleday issued *The Complete Book of
Outdoor Cookery* by Helen Evans Brown and James A. Beard. That year
Jim revised and edited *The Standard Bartender's Guide,* which dealt
with hard liquors, wines, and mixed drinks, about which he and
Isabel had been churning out pieces for *House & Garden.*

The fish cookbook was the first of his sustained efforts to reflect
his own history as an eater and a cook. In the introduction, he cites
his good fortune to have grown up in "a region that is remarkable in
its range of both salt- and fresh-water fish," and asserts further that
"many Americans eat fish regularly without knowing what fish they
are eating." Credit is given to Rose G. Kerr of the Department of Fish
and Wildlife in Washington, D.C., and to Helen Ridley and Frances
Smith of the National Fishers Institute (indications of government
interest in seeing more fish on home menus). But both recipes and
anecdotes throughout the text show glimpses of Jim from boyhood
on to his time as a pleasure-loving traveler, and leave no doubt about
his love of eating, as well as his nostalgia for Gearhart's oceanside and
nearby streams.

The proper way to clean a Dungeness crab, as practiced by
Elizabeth Beard, is given, and so is Polly Hamblet's recipe for deviled
crab, a buttery, green-pepper-dotted casserole topped with cracker
crumbs; this was one dish Joe Baum remembered with relish among
those that Jim served at gatherings in his apartment.* He could poke
fun at grandiosity in himself—as when he dramatically made his

---

*A cautionary note: "The Deviled Crab recipe in *Delights and Prejudices* is all wrong!" Mary
Hamblet said indignantly in 1989. True. That version calls for one good-sized green
pepper chopped in its entirety. In the other versions given in Jim's books, the amount of
chopped green pepper is two tablespoons, instead of, as Mary asserted, only one tablespoon.

Mary Hamblet and Jim, Gearhart, 1966

entrance with champagne spurting energetically onto sauerkraut—or he could serve a simple dish from home with the pride of one whose palate had been keen enough in childhood to know how good a simple thing can be.

A young neighbor who often dropped in was his New York godchild Kiki, for whom Jim made cookies. Her arrival would remind him that as a child he always had access to a familiar canister in a kitchen down the street. He might, in another mood, make a vast bowl of popcorn when a child visited, for it was, after all, the necessary accompaniment to his version of Carl Sandburg's *Rootabaga Stories* that pleased him enough to recall it in one of his columns. It was the variously embroidered fable of a Midwest summer as hot as a prairie fire. Mr. and Mrs. Huckabuck and their daughter Pony-Pony lived on a farm that annually produced acres and acres of corn for popping. Pony-Pony, like Dorothy in the *Wizard of Oz,* realized the potential fantasy of life on the plains but (as Beard's story had it) she wasn't quite ready when the big heat wave struck. The sun's rays were so intense that a hundred and fifty-six acres of corn popped at once, banging high into passing clouds, piling up on the arid ground until, like a snowstorm, it buried the Huckabuck house in white stuff; Pony-Pony and her parents had no choice but to move to Walla Walla, Washington, a place that suited the young girl's fancy because she too had been named twice. As an aside to his newspaper readers, Beard added archly (echoing Gore Vidal), "I'm always a godfather, never a god."

His stints as a teacher of youngsters, in Portland and in New Jersey just before the war, helped him to decide in 1955 that the time was ripe for an adult cooking school. There were a few others around, of course, including his friend Dione Lucas's Cordon Bleu school. Helen Worth had moved from Cleveland to set up a teaching kitchen for brides in midtown, and she offered a series of lessons aimed at men in gray flannel suits which was called "Learn Your Lunch." She gave her male pupils the chance to eat their mistakes as well as their accomplishments.

Jim teamed up with André Surmain, the urbane Frenchman he met on Nantucket. Both believed that first things must come first, that learning to cook begins with respect for fundamentals. All his life Jim was the champion of the principle that cooking starts with hands. In his *Theory & Practice of Good Cooking,* published when he was seventy-four, he wrote that "hands were the earliest tools for the preparation of food, and they have remained efficient, sensitive, and versatile. They are so sensitive that when your fingers touch or feel something, they transmit messages to your brain about texture and temperature."

Convening first in an upstairs room with a fireplace, and a tapestry on the wall, the partnership began in the building on Fiftieth Street which was to later house the restaurant Lutèce for many years. The James Beard Cooking School kicked off its long history with a class of ten that included Jim's friend Florence Aaron, Paula Peck, whose natural gifts soon began to develop into a career as a master baker, and Rita Wynn, who with her photographer husband had met Jim on Nantucket. They paid $125 for five lessons, Rita recalled, and "you could do anything as long as you kept to the principles." The first commandment was that you could beat, cream, fold, knead, pat, press, form, toss, tear, and pound. Beard's advice on dough was, "Take out all your animosities on it—throw it on the table and make it behave." Above all was his creed that freshness in ingredients is more important than anything else.

Rita Wynn kept the recipes of that first class, which ranged from corn bread, Cuban bread, and pie dough to snails aux champignons. Among many dishes, she learned Jeanne Owen's way to sauté *poulet à l'estragon,* the Beard way to serve broiled mushrooms on toast from the *Fireside* book, and how to toss anchovy, tuna, hard-boiled eggs, tomatoes, and greens together to make the then-unfamiliar salade Niçoise. The spinach soufflé recipe was one of those going into the manuscript of *The James Beard Cookbook.*

Jim and André Surmain both laid claim to having first memories that were olfactory. As a toddler, André also played in the kitchen, and in 1988, over lunch in his restaurant in Mougins, he called up the mingled childhood smells of pastry and clean laundry hung over the stove to dry. "When Jim and I met, I was supplying the food for Varig airlines, but I wanted to have more to do with cooking. Jim seemed to me a born teacher, so I talked him into the school. It was something we each could do by fitting other work around it. And we got Frank Schoonmaker and Alexis Lichine to come for sessions on wine, and Albert Stockli was a regular guest teacher." André was cheerful as he thought back over thirty-odd years. "It was fun, but we lost money— the school was ahead of its time, of course."

Deeply involved as he had become in Restaurant Associates, Beard kept the cooking school going when Cheryl Crawford's friend Ruth Norman became manager and assistant teacher. For classroom space, they were given the use of test kitchens that Joe Baum had established in the Hotel Lexington, and the school began to thrive little by little.* In the same kitchens, many more hours were spent on preparing and criticizing dishes for RA establishments yet to be opened. Mimi Sheraton was among those working with Baum, Stockli, and Beard. "We'd taste thirty-five dishes a day for the Four Seasons," she remembered. "They wanted the seasonal expressions of the whole world. Alert to Albert Stockli's lead, they searched out fresh herbs when everyone else was using dried, and they were the first to demand baby vegetables. Jim talked Joe into actually buying vegetable farms to supply the kitchens—one in Jersey and one upstate."

By this time, the Hotel Lexington had two RA restaurants with Stockli as chef—the Paul Revere Tavern and the Hawaiian Room—transforming the world of dining-out in Manhattan. "Albert," as Phil Miles remembered clearly, "had worked as a chef on boats sailing the Pacific. He really had ideas about Oriental, Polynesian eating. The Hawaiian Room went back to what Jim knew about Chinatowns on the Coast, and food in Honolulu. Albert began to develop dishes like Polynesian broiled shrimp, and mustard greens soup. Jim knew exactly how to handle Albert—get the best out of him. Together they worked out this *imu* thing with goat meat, carried in on sticks. There was Uncle Jim, as I called him—looking like a Hawaiian king, or a white trader—he made it a real show. Drums rolling, dancers shaking. Jim was immense then—like Sydney Greenstreet. He loved the show, the food, everything."

Baum also had Jim working with him in creating a place aimed especially at drawing male customers, and they called it Charley O's. With Stockli now as RA's executive chef, the two worked in the fifties on sixteen restaurant kitchens, each with a different cooking style, including La Fonda del Sol in the Time-Life building. Jim had

---

*In retrospect of three decades, Jerry Mason told me: "I think what did it for Jim more than anything else was the cooking school. He got a lot of publicity, first from Jane Nickerson, later Craig, and the students were really something at spreading the word."

brought Helen and Philip Brown from Pasadena to join in critical testing of new recipes at the Newarker. With Fred Rufe as manager, the Browns and Jim persuaded Elena Zelayeta, a highly gifted Mexican cook in Los Angeles, to be one of the advisers in creating the complex Latin American bill of fare at La Fonda (for which Jim found the designer Alexander Girard).

He may not have been instrumental in the menu here, but La Fonda scintillated with the same spirit that had uplifted Jim in Rio during the war. It was almost sentimentally his kind of eating place. The kitchen styles were Argentine, Brazilian, Chilean, Mexican, and Peruvian. It was centered, in a sense, around a hearth, a big open grill manned by three white-toqued chefs who maintained the spits that roasted piglets, sections of pork, lamb, beef, chicken, and fish over beds of coals. Everything was there to emphasize the provisions—corn, potatoes, tomatoes, chocolate—that had been the basis of the diet maintained by pre-Columbian Indians and incorporated into the cooking of colonists from Spain and Portugal. La Fonda was so much a dramatization of American food that the compelling activity at the hearth, plus the south-of-the-border decor, may have been too distracting. It was a unique restaurant, ahead of the times, and it set a spectacular example for the surge of Latin American food in the 1980s.

Travel writer Horace Sutton described it accurately: "Many will not be able to believe that it is a New York restaurant because people are not sitting all over people with their elbows in each other's conversation. As a matter of fact, the tables are spread all over the white marble floor as if nobody cared whether the cash box was stuffed or not. The Fonda del Sol gives an idea of what Latin America might be like if somebody like, say, Cecil Beaton were to stuff the best of it into one stage setting. . . . [It is hung] with as brilliant a collection of Latin American things as anyone has ever seen . . . woods from Brazil, floor tiles from Cuba." He added that the manager's name had been translated on his business card as "Federico Rufe."

The era of the "theme" restaurants was in full swing. The Baum triumvirate established the Forum of the Twelve Caesars as a place for the Roman Empire's opulent style of eating. Here the menus were studded with the kinds of lavishly prepared foods of the wilds that Jim had savored since childhood. And not only was there "Pheasant of the Golden House on a Silver Shield in Gilded Plumage" or "Truffle-Stuffed Quail, Cleopatra," there were "Wild Boar Pâté" and "Salad, the Noblest Caesar of Them All." Rockefeller Center, to which the Forum was adjacent, was a great power base of commerce and therefore needed, according to the Forum's creators, a salute to the Ancient World's political seat of power.

Restaurant Associates, however, did not need Suetonius or Apicius when the vision of the Four Seasons occurred to Baum. Beard had been waiting a long time to witness an *American* restaurant with ambitions, and he was ready to contribute ideas for "foods of the seasons to appear in their natural sequence," as he put it. "There would be the first asparagus, the first raspberries, things like wild mushrooms and fiddleheads that you seldom find on a menu. Baskets of fresh vegetables would be brought to your table to be chosen and cooked to order." Also to mark the quarterly shifts on the calendar, the decor of indoor trees, shrubs, and flowers followed the same seasonal pattern as the menus. Jim said in a column for syndication that one of his favorite specialties in any time of the year "has always been the Four Seasons steak with smothered onions, cooked and served in an iron skillet. A good thick cut of steak is sautéed in butter and a little oil, and then absolutely smothered with softly sautéed onions, cooked down until they are almost little strings, tender, flavorful, and aromatic." Jim's palate was not refined beyond redemption—nothing, perhaps, is more American than steak with onions, and he truly loved the combination.

A winter menu at the Four Seasons (said Michael and Ariane Batterberry in their illuminating account of New York hospitality, *On the Town*) "could only be treated with a kind of flabbergasted respect." Two feet long, just a sampling of its tastes can be included here:

> Small Clams with Green Onions and Truffles, 1.85; Iced Brochette of Shrimp, 2.50; Winter Farmhouse Terrine, 2.25; Virginia Blue Crab Lump, 3.25; A Tureen of December Fruit, .95; Steamed Mussels in Crock, HonFleur, 2.25; Crisped Shrimp Filled with Mustard Fruit, 2.35; The Four Seasons Mousse of Trout, 2.50; Beet and Lobster Madrilène, .95; Vermont Cheese Soup, 1.35; Barquette of Flounder with Glazed Fruits, 4.95; Red Snap-

per Steak—Grilled, 4.65; Carré of Meadow Veal, Mushrooms in Cream, 5.95; Breast of Chicken with Lobster, Nantua, 5.75; Jersey Poularde broiled over charcoal, 4.50; Amish Ham Steak, Apricot Glaze, 4.85; Spit-roasted Larded Pigeon with Candied Figs, 6.25; Bouillabaisse Salad, 5.25; Julep of Crabmeat in Sweet Pepperoni, 5.50; Zucchini and Hearts of Palm Lemon Dressing, 1.50; Soufflé of Artichoke, for Two, 3.85; Candied Harlequin Crêpes; Rose Petal Parfait.

Baum's imaginative relish for bountiful menus and Stockli's creative mating of fruits with meats and fish are here, and underlying all the Four Seasons bills of fare was Jim's enormous range of knowledge, the unfailing information about America's regional and seasonal harvests—the wild treasure as well as the yield of gardens and farms.

His influence at the Four Seasons never stopped after the rehearsal period when he was the avuncular drill sergeant who taught the dining room captains the *danse vendre* of service. His years of studious observation at Henri Soulé's Pavillon and his long acquaintance, professional and social, with Oscar of the Waldorf bolstered his own sure feelings of what impeccable service could do to enhance the satisfactions of dining in a restaurant. Jim had worked with Claude C. Philippe, who was Oscar's successor in personifying the Waldorf and who would be, in a year or two, briefly the replacement for Soulé after the latter's death. The Beard impact on the Four Seasons was nourished by the many kinds of gastronomical exposures he'd had.*

George Lang, the restaurateur, remembered meeting Jim in the Waldorf when Lang was beginning his career. "I was called in to Philippe's office and there was this large gentleman. He was like a Turkish pasha who knew the essentials of life. Philippe was there at his Louis XV table, looking through you, and Victor Borge was there." Having introduced Borge the entertainer as Borge the breeder of

---

*A couple of years before he died, Jim called my attention to this passage about restaurant service that he'd come across in Louise Brooks's nostalgic *Lulu in Hollywood:* " . . . when I was sawing away on a squab in the Colony, it scooted off my plate. One of the captains, Ernest, whisked it away and returned with a fresh squab, which I watched him carve on the service table. From then on, indifferent to the reactions of my dinner partners, I took instructions from the waiters on how to eat everything on the menu. There was how-to-bone-a-brook-trout night, how-to-fork-snails night, how-to-dismember-artichokes night, and so on until we came to the bottom of the menu, which included a dessert made up of the understanding and proper pronunciation of French words."

ViBo Rock Cornish hens, Philippe left. Jim sat up. "He suggested we do something amusing with the little birds—have a party with twenty-five hens, each boned and filled with a different stuffing. We hit it off right away. Later we thought it would be fun to transform the Waldorf ballroom into a midwest country tavern with a barbeque."

On the night of the dramatic event Jim was at stage center, cooking spareribs and hamburgers on an open grill, and neither he, George Lang, nor anyone else had given thought to fire problems. Flames shot up toward the high ceiling. Some of the Waldorf guests began to panic, but Jim had seen too many open fires to show any reaction. "While the fire department was being called, he was calm—hell, he was jolly, even though the flames were five feet high. His self-possession was enough to keep the evening going." Many dinner parties at the Waldorf were produced as in-house theater. With Elsa Maxwell reigning as the hotel's party-giver extraordinaire, Beard and Maxwell often found themselves together in food-and-entertainment ventures at the Waldorf. They had met in Paris when Elsa was developing her talent as a society hostess at a night club called Les Acacias, but they also had in common some youthful days in San Francisco. In the years when Jim would come down from Portland on the Southern Pacific to take in the opera, Elsa had met Tetrazzini when her father brought the singer home one day, and even so many years later, Jim couldn't get enough of the gossipy tales that Elsa liked to tell about Tetrazzini and her uninhibited ways.*

As Jim and Elsa Maxwell found common interest in music, so Jim also shared this interest with George Lang, who in his spare time played chamber music with the writer Joseph Wechsberg (who had profiled restaurant people ranging from a wine waiter at Maxim's and Roger Topolinsky at Laperouse to Fernand Point) and Arnold Gingrich,

*San Francisco was Tetrazzini's second home, and Elsa's father invited her to his apartment one day, Elsa told Jim. The soprano asked her host's daughter if she had a boyfriend, and after receiving a negative reply, cried, "Without love, child, you might as well be dead!" As it happened, during a hot fling with a handsome basso whom Tetrazzini had set her mind on marrying, the diva decided to elope. To elude her conductor husband, she encouraged him to drink until he was senseless. In Beard's version of the story, she and her lover stretched the sodden husband out on the floor, surrounded him with flowers, and, "like Tosca after bumping off Scarpia, they placed a lighted candle at head and feet and arranged a crucifix on his chest. Then they ran off. Of course it was not an affair of great duration."

the editor of *Esquire*. Lang's career crossed lines with Beard's in numerous ways, including a stint at Four Seasons when Lang managed it in the late sixties.

As a former prodigy on the violin who played in intimate groups, Lang had an ear for the affinities necessary for good performances, and he had a sharp eye for the things that distinguished the Four Seasons. "Joe Baum is brilliant at choosing the right person for the right job," Lang said to me one day in his book-lined garden office, "the way he did with Jim and Stockli. Jim was the spark plug; Albert was the engine. They bounced off each other. Albert was a very important part of Jim—he could execute his ideas beautifully. I remember their port wine sauce; it was so simple yet so good you would have an orgasm. You would never see veal smothered with cilantro, cumin, to kill the delicate flavor—the way you find it today."

In the words of Joe Baum:

> Being with Jim, he gave me such confidence—it was like watching a great artist, listening to a great singer. You never had to worry, you always knew that he was going to make the notes. When he worked in the kitchen the simplicity was one of elegance— unconsciously elegant—like watching some great sushi chef. He seemed to know *exactly* what he was doing. I sometimes felt that he must have lived with Colette. Who else would say, "And that reminds me of that wonderful little lamb stew I had the other night at Chuck Williams'—it was so wonderful you could cuddle it in your arms"?
>
> We went to Europe three or four times together. We had lunch in Saulieu at the Hôtel de Côte d'Or with Alexander Dumaine, whom he knew. Jim, you know, had poetic flights of appetite, and almost erotic times of satisfaction. To me, Jim could be expansively evocative about food; he gave life to the words. There were times when I needed that kind of stimulation. Once I asked him because I'd read, I think, in a collection of Mark Twain's where Mark Twain had done a whole page of just menu items.* So I asked Jim to do that—and he did. Wonderfully. Wonderfully. It began a lot like that when we first got together.

---

*In his travel book, *A Tramp Abroad*, Mark Twain complained, with no apparent tongue in cheek, about the inedibility of the fare that was offered him in Europe and said he was

A matter of sit down and talk. I'd say, "What do you think of this, Jim?" And he'd say, "Have you thought of so-and-so—you ought to read so-and-so."

People say he always agreed with you. Well, he didn't—he sounded as if he did, but people jump to first impressions. It's a matter of taking the trouble to hear what he was saying. You know, sometimes you have to peel something off to know what it is. I'd know that he'd maintained his position completely, and it was not a question of making trouble—it was just that he knew a

---

sending ahead his list of about 100 American dishes that he wanted to be ready for him upon his arrival. They included Philadelphia terrapin soup, canvasback duck, porterhouse steak, hot corn pone with chitterlings, lake trout from Tahoe, Connecticut shad.

lot of confrontation was not necessary, if there was another way to make the point.

It's hard to separate myth and legend, but with Jim I think it's not necessary. I always had the feeling he was living the second time around: "I've already done it, I've made my decisions." Like he could make you feel he really did care when he really didn't care—he'd seen it all. He had innate style. There was elegance in all that lusty strange self-irony—and maleness that made it all right for men to cook. There was that mixture of masculinity and social style, I think, that expressed so much of Jim. He was a treasure house of lives that I could never have lived, and of times that I could never have been a part of. Jim was so meaningful to my professional life—to my personal life. It's a treasure for me to horde. Nobody else was like him, he knew what it's all about. Jim had a life—not a mission.

And he had energy—energy to keep all those balls in the air. As his relationship with Baum was evolving, he had helped Leon Leonides to work out an American emphasis for food service at The Coach House, just as earlier he had offered advice when Eric Ladd had established a regional restaurant in one of Portland's traditional neighborhoods. In 1956, he renewed his interest in running a restaurant, and the experience soothed his memories of Nantucket. He'd been tapped for his services by Helen Sigel Wilson, a Philadelphia champion golfer who had inherited a family restaurant that had beguiled brokers, ad men, and the sports crowd with oversize drinks, and no more than a red-meat-and-potatoes menu. Coming in on a once-a-week consulting and teaching basis, Jim became a close friend of both Helen and her husband, Charles, and the Walnut Street eating place soon became known for such titillating innovations as chicken Paul Gauguin (baked with bananas, pineapple, and sausage) and crêpes ornamented by baked bananas, a filling of custard, and a caramel sauce flaming bright with Cognac. Jim then expanded this friendship by getting the Wilsons started in a suburban redoubt they called L'Auberge. As always, his ideas were innovative. Almost two decades before the campfire fuel of the Southwest was neatly described by Jim's friend Jeanne Voltz as "the wood of the moment," L'Auberge's menu was dominated by Specialties from Our Mesquite Grill, including a mixed grill consisting of a lamb chop, quartered chicken, and salmon steak.* Another of the Beard items on the menu was his carrot blini, served with caviar and sour cream (which turns up in his final book, *The New James Beard*). Also among dishes he devised for Philadelphia's Main Line—and also ahead of their time—were duck served with raspberries and a salad of apple wedges with crumbled Roquefort and a walnut oil dressing.

French touches like these seem to be fair enough in a country dining room called L'Auberge. They also reflect the travel schedule that took Beard on an average of two trips a year to Europe, as well as his alertness to good American cooking blended with that of countries from which so many immigrants had come. He was a consultant to another rural inn, near Brewster on Cape Cod, when one day in flicking through a French magazine he had an inspiration. He had come upon a reference to a cake composed of layered meringues and nut cream that reminded him of a similar cake made of stacked meringue shells that his friend Ann Seranne sometimes baked. It was just the thing, he thought, for a special dessert at the Chillingsworth Inn.

As he looked up from his reading, he saw his protégé John Clancy, down from Cape Cod on a weekend. It had been on Jim's advice that Robert Stevenson had hired Clancy as the chef of the Chillingsworth kitchen, and through Jim the inn on the Cape became the place where dacquoise began its American history as one of the most elegant of desserts. The moment meant so much to Clancy that he described it with enthusiasm in his book, *Clancy's Oven Cookery*.

As Jim translated from the French, reeling off the ingredients list, Clancy wrote it down. He recalled their excitement as Jim read aloud "the techniques for what turned out to be ground almond-filled meringues, and then the coffee butter cream to hold them together." As soon as he returned to Chillingsworth, he tried the

---

*In her *Barbecued Ribs and Other Great Feeds*, Jeanne Voltz says, "The chief advantage of mesquite, if you fall heir to a chunk or a bag of charcoal, is a hot fire, which sears the food quickly. Mesquite imparts a lightly woody flavor—best on beef, good on poultry, but sometimes slightly bitter on fish." In this fine book, she gives the recipe "from my dear friend Jim Beard" for grilled fillet with mushroom sauce; mesquite is optional.

recipe out at a tasting party for the press, with great success. Later, in the fall of 1959, Sheila Hibben of *The New Yorker* telephoned Jim in her search for new ideas in preparation for the Christmas issue. As Clancy remembered the episode, "Jim said, 'Call John Clancy. He makes a beautiful dessert called dacquoise. I'm sure he'll make one for you.'"

When Clancy, back in New York, became chef at The Coach House, he wrote, "I put it on their menu. Craig Claiborne came in and tasted it, then devoted a whole *New York Times* (Sunday) *Magazine* article to the recipe, along with a rave review."

Later still, Gino Cofacci, whom Jim had sent to study pastry-making in Paris, began turning out dacquoises to supply several New York restaurants, including the Four Seasons and Windows on the World. To keep up with the orders, he needed help, Gino said, and he managed to transform the Beard kitchen into an informal cake factory by dragooning other members of the ménage to volunteer as bakers. Two days a week, sometimes more, neighbors on Twelfth Street, enveloped in aromatic emissions, could not fail to recognize that Gino or his minions were at work.

Beard generally was well served by his disciples, but Clancy and he had some kind of falling out that left Jim unwilling to talk about Clancy's disloyalty, just as it caused Clancy to refuse to speak of Jim after the latter's death. Jim's experience with the Chillingsworth Inn, while it afforded him trips to Cape Cod with Gino as one of his companions, was scarred by some lack of appreciation on the part of Paula Wolfert, for whom he had also arranged a job in the inn's kitchen.

Wolfert, who was to become known with the publication of her *Couscous and Other Good Food,* had turned to Beard after a year's apprenticeship under Dione Lucas, and he had introduced her to the New York food scene by arranging a dinner which Paula was to cook. The guests included Clementine Paddleford, Helen McCully, and other food writers, and the result was the beginning of Wolfert's considerable impact on the food establishment. Jim then recommended the young woman as a caterer for a luncheon to be given by Mrs. Joshua Logan in Connecticut. The hostess had firm ideas about the menu but left the choice of dessert to Ms. Wolfert, who turned again to Beard for a cake that would be unusual. He suggested a recipe for a walnut roll, pointing out that it wouldn't be difficult to bring off. "It always works," he said sympathetically. "You can multiply the amounts for any size party. It's easy—and it's delicious." The walnut roll made a hit at the Logan party, and it became, in Paula Wolfert's eager hands, a favorite cake as her children were growing up and a constant reminder of Beard's inclination to help the new generation.

It was not uncommon, as Jim grew older, to have to deal with ruptures in relationships now and then. But the most remarkable quality about him continued to be his talent for establishing rapport with others. Among fellow professionals the woman with whom he shared a common commitment in basic philosophy (including skepticism) was the Nova Scotia–born Helen McCully. She championed Jim in numerous ways, including making available to the James Beard Cooking School the kitchens of *McCall's* magazine, where she reigned for seventeen years as food editor. Far more than such gestures indicate, she was his no-holds-barred friend and chief among those who called him daily before 7 a.m.

William North Jayme, friend of both, and one of McCully's collaborators, says that the greatest bond between Helen and Jim may have been their similar backgrounds, "Words hyphenated by such concepts as make-do, nothing-goes-wasted, and no-nonsense." Above all, the two early risers had unslakable appetites for gossip (or "gissip" as Jim liked to misspell the word in letters to Isabel Callvert). Before breakfast or afterward, depending upon who made the call first, they traded observations, often caustic, about the food world. As a mistress of four-letter expletives, Helen could make Jim laugh. (Jerry Mason's carefully chosen word for her is "effervescent.") She could also be abrasive in chastising her friend when he was less than letter-perfect in writing down recipe specifics. When they collaborated on an article for *McCall's* she would argue minor points with both affection and disdain. She was as close to him as any member of his appointed family with whom he shared the holidays.

She was the author of several cookbooks and albums of cooking information, one of which, entitled *Nobody Ever Tells You These Things*, is dedicated with the lines:

> For James A. Beard
> dear friend, dear mentor,
> who can tell you these things
> and everything else there is to know
> about food.

The sentimentality was typical of both of them. Her ears were all his when he felt like talking about the cooking school and its vagaries. Their mutual appetite for other people's foibles often meant shared amusement as when, for instance, the film star Gloria Swanson came to Beard's advanced class with her ingredients for macrobiotic meals— she wasn't there to brush up on haute cuisine, that was clear. And Clare Booth Luce, having retired from her ambassadorships, once telephoned Jim. "I've decided I don't want to be a slave to the slaves in my kitchen," he remembered her saying. "She had decided to cook for Harry herself." (That may have been an unlikely memory.) Mrs. Luce was a quick study at the stove, of course, and Jim checked in on her after she moved to Hawaii and found her still able to talk cooking with confidence, if not with as much enthusiasm as he hoped. She had taken a postgraduate course with Helen Worth. But like others of her background she seemed content to know just enough to be able to speak to her cook with knowledgeable demands.[*] Sylvia Jukes Morris, her biographer, says neither of the Luces had the remotest interest in food; nevertheless Mrs. Luce had an uncommon knack that she could reveal, to Jim's pleasure. Like him, she had learned as a youngster how to wring the neck of a chicken and, she recounted, had bowled over the strapping novelist Irwin Shaw when she dared him to match her lethal skill.

The James Beard Cooking School was moved after Helen McCully left *McCall's*. Jim had his own approach as always, and he said often that his chief aim was to convince his pupils that cooking is primarily

---

[*]Mrs. Worth reports that Mrs. Luce found Beard "so physically repulsive" she couldn't deal with his presence in a room as small as his kitchen, and therefore quit the class. Conversely, Leon Leonides, a classmate, found her "a good student" and was unaware of any rift.

fun, that the more people understand of cooking the more fun it is. His teaching plan was to set up lessons structured, as he said, on menus. His students learned how to time the preparation of a meal so that in having everything done at the right time, they mastered basic techniques of a variety of cooking methods. His buoyant personality helped to establish good chemistry with class members immediately, and some of them were so affected by his encouraging attitude that they became teachers themselves. And Peter Kump, who later founded his own professional school, was surprised when he asked Jim to come to dinner and the teacher of the new boy in class said yes. Jim seemed able to be as much at ease as a guest as he was as a teacher.

He fitted his teaching sessions into the schedule of the year with the same aplomb. He frequently managed to squeeze in time for relaxed trips to such places as Avery Island, to visit a Louisiana admirer, General Walter McIlhenny, and the rest of the Tabasco-making family; they had become close colleagues—as had Kate Titus Yutzy, of the public relations firm Dudley Anderson and Yutzy, who introduced them. As an almost unbreakable habit, a Beard trip to a new place seldom failed to add someone to his ever-embracing circle.

In those days there may have been a kind of madness in Jim's daily schedules. Jim had met a young writer and editor named John Ferrone, whom he sometimes encountered at dinner in the Jumble Shop in Greenwich Village, and he found in him a fellow enthusiast for antique hunting in village shops. At a party, Jim was introduced to Frank Taylor, sometime movie producer and editor-in-chief of Dell paperback books, for whom Ferrone worked. Immediately recognizing Beard's name, Taylor was inspired to propose the publication of the first soft-cover cookbook that would be basic and thorough enough to satisfy a mass market. With Isabel Callvert's agreement to come in as co-author, Jim added the *James Beard Cookbook* to his bag of projects. At the same time, the two collaborators continued with regular contributions to *House & Garden,* augmented with occasional articles for *Collier's, Look,* and *Woman's Day,* as well as a Baltimore periodical titled *Journal of the Societé des Gentilhommes Chefs.* As his list of followers increased steadily, the number of parties and informal buffet dinners grew accordingly.

And, of course, he was in constant demand as a dinner guest. He was frequently the attraction among the throng when Helen McCully gathered a mixed grill of people in her small penthouse above the restaurant Toque Blanche for a meal that might center around such a then-novel dish as *vitello tonnato.* Sometimes he was Cecily's only guest, and they argued "childishly" (Cecily's word) as transplanted Britishers, about how much suet was required in a proper pan of Yorkshire pudding. Kate Titus, the dynamic Madison Avenue executive, was a frequent and gracious hostess who served up her own good cooking when she entertained Jim and the elite of the food community. Squeezing in time to go out to Long Island, Jim played at clambakes with Kate, and once or twice he stopped for meals with the Italian family of Gene Poll, an account executive at DAY, as Kate's firm was called, for whom Jim served as consultant on the Florida Citrus account. Gene introduced him to her grandmother, who cooked *bagna cauda* and *polenta* at Jim's urging. " 'Come on, Nona,' he'd say [as Gene recalled], 'I'd love to have some of your Piedmontese secret specialties.' "

"Jim loved challenges," Gene Poll said one morning in her

flower-spattered office. "When I first talked to him about grapefruits, he said 'Fish. Have you ever thought of trying something like *seviche* with grapefruit?' Nobody then had ever heard of *seviche*. It was something he'd brought back from his South American days. I asked him to demonstrate *seviche* for the first time at a food editors conference in Chicago, and that's how this country came to recognize a native American way of 'cooking' fish without fire."

When it came to scaring up old recipes, Jim left no page unturned, no opportunity for "shop-lifting," as it were, bypassed. He had an instinct for finding comrades among homosexuals who had permanent relationships with others. Emil Kashouty, a DAY food stylist, once did a favor for Kate Yutzy by dropping off a package for Beard. Finding Jim whacked out at the end of a hectic day (as he described it), Emil hung around to prop him up with a large dose of admiration. When the talk touched on home cooking, Emil timorously suggested that Jim come for dinner and bring a friend so that Emil and his mate, Frank Hearne, could cook for their hero. The two planned a meal of roasted tenderloin with sauce béarnaise, and a dessert of cake custard; but they were uneasy about choosing a wine.

"I walked into Sherry's," Frank recalled, "and I was lucky enough to talk to Sam Aaron, who was so pleased that we were entertaining Jim Beard that he asked about the menu and suggested a modestly priced magnum of Pétrus. 'That will do beautifully,' he said. He made me feel so good that Emil and I forgot our fears. Jim and Gino arrived on schedule, and Jim immediately saw our collection of opera records. Dinner went just perfect. It turned out we liked the same singers, and the lemon thing was a wonderful old cake-pudding that my mother used to make and that Jim later put in his *American Cookery.*

"The evening was so enjoyable that before Jim and Gino went home at about three o'clock, I told him I'd read an article in the *Saturday Evening Post* about soufflés, adding that when I tried the recipe it turned out to be easy." Jim smiled at that, Frank remembered. Beard knew the article, which was soon republished in a book called *Cook Until Done,* the result of a collaboration between Ruth Norman and a writer named George Bradshaw. Jim told his new friends of Ruth's part in the cooking school, then invited Frank and Emil to come and make soufflés in his kitchen.

The foursome got on so swimmingly they spent holidays together on Cape Cod when Beard was helping the Chillingsworth Inn get started, and Jim was a visitor in Virginia when Frank and Emil moved south. As he had shown with Gene Poll's grandmother, he could win the trust of unsophisticated women as easily as he related to those of fashion and power; he and Emil's mother in Falls Church, Virginia, became cooking pals. Early on the first morning in the Kashouty house he'd been awakened by the sound of a heavy metal pestle pounding cut-up meat in a metal mortar. It turned out to be the preparation of baked *kibbeh,* his hostess's unusual variation of a Syrian lamb dish that was seasoned with allspice and pinenuts and baked in rows of sausage shapes. In *American Cookery* Beard points out how much a part of restaurant eating Middle Eastern food has become in this country.

Throughout his life he remained interested in recipes that were exchanged by neighbors of different ethnic backgrounds, and his discoveries influenced the guidance he offered restaurant clients, as well as the menus he used for his own parties. Often traveling in Pennsylvania Dutch country, he came to know the mother of his friend Fred Rufe, who was not simply a fine cook but a gifted quilt-maker who made several bedspreads for him. Mrs. Rufe also was the source of the recipe for the black walnut carrot cake included in *American Cookery.* Her soft lemon icing had proved to be such a success that her son licked his lips when he told me about it. Jim was, in the final essence, the insatiable *jäger,* a *chasseur* of recipes.

A dish he often served, called tapenade, "varies from town to town in Provence," he said, indicating that such a sauce for dunking vegetables lent itself to the imagination of cooks across the country. Among his students who worked professionally with him and had become cooking teachers themselves, a Chicagoan named Peggy Harvey gave a glimpse of her friend Jim in her book called *The Horn of Plenty,* and she introduced his way with tapenade: "When Mr. Beard serves it at a party in his colorful Greenwich Village kitchen (the classroom for his cooking school) he does not attempt to prettify it. However, for a large cocktail party at a food convention, when I assisted him, he added mayonnaise which made the mixture more appealing to the eyes of the uninitiated . . . " She also had an eye of her own for what there was about Jim that appealed to her and so many others like her.

"Jim is a big man; he has a big voice, a big appetite, a big reputation, a big heart and, as a result of the last," she wrote expansively, "a big group of friends to which I am proud to belong. His energy is as enormous as everything else about him. There is always a cookbook or a magazine article on the fire, so to speak. He is constantly just leaving on or just back from a trip involving a wine or food tasting, a consultation, or a demonstration. Occasionally these junkets force him to miss a Broadway opening or a Saturday afternoon performance at the Metropolitan but not if he can help it." She added that whether his kitchen was filled with students or with guests for a cocktail party or a buffet, "the jovial host is to be found looking as if he had nothing on his mind but the pleasures of the moment."

Peggy Harvey knew the pleasures of being among Beard's party guests, but with a husband and children in Chicago, she was not one of those (Fred Rufe, Les and Cleo Gruber, Helen McCully, the Callverts, Nika Hazelton and her husband, and various others on their own for holidays) who were brought together for Jim's familial feasting on the Fourth of July, Thanksgiving, or Christmas. When he finally had a garden of his own, he celebrated Independence Day outdoors to the sounds of firecrackers and hissing meat on the grill. On Thanksgiving, he might roast a joint of mutton to prove to doubters that it could be delicious and highly edible.

"He was a style-setter," says John Ferrone, voicing what is a near-unanimous observation. "His informal entertaining was elegant." He hated balancing dishes on knees, his table was set with oversize plates and cups, with interesting but unmatching pieces of china, ceramics, pottery, of faience picked up on travels. He chose dishes that enhanced the food and its display. "Whether or not the table settings mixed Chinoiserie with Italian," Ferrone points out, "it gave a kind of surprise and excitement."

From his fountain-pen apartment he had moved on to more commodious quarters on Twelfth Street, but he had unfulfilled dreams as always—he sensed that a house in Greenwich Village would serve as a status symbol, a small part of making the dream come true. And it had its practical reason as well—the cooking school needed space.

RECIPES

Cold Pumpkin Cream Bisque
▼

Beard and his friends the Browns were responsible for the hiring of Elena Zelayeta, a blind Los Angeles cook, as the creative chef of the restaurant La Fonda del Sol. Elena cooked as if she had no handicap, and she and director Fred Rufe turned out to be so well matched that she made him her unofficial son. He is also heir to some of the recipes that made the restaurant so distinguished, and this is one he contributed to the Beard treasure trove.

2½ pounds peeled pumpkin	salt
1¼ quarts chicken stock	freshly ground pepper
⅓ cup chopped onion	2 medium-sized ripe
6 scallions	tomatoes, sliced thin
1 cup light cream	1 cup heavy cream, whipped

Cut the pumpkin in pieces, put in a saucepan with the chicken stock, chopped onion, and the white part of the scallions, chopped. Bring to a boil and simmer until the pumpkin is very tender. Purée in a blender or food processor, then strain through a fine sieve. Set aside to cool. Stir in the light cream and season lightly with salt and freshly ground pepper. Pour into warm soup cups, and gently place a tomato slice on each portion so that it will float on top in the center of the soup. Decorate with a dollop of whipped cream and a sprinkling of minced scallion greens.   SERVES 8 TO 10.

Cucumbers in Sour Cream Cheese Sauce
▼

William Templeton Veach, friend and fellow cooking enthusiast, took note of this salad when Beard devised the dish for a buffet dinner in his Greenwich Village house. "It was a poem," was Veach's comment.

1 cup sour cream
1 tablespoon
grated horseradish
2 tablespoons grated
Emmenthaler cheese
1/2 teaspoon salt
1/2 teaspoon freshly grated
black pepper

1 teaspoon dry mustard
2 cucumbers, sliced very thin
(peeled only if waxed)
1 Bermuda onion,
sliced thin

Combine the sour cream with the horseradish, cheese, and the seasonings. Beat well. Toss the cucumber and onion slices with the sauce. SERVES 4 TO 6.

Paris Ritz Poached Egg Soufflé

▼

"I ate the most wonderful soufflé in Paris at the Ritz," Beard wrote to Isabel Callvert. "A very light cheese soufflé with no flour, according to me. Baked in a shallow oblong dish. Some of the mixture put in, then two poached eggs, the rest of the mixture, and some piped around the edge. Baked fast and it held up for the second helping!!! and was it ever delicious."

3 tablespoons white vinegar
salt
4 whole eggs
5 egg whites, at
room temperature
1 cup grated Swiss cheese
2 tablespoons soft butter

1/4 cup grated
Parmesan cheese
freshly ground pepper
2 tablespoons chopped fresh
herbs (parsley, chives,
and tarragon)

Fill a medium-sized skillet with water; add the vinegar and a big pinch of salt. Bring to a boil, then turn down the heat to a simmer. One by one, crack open the 4 eggs and carefully slip each one into the simmering water. Simmer each about 1 minute, until the whites coagulate around the yolks, then remove with a slotted spoon to a bowl of cold water. Beat the egg whites with a pinch of salt until firm peaks are formed. Fold the Swiss cheese into the whites, taking care not to deflate the whites. Have ready two small oval or round baking dishes which you have liberally buttered. Sprinkle about 1 tablespoon of the Parmesan on the bottoms of the dishes, then spoon about one-quarter of the egg-white mixture to barely cover the bottoms. Remove the eggs from the water with a slotted spoon, carefully roll in a paper towel to dry, trim away any ragged edges, then place 2 eggs in each dish. Season with salt and pepper. Spoon the remaining egg whites over and around the eggs and sprinkle the remaining Parmesan on top. Bake 12 minutes in a 400 degree oven, until whites are just firm. (Poke the sides with a pointed knife to make sure.) Sprinkle on the herbs and serve.   SERVES 2.

Carrot Blini à l'Auberge

▼

As both her great friend and her restaurant consultant, Jim helped create the menu for Mrs. Helen Sigel Wilson's L'Auberge in Philadelphia, where among the *specialités du chef* was this appetizer. Jim described it as a different and much simpler form of crêpe.

1 cup sifted flour	*1 cup milk, approximately*
3 eggs, lightly beaten	*1 cup shredded raw carrot*
3 tablespoons olive oil	*3 tablespoons butter*
1 teaspoon salt	*sour cream*
1/4 teaspoon freshly ground	*red caviar*
* black pepper*	

Put the flour in a bowl and stir in the lightly beaten eggs, oil, salt, and pepper, and just enough milk to make a thick batter. Stir in the shredded carrot. Heat enough butter to cover the surface of a heavy skillet and drop in the batter with a large spoon to make pancakes about 3 inches in diameter. Cook on both sides until lightly browned, adding more butter to the pan as needed. Serve with a dollop of sour cream and a teaspoonful of red caviar for each blini.   SERVES 8.

Persian Lamb with Rhubarb

▼

Jim liked nothing better than cooking in ways that celebrated the season. For an April dinner with us among those present he served this unusual lamb dish, saying that he had noted the recipe when he'd eaten the dish at a friend's home. He announced that the best time to make it is when spring rhubarb—preferably the brilliant red cherry rhubarb—first appears in markets.

2¹/₂ cups sliced rhubarb
³/₄ cup sugar
³/₄ cup water
4 tablespoons butter
1 large onion, chopped
1 pound lean lamb, cut in
  1-inch cubes
1 teaspoon salt

¹/₂ teaspoon freshly
  ground pepper
¹/₂ teaspoon cinnamon
¹/₂ teaspoon freshly
  grated nutmeg
1 cup chopped parsley
1 tablespoon cornstarch

Put the rhubarb in a bowl with the sugar and water and marinate for 30 minutes. In a large heavy skillet melt the butter and sauté the onion until translucent. Add the lamb cubes and brown on all sides. Season with salt, pepper, cinnamon, and nutmeg. Stir in the parsley and continue cooking 2 minutes. Drain the syrup from the rhubarb and add.

Transfer the meat mixture to a covered casserole with the onion. Cover with a round of wax paper cut to the same size as the casserole, then cover with a lid and simmer very gently for 30 minutes. Stir in the reserved rhubarb and continue simmering for another 20 to 30 minutes or until the lamb is very tender. Taste for seasoning. Combine 1 tablespoon of cornstarch with 1 tablespoon of cold water and stir into the meat mixture. Cook gently for 3 minutes, until the sauce thickens. (The rhubarb and onions will have melted down.) Serve over hot cooked rice.   SERVES 4.

Lamb Loaf

▼

A cook could win as much as $25,000 for a recipe entered in one of those Pillsbury Bake-Offs that Jim judged once or twice, but for the "Great Hamptonian Meat-Loaf Bake-Off," originated by Shana Alexander, the object was to bring some perky seasoning to Long Island winter doldrums. The commercial Hamburger Helpers were eschewed, perhaps in response to Beard's dictum that a meat loaf needed no better example than his mother's pâté for Oregon picnics. His own recipes sometimes were accented by ground ham, minced clams, or stuffed olives. Here is a basic loaf that is uncommon in its use of ground lamb.

2 pounds ground lamb	1 clove garlic, chopped fine
1 cup dry breadcrumbs	salt
1/4 cup finely chopped onion	1/2 teaspoon dry mustard
1/4 cup finely	2 eggs
chopped parsley	4 strips bacon

Mix the ground lamb with the crumbs, onion, parsley, garlic, a light sprinkling of salt, and the mustard, then break in the eggs. Form the mixture into a loaf on a shallow pan to collect the juices. Lay the bacon strips across the top. Bake in a preheated 350 degree oven for 50 to 60 minutes. Serve with deep-fried onion rings and a green salad.   SERVES 6.

Lobster Pizza Reprise

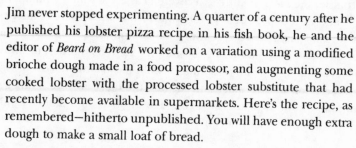

Jim never stopped experimenting. A quarter of a century after he published his lobster pizza recipe in his fish book, he and the editor of *Beard on Bread* worked on a variation using a modified brioche dough made in a food processor, and augmenting some cooked lobster with the processed lobster substitute that had recently become available in supermarkets. Here's the recipe, as remembered—hitherto unpublished. You will have enough extra dough to make a small loaf of bread.

Dough:

1 tablespoon active dry yeast	2 large eggs
1/4 cup warm water	1/4 cup nonfat dry milk
2 teaspoons sugar	dissolved in 3/4 cup water
3 1/2 cups all-purpose flour	dusting of cornmeal
2 teaspoons salt	
3 tablespoons butter, at room temperature	

Filling:

12 ounces cooked lobster in bite-sized pieces (combined, if desired, with processed lobster substitute)	8 scallions, sliced, including tender green
	1 good-sized red bell pepper, chopped in small dice
	drops of fresh lemon juice

3/4 cup ricotta cheese
5 ounces shredded mozzarella
salt
freshly ground pepper
4 tablespoons chopped fresh
*   tarragon or basil*

4 tablespoons freshly grated
*   Parmesan cheese*
2–3 teaspoons olive oil

To make the dough: Dissolve the yeast in the warm water and stir in the sugar. Spin the flour with the salt in a food processor. With the motor still going, add the butter and eggs, then the dissolved yeast and the milk. Process until the dough forms a ball around the shaft, adding a touch more water if necessary. Turn the dough out and knead it briefly by hand. Transfer it to a large buttered bowl, cover, and let rise in a warm place until doubled in volume, about 1 hour.

Preheat the oven to 450 degrees. Tear off 2 pieces of the risen dough that are slightly less than the size of a tennis ball. (Punch down the remaining dough and put into an 8-inch buttered loaf pan; cover loosely.) Roll each of the balls of dough out on a floured surface to circles 9 inches in diameter. Transfer the disks to baking sheets that have been sprinkled with cornmeal (or to a paddle, if you have an oven lined with baking tiles and can slip the pizzas directly onto the hot tiles to bake). Arrange equal amounts of the lobster meat, scallions, and red pepper over the 2 circles of dough. Season with drops of lemon juice, then spread the ricotta around, sprinkle mozzarella on top, and season with a little salt and generous grindings of pepper. Sprinkle the herbs and Parmesan on top and drizzle a little olive oil over. Bake for 12 minutes, until the dough is lightly browned and the filling bubbling.

(For the loaf, turn the oven down to 350 degrees after the pizzas have baked and, when the dough has doubled in volume, bake the loaf for 45 minutes.)　　　SERVES 2 TO 4 DEPENDING ON APPETITES; PLUS 1 LOAF BREAD.

Basil Buttermilk Bread

▼

Jim never could ignore a good bread. After his own *Beard on Bread* had become a huge success in Japan, he made a trip to Australia and, as always, continued collecting recipes—this one turning up in a country inn not far from Melbourne. It does not require yeast, and can be made with dried basil, but it won't be as aromatic.

3 cups all-purpose flour,
  sifted, plus extra
  for dusting
1¹/4 teaspoons baking soda
¹/2 teaspoon salt

¹/2 cup chopped fresh basil
¹/2 teaspoon freshly
  ground pepper
2 tablespoons melted butter
1¹/3–1¹/2 cups buttermilk

In a bowl or an electric mixer with a dough hook, combine the sifted flour, baking soda, salt, basil, and pepper. Rub in the melted butter. Make a well in the center and mix in the buttermilk until you get a soft sticky dough, adding more flour if needed. Turn out on a floured board. Knead just enough so that the dough becomes smooth and holds its shape. Soda bread doesn't require much kneading. Form into a round loaf, flour the top heavily to give the loaf a crusty finish, then place in a well-buttered 8- or 9-inch round cake pan. Bake at 450 degrees for 40 minutes. Allow to cool.   MAKES 1 LOAF.

Jim's Walnut Roll

Having grown his own walnuts as a youngster, Jim always liked to find unusual ways of using the nuts. Outdoorsmen who know his books about cooking at a campfire learned to roast walnuts in the coals and indoor cooks followed his lead by adding walnuts to salads and vegetables such as eggplant and zucchini. Generous as always in sharing recipes with colleagues, he recommended that Paula Wolfert (see pages 216–17) use this recipe for dessert when, as a beginner, she catered a luncheon party.

5 eggs
¹/2 cup sugar
¹/8 teaspoon salt

¹/2 teaspoon baking powder
5 ounces walnuts, finely
  ground (1¹/4 cups)*

Filling:
¹/2 cup milk
6 ounces walnuts, finely
  chopped (1¹/2 cups)*
¹/4 pound unsalted butter

²/3 cup sugar
2 tablespoons cognac
1 cup heavy cream, whipped
confectioner's sugar

*Walnuts may be ground or chopped in a food processor but do only a few ounces at a time and add a sprinkling of the sugar to keep them from becoming oily.

Separate the eggs. Beat the egg yolks until lemony, then add the sugar slowly and continue to beat until fluffy. Add the salt, baking powder, and ground walnuts. Beat the egg whites until they form firm peaks and fold them into the batter. On both sides generously butter wax paper cut to fit the bottom and sides of an 11 × 17-inch jelly-roll pan. Line the pan and pour the batter in, spreading it evenly. Bake in a preheated 375 degree oven for 12 to 15 minutes. Meanwhile, make the filling. Heat the milk and pour it over the chopped walnuts; set aside to cool. Cream the butter and sugar together, then beat in the nuts and soaking milk, and the cognac. Fold in the whipped cream. When the cake is done (a straw inserted in the center should come out clean) invert it onto a towel dusted with confectioner's sugar. Peel off the paper and roll the cake up from the narrower end, the towel inside. Let cool on a rack. To fill, unroll the cake, spread the filling on, and then roll the cake up, using the towel to help roll it. Turn onto a platter and dust the top with confectioner's sugar. SERVES 8.

9

The Upward Curve

He would never be cured of his compulsion to travel nor entirely relieved of his yearning to own a restaurant or to be a country innkeeper. But when Agnes Crowther White called him about a house she had found for him to buy, he was on the verge of an equally important fulfillment.

Agnes, the Portland interior decorator who had become a New Yorker and skillfully manipulated the spaces of Jim's tiny flat, had since married the real estate broker William White. She was one of Jim's foster siblings—not a childhood playmate as was Mary Hamblet, not a fellow thespian as was Harriet Cass, not like any of the others. She seemed a bit odd, even reserved, to some of the "family," always quietly dressed, husbanding her creativity for the interiors she designed for others. "She could tune in on Jim's personality," was the way it seemed to John Ferrone. "She could put personal things together sensitively and imaginatively to express Jim's taste in whatever he might require."

Ferrone is persuaded that Agnes White gave Jim a lot of the style "we recognize as Jim's." But the Beard taste in collecting pieces of porcelain and objets d'art began with his mother and the interest she shared with Mary Hamblet's mother which she had expressed in buying Canton dishes. Mary and Jim carried on the tradition as they visited antique shops together, or gave each other things they found in their separate sorties. Jim was an inveterate pot-hunter in dark and cluttered bric-a-brac emporiums, and many friends, Frank Hearne among them, served him as foils as he pursued his interest in old pottery. John Ferrone himself observed Jim's taste as they set out together on antique hunts in London once or twice, and in the aisles of Hamilton-Hyre on Bleecker Street.

The decor of the townhouse that Jim purchased through Agnes White began almost at once to take on the complexion and sense of style that these two had in common. As background there was wallpaper that bore the conventionalized design of outsize pineapples, each bigger than Jim's massive skull. Upstairs, there may have been one of the first examples of the trend toward modern home kitchens conceived as rooms to be decorative, as well as efficient. The floors were of rosy terracotta Spanish tiles. Among the collected ceramics were oyster dishes hung on the wall not far from antique copper molds, and there were vintage wineglass-rinsers in amethyst, amber, and white Bristol glass.

As a new homeowner, Jim drew on his accumulated theories about kitchens as well as on the research for his introduction to a facsimile edition of *The Modern Housewife,* written a century earlier by Alexis Soyer, noted Victorian gastronome. "All the great developments kitchen-wise, of our day," Beard wrote, "can be traced to this creative brain whose genius really revolutionized cookery. . . . His inventions have remade the labor of kitchens into the easy thing it is today. . . . he published kitchen designs for average homes, for small cottages, and even for bachelor's quarters. One of his inventions attracted unusual attention, the portable Magic Stove." Jim pointed out that much of the contemporary efficiency of home kitchens—and the backyard grill, to boot—had to be credited to Soyer, the chef of London's Reform Club.

The focal point of the new Beard kitchen was a horseshoe-shaped counter embedded with electric cooking plates. The unit could be covered with Formica that was tailored to fit so that it furnished an attractive surface on which cooking students could eat the meals they prepared; and the same effect worked well at the big parties that were always centered in the kitchen. In spite of criticism, Beard remained all his life "an electric cook," as he put it, and he pointed out that there was an admirable likeness to his mother's

Clay with Jim

wood-fired range on which cooking pots could be slid easily from a spot of intense heat to another moderate hot-spot.

In the garden behind the house was the bronze bust of Beard by André Surmain's father, who sometimes entertained Jim in Majorca, and, near the bed of kitchen herbs, was the form of a Périgord truffle-hunting pig that once had been a charcuterie sign. The four-story house and all it held was (in a long-looked-forward-to way) a celebration of Jim's recent success with his latest book. More significant than any of the tangible acquisitions was the addition to his ménage of Clay Triplette, a young black man who had grown up in upstate New York, but had a soft Southernness about him. (Yet he was quick on his feet, zipping around, flicking a towel—and he was charming. His big smile, infectious laugh, and ease with people were to be just the thing to add zest when he helped with cooking classes.) In his search for work, Clay had made the kind of impression on André Surmain that caused André to call Jim Beard. Jim took one look at Clay and said, as the latter remembers, "I just want you to come in and completely take over."

Clay took over the housekeeping, took over the food shopping from Ruth Norman, took over the role of a short, sassy concierge at 119 West Tenth Street. He became the star's dresser, his sometime assistant (a mere walk-on part) in demonstrations, and, to boot, the household seamstress, who received the shipments of designer fabrics that Jim was to send home from his travels for the making of robes and kimonos. He and Gino Cofacci, Jim's frequent opera companion and sullen ward, sometimes scrapped, yet of all the Tenth Street cortege they alone finished the play.

The spring collection of *The James Beard Cookbook* was a singular event, the first soft-cover, pocket-sized collection (publisher Frank Taylor's cocktail-party inspiration) of hundreds of recipes, and it was an event that was roundly hailed by *Publishers Weekly,* the voice of the book industry:

> James Beard's latest publication, *The James Beard Cookbook* (Dell), is a runaway, outselling even the firm's current top fiction title, *The Anatomy of a Murder,* in New York. The day before publication the *New York Times* ran a half-page feature about the book. . . . Stores and newsstands all over town were immediately sold out. The *Times* woman's page department had so many inquiries that it had to shut off its telephones. The *Times* story, which pointed out that Mr. Beard's book tells the housewife everything, including how to boil water, was picked up by CBS.

Publishers Weekly noted, several years before the beginning of television's coast-to-coast attention to the increasing interest in food, the evolving recognition of how Americans cook:

> More than any other author of cookbooks, perhaps, [Beard] had introduced Americans to gourmet food, though he says he dislikes the word "gourmet" and wishes he could invent another word for imaginative, well-cooked meals. He favors what he calls a "narrative type of recipe," and he writes in a rather chatty style.

In being interviewed for the article, Jim found the chance to reiterate his musings to Helen Brown about "home economics" attitudes: "A cold approach scares the housewives. It's like giving them a chemical formula." The article went on to say that Beard endeavors to convey the idea that cooking is fun, and that he wants to take the snobbism out of fancy food. "People still like to eat, even though they are literally unable to eat as much as they did a century ago," he said.

Another change had been noted. *PW* had clearly been impressed by the fact that the *Times* had devoted a half-page with pictures to a review of *The James Beard Cookbook.* As the writer of the piece, Craig Claiborne (who had replaced Jane Nickerson) was himself a symbol of the emerging importance of food in the lifestyle Americans were assuming. Claiborne's review of the book, on what was then the "Food Fashions Family Furnishings" page of the *Times,* observed that "the recipe range is vast. There is not a gastronomic cliché in the book, and the principal reason undoubtedly is that Mr. Beard is not an armchair cookbook author. He is a kitchen wizard." Claiborne pointed to a remarkable fact about the new volume. "This book, which will be available at many of the nation's newsstands, bookstores and supermarkets beginning tomorrow, is a paperbound volume. It costs seventy-five cents."

The price was right. Few neophyte cooks thought then of shelling out money for a cookbook when they already had one, but a paperback was worth the risk. It was a time when most households relied on one or two basic texts—*Fannie Farmer* or *The Joy of Cooking,* plus occasional boxtop recipes suggesting new uses for dehydrated soup and cornflakes as a quick casserole topping. It was a time when the food industry continually hammered at consumers trying to persuade them that the modern pace of life left no time for traditional cooking—leaving women who liked to cook feeling vaguely guilty.

Jim's idea-packed book offered an enormous variety of appetizing recipes in clear, concise, and—best of all—reassuring language. Now, instead of having standard weekly roast chicken, one could vary things—chicken with olives and chilies, chicken with tomatoes and bacon, chicken in white wine with tarragon butter sauce, chicken in red wine, chicken with cream and prosciutto, ad infinitum. Entertaining friends at home was not drudgery; it was drama, Beard style.

The *Times* review had less to do with the attention allotted to a paperback than its shift in editorial policy. Cultural affairs were beginning to get daily attention, and the review of a paperback book, unusual in itself, fitted into the scheme of giving space to feature articles based on the new interest in food and its place in social history.

Claiborne had entered the New York food world after graduation from the L'Ecole Professionelle de la Societé Suisse de Hôtelier. He had applied for a job with Helen McCully but was rejected because she scoffed at a notion he held in common with Beard—that serious cooking by average persons was a part of the future. So instead, Craig managed to get a job with Ann Seranne at *Gourmet*. Later when Ann left the magazine and formed a public relations office to handle food accounts, Claiborne went along, and through Ann he met Jane Nickerson, just as she was resigning from the *Times*. Still working for Ann's agency, however, Craig had a bad beginning with Beard, who was a guest at a press party. What happened—in the opinion of Craig and other Beard-watchers—was typical of Jim. He passed around the platter of shrimps that Craig had fried in beer batter with accents of sherry. "Graciously, Jim picked up the platter and offered the shrimp, so that people got the idea he'd done the cooking. But he never said a word when the crowd mistakenly gave him credit, and that's the way he was a lot of the time," Claiborne said. "Somehow he got credit for other people's things."

Less specifically, others who knew Jim well and held him in affection told of similar instances. Yet in this case, perhaps unaware of the vibrations, Jim often entertained Craig—as entries in a daybook for the period make clear—in spite of Claiborne's certainty that he remembers no such occasions. Ann Seranne, however, did remember times when she and Craig went together to partake of Jim's largesse. Still, no comradeship developed between the two men.

After he was hired to succeed Nickerson, Claiborne's rise was swift. With the *Times* readership at his command, he soon became the critic that restaurateurs had to respect for the effect his reviews had on diners, and it wasn't long before his name also was emblazoned on *Times* delivery trucks in much the same way as the newspaper exploited sports writers and other columnists. The recognition of the importance of food as a subject of general interest confirmed Jim's years of commitment and his preeminence as a pioneer of American cooking.

"Within a year," Craig wrote in *A Feast Made for Laughter* about his joining the *Times*, "I had traveled around the world on an eating expedition with James Beard, Lester Gruber, owner and host of the London Chop House in Detroit, and his wife, and Helen Evans Brown, the well-known West Coast cookbook author." Jim, as usual, was the catalyst. He had earlier introduced Craig to Mrs. Brown by describing him in a letter as "a really marvellous cook." There wasn't any question about Craig's ability—with the training he had had in the tile-roofed academy for chefs on Lake Geneva. In contrast, Craig minimized Jim as an unsophisticated cook, although he characterized *The James Beard Cookbook,* twenty years later, as "one of the first and best basic cookbooks to be published in the present age . . . the recipes are excellent for the beginning cook." He made a point of adding that Beard had had "the invaluable assistance of Isabel E. Callvert."

Of the round-the-world trip, Craig pointed out, when we talked, that because of his size Jim had to travel first class to be able to sit. "He hated eating in Japan, because he couldn't sit comfortably on the floor." Maybe. But it is instructive to remember that Jim, as an incurable romantic about picnics, was never known to be unable to lower his body into position for eating at ground level—often managing to balance champagne poured into Baccarat stemware.

When the globe-girdling party was in Teheran, Craig ate a salad bowl of caviar while delayed at the airport, and Jim and the Grubers and Helen Brown went restaurant-hopping, and otherwise canvassing the food scene. Jim recalled "with much nostalgia" a dinner under the trees in Iran "that started with masses of caviar, and then went on to skewers of charcoal-broiled sturgeon that had been marinated in yogurt and herbs. This was served on a bed of cracked wheat, with its lovely nutty texture and flavor." Claiborne caught up with the rest of the troupe and he and Jim met frequently thereafter, but Craig harbored his first impression of Jim as a man he judged to be all-too-often making use of ideas he picked up from others without credit.

Jim, no less than other food writers, did use recipes from various sources—from old cookbooks and old friends, from strangers who mailed them to him, from friends he often credited and from some he didn't. He liked to point out that there were no really original recipes.* He had no compunction about accepting free breakfasts, lunches, and dinners. Sometimes he was conveniently absentminded about what he had received from others. But in the view of his friend Leon Leonides, proprietor of The Coach House restaurant, however, "He was the most generous and unassuming man I ever met. He loved people and was always eager to share his vast knowledge of their history and the development of the American cuisine. He never hesitated to share his personal recipes with anyone who wanted them."

Some friends tended to laugh behind his back at Jim's ease in letting others pick up the check; they said his arms were too short and his pockets too deep. There were some who, when he wasn't present, criticized him for taking money for the use of his name, and he was aware of the resentment. He needed money, however, and there seemed never enough royalties, fees from magazine articles, demonstrations, or lectures to completely cover the cost of life as he thought it should be lived. He said he had to accept payment for endorsing products in which he believed in order to pay his bills.

Free-lancing was precarious. He needed to be in charge of his own calendar, going and coming, and he also had to have sources of income which paid more liberally than most editors, restaurant owners, or the nonprofessional promoters of lectures or demonstrations. Public appearances were essential to his design for living. They got him to new places, into the heart of America—before the media had made a commonplace thing of exploring ordinary lives. Much of the time his trips took him into the kitchens of everyday people in small towns like Le Sueur, Minnesota, or the mountain cabins of Basque shepherds. He and Ruth Norman periodically booked the cooking school as a two-person traveling show called "The Art of Cooking," with appearances sometimes sponsored by the French National Association of

---

*His credo: "When I wander into a market... I may see a different cut of meat or an unusual vegetable and think 'I wonder how it would be if I took the recipe for that sauce I had in Provence and put the two together?' So I go home and try it out. Sometimes my idea is a success and sometimes it is a flop, but that is how recipes are born. There really are no recipes, only millions of variations sparked by somebody's imagination and desire to be a little bit creative and different. American cooking is built, after all, on variations of old recipes from around the world." From *James Beard's Theory & Practice of Good Cooking*.

Cognac Producers—but with modest monetary rewards. The fun was in being James Beard. Wasn't he born to be a star?

Yvonne Rothert of the Portland *Oregonian* described one of his arrivals at a downtown hotel. "A giant of a man, wearing a vast opera cape, swept dramatically across the lobby, plainly savoring the glances that followed his progress toward the elevator."* Of his stage appearance, Rothert said to me, "The pace was frenzied. Beard dominated one cooking station, his associate was at another, and someone from the audience at a third, and the action was swift as Jim called the shots in bringing a recipe alive. Writing the story, I couldn't resist using the baseball triple-play metaphor—Tinkers to Evers to Chance. When I showed him the piece, Jim roared with laughter. He *knew* he'd been a hit."

It was in Paris that there came an upsurge in his career that must have been a surprise. Cecily Brownstone, there on a food junket sponsored by Pillsbury, introduced him to Bill Powell, the flour company's promotion man. "We had a Scotch together at the Ritz bar, and we hit it off," Powell told me over breakfast one day. He pulled out of his pocket a silver object. "Jim gave me this," he said. He turned the top of a small ornamental grinder, dusting his eggs. "It's a pepper mill—Jim would order a martini, straight up, no lemon rind, no olive. Jim would pull this out and grind black pepper on his gin."

The two kept in touch. "The next year I talked him into doing a cooking course for our top management. None of them knew how to cook, that was women's stuff. Jim put on a show that pricked their complacency and, after a solid week of classes, turned them into good enough cooks to put on a fancy dinner. They loved showing off to their wives. And that was when Pillsbury bought the promotion idea that cooking can be fun, for everybody—and we ran with it."

Bill Powell was an enthusiastic hobby-cook who was alert enough as a food professional to realize *Gourmet* magazine was on the right

---

*"Beard is fat, for instance, but fat in a way that makes thin people wistful," John Skow wrote in a magazine piece. "Most cooks are fatty, which is not the same thing; they are puffed and pounded from a lifelong battle with cream sauce. Beard's great body is that of the rare athlete who is exactly sized for his specialty. He has a thick, powerful neck and small, pointed ears. He looks like a wrestler who has begun to melt, a genie who has started to solidify."

track. On liquor shop counters, he began to notice a give-away magazine called *Bon Appétit* at a time when there was an industry rumor that both Time, Inc., and American Express had tried to buy out Earle MacAusland. "I talked the situation over with Jim, and I talked him into being the editor of *Bon Appétit*—if I got Pillsbury to buy it." Powell had to smile at that. "But the board of directors didn't want to risk it."

Beard and Powell remained friends, and Jim's counsel helped Pillsbury's research and development division to solve technical problems in creating refrigerated crescent rolls as Americanized *croissants*—a product that was as effective as pita bread (a gift to the average United States kitchen from Middle Eastern immigrants) in enlarging common attitudes toward what a sandwich could be. From time to time flying into Minneapolis, Beard was a free-thinking influence on the meetings at Pillsbury that resulted in the new promotion of home-baked bread, as well. Before he wrote his own bread book, in 1978, he had published (in *James Beard's Treasury of Outdoor Cooking*) his basic formula for what he called "Cuban bread," an easy-to-do homemade version of the French *baguette* that his friend Julia Child was to help establish in America through the second volume of *Mastering the Art of French Cooking*.

Before he and Mrs. Child were to meet, Jim had become a frequently called-upon adviser to the Green Giant Company, an assignment which required, as did his Pillsbury connection, recurrent trips to Minnesota. The first of these was the result of a casual call on André Surmain in New York by Edward Ritchell, a Green Giant food technologist (almost as much an opera buff as Jim, who, as luck would have it, happened to be present). Ritchell and Beard, with participation by Green Giant's advertising agency, became deeply involved in producing a booklet of recipes for which Jim provided such culinary tips as "No vegetable exists which is not better slightly undercooked"—a thought that then hadn't occurred to a lot of Americans still boiling green beans for forty minutes.

Working with the company staff, Jim developed a butter sauce for peas that was packaged in a pouch contrived especially to hold the vegetable for cooking briefly in boiling water. With Helen Evans Brown once more his partner, he worked out new recipes for cooking

Green Giant vegetables as accompaniments to meals prepared over outdoor fires. One was called Green Giant Pea Pie, an adaptation of the tart of peas which his friend June Platt had given him for use in his *Fireside Cook Book.* For broiling over the edge of glowing charcoal, he suggested seasoning Niblets corn and Green Giant peas with basil to stuff ripe tomatoes wrapped in foil.*

Sometimes he worked on the recipe development in his own New York kitchen, but he was often at the stove (with his protégé John Clancy as an assistant) in the company's test kitchens in Le Sueur in the Minnesota River valley. He became as much a local hero as the Green Giant himself when it came to eating out, and his gargantuan appetite is still remembered at the former Holland House, an inn on the river, and at the Blue Horse restaurant in St. Paul, where the menu for years included "Oysters James Beard."

Jim Martell, who owned the Holiday House, was considered "a magician with food" by Beard. One of the specialties was a steamed cranberry pudding with "baked-on frosting" that was a mixture of brown sugar, butter, sour cream, and grated coconut put under the broiler until it bubbled and turned golden. The stuffed pork roast was a meat course typical of southern Minnesota kitchens, and Martell's rendition was a memory Jim kept. He knew enough about American food to have no doubts about what was good and what was bad about it.

His fellow diners at Holiday House, and other places in the hinterlands, remembered Jim's capacity. "He could clean up a platter of peeled red peppers all by himself," Ritchell said to me, enviously, "then do away with a whole order of polenta." But he disdained the wild rice for which Minnesota Indians are famous, telling Ritchell it wasn't rice at all and had an unattractive musty flavor.

Jim is equally remembered for his Holiday House run-in with a bathroom shower designed for average human beings. When Jim got in it, after one of his huge meals, he had to call for help. He was told to use more soap and to keep the water running so he could free the flesh from the pebbled glass sides—in order to slide himself out.

*When he was in London for a promotion party sponsored by the company, Helen Brown wrote, in vexation: "Damn Green Giant! Are they going to dress you up in green corn stalks?"

The vicissitudes of travel were part of a thespian's life and added to Jim's sense of "being on" all the time. He didn't like airplanes but for many domestic trips he had to use them ("I think I was born with an airplane ticket in my mouth," he once said). Still, "half the pleasure," as advertisements in the fifties and sixties said, was "getting there"—if he could go by sea. He often told friends that the S.S. *France* was his favorite vessel, and it might be that the special attention he habitually got on board had something to do with it. His steward knew he had an insatiable yen for white bread sandwiches made with white meat chicken and a little butter; every night there would be left for him in his cabin a large plate with a white napkin protecting the sandwiches. Yet, he loved *all* luxury liners, and he preferred to go to England and France by ship. Details touched him—he remembered "the beautiful bowl of crystallized ginger" at the entrance of the *Queen Elizabeth I*'s roof terrace dining room.

He invariably made it a point of getting to know the kitchen staff, the captain, and many of the ships' crews, and he was considered an attractive addition to passenger lists. On one April sailing of the S.S. *United States*, he drew as table mates Donald Morris, a young American naval officer, and his "ravishing" wife Sylvia; she was the daughter of Lawrence Stallings, the playwright he had known in Hollywood. And Jim also knew Lewis Gannett who was Sylvia Morris's boss at the book section of the New York *Herald Tribune*. The other passengers included people whose names were celebrated in the period. There were C. W. Ceram, whose *Gods, Graves and Scholars* had become a surprise bestseller, the screen writer Garson Kanin, and Rita Hayworth "who remained secluded in her suite the entire voyage. The first evening, *inter alia*," Donald Morris said in a letter to me, "we discussed an anthology of wine short stories, and I pointed out that the field was pretty thin—all by Dorothy Sayers, and one by Roald Dahl. Beard, who seems to have been a whodunit fan, mentioned that there had never been a good wine murder."*

---

*Twenty years later Beard's younger contemporary Alexis Bespaloff published *The Fireside Book of Wine*, an anthology which includes Dahl's chilling story entitled "Taste," an extract taken from Dorothy L. Sayers, and a witty anecdote from Julian Street about wine as a tooth-brushing liquid.

Morris found his fellow traveler "shockingly obese," and estimated his weight at about three hundred twenty-five pounds. He thought Beard didn't look healthy, although "he was lively and vivacious, and appeared in a dinner jacket every evening." Commander Morris draws from his daily journal to provide a portrait of Beard as a social animal in the late fifties, and it ripples with insights:

> The second evening there was a bit of a roll, but Beard was a good sailor. We met him for cocktails before dinner, and he started rolling his eyes and announcing in a melodramatic, side-of-the-mouth stage whisper, "I have much dirt." He turned out in fact to be a walking compendium of all scurrilous ship-board gossip; he knew and listed exactly who was sleeping with whom (including a couple of closet gays); I honestly think he must have bribed some of the staff to report to him. Included was a gorgeous Hindu maiden, traveling alone—born in Trinidad and at one point a café singer in Cairo. Beard knew her entire history, including past and current boyfriends.
>
> He then spent an hour with Sylvia discussing Martin St. Rémy and Christian Dior. [Beard continued to find ways to exercise his enchantment for the worlds of fashion and design.] I remember at one point Sylvia asking his advice on the ship's wine list and his remarking it made absolutely no difference since no French wine could travel; once they'd been subject to an ocean crossing they were ruined anyway.

It was all in fun, of course. Extravagant moments were not uncommon, and good brandy after dinner, or a few jolts of Glenlivet sometimes released him from his expert-witness disciplines with bursts of prodigal theatrics. Later, in a sober, relatively stuffy mood, he wrote an article for *New York* magazine on what diners should know about wines: "You can't fool a good sommelier. But if you find a bottle that is corky, that has gone 'over the hill,' or that is disagreeable, don't be afraid to say so. It is unlikely that your taste will be questioned." He advised calling the owner in the event of trouble. "And if he won't give you satisfaction, then refuse to pay for the wine, as I did once in Carpentras, in the south of France. Although I was accompanied by a wine expert and a friend with excellent palate, both the captain and the owner argued that the wine was good." Unfortunately, the place had one star in the *Guide Michelin*. "Not only did I deliver a speech to the patronne, but I wrote *Michelin* a lengthy protest. Perhaps there were other complaints because the following year the restaurant was missing from the *Michelin* ranks."

What had happened, as observed by Ferrone, who was present, was that Jim had tasted the wine and declared it to be *maderisé*. He had noted that the Château Grillet they had ordered had acquired a brownish tinge, possibly a result of having been left in the barrel too long before bottling. "We asked the waiter for a fresh bottle, which brought forth the *patronne,* a stony-faced woman," according to Ferrone, "who said her restaurant never served bad wine—*Monsieur* was mistaken. Beard said he knew bad wine when he tasted it. They began to shout at each other, and the regular customers looked up with interest from their omelets and entrecôtes. When Beard got really mad he could bellow like a bull. Madame wouldn't surrender. We ate some of our food, which had already been served, paid our bill—we refused to pay for the wine—and stormed out. It was a rude comedown from the reception at starrier places. In Carpentras M. Beard was just another customer." Ferrone added that, whether or not Beard's protest was joined by others, the incident proved the Michelin to be responsive to criticism.*

Michelin fails to cite any restaurant at all in Maillane, the birthplace of Frédéric Mistral, but the village bistro there (along with many other Provençal eating places) made Beard more than welcome. He had won the heart of its patronne, Ferrone observed, and they ate well, if simply, of such good things as tians, *courgettes gratinées,* and daubes, which have been favorites among Provençal diners for generations.

In Paris, after one of his Atlantic crossings, Jim told Art Buchwald that an American *Guide Michelin* wouldn't work because the cost would make it impossible, "and besides there is too much of a turn-over in the restaurant business in America. As soon as a restaurant becomes successful in the U.S.," he assured the columnist, "it is

---

*After having had dinner at a restaurant recommended by Beard, one of his friends reported: "They served us a Pouilly-Fuissé wine that I felt was not good and I returned it as he [Beard] suggested I should. When I received the bill, I was billed for the bottle I returned plus the bottle that replaced it, which I thought was very unfair. [Beard] said that since he was their wine consultant he couldn't handle the complaint."

either sold for a capital gain or enlarged." He added, "I've just made a study with Helen McCully, of *McCall's* magazine. We found only a hundred and fifty worth mentioning."

When Jim got together over an *omelette aux truffes* with Henry McNulty and Buchwald at the Restaurant Aux Bonnes Choses, the *Herald Tribune* columnist got Jim to speak his mind on a pet peeve. "The word 'gourmet' has been run into the ground," said Beard. "Anybody's cousin who drinks wine with his meals, or who substitutes broccoli for potatoes considers himself a gourmet. It's become a dreaded word in the American language."

As the three sat at a table with a paper tablecloth in the Montparnasse bistro, Jim went on to say that he considered the word "epicure" to be more honest as a distinction. The trouble was, "people who like to be considered gourmets are all bolixed up and don't know what they're eating." He added that scrambled eggs "can be a work of art—the epicure wants to preserve simple dishes. He's a man who likes food—a 'gourmet' is one who likes talking about food."

Jim and Henry McNulty had become such close companions that when Henry married Bettina Coffin, it was Jim who went with her to the Costa Brava instead of the bridegroom. The latter had been held in bondage in Paris when his boss arrived from New York and called a conference demanding McNulty's participation. Bettina and

Jim, they both liked to say, spent the honeymoon together, until Henry's release, when the threesome shared a small house at Palomas on a two-mile stretch of beach. The house had been found for Jim by Frank Schoonmaker, and came with the services of Mercedes Figueras, a gifted local cook who, like so many others, found herself almost enslaved to "Don Jaime." Jim was there to work with Schoonmaker, and as usual to steep himself in regional cooking styles.

The McNultys and Jim, with Schoonmaker and his wife and child, ate chickpeas and sausages together, and Bettina and Jim absorbed Mercedes's tricks for turning out a simple classic potato omelet, as well as the Spanish garlic sauce called *all-i-oli*. Sometimes, Bettina recalled, they would meet Mercedes at the market in the morning. "Jim's aura of benevolent giant appealed to the Catalans, and he always caused a stir strolling in the early evening in the *paseo*, or when he appeared in the *mercado* in the morning."

Wherever Beard lingered in travels through Europe, he found something like an entourage—an equivalent of his Greenwich Village family. "With Jim," Henry McNulty said reminiscently, "Bettina and I sampled many of the places he and Sandy Watt had described in *Paris Cuisine*. Together we three had jambon tastings at home, shopping for as many different types of smoked or otherwise cured hams as we could find. Oyster tastings were another experiment—there are at least ten different kinds of oysters available in season in France, all deliciously worth trying. We even put our palates to testing mineral waters from all over France, Belgium, and Germany."

In Paris, Beard won over Alice Toklas, now alone after the death of her companion, Gertrude Stein, when he discovered her *Alice B. Toklas Cook Book* and wrote about it. They remained friends who corresponded until Alice died.* In *Delights and Prejudices* he tells of

---

*In a 1955 letter to John Schaffner, the literary agent who represented them both, Miss Toklas wrote of her book called *Aromas and Flavors of the Past and Present* that her friend Jim "was too indulgent about the book of recipes. He saw two pieces I did [for *House Beautiful* whose food editor was Poppy Cannon, a Beard colleague] or perhaps only one on cooking with champagne, which he said required amplification—more anecdote—more preparation— more comment— more introduction. It was I knew hopeless advice—there wasn't a word more in me . . . I was very ashamed to appear ungrateful to Mr. Beard whose visit had been a real treat." Jim Beard and Alice Toklas had met through a friend, the Paris *Herald Tribune* columnist Naomi Barry, about the time of the *Alice B. Toklas Cook Book* publication.

picnics he and the McNultys shared in the fifties, "notably one when Alice Toklas roasted as delicious a chicken as I ever ate, and I, who was settled in a hotel, had searched around early on Sunday morning [to find] a pâté of duckling *en croûte* that Alice praised as the best she had ever eaten, some remarkably good cooked ham from Milan, a selection of cheese and salad greens." Magnums of champagne were de rigueur. Picnics were a passion of Jim's life, as we have seen. As Bettina remembered, "We all went in Henry's little Triumph Herald to a bucolic spot looking across at Montfort l'Amoury. Alice was game about finding the right site as soon as we'd humped the picnic stuff through a hedge—no cow pods and not too slopey." Henry added,

"Alice, in her black lacquered hat, with a feather pompom straight up in front like a feather duster—she was then well into her seventies—was invited to sit on the uphill side. 'Oh no,' she exclaimed. 'I never face the view. It takes my mind off eating!' "

Eating al fresco was the subject of Beard's next book—so lavishly illustrated that it reproduced such paintings as *Déjeuner sur l'herbe* by Edouard Manet, *The Feast of Achelous* by Peter Paul Rubens, and other works by Fragonard, Picasso, and Renoir. The book was *James Beard's Treasury of Outdoor Cooking,* published by Jerry Mason and Simon and Schuster. A more expansive work than his other books on the subject, its recipes, in elegant typography interspersed among color illustrations, ranged from ways to grill to how to plan large beach parties, and touched base with his mother's feasts at Gearhart, as well as tailgate hot food that included a "quick cassoulet." In the chapter on drinking outdoors, there is this tip: "Wine, like modern art, hi-fi, and growing a good lawn, can be as esoteric a specialty as you care to make it."

Wine and brandy were the attraction (after leaving behind the resolute Miss Toklas) when Jim and the McNultys met Philip and Helen Brown in Paris and drove south for a five-day tour of the Cognac region and Bordeaux. Jim's "very dear friend in Cognac, M. André Renaud," the head of Rémy Martin, gave them lunch—including roast baby mule as the pièce de résistance. Jim wrote home to Isabel to say, "and now I know where all the lamb in the U.S. comes from. It is exactly the same." He added, noncommittally, that the uncommon meat for roasting had been given to Renaud, and that his host "had saved it for me to taste." One can only guess that the roast was appreciated. (As the McNultys recalled, "Renaud liked to surprise his guests with odd dishes—another time we tasted ostrich meat.")

The friends took part in the *intronization* of Helen Brown and James Beard as *Grands Brûleurs d'Honneur* of the *Confrérie des Alembec Charentais,* the Cognac honorary society, then went on to Bordeaux for Jim's installation as a member of the *Commanderie du Bontemps de Médoc.* It was a merry month of May. "We had a long and strenuous weekend in Cognac," Beard wrote to Isabel; "it was gastronomic to say the least and fun, for the Browns became the talk of the town in every way, and Philip was in his best humor and created a never-ending laugh."

Philip Brown, Bettina McNulty, Jim, Helen Brown,
unidentified friend, and Henry McNulty

They went out to Margaux to visit Alexis Lichine at Château Lascombes, taking in the cabernet vineyards, the ancient vat room built by monks, and the rhododendron woods where Jim, on another occasion, had gathered large musty-orange *cèpes* with Lichine, his old comrade from Sherry wine shop days. "To feast on M. Dumaine's food" before the chef's impending retirement, Jim planned a trip to the incomparable Hôtel de Côte d'Or, and then the friends drove to Rheims, where among others they saw Jean Seydoux of Champagne Krug, to be reminded, as Henry McNulty recalls, that "Krug is the Rolls-Royce of Champagne—there is only one model."*

---

*McNulty recounts the history and folklore of sparkling wine in his book *Champagne,* published by Chartwell Books, Inc., 1988.

Beard's heartfelt views on champagne as a drink appear in his collection of columns, titled *Beard on Food:*

> ...while crossing to Cannes on the S.S. *France,* I was struck by the amount of champagne that was consumed aboard—French champagne, naturally. The *France* has probably the most complete stock of this delightfully festive wine you could find anywhere, some seven thousand bottles in sixty-seven varieties from twenty-eight houses, ranging from the famous names—Bollinger, Moët & Chandon, Veuve Clicquot, Krug, Heidsieck, Mercier, and Mumm—to the lesser known, such as Gauthier, De Venoge, Canard-Duchene. In fact, if you happened to be a champagne fancier, you could spend a month or more on this supremely luxurious ship and never drink the same wine twice.
>
> Champagne was the bon voyage drink, it was the favored apéritif before lunch and dinner with those passengers who knew that this was the best of all preludes to magnificent food and wine, and it was invariably served at most of the parties I attended, from a private luncheon in the captain's quarters to the head purser's cocktail party on Gala Night. Champagne might have been made expressly for shipboard life. One doesn't want to be stupefied by a lot of alcohol, and the bubbling charm and lightness of champagne fits most graciously into the relaxed pattern of one's days, making the trip more glamorous, gay, and elegant.

Neither his appreciation of champagne nor his memories of it failed him as the years progressed. He was alert to the upsurge of California-made sparkling wines, and pleased to applaud the achievement of his friends Jack and Jamie Davies of Schramsberg Vineyards near Calistoga, for they had formed a partnership with André Renaud. He told readers of his column that Schramsberg produced five "champagnes," each from a special blend of varietal grapes. He saluted Jamie as a good cook, as well as winemaker, and the thought of the first lunch he had at Schramsberg stayed with him. "She served pignatelli fritters with Schramsberg Blanc de Blancs, which is still my favorite of their champagnes." Her cheese soufflés triumphed, and were accompanied by asparagus, croissants, and a green salad. "The meal ended with ripe strawberries and a champagne sauce. The lunch was so perfect," he ended his column, "that I remember it distinctly." Was there ever a meal he didn't remember distinctly?

As fellow employees of the Edward Gottlieb promotion office, Beard and Henry McNulty both kept abreast of California's burgeoning sparkling wine production, and the McNultys were occasionally in the States after McNulty became one of *Vogue*'s correspondents. Jim and his two friends again made champagne a priority when they chose a Labor Day weekend for a picnic on Maryland's Eastern Shore. Reached by ferry, the peninsula was a watery region Jim had come to know by serving as a judge at Delmarva chicken-frying contests, though he was more interested in the blue crabs, which he appreciated almost as much as the Dungeness of his native surf.

The light was fading as they drove south past marshes and the crab country that made Jim mindful of Oregon's Dungeness shores; they had every intention of having one of those picnics that Jim doted on whenever he could find a rustic excuse. But the highway traffic was against them, as it can often be in the summer on the Eastern Shore. Finally, as they headed for the Choptank River, night fell, as Henry remembers it, before they found a scenic spot, and they had to settle for a Howard Johnson parking lot under klieg lights put up for trucks. "But we had our Baccarat, our good damask, our china, we ate filet of beef, salad, bread and cheese, and we wondered if people were ever puzzled by the champagne bottles we left behind."

Bettina said, "We'd been lackadaisically looking for an inn that Jim might buy—a constant ever-present dream of his. When we found out that Labor Day was the biggest and almost only weekend on the Choptank, Jim lost heart." But he compensated. He was up early on Saturday morning knocking on the doors of the antique shops. At breakfast he was "crowing over the just-bought Crown Derby china—a passion of his."

It was a period in which he was as often in the United States as in Europe, or vice versa, and he had as many friends abroad as in America, it seemed. The San Francisco–born William Templeton Veach, his sometime host in Florence, owned a cottage in the village of Bonnétable, in Sarthe, not far from Le Mans, and Beard and Veach (once Philip and Helen Brown were his guests) cooked together such provincial treats as *oignonade à la Bretonne,* a comforting baked dish of chicken breast braised in a bed of tiny onions with some sautéed mushrooms, heavy cream, and chicken stock. Jim dropped menus into his conversation as satisfyingly as someone else might give a description of a landscape.

One of Jim's accounts of the food in the fishing village of Carry-le-Rouet, west of Marseille, lured the Grubers to join him overnight, even though he suggested to Isabel beforehand that he thought the Detroit couple might not be up to the rustic plumbing in the private home that took him in. It was at the portside restaurant named L'Escale, whose terraces overhang the gulf, that he had discovered one of his most admired bouillabaisses, and where he and his British friend Elizabeth David relished the fish stew called *bourride,* as it was prepared in those days by Charles Berot—he had been *chef des cuisines* of the *Ile de France* when the liner was most celebrated for its good cooking.

Jim was almost as compulsive about making friends with restaurant chefs as he was about the act of eating itself. In introducing Alan Lewis of Restaurant Associates to chefs whose names had appeared in *Paris Cuisine,* he and his friend got into an amiable argument about where to have lunch on Lewis's first visit to the French capital. As Lewis remembered it, "One day we ended up at lunch with each having two complete plates, then walked through Les Halles and had coffee in between, and in the evening for dinner went to two different restaurants and had two separate dinners apiece. I sent Jim rolling home in a fiacre."

Lewis was as pleased that his own capacity matched Jim's as he was to be taken to Le Grand Comptoir, where Jim knew all the specialties (such as fresh-grilled outsize sardines) and where M. Buisson greeted him by name. Lewis went with Jim to Beaune and got to know Marc Chevillot of the Hôtel de la Poste, and his friends introduced him to Alexander Dumaine and to the Hiely family in Avignon, who knew Jim well, as Lewis discovered.

When Beard spent months, at intervals, in nearby St. Rémy-de-Provence, he referred to the splendid L'Oustau de Baumanière, a short drive through rugged troglodytish terrain, as "my local bistro." He and his guests, whoever might be with him at the moment, often drove down into Les Baux to sit at poolside or at one of Raymond Thuilier's tables in the gracious dining room. L'Oustau is one of the world's most famous restaurants, and Jim admired Thuilier because he had chosen, in midlife, to give up all else for food. Jim saw him as a poet in the kitchen—like the American poet, Wallace Stevens, whom Jim admired, Thuilier had been an insurance executive until he founded his restaurant. He was a painter as well, and one day, while eating lunch with Mary Hamblet, Jim persuaded Thuilier to give Mary a souvenir menu which bore Thuilier's watercolor of delphiniums on its cover.

In a booklet Thuilier had written, Jim found the essence of his cooking-school philosophy, he said. He often quoted the Provençal chef: "Culinary art is not solely the making of a sumptuous dish—not at all! It can be magnificiently achieved in the preparation of the most common and simple dishes." Three years after Beard's death, when I talked to Thuilier, the ninety-one-year-old restaurateur (incidentally he was then running for mayor of Les Baux) remembered Jim as an appreciator of food. "Monsieur Beard was," he told me, *"passioné sur la cuisine."* He paused and with a thin Gallic smile added, "And that in itself is *extraordinaire* for a culture like yours which does not involve itself truly with food." He went on: "Monsieur Beard's métier was his curiosity—he was always attentive, each time more curious. He would *replonger* into French cuisine each year he returned. And he understood that it is always necessary to cook for a few persons only."

But the *replonger-* ing—immersing himself in food (sampling dish after dish, and he was never one not to clean his plate)—took its toll. He was constantly being reminded about his increasing girth by doctors, by the concern of Jeanne Owen delivered indirectly after the rift, by sisterly concern from such friends as Helen Brown, whose letters now might end with a postscript—"For God's sake, take it easier!"

To Helen, he could occasionally admit some of the health problems that plagued him in the early fifties. He told her that as the result of cardiograms his doctor had diagnosed "a slight irregularity, and has given me an acre of lectures and has put me on my honor..." He assured his friend he wouldn't drive himself "so horrendously as I have been," and he had noted the night before that as he began to lose weight, "my dinner jacket almost seemed as if it had been made for me."

"James, darling," Helen wrote in response four days later, "I am worried about you. Do you really think that you will be good on the 'honor system'? I think you ought to go to the hospital, and at once. Don't be a nonny. You have only one life, you know. And you keep talking about taking it easy and in the very next breath you say that next week will be hell. What kind of rest is that?"

Here is the final paragraph of Helen's letter in capital letters, as she typed it:

"TAKE CARE OF YOURSELF, STOP ENTERTAINING, STOP DRINKING, STOP GOING PLACES, STOP EATING TOO MUCH, STOP ALL JOBS BUT THE ONE THAT PAYS THE MOST OR YOU WILL STOP LIVING. I am serious."

But his good intentions seldom prevailed. His interest in food remained passionate—even more emotionally so than Thuilier recognized. Perhaps it was Jim's understanding that cutting down on eating meant cutting down on life that caused him to think about telling his own story in a book. One of Helen Brown's letters to him makes it clear that, soon after the success of *The James Beard Cookbook*, he broached the possibility of an autobiography and sought her reaction.

"It was a good letter from you," she wrote later, in January 1960. "Yes I think it is time you did your memoirs. A good long thoughtful book with you, not Isabel, coming through." Helen appreciated how much Isabel Callvert gave to the writing that bore the James Beard name, and she was aware that Jim had a way of typing out facts on a subject, expecting Isabel to provide organization and a sense of Jim's personality in each of their collaborations. She knew too that he could be easily distracted—he had no ability to ignore telephone calls, whether they offered possibilities to advance his income or came from readers who wanted their hands held by the master as he talked them through a recipe. Knowing her man, Helen used the letter of encouragement to give him a firm push. "And I think you should go away to do it, or you will be constantly interrupted."

Jim being photographed by Bill Fotiades on the Grand Canal

It was sound advice, all right, but the going-away that Jim found time to do was as full of distractions as staying at home with the scrapping household that included the ever-present, grumbling Gino, sometimes unasked-for comments from Clay, and part-time secretaries. When he was away from the new house and its occupants, the distractions could be irritating. "I think the Parthenon should be seen at a distance," he wrote to Isabel, showing his annoyance at tourist hordes in Greece. "As a matter of fact I would have been happier if I had not gone to the Acropolis."* On the other hand, "seeing Ephesus

---

*His feelings about the Ancient World were ambiguous, and so were his leanings toward pre-Columbian America. After spending time in the Yucatán, he had urged Ron Callvert, with Isabel as a cohort, to pursue Ron's archeological bent by specializing in the Olmec ruins of Mexico.

was a dream voyage." In the same letter, he showed some of the real pleasure he found in a cruise through the Middle East. "I have made a list this morning of the recipes I have picked ... I think I have about 200 brand spanking new ones" and he wanted them culled to be sure there were no duplications. It was the satisfactions to be found in work abroad—or back home at 119 West Tenth Street—that refueled his capricious drive.

One day on his doorstep on Tenth Street, there arrived an advance copy of a large and handsome volume, *Mastering the Art of French Cooking,* by two Frenchwomen and an American named Julia Child. Jim recognized immediately that this was an important book. What Julia Child had done for French cooking had never been done before. Jim was familiar with the recipes—they were the backbone of the cuisine of France. But the new tome was more than a compendium of recipes; it was an attempt to translate French cooking for Americans— to tell them all the whys and wherefores of classic techniques. The answers were here: what to expect, what to do if something goes wrong, how to choose substitute ingredients when supermarkets failed (as they so often did) to have the right ones on hand.

Jim knew at once that here was a great teaching book, and he remarked to a friend that he wished he had written it. But his approach to cooking was not analytical as Mrs. Child's is. He taught by instinct. He bent the rules rather than codified them. And, recogniz- ing a masterpiece, Jim went all out. As nobody else could do as well, he made it his role to see that the fledgling American food establish- ment did what was necessary to put *Mastering the Art of French Cooking* on the map. He rallied colleagues—Helen McCully, Cecily Brownstone, Clementine Paddleford, June Platt, Jeanne Voltz, et al., for a party in Dione Lucas's restaurant, called the Egg Basket, on the eve of publication. With a send-off by Craig Claiborne in the *Times,* rave reviews across the country, and a year or so later the first network broadcast of Julia Child's "The French Chef" on public television, the book changed American thinking. Jim wrote a note of congratula- tions to the publisher, his friend Alfred Knopf.

For the authors of *Mastering the Art of French Cooking,* as Julia Child put it, "The idea was to take French cooking out of cuckoo land and bring it down to where everybody is." In an interview with Chris

Chase, author of *The Great American Waistline,* she added, "You can't turn a sow's ear into Veal Orloff, but you can do something very good with a sow's ear." Knopf's editor, Judith Jones (who is my wife), told Mrs. Chase, "It was like having a teacher right there beside you in the kitchen, and everything really worked."

As *Mastering* was beginning to take hold in America, Jim was in Europe tapping out his memoirs. He finished his own book, a smattering of charming recollections interspersed with recipes, in New York, in Geneva, and in the village of St.-Rémy-de-Provence. In France he had the companionship of Mary Hamblet, who served as his driver one year, and later of John Ferrone, who took over as editorial assistant in place of Isabel Callvert when the latter's health persuaded her to decline the project.

The journalist Naomi Barry, who had a nearby *mas,* found the house on the edge of St.-Rémy where Jim was working. The bedroom was his, his childhood friend slept in the living room, and for these long-ago Gearhart cronies there was time for afternoon bullfights (much loved by Jim), for exploring adjacent vestiges of occupation by the Romans, and the kind of juvenile pranks to which Jim was sometimes given. "The place," Mary said, "included a horse which delighted me because I loved to ride. But that damn Jamie taunted me about taking a jump I knew was impossible. Of course, I didn't make it. The horse balked—I went flying, and broke my nose."

The furnishings of the house made it a nineteenth-century museum because Mme. Baudin, the owner, wouldn't put up with anything contemporary. In spite of a tiny primitive kitchen, however, Jim cooked a lot, as Mary recalled one day in her Portland home. "There was local wine, in bottles with porcelain stoppers, delivered twice a week. Another wagon came with a toot-toot [a Harpo Marx horn with a bulb to force out the sound], and it had everything: spools of thread, cheese, sausages." The two Oregonians were undaunted by the old-fashioned provincial life until the fly season. "The flies drove me up the wall," Mary recalled, "so much so, I said I was going home." To stave off Mary's seriously intended threat, Jim went to the village to find rolls of sticky flypaper that he could hang from the chandeliers. "If Madame sees this," Mary remembered Jim saying, "she'll throw us both out."

*Jim introducing Julia and Paul Child to the director
of the Culinary Institute of America*

The possibility of a set-to over such a prospect was avoided when
the flypaper went undiscovered. But Mary Hamblet knew, like many
others of Jim's extended family, that vexing annoyances often set off
tirades, not unlike the childhood conniptions Mary had witnessed at
the beach. St.-Rémy, though, was a reassuring environment in which
Jim thrived in spite of occasional complaints about varicose veins and
foot pains that sometimes resulted from long walks.

John Ferrone observed the pleasure that Jim took in marketing
almost daily—"sniffing, tasting, and pinching his way through bins of
fruits or vegetables, or having a good chat with the baker or charcutier."
Beard told Ferrone that he felt strongly that American influences
were behind the decline in the quality of French food; he was
unhappy to see supermarkets and convenience foods taking hold. But
he had made himself a familiar figure in the village to which they
walked once or twice through eddies of scent from the fields of
lavender and the pungency of thyme and rosemary plants.* He had
tried all the breads available in order to find the one he liked, and he
had become a friend of the best butcher.

---

*Ferrone said he was so intoxicated by the scent of lavender "he tried to bottle it, making a
mixture of lavender oil and alcohol that served as a crude cologne."

He knew where to find the best linens as well as the best saucisson. [Ferrone wrote in a memoir of his time at St.-Rémy.] We stocked up on items for our larder, and he couldn't resist a tall can of white asparagus, a weakness from boyhood, when his mother used to can her own. We had the asparagus with a vinaigrette sauce for a first course that evening, and then a shoulder of baby lamb roasted with plenty of garlic and rosemary, peas from the garden, and madeleines with apricot preserves. Beard expected his guests to pitch in and work along with him in the kitchen. I liked to watch the unhurried way he shuffled from table to stove, handling food without fuss, plopping a chicken or roast into a pan and sprinkling it generously with herbs and seasonings. It was cooking done with a broad brush.

Ferrone reported that work on Jim's autobiographical book went along at a similar pace: "We worked until lunch time, Beard punching away on his portable typewriter, whose erratic habits I knew well. The space bar stuck and produced clusters of words that looked like ciphers. Beard seldom reread what he had written but just churned out an easy flow of words that sounded exactly like him."

The resulting manuscript, which Ferrone edited and assembled in thirteen chapters that swing uninhibitedly back and forth in time (although not the "long thoughtful book" that Helen Brown seemed to have had in mind) was a life sketch as winning as any professional American gastronome has left behind. While the text is punctuated by recipes that enhance the memories as much as the illustrations by Earl Thollander do, Jim's fanciful side prevailed over pragmatic advice when he chose the title. A month short of his sixty-first birthday *Delights and Prejudices* was published; the review in the *Times* opened with the following paragraph:

Jim Beard, who has frequently been called America's best-known gastronome, is a practicing cook who revels in standing behind a stove as well as sitting at a feast. He is a portly, good-humored man in all seasons, a connoisseur of wines and a gentleman with the most incredible memory where the art of the table is concerned. He can recall in depth the delicacies of his childhood as well as those of the present day and he has done so in a volume of memoirs that is readable and amusing and will surely tempt the reader's palate.

Appearing at the top of page 36 on a Thursday morning in April, that lead paragraph was a poignant Claiborne tribute to a colleague who, for a quarter century, had been an exemplar. Claiborne's review sketched the biographical trails—from the Gladstone Hotel to the youthful disappointment in the romanticized cuisine at Maxim's—that Jim had blazed. The period about which *Delights and Prejudices* concerned itself had been an age "when no one cared about cholesterol, when everyone who could afford it ate and drank without stint." Four recipes followed the review. As significant as any of them, for an American who so loved outdoor celebrations, was the one titled James Beard's Pâté for Picnics.

Just as five years earlier the *Times* review of *The James Beard Cookbook* had started the author off on a promotion tour beginning with appearances on the Arthur Godfrey television program and another called "The Galen Drake Show" that was seen from coast to coast, the review of the new book cranked up a lot of interest. He was persuaded to do a Chicago TV broadcast, and his book was treated handsomely by *Time* magazine. Jim's schedule of department store demonstrations included a tour of regional cities (about which he wrote to Helen Brown from Florida). Similarly the *Times* nod to *Delights and Prejudices* was the first sign of the attention his autobiography was to draw as he headed for the airport.

As before, he had been asked not only to sign copies for bookstore customers, common enough for authors in general, but he was booked to turn up in department stores, where kitchen equipment was sold, to give cooking demonstrations. In one week in April 1964 he appeared at Meier and Frank stores in Portland and Salem, Oregon, and conducted a cooking school in two sessions on a single day at the Neighbors Woodcraft Hall for a children's school benefit. His years of barnstorming in the interest of American cooks everywhere had set a pattern of "book tours" for the food establishment that were to become a cliché in the seventies and eighties.

RECIPES

Cold Stuffed Vine Leaves

▼

Jim welcomed to his cooking school guest teachers like Leon Leonides, who demonstrated the art of Greek cookery, and he almost as frequently saluted the authors of cookbooks from abroad at the parties he gave. American cooks, he believed, were interested in adding new ethnic techniques to their kitchen skills. To introduce Claudia Roden, one spring evening he gave a garden party in honor of her superlative *Book of Middle Eastern Food,* and in turn she gave him her recipe for dolma.

Filling:

3/4 cup long-grain rice
2–3 chopped tomatoes
2–3 onions, finely chopped
2¹/2 tablespoons chopped
    mint leaves
2 tablespoons
    chopped parsley

1/4 teaspoon
    ground cinnamon
1/4 teaspoon ground allspice
salt
freshly ground pepper

1-pound jar or can
    vine leaves
sliced tomatoes
3–4 cloves garlic
1/2 cup olive oil

1/2 cup water
1/4 teaspoon powdered
    saffron (optional)
1 teaspoon sugar
juice of 1 or more lemons

Mix the filling ingredients well. Place the leaves on a plate, vein side up, and put a heaping teaspoon at the center near the stem edge. Fold the stem end up over the filling, then fold both sides toward the middle and roll up—like a small cigar. Squeeze lightly in the palm of your hand. Pack the rolls tightly in a pan lined with slices of tomato (this prevents the leaves from sticking to the pan and burning) and slip the garlic cloves in between the rolls. Mix the oil and water with the optional saffron, sugar, and juice of 1 or more lemons. Pour this over the vine rolls, then put a small plate on top to prevent their unwinding. Cover the pan and simmer very, very gently for at least 2 hours, until thoroughly cooked. Add water occasionally, about 1/2 cup at a time, as the liquid becomes absorbed. Let the rolls cool in the pan before turning out. Serve cold.   MAKES ABOUT 40 STUFFED VINE LEAVES.

Chicken Liver Timbales

▼

Gerald Asher, author of the fine autobiographical book *On Wine*, is one of those who shared with Jim a deep admiration for Elizabeth David. He was also one of Jim's sources of recipes, including this savory custard which Asher relayed from Yvonne Geoffray, a friend in Beaujolais, and which Beard adapted. "The recipe is delightfully quirky, and I had to make some educated guesses! Mme. Geoffray recommends serving it with a tomato sauce flavored with mushrooms," he wrote.

1 large chicken liver	*salt*
2 cloves garlic	*freshly ground pepper*
4 sprigs parsley	*2 cups milk*
fresh tarragon to taste	*1/2 cup cream*
5 eggs, beaten lightly	*pinch of bicarbonate of soda*

Chop very fine the chicken liver, garlic, parsley, and tarragon. (Use 1/2 teaspoon of dried tarragon if fresh is unavailable.) Season the beaten eggs lightly with salt and pepper. Heat the milk and cream and add slowly to the eggs, stirring all the time. Stir in the chopped liver and herbs and add a pinch of soda (*"Une petite précaution pour la composition ne tourne pas,"* says madame, *"ajouter une pincée de bicarbonate de soude"*).

Line the bottom of a 4-cup charlotte mold or a soufflé dish with a round of wax paper, butter it and the mold well, and fill with the mixture. Set in a baking pan partly filled with hot water and bake at 310 degrees for 1 1/4 hours. Loosen edges with a knife and turn out onto a platter.   SERVES 4.

Beard on Tians

▼

Jim brought Provençal tians to the attention of American cooks with a spot in their hearts for casseroles that have character and style. Visiting the Frédéric Mistral museum in Maillane, not far from Avignon, he was reminded of the French poet's dictum that *"le tian véritable"* is a combination of green vegetables, garlic, and cod, accented by cheese. There are many variations.

1 pound salt cod,
* soaked overnight*
1¹/2 pounds spinach, washed
1 onion, chopped
6 tablespoons olive oil
1 medium zucchini, diced
1¹/2 cups crustless bread* torn
* in pieces and soaked in*
* 1 cup milk plus*
* additional milk*

salt, freshly ground pepper,
* and nutmeg to taste*
2 cloves garlic, minced
¹/3 cup breadcrumbs
5–6 tablespoons Swiss or
* Parmesan cheese*

Drain the cod and put it in a saucepan with enough boiling water to cover by a couple of inches. Bring to the boil and simmer 5 minutes, then drain. Cook the spinach in lightly salted water 3 to 4 minutes, depending on tenderness. Drain, chop, and squeeze dry. Sauté the onion in 2 tablespoons of the oil until golden. Add the spinach and zucchini and cook, stirring, 5 minutes. Squeeze out the bread pieces and add them to the skillet, breaking them up. Add the drained milk along with enough more to make 1¹/2 cups, and cook, stirring, over low heat for about 10 minutes, until the liquid has been absorbed but the mixture is still soft. Season with salt and pepper and nutmeg to taste and stir in the minced garlic. Put half the vegetable mixture in the bottom of a fairly large, shallow, oiled earthenware casserole. Arrange pieces of cod on top, then spread on the final layer of vegetables. Sprinkle on the breadcrumbs, drizzle the remaining olive oil over, and scatter the cheese on top. Bake in a preheated 425 degree oven for 10 to 15 minutes, until brown on top. SERVES 4 TO 6.

Cèpes à la Cuisine de l'Enfant Barbue

▼

"This is a Bearded Child recipe," Jim Beard told a gathering of mushroom scientists. He said it evolved when he and Julia Child found "a great mass of fresh cèpes in the market in Nice." In Julia Child's Provence kitchen, "contrary to the Bordelaise fashion, we sliced the caps rather thinly and chopped the stems fairly coarsely . . . and they were absolutely divine eating."

2 pounds cèpes (Boletus)
3 tablespoons butter

3 tablespoons olive oil
salt

*Use unsweetened bread, preferably French or Italian.

freshly ground pepper   *3–4 cloves garlic*
1/4 cup finely
   chopped parsley

Wash the cèpes and remove any spots. Separate stems and reserve. Slice caps in 1/4-inch slices. Chop stems coarsely. Heat 3 tablespoons of butter and 3 tablespoons of olive oil in a 9- to 10-inch heavy skillet. Toss in the sliced caps and sauté very quickly, turning well, until evenly browned. Add salt and pepper to taste. In a small skillet, sauté chopped stems lightly, tossing well. Combine the sautéed stems with the sliced caps. Add parsley and garlic and stir until well mixed. Serve with beef or game.   SERVES 4.

Linguini with Scallops and Cherry Tomatoes

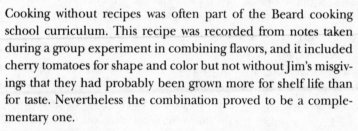

Cooking without recipes was often part of the Beard cooking school curriculum. This recipe was recorded from notes taken during a group experiment in combining flavors, and it included cherry tomatoes for shape and color but not without Jim's misgivings that they had probably been grown more for shelf life than for taste. Nevertheless the combination proved to be a complementary one.

3/4 pound linguini   *1/2 cup chopped*
1/4 pound butter   *flat-leaved parsley*
4 plump shallots, minced   *salt and freshly*
1 pound bay or sea scallops   *ground pepper*
20 cherry tomatoes, peeled   *1/2 cup dry white wine*

Plunge the linguini into a large pot of salted boiling water. Heat 4 tablespoons of the butter in a large skillet and sauté the shallots about 2 minutes, then add the scallops (cut in half if they are large sea scallops) and continue to cook over high heat, tossing, for about 4 minutes. Add the tomatoes, parsley, and salt and pepper to taste, and cook just long enough for the tomatoes to heat through, not disintegrate. Drain the pasta when it is done al dente, toss with the remaining butter, season with salt and pepper, then spoon the scallops and tomatoes on top. Quickly pour the wine into the skillet, reduce slightly over high heat, scraping up browned bits, and pour over the pasta.   SERVES 3 OR 4.

Carbonnade Flamande

▼

Jim's *Gourmet* colleague Louis Diat seems to have introduced this Belgian dish to Americans at the New York Ritz, but Jim adapted the recipe to his own electric-stove cooking techniques. Old Flemish cooks used a dark red beer to give rich color; Beard got appetizing results from various American brews.

3 tablespoons butter	*2 teaspoons or more salt*
2 pounds onions, sliced thin	*1/4 teaspoon or more*
3 pounds chuck steak, cut	*freshly ground pepper*
in 2-inch cubes	*2 cloves garlic, chopped fine*
flour	*1 cup beer*
3 tablespoons beef fat, lard,	
or goose fat	

Melt 3 tablespoons butter in a 10-inch skillet and sauté the onions until soft and lightly browned. Dry the cubed beef and sprinkle lightly with flour. In a Dutch oven or enameled iron casserole, melt the fat and brown the meat, a few pieces at a time, over medium-high heat; don't crowd the pieces or they won't brown. When each cube is browned on all sides, add the sautéed onions from the skillet and season with 2 teaspoons salt and 1/4 teaspoon pepper. Add the garlic and the beer, cover, and reduce the heat. Simmer about 1 1/4 hours, until tender. Mix a little flour and butter into a paste and stir into the juices, cooking until the sauce thickens. Add salt and pepper if needed. SERVES 6 TO 8.

Ham Soufflé with Parmesan

▼

In San Francisco, Prentice Hale always had a box at the opera that was available to Jim, and his wife, Denise, was one of the few Beard friends who ever had private cooking lessons from the master. One time, he made her do nine soufflés in a row until she got it right. Finally, while they took time for lunch, her last soufflé rose perfectly. "You see," Jim said to Denise, "I knew you had a mental block." Not true, said Denise. "It was just that by that ninth soufflé I was so mad I forgot about the tension I thought I was under!" The Beard philosophy was that all soufflés are easy to do—the trick is to relax.

3 tablespoons butter
4 shallots, minced
3 tablespoons flour
1 cup milk
salt
freshly ground pepper
4 egg yolks
1 cup minced country ham

1 tablespoon chopped fresh
  tarragon, or 1 teaspoon
  dried, crumbled
Tabasco sauce
5 tablespoons grated
  Parmesan cheese
5 egg whites

Melt the butter in a heavy saucepan and sauté the shallots until soft. Stir in the flour and cook gently 2 to 3 minutes. Add the milk and whisk over heat until thickened. Season to taste with salt and pepper. Beat in the egg yolks one at a time. Add the ham, tarragon, several dashes of Tabasco, and 3 tablespoons of the Parmesan, and let cool slightly. Beat the egg whites until they form firm peaks. Mix a few tablespoons of the whites into the soufflé base, then fold in the rest. Butter a 1½-quart soufflé dish and sprinkle the bottom and the sides liberally with the remaining Parmesan, then spoon the soufflé mixture in. Bake in a preheated 375 degree oven for 30 minutes—a little less if you like it quite soft in the center.   SERVES 3 OR 4.

Brown Sugar Custard in Brioche

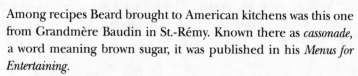

Among recipes Beard brought to American kitchens was this one from Grandmère Baudin in St.-Rémy. Known there as *cassonade*, a word meaning brown sugar, it was published in his *Menus for Entertaining*.

Brioche Dough:
1 teaspoon active dry yeast
½ tablespoon sugar
3 tablespoons warm water
dash of salt

1 cup flour
¼ cup melted butter
1 egg

1 cup brown sugar
4 egg yolks

1 cup heavy cream

Make the dough: Dissolve the yeast and sugar in the warm water. In a bowl or in a food processor mix the salt and flour, then add the melted butter, egg, and the yeast mixture. Beat or process until smooth. Turn into a buttered bowl and let rise in a warm place, covered, until doubled in volume—an hour or more. Punch down the dough, roll out, and fit into a buttered 9-inch pie plate. Let rise 5 to 10 minutes. Sprinkle the brown sugar over the brioche. Mix the egg yolks and cream together and pour over the sugar. Bake at 425 degrees for 10 minutes. Reduce the heat to 350 and bake until the custard is set. Cool and serve. SERVES 6 TO 8.

Katie's Prune Cake

Ordinary prunes, Jim once wrote, were laughed at as "boarding-house food," but he learned—from his mother, of course—that this fruit is good for many delicious things, including cakes. This recipe comes from Catherine Hindley, one of Jim's collaborators on *American Cookery,* who had previously been food editor of the *Oregon Journal.*

<table>
<tr><td>1/2 cup shortening</td><td>1/2 teaspoon each of</td></tr>
<tr><td>1 cup sugar</td><td> baking soda, salt,</td></tr>
<tr><td>2 eggs</td><td> nutmeg, and cinnamon</td></tr>
<tr><td>1/2 cup buttermilk or</td><td>1 teaspoon vanilla</td></tr>
<tr><td> prune juice</td><td>1 cup cooked, drained,</td></tr>
<tr><td>2 teaspoons single-action, or</td><td> pitted, and</td></tr>
<tr><td> 1 teaspoon double-action,</td><td> chopped prunes</td></tr>
<tr><td> baking powder</td><td>1/2 cup chopped walnuts</td></tr>
<tr><td>2 cups sifted</td><td> or filberts</td></tr>
<tr><td> all-purpose flour</td><td></td></tr>
</table>

Cream the shortening, adding the sugar, until fluffy and light. Add the eggs one at a time and beat thoroughly. Add the buttermilk or prune juice alternately with sifted dry ingredients. Stir in the vanilla, the chopped prunes, and the nuts. Pour into two greased 8-inch layer-cake pans. Bake at 350 degrees for 25 to 30 minutes. MAKES TWO 8-INCH CAKES.

Polenta Christmas Cake

The enthusiasm for Christmas felt by the Beard family stayed with Jim and caused him, one season in Venice, to buy a fruitcake made with polenta. He liked it so much, that, failing to find the original recipe, he went back to New York to try to work out the formula. After four or five experiments, he said, he got it down pat.

1/2 pound butter	*1/2 teaspoon salt*
1 cup granulated sugar	*1/2 cup candied fruits*
3 whole eggs	*1/2 cup mixed raisins*
1 1/2 cups all-purpose flour	*and currants*
3 teaspoons baking powder	*2 tablespoons cognac*
1 cup yellow cornmeal	

Cream together the butter and sugar until very light and fluffy. Add the eggs one at a time, beating well after each addition. Stir together the flour, baking powder, cornmeal, and salt. Add to the butter-sugar mixture and blend well. (If you have an electric mixer with a paddle attachment, use this. It creams the butter and sugar 0904incorporates the eggs and dry ingredients perfectly.) Remove the bowl from the mixer. Lightly flour the candied fruits and mixed raisins and currants and fold them in. Add the cognac as you fold in the fruits. Butter a deep 9-inch cake tin, line it with wax paper or cooking parchment, and butter the paper. Spoon in the batter. Lift the tin about one foot above the counter or table and drop it down on the board once or twice—this settles the batter and removes any bubbles. Bake in a 350 degree oven for 50 to 60 minutes; test with a toothpick or wooden skewer after 45 minutes to see if it is cooked through. Cool 10 minutes. Invert onto a rack, then quickly invert again onto another rack. This makes a cake about 2 1/2 inches high that slices well. It will keep two weeks in the refrigerator when wrapped in plastic.   MAKES ONE 9-INCH CAKE.

10

"IN THE BEGINNING..."

In New York Jim turned to the *Daily News* to revel in the comics and the paper's gossip columns before he read the *Times*. Wherever he might be in the United States, he bought the local newspapers for the pure indulgence of following the comic strips with the sort of pleasure he had found when he'd helped to dramatize the funnies as a West Coast actor. He pursued his serious appetite for a wide range of reading, but there was always a tendency as well toward anything he found amusing.

In 1968, in *New York* magazine, a piece by Nora Ephron was as entertaining as any news published that day. "In the beginning," her breezy article on the current food scene asserted, "there was James Beard and there was curry and that was about all." In the beginning, or a generation earlier than the year then being hailed for its "food revolution," there had been assorted curried tidbits in Beard's *Hors d'Oeuvre and Canapés,* and there had been Let's Secret Curry Sauce in Jim's childhood. But the curry that had been cited with arched eyebrows by Ephron was apt to be a main dish to offer guests in certain "gourmet" circles—a combination of cooked chicken pieces and sliced apples served over rice, in a white sauce faintly seasoned with tinned curry powder, and accompanied by sliced bananas, nuts and chopped egg, and other condiments.

That sort of supper dish wasn't really all that new. Curry powder had been on hand in America's colonial pantries, and it was the aromatic that distinguished the smothered-chicken casserole known as Country Captain. For a couple of generations a half-teaspoon of curry powder was considered the tonic that could bring new life to leftovers at family meals. But there was a sudden resurgence of the use of curry in the 1960s, just as James Beard, through publication of a shelfful of volumes about American cooking, was beginning to be discovered by new home cooks. Beard's books gave confidence to those too ill-at-ease in the kitchen to attempt anything as challenging as haute cuisine. For its part, a meal of curry, with its sambals and chutney, gave average dinner guests something to talk about.

"Dinner parties in fashionable homes featured curried lobster," Nora Ephron reported. "Dinner parties in middle-income homes featured curried chicken. Dinner parties in frozen-food compartments featured curried rice. And with the arrival of curry, the first fashionable international food, food acquired a chic, a gloss of snobbery it had hither-to possessed only in certain upper-income groups." Beef Wellington, a fillet wrapped in puff pastry and baked in a hot oven ("I hate the stuff," said Craig Claiborne), soon began to supplant curry as a fad. However, good cooks, as opposed to so-called gourmet cooks, were beginning to learn about the artful use of spices, and of fresh herbs, and of the pleasures that could be found in home cooking.

Jim could enjoy Nora Ephron's accuracy of eye. He and she talked about the new "food fraternity," as *The Saturday Review*'s Horace Sutton had dubbed the covey of self-anointed food writers that were gathering, and Beard told her (describing a recent shindig), "You could barely move around at the party for fear someone would bite you in the back." He was talking about the johnny-come-latelies who recognized Beard, Child, Claiborne, and Michael Field, of Time-Life's Foods of the World series, as the fraternity's "Big Four."

Beard and the other three were wont to treat each other as peers, and he and Julia (so she became universally known) turned to each other as brother and sister. It was not only because they found each other almost invariably the tallest persons in a gathering: their affinities for honest food transcended differences in their styles, and Julia and Paul Child became Jim's lasting friends.* Michael Field and

Jim had known each other since the former had quit his concert career as a pianist to become chef of his own restaurant in the Hamptons. Michael vied with Helen McCully in early-morning telephone queries aimed at tapping Jim's encyclopedic knowledge of food as much as in expressing real affection. He and Jim and Julia became involved in the Time-Life cookbook series, the mail-order venture that discovered half a million new cookbook buyers across the land.

Beard served Time-Life in much the way that he was an adjunct of Restaurant Associates. He was again the family doctor on call, this time sought out for his understanding of cultural cross-currents in the American hinterland as much as for his ideas about food. It was like him to be more open-minded about mass marketing than many other cookbook writers, who saw the mail-order ideas as an encroachment upon their own independent efforts. Jim was farsighted. He viewed mail-order as an opportunity to awaken more Americans to the cause

*"I'll never forget," Julia Child said to me, "how kind he was to Simca [Simone Beck] and Paul and me when our first book was published. We were nobodies from nowhere, yet he took us right in hand, introduced us everywhere, and really gave us our start in the New York food world."

of good cooking, to reach hundreds of thousands in areas in which bookstores did not exist.

In addition to becoming a Time-Life consultant, Jim took in Time-Life editors as freshman cooking students who came to his small kitchen to learn basics. He was involved in all the books of the series to a varying extent, and his pupils included editors and writers like Dale Brown and William Goolrick, who had been hard-news correspondents, and other staff members like Beatrice Dobie and Grace Brynolson. At his instigation, Michael Field had brought in Irma Rhode, his Hors d'Oeuvre Inc. partner who had studied cooking with the Grand Duchess of Baden. As researcher Lyn Stallworth remembers, "Jim and Michael played off each other as if they were in a tennis match." But those at Time-Life who were outside the competition observed that Jim was sometimes overcome by depression. Stallworth says: "We thought he was moody. He was a mixture—bitchy sometimes, but basically nice."

He was sometimes diverted by worry about his next book, and he needed publication on his own to keep his name and reputation continually burnished. Not that he had lost the qualities that brought public recognition. He couldn't shop anywhere without being approached or simply stared at by people who suddenly recognized him. In Greenwich Village, where for thirty years he had felt at home, such incidents sometimes warmed his spirits, adding to the satisfaction of picking out vegetables at Balducci's, or ordering meat at his favorite butcher. In the Jefferson Market one day in 1968 an encounter of this sort gave him pause. A vivacious woman came up to him as he was discussing a veal roast with his friend John Mantuori at the Jefferson meat counter. "When I said I wanted to take cooking lessons," Betty Ward recalled, "he told me he was booked for three years. So I just went back to my apartment and wrote him a letter, telling him that having worked for Juliet Prowse I understood celebrities. I offered to trade secretarial work for cooking lessons." Beard called her and asked her to come over, and she found herself installed at a big library desk "piled with books and manuscripts." It wasn't long after she started working as his secretary, she said after his death, that she found that Jim's annual income was $40,000. "He was going to Portland to do a demonstration and was being paid only five hundred dollars for the deal when it cost him a thousand to keep the date. I told him he was crazy." But she stayed to work for him. "While I was with him, Dupont brought out Teflon, and Jim loved it. When they called and asked for his endorsement, I got on the phone and set the price at twenty thousand. Jim was furious, said they'd cancel. I told him, 'They'll pay because you're James Beard'—and they did. Right away I ran the yearly take up to a hundred eighty thousand.

"Jim could be generous enough with time and things like the use of his house. Everybody knew him—the girls at the women's prison across the street never let him walk to the corner without calling out. They thought he was somebody, and he was. But he was tight. After all the extra fees I pulled in—finally up to four hundred thousand a year—I asked him for a raise to three hundred a week. I quit when he refused." Betty Ward was one of those who saw Jim as the spoiled brat his mother had brought him up to be.

Having worked for a movie star, Betty could overlook most errant behavior, and she took pride in Beard's accomplishments. She claimed large slices of credit for his increased financial status over the six years she worked for him. She was the one, for example, who egged him on as he signed up as consultant to Omaha Steaks. And she felt he never got the credit he deserved for introducing the revolutionary machine that became known as the Cuisinart food processor.

In the introduction to the booklet called *Recipes for the Cuisinart Food Processor*, Beard tells the story of how the French kitchen tool became a necessity for American cooks. When visiting a restaurant owned by a friend, George Garin, in the south of France, he and several others were making a mixture to force under the skin of two chickens to be roasted. "We used a machine that I had never seen before to chop the ingredients that went into the stuffing." He said he was filled with "awe and wonder at this incredible machine" which instantly chopped mushrooms, shallots, and crumbs as fine as one wanted.

He found the name of the manufacturer and the shipper, and had one delivered to his home. When it arrived, he recounted, he spent almost twelve hours trying it out on all kinds of things. "It was one of the most profitable play days I have ever put in." The immediate success across the country cheered Beard, he said, "because I realize that there are still some kitchen snobs who will not accept the fact that modern technological perfections are to be used and talked about . . . "

It was no surprise to Jim that his friend Julia, a stickler for not ever giving the use of her name, wrote of "this marvelous machine" in *From Julia Child's Kitchen,* in addition to demonstrating its efficiency in her telecasts. They were bound by different ethical standards on some points, but it was real camaraderie that Jim and Julia held onto. Both genuinely friendly people given to helping others, they had the ability to engender respect, or the next thing to it, from others. Both by second nature admired the European way of life, and they shared friendships among some of their peers in England and France.

In London, the person most often compared with either of them was Elizabeth David, whose books (on Mediterranean food, Italian food, summer cooking, the cuisine of Provincial France, spices and other aromatics, plus an exhaustive exploration of the subject of bread) were considered models on both sides of the Atlantic. She was a much-traveled Briton who wrote eloquent profiles of the distinguished London restaurateur Marcel Boulestin, the French gastronome Edouard de Pomiane, and of Norman Douglas, and Jim sent his friends to her for help. To one of these he cautioned, "Always bring two bottles of the best wine for lunch. One for her, one for you." She was enormously generous, the friend says.

Her kitchen shop near Sloane Square became for Jim as important a place to touch base in London as his favorite hotels, restaurants, and the other haunts of his years as a hopeful opera student. Julia also became a frequent visitor here. Their mutual California friend Chuck Williams, whose Williams-Sonoma kitchen supply shop pursued the same standards of equipment for cooks in a larger way, was as close to Elizabeth David as any American. He was among many of his countrymen who made pilgrimages on their own to the Sloane Square emporium.

Often including Elizabeth David, Jim made a point of getting together with his gastronomically inclined colleagues, and in checking the stores where British editions of his books sold well. In Mrs. David's

Jim with Chuck Williams and Paul Prudhomme

company he saw Bettina and Henry McNulty (whose first guest he had been, after they settled in London, when Bettina served "platter-sized mushrooms with thumbnail-sized lamb chops.") With Bettina he drove to Brighton Pavilion to inspect Carême's vast kitchen.* And he and Bettina and Henry went to Farley Farm near Muddles Green in Sussex, where Lee Miller Penrose, the former *Vogue* photographer and war correspondent, cooked for him, and he for her. Lady Penrose was as ardent and creative a cook as she had been a photographer. She had been Man Ray's protégée, but after settling in England she seldom touched a camera—an exception occurring when she photographed Jim on a picnic in a madras shirt and a chalk-stripe apron. He was displaying a freshly caught three-foot fish and the shot was later used on the jacket of the revised *James Beard Cookbook.* In Lee

---

*Beard wasn't often awed. "The first time I walked in there," he said in one of his columns, "I decided it was my spiritual home." The Brighton kitchen of the Prince Regent displays, among other showpieces, 11,000 items of "lovingly polished copper."

Penrose Jim had found another woman of affluence and highly cultivated style of life who reinforced his feeling that riches, plus the taste he thought necessary to use money well, were his due.

Work on *American Cookery,* which for years was sandwiched between other assignments, remained on his mind, and so he asked Catherine Laughton Hindley, the lifelong chum who had worked as food editor of the *Oregon Journal,* to join him, with her two boys, in a Kensington flat. Together, Katie and Jim tested recipes for the book that was so long in progress, and for three weeks in the summer of 1966 they worked at getting baking and dessert techniques down on paper, while weekends were reserved for outdoor festivities with the Penroses, McNultys, and others at Farley Farm.

He loved the English landscapes and he shared them with readers of his columns. "When I was in London recently," he might begin one of these pieces, "I spent a perfectly delicious day motoring up to visit Robert Carrier at Hintlesham Hall . . . out into the country-side and a breathtaking English spring." Carrier's parkland restaurant in a cream-colored Tudor house was the stuff of dreams—dreams that Jim on occasion could deny he had, but which he held on to until the end. "I wish I had an early Stuart brewery and stable block to renovate!" he once wrote.

With persistent memories of his mother's substantial meals, he remained a sentimental champion of British food. (He loved Carrier's mussels with bacon and mustard sauce.) Yet it may be that it was eating among the English that made him feel like an Edwardian gentleman surrounded by the best of everything. Years before the cooking styles of India established a beachhead in midtown Manhattan, he wrote, "My friend Elizabeth David took me to lunch at Shezan, a new Indian-Pakistani restaurant in London, and I was so impressed by the extraordinarily good cooking that I've been back quite often." Pointing out that in spite of the inconstant American enthusiasm for dishes called curries, "Indian food is a mystery" (he wrote) that warranted investigation.

And with Mrs. David, the McNultys, the wine writer Hugh Johnson, and restaurateur Robert Carrier, he dined with Simone Prunier, in whose restaurants in London and Paris he had been a welcome guest since his first trips abroad. He and Elizabeth David corresponded irregularly, trying to fit in a trip together to Amsterdam to take in the "wonderful cookery/pastry museum" on Wibautstraat, and meeting in Provence, where they both had similar enthusiasm for "the world's best *bouillabaisse*" at Carry-le-Rouet.

No one did more to spread the enthusiasm for Elizabeth David's work in the United States than Jim. "This shy, charming, knowledge-able English woman, whom I have known for years and count as one of my dear friends, could write," he said in *Beard on Food*, "with greater style and perception than anyone I can think of. She is a purist in many ways and can't stand what she calls 'bogus expertise.' Her books, which are intensely personal, give you an insight into her character, her sincerity, and her honest approach to the principles of foreign cooking." Both were alert to ethnic trends and, not surprisingly, they both were to write books on the subject of bread. (His, she wrote to him, seemed to her to be the best of anything he had done.) Jim's was dedicated to Elizabeth, a salute she described as an honor. Yet they did not get together when her American visit took her to California without a New York stop. After Beard's death, she wrote to me to say that while she liked *Delights and Prejudices,* she didn't find his other books original; she was among those who thought his "commercial interests such as Green Giant corn" suspect.

It's almost certain that because of her affection for Jim as a friend he was spared her critical assessments of his career. In letters that he kept, she told him that she looked forward to his visits to London, and she seemed regretful that the possibility of a trip to Vienna didn't work out. Jim understood the fact that frequently their schedules didn't mesh, but the daybook, in which he scrawled in his looping hand bits of observations on some of his travels and the menus of some of the meals he consumed, is chockablock with signs of constant companionship with friends from home and abroad. He had a ren-dezvous with Michael Field and his wife, Frances, in Nice at the end of 1968, and on New Year's Eve he had dinner near Cannes at the home of Simone Beck, Julia Child's collaborator. On New Year's Day, in Simca's kitchen, "Julia and I prepared luncheon for 2 o'clock—Fresh *foie gras panné, 2 fois*—Sauté in clarified butter, truffle sauce—Admiral's filet of beef—Salad—Apple tart—All superb!!!"* As a guest next door, at the house of Julia and Paul, he was able to do some work on a series of instructive articles for *Gourmet* magazine called "Cooking with James Beard."

Ten days later he met *Gourmet*'s editor, Jane Montant, in Paris and they sat down for a cheerful exchange of the gossip for which they both had large appetites. Jane's news of New York tempted her to lead him again to the story of how the cooking lessons that he was writing for the magazine had come to be. The idea had been Jane's and, in order to sell it to Earle MacAusland, who had soured on Jim twenty years before, she had arranged a lunch at the Pavillon. Neither she nor Jim made a note of the food, but they did remember that Delores Del Rio, a sultry brunette Hollywood star, was at the next table. When Jim couldn't ignore the fascination with which MacAusland gazed at the actress, he began on his mother lode of anecdotes about movies in which Del Rio appeared, and his own days in the movie colony, and the publisher became suddenly mellow enough to agree to Jane's plan for the series.

When Jim parted company with Jane, he was off on a brief spate of opera going. In Salzburg he caught up with Janet Wurtzburger, a wealthy supporter of the Walters Art Gallery in Baltimore, where he had given lectures and for which he had arranged periodic cooking demonstrations by Michael Field, Philip Brown, José Wilson, and others. The gallery's book of recipes, *Private Collections,* is illustrated by more than two hundred of the museum's works of art, and Jim's introduction to the volume makes a point of noting that other community cookbooks (much less lavish in design) comprise a major source of authentically American recipes. Among the recipes, which are followed by donors' names, are a few attributed to "G.O.K." This was Mrs. Wurtzburger's way of distinguishing her own contributions. The initials stand for "God only knows."

---

*When Mme. Beck published her own book, *Simca's Cuisine,* in 1972, she included a recipe which she entitled *La tarte pour Jim.* It had a pastry shell layered with apricot jam and a custard filling of pulverized almonds, raisins, and, for American cooks, "apples like Rome Beauties." The tart symbolized the affection between the two; Jim helped establish Simca's reputation as a cooking teacher in the United States and in France as well. Both were published by Alfred A. Knopf, Inc. Having been entertained by the publisher but unable to receive him in her home, Simca included in her book recipes for *"Un menu somptueux pour Mr. Knopf."*

A stylish, nurturing woman of considerable inheritance, Mrs. Wurtzburger had created a personal outdoor gallery of high repute in Baltimore. Her handsome suburban residence is surrounded by a scattering of life-sized sculptured figures that come as a surprise when discovered among the trees. She had taken cooking lessons from Jim, and in the resulting friendship he had become a frequent houseguest, often made comfortable in a bedroom suite that offered all the intimate appointments that might be at hand in a hostelry like London's Dorchester. Jim found in her house the kind of welcome he so often sought, and he and his hostess remained close until, one Christmas on a walk along a Caribbean country road, she was killed by a hit-and-run driver. The news of her death devastated Jim.

Mrs. Wurtzburger had fostered the idea of matching interest in the art of cooking with a network of museums in America. She and Beard found new audiences for cooking demonstrations among collectors of paintings, sculptures, and other works of art as well as among enthusiasts who lacked the money to invest. With Jim as a kind of avuncular member of the Wurtzburger family, both Janet's daughter and granddaughter were students in his cooking classes. He and Mrs. Wurtzburger toured Europe's museums, and they had favorite operas in common. His daybook reports critically on evenings of music and dining with equal commitment. In Vienna the two were disappointed with Demel's, and not happy about a dinner at which "Janet had a bad paprika chicken, I a poor *tafelspitz* —really bad." However, "*Bohème* was marvellous." Next day, after a visit to St. Stephen's there was a "superb *Trovatore* —great!" He added, "The days with Janet were lovely."

The number of female companions who cheered his travels at home and abroad should suggest, perhaps, that his ardent interests in specific men were sporadic. His associate Burt Wolf says that he disdained the description "gay," and thought it should be reserved for those prone to call attention to their feminine mannerisms. Among strangers, Jim was accepted by most as a heterosexual. He himself, he told Wolf, thought it was nobody's business what the sexual preferences of anyone might be, and his masculine deportment was such that many of his women acquaintances would have resisted the idea that he was "really different."

In his social circle, there were always homosexual couples, and there were also important male comradeships that included numerous husbands who met Jim through their wives. Choosing close friends, he served his need to appreciate people for themselves, for their individuality and the values they shared whether they were of the theater world or that of food. His passion for opera added dimension to his place in San Francisco society and New York, as it did in Europe. Mateo Lettunich and Jim found that they had had separate friendships with Cheryl Crawford, and Lettunich had tried to bring back the affection Jim had had for Cheryl. "But Jim," Lettunich said, "behaved like a diva. He thought Cheryl had lost her touch as a producer."

Beard doggedly maintained his interest in actors, and he was in Portland one spring evening in 1971 when he was matched at the dinner table with the television star Robert Cummings. The subject was healthy eating, with Jim goading the handsome leading man—a declared believer in organic food, as were thousands of Americans in that period. "Organic food people scratch for their lives," Jim said to Cummings. He outlined his thinking about healthy eating. "A simple menu, balancing elaborate dishes with something not so elaborate—I'm really convinced most people eat too much." Cummings told Beard that he stuck to his chosen diet to keep himself young. As it turned out some months later, Beard's own liberal diet caused him to check into the Clinique Medicale et Dietique Grassoise in the south of France.

After three years in which he returned annually to the rented house in St.-Rémy-de-Provence, Jim's friendship with Julia and Paul Child, and Simca too, made him regularly welcome in the village of Plascassier, often in the Childs' house, which they called La Pitchoune. It was turned over at times by the Childs to friends, including Frances and Michael Field and M.F.K. Fisher, who had been sought out by Time-Life to write the first volume of the Foods of the World series.*

---

*For my benefit when I was working for Time-Life, Beard wrote a memo from Plascassier in which he surveyed the then current American food scene. His review of regional United States eating patterns, along with his historical perspective, ended with the admonishment that researchers should not miss the agricultural elements considered essential to the gastronomical story.

When Beard was ensconced at La Pitchoune his frequent visitors were various—Mary Hamblet; fellow opera-followers like Mateo Lettunich and his brother Nicholas, a good cook; John Ferrone, the editor; and the McNultys.

He had the companionship of Mrs. Fisher after he signed himself into Grasse clinic. There he was sentenced to a salt-free diet, his daily intake rigidly controlled, with all his food weighed. As a fellow Westerner and friend, Mary Frances took him for drives, and they shared their sense of Provence's mystery. For her, it may have been an unexplained feeling of belonging to the chalky, craggy land, or thriving in the "play of the pure clear sunlight of Provence." For Jim it was a place of Roman vestiges, of troglodytes and troubadours as well, land that nurtured bountiful food and wine, earth that could be turned into tiles or pottery. Oddly perhaps, their paths in the world of cooking had first crossed in Johnny Kan's restaurant kitchen, where the friend of Jim's Portland childhood had taught the author, M.F.K. Fisher, to cook asparagus. They had many appreciations in common.

Together that summer they took in the Maeght Museum near St.-Paul-de-Vence and, in Moustiers-Sainte-Marie they stopped at the faïence museum, because of Jim's much-exercised interest in collecting glazed pottery. As they drove through the foothills of the Alps, he told Mrs. Fisher that when required to name a single food on which to subsist exclusively for seven days at the clinic he had chosen potatoes, which he considered "glamorous aristocrats among vegetables."

Down on the Côte d'Azur, when he was working on *American Cookery* at the home of the Childs, he had Katie Hindley again helping him to test recipes in the efficient kitchen, much as she had done when she had joined him in London earlier that year. His characteristic even-keeled complacence about the books he had undertaken to write was threatened in the big project which at the time he saw as his magnum opus. He honored his friend Julia's achievement in *Mastering the Art of French Cooking* as well as her success at using TV to stimulate and teach thousands of Americans. In his own *James Beard Cookbook* his ability to communicate had brought confidence to uneasy but easygoing cooks. Different though it was in approach, *American Cookery* was aimed to do for the subject of food in the United States something similar to what *Mastering* had accomplished for

French cuisine. The worry was on his mind, and his health eroded his inner strengths. "He was having terrible pains in his legs," Mrs. Hindley recalled, "and there were tantrums, terrible arguments about recipes when I tried to share some tips on bread." His health was an understandable vexation, but there was also the problem of male rights. Philip Hindley thought Jim demanded too much of his wife's time, while Jim, nevertheless, often felt a need to have dominion over those who worked with him.

"We found that Jim could hardly stand to be alone," Catherine Hindley told me. "That made it a big deal to get to go sightseeing on Sunday—when Jim would otherwise have worked, just to get me to be with him in the kitchen. Somehow Phil won out a few times, and we would drop Jim in Nice and, after our drive along the coast, pick him up in the evening."

There were bursts of lonely weekends throughout Jim's life. When he was in residence in Greenwich Village there were strings of Saturdays and Sundays when he had shut himself off from Cheryl Crawford's country house, when Gino Cofacci would go off on his own, when there was no secretary to keep him occupied; there was the dread of loneliness that caused him to make Sunday phone calls to Portland and San Francisco friends. Times when the Saturday-afternoon opera season was over, and Broadway had nothing to offer. Sometimes he used the hours alone to write letters to Isabel Callvert, until her health no longer supported the taxing life as his editorial assistant and he arranged a calmer job for her at *Gourmet*. To Helen Brown until her death from cancer. To John Ferrone as editor and friend. To Mary Frances Fisher, and less regularly to others. ("He needed me because he was lonely," one close friend said. "He was gregarious, yet very dependent. He said many times, 'The saddest thing for me is I've never loved anyone.' In his mind, he was always apart, special. He had no sense of equality.") He was always at the center of the circle.

As the circle widened in the passage of time, Richard Olney (who was a painter as well as the author of cookbooks much singled out by Beard) became a friend, as did Marion Cunningham of California, who accompanied him on a European trip during which they stopped at Olney's cliffside house a few miles northeast of

Marseille. Some of Jim's friends found it irresistible to describe this place. Mrs. Cunningham wrote of "the wonderful setting, garden, arbor, hanging grapes, the table set under it with a plastic cloth and dish towel napkins. . . . Richard, the artist," she continued, "has created a perfect picture of what the American would like to think French country life is like." She sketched the menu prepared especially for Jim: "lamb's feet and tripe with lean bacon, parsley and herbs."

When Jim had written to M.F.K. Fisher of visiting Olney, she responded in kind. She recalled in the letter her own visit to Richard's "eyrie," as she dubbed the house on the height:

> The more I think of doing one of the climbs without a flashlight in pitch dark, the more I wonder *how*. The road was impassable, except to herds of sheep and Sybille Bedford and me. Richard and Eda Lord pranced up and down through the abandoned quarry, but once was enough for me . . . I am not good at heights and depths, and more, especially without lights, air, guard-rails, even steps . . .
>
> Of course dinner was superb. Endless. The wines were very-good indeed, and also endless. The talk, which with Sybille racing a hundred words a minute, was mostly about those two subjects, wine and food, it was endless. We reached the bottom of the cliff at a very early hour, barely pre-dawn, and Sybille stopped at every fountain in the village to judge the waters. (I think I've written this to you . . . it's etched on my memory at least . . .) She was right: each fountain was different, even to my comparative[ly] untrained palate."*

M.F.K. Fisher and James Beard both loved to trade observations of friends' idiosyncrasies. When she and Michael Field, along with his wife, had been at La Pitchoune, the fact that the refrigerator was always empty delighted her, for what it revealed about the editor of the Time-Life cooking library—to Michael, away from the desk meant away from the stove; he was there to learn more about Gallic culinary

---

*The novelist Sybille Bedford's knowledge of food is direct and unimpeachable. In *The Artists' & Writers' Cookbook* she wrote: "I have loved all food at its hour. From the chicken leg devoured in hand to the *suprême velouté* to the dish of boiled bacon and greens. But what I love most—now—is an abundance of simple food of perfect quality and staggering freshness, very simply and respectfully treated, tasting strongly of itself." The same sentiment was often expressed by her friend Beard.

fundamentals but the food of chefs interested him more than what French families were cooking for themselves. When Mrs. Fisher was back in the Sonoma Valley, she and Jim gossiped occasionally by phone. "Thank you for calling," she wrote to him after a long telephone chat. "You sound well and strong." She apologized for having seemed impatient when he said he planned to do a small book on pasta—even though, she assured him, "I know it will be very good, and very much Beard. But I do want you to get to that personal, very Beard, post-script of DELIGHTS. *I* want to read it, and Time is turtling."

Occasionally he dictated a recollection to be used in a more extended autobiography, but he needed others to get him to settle down to it, as she wished. When he was in San Francisco, on the frequent trips he never stopped making to the West Coast, he would find one of their mutual friends willing to drive north for a visit. But Mrs. Fisher failed, as had been true with Helen Brown, in her effort to persuade him to take his life story more seriously. She remained at the top of his list of California comrades, which included James Nassikas at the Stanford Court Hotel, John and Helen Kan, and Chuck Williams, whose kitchen business had become a significant part of the increasing popular interest in eating and cooking. The same period brought the republication of M.F.K. Fisher's classic works, and in the trend that had been noted in the Ephron piece, there was much fervor that continued to mount in various ways.

Even Craig Claiborne, after savaging Time-Life's treatment of French Provincial cooking, had agreed to become one of the series authors, and other collections of recipes were being published almost in abandon. In 1969, 229 new or revised cookbooks had been published; ten years later the annual number would almost double. The country seemed to be in the process of transforming itself from a proverbial land of bounty and not much gastronomic style into a nation set on honoring the art of gourmandizing.

Julia Child's success on television had a great deal to do with it, but the accumulated importance of Beard's contributions was now being recognized more generally. At last *James Beard's American Cookery,* a giant volume with 839 pages of recipes, was published by Little, Brown and Co., and a weight fell from Jim's shoulders. The review in the *Times* by Nika Hazelton called it "the value of the year, and as good for us as it will be for our children. The author, who has done more than anybody else to popularize good food in America, puts a lifetime of experience into the pages. . . . This cookbook is also a good reading book, on just what the title says, American cookery and its origins." The measure of Jim's contribution was underscored in other reviews.

"Now, with the publication of 'James Beard's American Cookery,'" said William Rice in the Washington *Post,* "he has become a historian as well. . . . I know of no other person more qualified than Beard to attempt such a work and no other person could have created this book." Yet Bill Rice, admirer and friend, added judiciously: "But don't throw away the 'Joy of Cooking.' Though a fine teacher, Beard has never written in the step-by-step, learning-to-walk style employed by Michael Field and others." Rice's final words are worth repeating. "He finds improvement in American cooking and eating habits over the years, but does not fail to decry the lack of flavor in today's chicken and beef or 'the soft, rather flabby substance which we are fools enough to accept as daily bread in this country.'"

American Cookery, in spite of the years he had spent gathering its contents, turned out to be ahead of the times. In a season that offered such "gimmick" books as *Eat to Your Heart's Content* and *Cooking for Compliments,* Beard's was not the bestseller; its total sales over the years were only 15,222 in hardcover, and later the paperback edition sold 69,981. Those figures cast a pall over his long relationship with Little, Brown. In spite of his own promotion efforts (Jeanne Voltz in the Los Angeles *Times* reported that his schedule would "murder a younger, less enthusiastic person"), the book's earnings didn't come close to paying a living wage.

Beard had now a baker's-dozen books to his credit in spite of periods of bad health that sent him for days at a time to the hospital for treatment—he'd had much of his innards removed and the bouts with phlebitis were recurrent. Still he rose early, and his daybook was crowded with scrawled references to the demands on his time. For a couple of years he'd been lunching occasionally with Judith Jones, the Knopf editor who was looking for the right person to do a book on the subject of bread. He was intrigued. In *The New Yorker,* M.F.K.

Fisher had taken on the subject, citing among other recipes the one for French bread that had been perfected by Julia and Paul Child. The burgeoning awareness of food in general encouraged neighborhood bakers to sense a market for good loaves, and at last Beard agreed that there was no one else, after all, more likely than he to produce the kind of book that would make bread making seem within the reach of everybody.

Jim and Gino observing the making of Norwegian flatbread

His memory held stockpiles of bread recipes that began with a raisin loaf his mother had baked for benefit teas that she had given for the British Red Cross during World War I in San Francisco's Palace Hotel. Brought back from an Ireland trip was Myrtle Allen's Brown Bread, and from his Norwegian tour there was a loaf he had learned how to make at Mrs. Ovenstad's farm near Oslo.* He remembered breads baked by his friends—Emil Kashouty's pita, Janet Wurtzburger's

---

*He had been called to Norway by the government travel office as a consultant on ways to please American tourists—and how to please Americans at home in the preparation of sardines, herrings, and other fish for the United States market. Packers who sensed the growing calorie-consciousness across the Atlantic listened as he discussed the possibility of substituting herb-flavored water for the usual oil in cans of fish.

health bread made with home-ground flour, and one of wheat germ and potatoes created by Carl Gohs, a Portland writer.

"By accident I even learned how to broil bread . . . " It was a time he deemed one of his most rewarding. "I find it always pleasant at the beginning of a day to 'proof' the yeast, to plunge my hands into the dough and bring it to life, to watch it rise, to wait for the moment when the finished loaf can be taken from the oven." When *Beard on Bread* was published, he waited as the book was reprinted seven times in its first year and then went on to sell more than 264,340 copies. The success pleased him in terms of income, of course, but his good common sense caused him to turn down a suggestion from Knopf's editor-in-chief to write a similar volume devoted to soup recipes. "Soup?" he said to his editor. "Good soup doesn't need recipes. You look in the refrigerator, see what's there, and that's how soups are born."

At seventy he had lost no lust for life. "A James Beard is a phenomenon forty years in the making," a friend said. The measure of his achievement was not alone in his books, however; his years as a consultant left other traces. The Chicken Hash James Beard on the menu at Joe Baum's new restaurant (Windows on the World, which viewed the city from one hundred and seven floors above Wall Street) was a mere fingerprint of his continuing advisory capacity, just as was the Smithfield ham mousse served at Chicago's The Presidents. He was drawn further into the Midwest when he was asked, along with Mimi Sheraton, to act as consultant in Kansas City at the new restaurant called The American.

There in the heartland, where there hadn't been many eating places worthy of mention, the Beard conviction that an American cooking style needed only to be uncovered was being demonstrated. "We are barely beginning to sift down into a cuisine of our own," he had written in his *American Cookery*. Now he was continuing his crusade, and Kansas City's American restaurant had a menu distinguished by such regional specialties as veal from Minnesota, trout from Idaho, lime-lettuce from California, Michigan wild mushrooms, and Florida turtle. When the restaurant's manager was asked then by James Villas if he could envisage a day when the staff, including those in the kitchen, would be exclusively American, there was no hesitation.

"By all means!" was the answer. The kitchen had an apprentice program already established.

Beard liked to hear this kind of thing. His encouragement of young Americans who wanted to be chefs increased, but he wanted them first to understand the word. ("Don't call me chef," he said repeatedly. "I don't have the credentials.") Only a person who had gone through apprenticeship and had been trained to take charge of a professional kitchen could earn the title. He tipped his hat to young Americans who got themselves hired in European kitchens and who returned to the States to apply their new skills in cooking. He was at least as moved by unpretentious ambitions focused on local ingredients, or even by short-order coffeehouses. He wrote an introduction to a cookbook compiled by two young women whose restaurant, not far from Gearhart, specialized in all the Pacific seafood his mother had cooked.* It sometimes seemed that there wasn't a venture too modest for his professional interest.

At the urging of his friend the restaurant designer Charles Mount he made time for a consultation with three young owners of the newly opened American Café, in the District of Columbia. His dress that day was typical of his year-round sense of style. He wore a blue-on-blue striped shirt, a pink and orange striped tie, a glen plaid suit; and he immediately settled into the chore of sampling the café's new menu items. He tasted the "barbecue" sandwich, the outsize croissant stuffed with pâté—and the Chinatown special (marinated pork, alfalfa sprouts, and pineapple) caused him to cry out, "I love this!" It didn't unsettle him to know that a reporter was present who would publish the proceedings verbatim. He was as sure of his ground at the modest American Café in Georgetown as when he and Joe Baum dealt with the tastes of Manhattan.

Nothing pleased him more than proving himself a man for all seasons and all generations. His success as a consultant to restaurateurs

---

*In Jimella Lucas's words: "He had the ability to walk in the restaurant and take in everything from the tulips outside to the way we prepared the sole on his plate, to his mother's strawberry shortcake that we had prepared that night. Most things he spoke of rang up memories of the way I was raised—to cook and eat and enjoy the beauty of the seasons in my own region. . . . Beard played an important role in what we see happening around us in Northwest restaurants, predicating their menus on the gifts of the seasons from their own backyards and waters."

was due as much as anything to his undiminished love of all kinds of food. His admiration of haute cuisine remained, and he went often to Lutèce, the restaurant founded by André Surmain in the house where Jim and his friend had started Beard's cooking school. When ownership was passed from Surmain to the young chef André Soltner, Lutèce began its rise to greatness, and Jim remained a friend and adviser. Soltner remembers when Surmain, in jest, introduced Jim as the Curnonsky of America.* But Soltner viewed Beard as a modest man, always ready to help. "Over the next twenty years," says Soltner, "when I wanted to know something or other about American cooking, where to get produce that was scarce, I would ask Jim—he always knew." His reputation as a walking encyclopedia never diminished, and when he found a new colleague in Marcella Hazan, author of *Classic Italian Cooking,* who was herself encyclopedic on Italian food, she became as dependent as Soltner on Jim's wide command of the American culinary scene. "Jim for me," she said, "was a monument."

His information storehouse was the foundation of his rapport with all in the restaurant business, and it enlarged his friendship with magazine editors like Helen McCully, Glenna McGinnis, and José Wilson. (Wilson was about to leave her editing job at *Vogue,* and not long afterward took over as Jim's ghostwriter and, for the last years of her life, his collaborator.) Jim relayed, to anyone who asked, the information he gathered, almost automatically, on the road. For instance, he would not go to Cincinnati and leave immediately after a demonstration. He stayed, to establish lasting relationships among people who appreciated music and art, as well as among others who knew the markets or kept track of the sources of cooking ingredients.

"He changed things," Soltner says with conviction. In those days a restaurant couldn't get directly in touch with farmers or with the people who raised special vegetables, or knew where wild food could be found. "It seemed that nobody else could get to know as much about the bounty of the whole country the way James Beard could."

---

*As France's "Prince of Gastronomes," Curnonsky was a famed writer who was found attending his windowsill herb garden when Beard visited him before his death in 1956. The Frenchman took his pseudonym from the Latin words *cur non* (why not), adding *sky* in recognition of the White Russian noblemen who were highly respected in Paris before the wars.

Yet Soltner also pointed out that the same insatiable need to know caused Jim to ask the gifted chef what it is that results in the unique crispness of crust in a Lutèce onion tart.

His memory for such details was like his taste memory, which he always equated to perfect pitch. Nobody ever saw him take a note, whether for a recipe or for the basis of a column he might write weeks or months later. Pat Brown, as editor of *Cuisine,* took him to Leon Leonides's Coach House and got him talking about memorable dinners. (Jim's main course that night, she said, was three bowls of Leon's tripe soup.) Can you remember the first meal you ever ate at Fernand Point, Jim? she asked. "He proceeded to describe not only that entire dinner, but how many times he'd eaten at the Pyramide, and what the food was," Pat recalls. "He could remember exactly."

Neither telling stories nor expounding on the lore and legend of food ever bored him. If you asked him about rice birds he'd give you chapter and verse—the rice birds of the Carolina low country are the reed birds of Main Line Philadelphia, the bobolinks of New England that fly south to the rice fields in late summer. The early-nineteenth-century cookbook *The Carolina Housewife,* he might say, tells you to permit no sacrilegious hand to remove the head because the most succulent part is at the base of the brain of the rice bird.

Young cooks with dreams of a *toque blanche* of their own thought of Beard as the father of American cooking. Jimmy Schmidt inherited his role at the London Chop House after Beard had seen his talent developing at Madeleine Kamman's Modern Gourmet Restaurant in Boston—he had great admiration for Kamman's teaching skills. Les Gruber took his friend's advice and hired the young cook to move to Detroit. There, as Gruber and Beard urged the neophyte chef to flex his muscles, Schmidt, always giving credit to his Boston teacher, impressed the food establishment with his skill at building menus that emphasized American ingredients. With Gruber he visited Jim in New York a dozen times a year. "Once at Leon Leonides's Coach House," Schmidt recalls, "we all spent most of the night just talking beans—all kinds, all countries. James Beard taught me there is no limit to what makes good cooking. He brought shark's fins to Les Gruber's house and left them soaking in the sink—when the housekeeper found them, she literally fainted dead away. But the soup that resulted proved the point. You get rid of your prejudices about ingredients that are unfamiliar."

Larry Forgione, a graduate of the Culinary Institute of America, worked for two years in the kitchens of the Connaught Hotel in London, and then became chef at the River Café on the Brooklyn side of the East River. When he called Jim, he explained that he wanted to use his Connaught training in haute cuisine as a basis for evolving his own American style of cooking.* He had been trying to find sources of foods that were not usually available to New York restaurateurs. Forgione was interested in the country's wild bounty—woodland mushrooms, fiddlehead ferns, sea urchins. He had his grandmother's cooking in mind; he wanted to find a supply of chickens that tasted as good as those his grandmother had raised herself.

When he located some gatherers of wild food, he developed a steady supply of chanterelles and morels and he brought some of the good things to his new friend Jim. Together they talked about bounty as the fundamental to all American cooking styles, and Jim encouraged Larry's determination to emphasize natural flavors. With Beard's help in locating suppliers of such arcane items as sweet cream butter produced on an Iowa farm with no middleman involved, Larry continued to seek Jim's counsel in developing menus for a new restaurant. He called it An American Place when it opened on Lexington Avenue. "He pushed me into using his library of books on American food, and I got to know the things that make cooking in this country what it used to be," Larry says. He smiled when he added that he'd become an expert on desserts like apple pandowdy.

"I was too serious in the beginning," Larry remembers. "I'd show him a dish. Was it fun? His whole thing about food—it must be fun. Seeing it, creating it, must be fun, not precious. He changed me. In '79 I was proud that I'd never served anything made in a deep-fat fryer; now I know I can use it to good effect. He taught me about

---

*Working in the Connaught kitchen, he'd been razzed unbearably, he thought, by European fledgling cooks who held him responsible for the American penchant for surviving on hamburgers, hot dogs, and little else. "I promised myself I'd never again have to apologize for American food," Forgione says.

fresh-made biscuits, muffins—warm—fresh berries, cream. Food can't get any better than that. Maybe fancier, but not better. A plate doesn't have to be arranged like an abstract painting."

In a newspaper article, Beard hailed Forgione's development of menus that emphasized game, and cited the variety of foods that included Florida pompano, Calistoga goat cheeses, Smithfield bacon, Maine oysters and lobsters, bear steaks, "such rare items as marsh rabbits and beaver," along with the menu that started with "fillet of venison smoked on the premises and served paper-thin with shredded celery root in mustard sauce" and Muscovy duck.

"I must include Larry," Beard wrote, "with such people as Alice Waters, Jeremiah Tower, Mark Miller, and a few other brilliant young chefs who are making the effort to create a cuisine that is distinctly American and capable of rivaling any other in the Western world. This movement is not a flag-waving proposition as much as it is a justification of the excellence of our own products, which many people have hesitated to accept because they felt they couldn't possibly be as good as the imported articles."

Indeed in many ways Jim was just what the new wave of young American professional cooks was looking for. A grand, vintage star who still had instant rapport with the sort of style and iconoclasm which permeated the ideas held by many of them. "Whenever any of them came to the city there was a pilgrimage to Jim's house," Larry said. "I'd be there talking—suddenly one of the others would walk in or phone."

This was Jim's last house, a four-story building next to a private school on Twelfth Street. ("Those kids," Jim said, "they study nothing but recess.") He had been bamboozled into the purchase by Agnes Crowther White, who never quite succeeded in burying her own opportunistic nature. Jim was unable really to like the place, even though it had several attributes—a top apartment to be rented, along with a third floor in which to install Gino Cofacci (whose clinging presence Jim bore like a cross that reminded him of past sins). Although the decor changed from time to time, it was as remarkably offbeat as his haberdashery. Once, kitchen walls and ceiling were covered by gigantic, delicately colored maps of the world (Jim's world in its entirety), as if they papered the chartroom of the gastronomic

Magellan he had become. The floors were of rosy terracotta and there was a garden. In the remodeling that came later, an effort was made to make up for the lack of size and space by adding a two-story greenhouse that extended the space for living and for work into the north light. A bath and shower were included in the uninhibited addition, which gave Jim a new chance to shower with only glass separating him from the open sky while neighbors with windows overlooking the garden could look down on his bald head.

With his love for seeing and being seen, he had arranged his work desk so close to a big window on the lower floor of his house that he could observe any sidewalk activity there might be. Just as he liked to be recognized through the glass-fronted restaurants he often patronized, he enjoyed the fact that people could see him when he worked at his desk. Often a passerby who was recognized by Jim would be stopped by the sound of his tapping on the windowpane. "It was his way of demanding that I stop and come inside," his friend, Zack Hanle, a magazine editor, recalled. "What he wanted was to stop awhile for some good gossip—what he loved to call 'gissip.' He had his own way of dealing with everything."

His sense of decor reflected the same disregard for conventions. With the sculptured Grecian ladies still a dominating factor in his eclectic design scheme—a gilded and brocaded Mandarin coat was spread out and pinned to a wall of the alcove in which, for lack of sufficient space, Jim slept. There was Chinese porcelain and majolica on view. The place was much photographed, and appeared often in magazine articles that paid tribute to the lifestyle of the country's gastronomic doyen.

Among the frequent visitors Jeremiah Tower, who had met Jim while working with Alice Waters at Chez Panisse, recalls it was a privilege to talk alone with Jim—"like being at a French court. He was really at his greatest as personal adviser." The reminiscences would flow . . . talk of the great ocean liners to whose luxuriousness Jeremiah, young as he had been, had been exposed by his globe-trotting family. Europe's grand hotels that Jim's memories brought to life. Henri Soulé and the Pavillon and the French chefs who worked at the '39 World's Fair and stayed on to change the New York restaurant scene. "Jim was a chameleon," Tower says. "Everyone thought they had a

private Jim. He always listened—was always objective. I could get him to tell me always what my next step should be. He talked over power plays, and moves. He was like J. Edgar Hoover—he had everybody's file." The quality that impressed this San Francisco restaurateur was (as it was to many) Beard's sense of presence. "Not just size—a special kind of awareness; he taught me how to turn on a spontaneous smile as soon as a camera appears."

There is a temptation to remember that Norman Mailer had described a metaphysical presence that he says accompanies him everywhere—which consists of half of what he pretends to be and half of what others expect him to be. For Jim there may have been a similarity, but it had its distinction. Different people needed different Beards; thus he was free to invent himself. His own generation of food professionals tended to take him for granted as a peer who had some special gifts; the new generation recognized him for what he had become.

Alice Waters of Chez Panisse says, "We wouldn't have been what we were without him. He put Chez Panisse into perspective in relation to other restaurants in the country." Beard appreciated the fact that Alice, unlike most of the young cooks who were succeeding, was a self-made cook, as Jim was too. He had first heard of Chez Panisse from Marion Cunningham, the California housewife who had been keeping abreast of the times by joining cooking classes, the more variety in ethnic styles the better. With Marion he often came to eat at the restaurant, sometimes with their friend Chuck Williams along. "Jim talked us up to everybody," Alice says. Gael Greene, the food critic of *New York* magazine, was brought to Chez Panisse by Jim.

But it was Marion Cunningham who was the essential link between Jim and most of the young restaurateurs of the San Francisco Bay area. She had had an intense fear of travel, had never before left California, when one day in her late forties she and a friend boarded an airplane for a flight north to Oregon, to enroll in the James Beard Cooking School at Seaside. In her introduction to the man she chose to call "James" but never "Jim," she met the most important person in her life and he met his Galatea. In the cooking classes, Marion became Eliza Doolittle and he Professor Higgins.

Middle-aged and mother of two, she was a tall, blond, blue-eyed Californian whose smile lit up her face like sudden sunshine, and she was engagingly smitten by Jim from the outset. They played into each other's hands—he needed a worshiping daughter; but, most of all, she needed him—to take care of solicitously, to hover around, putting up

with his moods and tending to his health—in order to immerse herself in his wisdom.

The extension of the cooking school into summer sessions, at the beach which had been his boyhood playground, was a result of the homing instinct that drew him constantly back to Oregon. Once he spent six months in residence near Tillamook Head, searching for the right house, a year-round dwelling to which he could retreat at whim. With his friend John Carroll as his driver, he traversed old roads, stopping to eat junk food as he had as a youth.* He was entertained by Portland's best families, only to decide that his affinity for New York was greater. He decided on a seasonal school instead of a full-scale move, and it injected Jim's old age—years that others gave to retirement—with new energy in spite of physical deterioration. He became the Mohammed to whom the mountain moved—cooking enthusiasts from far places signed up to be taught by Beard in Maryon Greenough's teaching kitchen in Seaside High School. From New York, Jim shipped more than a dozen crates of pots, pans, knives, and small appliances and brought a professional enthusiast named Felipé Rojas-Lombardi to be the summer school's assistant instructor that year, while José Wilson served as his aide-de-camp and collaborator on the columns.

Felipé, who later opened the Ballroom Restaurant, with New York's first tapas bar, had grown up in Peru and had cooked in several countries, but found himself "absorbed" by Jim's enormous culinary knowledge. ("Little by little, he absorbed all my time. He was my teacher. He never asked if you could do something. When we were testing recipes, he would just say 'I have to have it tomorrow.'") Felipé was with Jim on a European trip during which they were accompanied by Felipé's mother, who had come on from Peru. "She and Jim became inseparable," Felipé said. "She didn't know any English, but they talked incessantly, French, Spanish, anything." Felipé felt so attached to his mentor that he gave Jim a fur coat which, with all the rights of a seigneur, Jim wore in New York. "It was just to cheer

---

*"He straddled two worlds, from the *Queen Elizabeth II* to street corner sausage," a New York business associate says. "Jim told me what this country needs is a 'Junk Food Day,' and for himself at least he meant it."

him up," Felipé says. "It was a challenge—he agreed to lose twenty pounds. He did, and he got his coat. In winter he loved to wear fur hats. They made him look like a hussar."*

José Wilson, after years as editor at *House & Garden* and as a free lance, had for some time spelled her name as if it were Spanish but pronounced it "Josie." She consistently sought out men who lived in fear of the female sex; as a result she was restless and unsatisfied, but somehow she fit in as a member of the Beard entourage and she had little new to learn about Jim.

Felipé, recollecting his jobs in European kitchens and his professional training, recalled that Jim gave him the finishing touches as a cook. "He gave me the patina—he opened my eyes." Marion Cunningham, for her part, learned that Jim understood her so well that he could open the future for her. He began to treat her as an associate and confidante, and soon she was working with Chuck Williams, and later Jim Nassikas, in organizing cooking courses at the Stanford Court Hotel in San Francisco.†

Like the majority of her classmates, she took some notes when Beard held forth on his philosophy of cooking. In the back of her brand-new copy of *American Cookery,* she jotted, "Cooking is theater—not what you feed people but hospitality you put forth—people need less food due to easier environment." Among some other Beard quotations copied: "Too many people never bother to read a recipe and that spells peril. You can be creative in the kitchen, but not until you have mastered the basic recipe. It is the same as music. First you

---

*He may not have lost enough weight, however. The story goes that Jim found the coat too small eventually and passed it on to Clay Triplette, for whom it was retailored.

†Often when they shared relaxed moments, Jim went back to troubles with his mother— "having terrible fights with her," Marion recalled once, "usually about some dish. But he always had great admiration for her. He even told me how he'd go to the corset-fitter and sit in a cubicle, waiting."

must know how to play, then you can have variations." And, most typical of the cheerful teacher: "If you are going to cook well, you have to have fun shopping."

Beard's teaching, on the West Coast, in New York, or in such regional centers as Dallas or Toledo, always emphasized basics. Back in 1962, when he set out to help Julia Child and Simone Beck after the publication of *Mastering the Art,* they found, when he invited them to his Greenwich Village class, that his students were happily plunging their hands into the egg whites. "Good cooking is in your hands" was a Beard maxim.* While students from across the country continued to sign up for his annual Seaside classes, he began a series of more than twenty articles on learning how to cook for *American Way,* the airline magazine. He wrote, "I find many people have difficulty learning to fold in beaten egg whites with a spatula and tend to overfold, but if you learn to fold them by using the side of your hand to cut down, and the palm to fold up and over, you soon grasp the technique of quick, light folding that doesn't deflate the egg whites."

To teach the most elemental form of using heat in cooking, he started students off with the baking of crêpes. "Nowadays baking is generally assumed to mean cooking in the oven," he would say, "but that's only the half of it." Pancakes of all kinds—French crêpes, Russian blinis, Indian poori, Mexican tortillas, whatever—evolved before there were even primitive stoves, when much cooking was done on smooth hot stones. Now crêpes, and other pancakes, are baked in pans, and the process is a fundamental way of learning how to judge the degree of heat required to cook simple batter, taking care that it doesn't burn yet gets cooked through before the crêpe is turned—with the hands, of course.

Without undermining the importance of learning manual skills among the basics, Jim applauded the new kitchen technology. For Marion and others, his Oregon classes served to introduce the food processor he had discovered in France. He also introduced, during a

---

*He collected sculpted hands when he went exploring in antique shops and they became, as he scattered them here and there, his household icons. For a time, there were carved wooden "salad hands," designed for serving tossed greens, on sale under Beard's name in specialty stores.

class in outdoor cooking, a new grill, with the admission that, since he and Helen Brown had written the classic *Complete Book of Outdoor Cookery*, cooking roles had changed. He said it was no longer the exclusive role of men to do the outdoor meals, and added that he knew women that are "damn good grillers," one of whom was his new colleague, Marion Cunningham. It was Felipé, however, who was in charge when a piglet was roasted.

In Marion Cunningham he had recognized the person he was to recommend to Judith Jones at Knopf, who had discussed with him her quest for the right kind of woman to take on the mantle of Fannie Farmer and the challenge of revising the best-known American cookbook. Without telling her what was in the wind, he asked Marion to begin perusing early versions of the Boston Cooking-School book, at the same time stressing to her his need to have her help in classes at the Stanford Court Hotel.

In spite of continued vascular and intestinal problems that caused repeated hospitalization, Jim's life had again shifted gears. Increasingly he had been assuring himself that teaching gave him as much, or more, pleasure as any of his myriad activities. Wherever classes were scheduled, applicants had to wait in line, as it were, booking admission months ahead. No doubt, he was doing a star turn—the country's most famous purveyor of the culinary art. In earlier days, Mimi Sheraton says, he had brought the image of food to people all over the country. "He seemed to be central casting's idea of what a food editor looks like."

Even his most indulgent friends couldn't overlook some flaws in his character, however. In retrospect, Marion Cunningham says, "He was like Tom Sawyer. He could always get someone to paint the fence for him." Chuck Williams admitted to colleagues that there were times he thought Jim forgot that he could be hurtful. "He always tried to get everything he could out of people." As a volunteer helper in classes both in Oregon and San Francisco, Williams viewed his friend close up, and sometimes he'd get disgusted at the treatment by Jim of those who looked on him with something verging on awe.

Along with periodic tendencies toward imperiousness, Jim became more intent on the possibility of singling out one or more protégés, and he had a weakness for pitting his favorites against each other. Of these, one used Marion's friendship to increase his standing with Beard. He was an aggressive young man named Carl Jerome, a part-time New York cab driver who moved into the Beard household and soon became the self-proclaimed "Director of the James Beard Cooking School."

RECIPES

Cream of Artichoke Soup
▼

Because he held classes in San Francisco's Stanford Court Hotel, Jim was often consulted by his friend Jim Nassikas, the hostelry's director. They shared a belief in old-fashioned service and in offering the best meals in town to the hotel's dining room patrons. This artichoke soup, Jim said, was an example of the originality with which the Stanford Court made use of California vegetables.

4 medium or large artichokes	*3 tablespoons rice flour*
lemon juice	*salt*
4 cups homemade chicken stock	*freshly ground pepper*
1/4 cup blanched hazelnuts, toasted, then crushed very fine	*1/2 cup heavy cream*
	1 tablespoon dry sherry

Cut off artichoke stems about 1 inch from top and snip off the prickly tips of leaves. Cook in boiling salted water with a squeeze of lemon juice for about 40 minutes. Remove with tongs and drain on paper towels. Remove leaves, scoop out the fuzzy choke, and drop the artichoke bottoms into a pot containing 4 cups of chicken stock. Add the nuts to the stock, bring to a boil, reduce heat, and simmer artichoke bottoms and nuts for a half hour. Purée the mixture in a blender and return to the pot. Mix the rice flour to a paste with 6 tablespoons of cold water, stir into the soup, and gradually bring to a boil, stirring. Reduce the heat and simmer for 15 minutes. Taste for seasoning and add salt and pepper to taste. Stir in the heavy cream and sherry.

SERVES 4.

Italian Mixed Vegetables
▼

Always open to new experiences, Jim accepted a luncheon invitation from Ellie and Ed Giobbi at their house near Katonah, New York, and the new friendship resulted in the exchange of numerous tales of eating. Ed, a painter whose work is internationally exhibited, is an inventive cook who had postgraduate courses from two Italian grandmothers. This is the way he made the *verdura mista* he served to Jim with stuffed veal breast and some of Ellie's freshly baked bread.

1 very large potato, peeled and diced	*¹/₂ pound Savoy cabbage, chopped*
1 stalk celery, cut in 1-inch pieces	*3 tablespoons olive oil*
1 pound fresh spinach, washed and chopped	*2 cloves garlic, finely chopped*
¹/₂ pound escarole, chopped	*salt*
	freshly ground pepper

Put all the vegetables in a deep pot and pour boiling water over them to cover. Return the water to the boiling point, then drain the vegetables, reserving ¹/₂ cup of the cooking water. Heat the oil in a large skillet, sauté the chopped garlic until it begins to take on color, then stir in the drained vegetables; season lightly with salt and pepper. Cover the pan and cook the vegetables over low heat until tender, adding some of the reserved cooking liquid if the mixture gets too dry.   SERVES 4.

Mushroom Roll à la Oregon

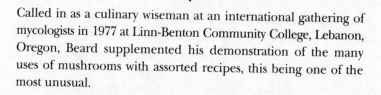

Called in as a culinary wiseman at an international gathering of mycologists in 1977 at Linn-Benton Community College, Lebanon, Oregon, Beard supplemented his demonstration of the many uses of mushrooms with assorted recipes, this being one of the most unusual.

¹/₃ cup dry breadcrumbs, approximately	*salt*
1¹/₂ pounds mushrooms, chopped fine	*freshly ground pepper*
6 tablespoons melted butter	*freshly grated nutmeg, to taste*
5 eggs, separated	*³/₄ cup fresh breadcrumbs, approximately*

Filling:

about 6 eggs, scrambled, or 1 pound asparagus, cooked (pp. 193–4)

Grease an 11 × 15½-inch jelly-roll pan and line it with wax paper, leaving an overhang of about 1 inch of paper at each end. Grease the paper and sprinkle with dry breadcrumbs. Set aside. Put the mushrooms in a dishtowel and twist very hard to squeeze out all the moisture. Put them in a bowl and mix in the butter, egg yolks, a sprinkling of salt, pepper, and nutmeg, and just enough fresh breadcrumbs to make the mixture hold together. Beat the egg whites until they hold soft peaks, as for a soufflé, and fold quickly and thoroughly into the mushroom mixture. Turn into the prepared pan and smooth the top evenly with a rubber spatula. Bake in a 350 degree oven for 12 to 16 minutes or until the center feels barely firm when touched. Put a sheet of buttered wax paper or foil over the top of the roll and invert onto a warm platter or long board. With the aid of the overhang of wax paper, carefully peel away the paper adhering to the roll, gently loosening it with the point of a knife where necessary. It doesn't matter if a little bit of the surface of the roll sticks to the paper, since this is the side you will fill. Fill the roll with scrambled eggs, or with asparagus tips that have been cooked in salted boiling water until just done but still crisp to the bite. Roll up with the aid of the wax paper or foil and serve as a luncheon or supper dish.

SERVES 4 TO 6.

Rockfish with Mustard Mayonnaise

Jim failed to find the country inn he dreamed of buying, but on Maryland's Eastern Shore he found "winding streams like the Choptank. High summer there is hot, watery and beautiful." He proposed this fish course for "a cheerful beachside lunch."

2 quarts water	1 clove garlic, peeled
2 cups dry white wine	1 teaspoon salt
1 onion, stuck with 2 whole	1 strip lemon peel
cloves	2 sprigs parsley
1 rib celery	4 pounds rockfish fillets

Mustard Mayonnaise:
1 cup mayonnaise mixed
   with 1 tablespoon dry
   mustard or 2 tablespoons
   Dijon mustard

Make a courtbouillon by combining all ingredients except the fish in a poacher or a large pot. Bring to a boil, reduce the heat, and simmer covered for about 20 minutes. Add the fillets and simmer 3 to 4 minutes longer. Carefully remove the fillets to a platter. Serve with mustard mayonnaise.

SERVES 8.

Jeanne Voltz's Grilled Fillet for Beard

"This lightly hickory-smoked fillet is a favorite of my dear friend Jim Beard. He liked it very rare," Mrs. Voltz wrote of this recipe that she sometimes served her barbecue mentor on her Manhattan terrace. "The sliced fillet also makes good luncheon sandwiches," she added.

1 beef fillet, about	*1 tablespoon herbes de*
4¹/2 pounds	*Provence or other*
1/2 cup red wine	*herb blend*
1/4 cup oil	*Mushroom Sauce*
1/4 cup minced onion	*(recipe follows)*

Buy prime-grade fillet, if possible, and trim it well. Fold and tie the tail to the meat to form a roast of uniform thickness (or have the butcher do it for you). Place the meat in a plastic bag. Mix wine, oil, onion, and herbs. Pour over the meat, close bag tightly, and turn it to coat the meat with marinade. Place bag in a dish and marinate 2 hours at room temperature or overnight in the refrigerator. Drain, reserving the marinade.

Grill meat 4 inches above hot coals, turning to brown all sides. This takes about 10 minutes of undivided attention so you can put out any flash fires. Add damp hickory chips or small hickory sticks. Move meat to edge of grill or cover grill and cook 15 to 20 minutes longer for rare, 20 to 25 minutes for medium-rare. Slice and serve with Mushroom Sauce.

SERVES 6 TO 8.

Mushroom Sauce

2 tablespoons butter	*8 ounces fresh mushrooms,*
2 tablespoons minced onion	*cleaned and sliced*
2 cloves garlic, minced	

> 1 teaspoon meat glaze
> (Bovril) or broth
> seasoning mix
>
> reserved marinade for fillet
> red wine or beef broth,
> if needed

In a medium skillet melt the butter, add the onion and garlic, and cook until the onion is tender but not browned. Add the mushrooms and cook, stirring gently now and then, until well saturated with butter and most of the juices exuded from the mushrooms have evaporated. Stir in meat glaze. Add reserved marinade and, if needed, a few tablespoons of wine or broth to make a light sauce. Serve hot with the grilled fillet.

Rio Grande Beef and Pork

▼

John Siddeley, Lord Kenilworth, a British writer for the French magazine *Vogue,* talked food one day in the Beard garden on Twelfth Street. He found Jim garbed in faded blue jeans and a quilted jacket and full of enthusiasm about Latin American influences that were becoming popular in the 1980s; he went away with this version of simmered meats redolent of powdered sweet pepper and accented by bitter chocolate.

> 3 tablespoons butter
> 3 tablespoons olive oil
> 2 large onions, chopped
> 3 fat garlic cloves, minced
> 2 1/4 pounds beef chuck, cut
> in 1-inch pieces
> 1 1/2 pounds pork loin, cut
> in 1-inch pieces
> flour for dredging
> salt
> 3 tablespoons paprika
> 1/2 teaspoon dried oregano
>
> 1/2 teaspoon ground cumin
> 1 tablespoon tomato purée
> (preferably homemade)
> 1 cup dry white wine
> 2 cups beef or chicken broth
> 1/2 ounce (1/2 square) bitter
> chocolate, coarsely grated
> 3–4 teaspoons sesame
> seeds, toasted
> 3 tablespoons chopped
> cilantro (or
> Italian parsley)

Heat the butter and oil in a heavy casserole and sauté the onions until golden. Add the garlic and sauté a few more minutes. Meanwhile, dredge the meats in flour. Set aside the onions and garlic. Brown the beef quickly in the same pan, removing the pieces when they are brown; do the same with the pork. Return everything to the pan, season with salt, paprika, oregano, and cumin, stir over heat 1 minute, then add the tomato purée, wine, and broth. Cover and cook slowly for about 1½ hours, until tender. Stir in the chocolate and sesame seeds and cook another 10 minutes. Taste and correct seasoning, then sprinkle cilantro on top.   SERVES 6 TO 8.

Love-Letter Banana Cake

The Beard summer cooking classes at Seaside attracted students of all ages and from most points of the compass. One was a fledgling journalist from Louisville named Sarah Fritschner. She reported that she wrote a three-page love letter to Mr. Beard, saying she thought he was the most wonderful cook in the world: "the one quality that sets Beard apart from other cookbook writers is the way he *feels* about food, and how he gets that feeling across to his readers." She was ecstatic when she was accepted for the summer of 1978 and when she got back to her job her account of the experience included this recipe, "Not because it was the most scrumptuous, but because it was so plain and simple and not oversweet."

½ pound unsalted butter, at
room temperature
2 cups sugar
4 eggs
3 cups sifted cake flour
4 teaspoons baking powder
½ teaspoon salt

1 cup milk
1–1½ teaspoons vanilla
2–3 bananas, sliced
1 cup heavy cream,
whipped, sweetened
slightly, and flavored with
brandy

Cream the butter, then beat in the sugar until fluffy. Separate the eggs and beat the yolks into the butter and sugar. Sift the flour with the baking powder and salt and add alternately with the milk and vanilla. Beat the egg whites until stiff and fold them into the batter. When smooth, pour into three 8 × 9-inch layer-cake pans. Bake in a preheated 350 degree oven for about 25 minutes, until the cake springs back when touched with the fingertips. Cool on a rack for a few minutes, then loosen from the pans and turn out onto a rack to cool completely. Top each layer with sliced bananas and the flavored whipped cream.   SERVES 12.

Corn Bread Apple Pandowdy

▼

Of all the young chefs to seek Beard's guidance, Larry Forgione was one of the closest to him professionally. He was also inventive in a way similar to Jim. Here is Larry's version of a colonial dessert that Jim described in a column as "so seductive that we all managed to have a tiny second helping because we just couldn't believe our palates."

8 slices corn bread
softened butter
light brown sugar
3 apples, peeled, cored, and
* sliced thin*
3 tablespoons molasses
1/2 teaspoon cinnamon
1/4 teaspoon freshly
* grated nutmeg*

2 tablespoons dark rum
2 tablespoons fresh
* lemon juice*
1 tablespoon vanilla
4 tablespoons unsalted
* butter, cut in small cubes*

Cut the bread in rounds to fit individual baking dishes; spread each slice evenly with softened butter and sprinkle with brown sugar. Put 1 slice on the bottom of each of 4 baking dishes, buttered side up. Toss together the apple slices, molasses, cinnamon, nutmeg, rum, 3 ounces of light brown sugar, the lemon juice, vanilla, and the diced butter. Turn until seasonings are evenly distributed. Divide this mixture into 4 lots, and spoon into the baking dishes. Place a second slice of buttered bread, buttered side up, on top of each dish. Put the dishes in a baking pan with enough water to reach halfway up the sides. Bake in a preheated 375 degree oven for 25 to 30 minutes. The tops should be buttery brown. Serve with sweetened pouring cream.   SERVES 4.

Gino's Rum Chocolate Cheesecake

▼

Gino Cofacci, sent by Jim to learn the art of pastry from a world master in Paris, was also a friend of Chuck Williams, to whom he gave this recipe. "He and Jim Beard," Williams wrote in his own cookbook, "used to cook up a storm together, and this cake was a great favorite of theirs. Gino has made it for years for several very good New York restaurants."

1¹/4 cups graham
cracker crumbs
³/4 cup plus
2 tablespoons sugar
4 tablespoons butter, melted
6 ounces semisweet chocolate

¹/4 cup rum
1 pound cream cheese
¹/2 cup sour cream
1 tablespoon vanilla
5 eggs

Butter the inside of a springform pan well and cover the outside with a sheet of heavy-duty aluminum foil, shiny side out. This reflects the heat away from the cheesecake and prevents it from baking too fast and becoming overcooked. Mix the graham cracker crumbs with 2 tablespoons of sugar and add the melted butter. Press the mixture evenly on the bottom and sides of the pan and refrigerate until ready to use. Cut chocolate into small pieces, combine with rum in top of a double boiler, and place over barely simmering water. Stir gently until the chocolate is melted and smooth. In a bowl of an electric mixer beat the cream cheese until it is light and fluffy. Gradually beat in the remaining sugar, sour cream, and vanilla. Add the eggs, one at a time. Mix well, then remove bowl from the mixer stand. Place it over a pan of hot water and mix until smooth. Pour about 1¹/4 cups of this mixture into a separate bowl and set aside. Whisk remaining batter with the chocolate, then stir over hot water until smooth.

Take the springform pan from the refrigerator and fill with the chocolate batter. Gently pour the plain batter over the top and make swirls down into the chocolate batter with a fork. Place on the middle rack of a 325 degree oven, and bake for 50 minutes. Cool to room temperature, remove the foil and the rim of the pan, and refrigerate overnight.   SERVES 10 TO 12.

Jim's Melting Moments

▼

His yen for British food never diminished, especially in regard to comforting nibbles. Traveling in England and Scotland, Jim came upon original versions of the cookies, called Melting Moments, which are as popular in country homes today as they were in Jim's kitchen in his old age. Caroline Stuart produced for Jim many a melting moment, at his behest.

¹/₂ cup butter
³/₈ cup sugar
1 egg yolk
1 teaspoon vanilla
1 cup all-purpose flour

2 tablespoons cornstarch
¹/₄ teaspoon salt
³/₄ teaspoon baking powder
rolled oats

Cream the butter and the sugar. Beat the egg yolk with the vanilla. Sift together the flour, cornstarch, salt, and baking powder, then stir in the butter-sugar mixture. Shape into balls the size of a marble, and turn in the oats to cover. Put a greased cookie sheet in a shallow pan to fit. Arrange the cookies on the sheet and bake at 375 degrees for 15 minutes.

MAKES 36 TO 40 COOKIES.

Beard-size Cookies

A couple of years after Jim's death Christine Whited, who calls herself a psychic consultant, claimed that the ghost of James Beard had visited her in her Greenwich Village kitchen and was dictating recipes to her. Beard friends were skeptical, particularly since the recipes were full of health food ingredients like tofu and carob—hardly Jim's notion of good eating. In her eagerness to prove that the recipes were Beard-inspired, Mrs. Whited sent over a bag of "their" chocolate chip cookies to the Beard Foundation, now located in the Twelfth Street house, and as spirits would have it, a TV crew arrived out of the polluted summer air. The camera bore down as a sample cookie (tangible enough) was gingerly tasted by Clay Triplette, who asked the sensible question: "If Mr. B. was going to send recipes back to earth, don't you think he'd send them through me?"

It was Percy the pug, however, who had the last bark. When the bag of cookies was offered to him he sniffed, clutched the bag in his teeth and swung it across the Beard kitchen. He knew what *real* cookies should taste like.

Here is an example of what Beard considered the real thing—plate-sized crispy cookies made with plenty of butter.

1 cup (1/2 pound) butter   *2 1/2 cups flour*
1 cup sugar
1 cup smooth or chunky
  peanut butter

Cream together the butter and sugar until light and fluffy; add the peanut butter and flour and mix thoroughly. Scoop up the mixture in lots of about 1/3 cup and drop on a well-buttered cookie sheet with plenty of room between mounds. When you have 12 mounds, dip the bottom of a 9-inch pie plate in sugar and press each mound firmly, flattening to form 6-inch cookies. Bake in a 375 degree oven for about 15 minutes. Remove from the oven and allow at least 5 minutes before carefully lifting with a wide spatula or egg turner, so they won't break.   MAKES 12.

11

NAME ABOVE THE TITLE

Long ago Paul Child told me that he and Julia were always impressed by the entourage that followed their friend Jim wherever he went; there seemed always to be acolytes with him, or "minor experts," as Paul said. With all his friendliness there was a somewhat muted regal air about Jim. When he'd been a guest of the Childs and sleeping in a room in the next house, Paul remembered him at breakfast time "sailing slowly across the way enveloped in a Japanese kimono, looking like a balloon jib." It was a phrase I didn't forget, and it reminded me of Joe Baum's image of Beard at the Baum country house "walking down by the pond in the morning in a green silk robe and a tasseled cap."

All of us who knew Jim in our various ways saw him as someone set apart. Sam Aaron, his intimate friend for forty years, thought of him as unique: "In art there was Picasso," Sam liked to say extravagantly; "in science, Einstein; in wine, Schoonmaker; in food, Jim. Jim was the trailblazer of American cooking." His peers in the food establishment all saw him not only as the one person who had contributed the most to the new gastronomical awareness but as a human being in a class by himself. "He was a mixture of masculine and social style," Baum told me. "There was a sure sense of style there—like listening to a great artist; Jim never worried about whether he was making the note. He just went on with his role." No wonder the food world followed him, or beat a path to his door.

From Richard Olney there had come a letter to the Beard house in New York after Jim had reviewed *The French Menu Cookbook,* citing the author as the only other American besides Julia Child to have "absorbed the essence of France and its cooking." In a note of thanks, Olney was grateful for Jim's public generosity because, he wrote, "The tight little island of American gastronomic journalism is, as I understand it, highly competitive and newcomers are not always welcomed with open arms." Jim's welcome of the Olney book was followed sometime later by Naomi Barry's article in the *International Herald Tribune* in which she augmented the Beard estimate; and her piece asserted that the book has "hoisted Richard Olney into the class of Julia Child, James Beard, and Craig Claiborne." Jim, again, had started the ball rolling, and for Olney's next book, *Simple French Food,* there was an introduction by Beard.

There is criticism that he spread himself too thin—too many introductions of other people's books, too many blurbs praising the work of others, too many commercial endorsements of such products as cookware and stoves, wine, flour, nuts, spices, chocolate, frozen vegetables, and meats. His defense was that he needed money, yes—also that he tested and approved each product, and that he refused many offers. A secretary said he turned down $100,000 from Aunt Jemima because he found the pancake mix not good enough.

He had been out there first and, with the precedent established, he had no reason to follow his friend Julia's decision never to lend her name to endorsing products or writing blurbs for other books. Like Jim, the Childs appreciated Richard Olney's talents, and they were also among the visitors who climbed to his eyrie, and Julia called attention to his creative cooking. Jim's endorsement included welcoming Olney among the teachers who had periodic stints in the James Beard Cooking School, by now an institution almost thirty years old.

There were occasional problems with the school—it was the ménage that much of the time seethed with temperamental differences. "Sometimes my house is like a Byzantine court," Jim said more than once. The home-base entourage was a floating, erratic population with Gino and Clay as permanent fixtures (although Clay, prone to cutting corners, had once been fired in one of Jim's furies). Betty

Ward, having quit over the salary dispute, had been replaced by a neighbor named Emily Gilder, an American caricature of his mother, whose gruff, teasing humor often sparked contention with whatever staff member might be present. The intrigues that Jim labeled Byzantine began to be more noticeable when Carl Jerome moved in, and Jim, in his seventies, fell in love—his senses closed to critical vibrations. Carl aimed to be his benefactor's alter ego, and he came close, as he alienated the ménage as well as friends of a lifetime.

How can you? Mary Hamblet wrote. How can you let him destroy the friendship we've always had? By most accounts of the Jerome relationship, Jim was besotted—he'd always had an eye for

pretty boys, old comrades said. Aging, and worn-out now, he was titillated by the presence of youth. Carl got him to take up smoking cigarettes again, and to dress in blue jeans and T-shirts broadly striped in horizontal bands of primary colors and white. Now, friends say, Jim told stories of using drugs in Chinatowns he'd frequented, and in Morocco and Hong Kong. It also seemed to please him that Carl  manifested respect for his knowledge and was outwardly solicitous of his well-being. When others of the household made themselves scarce to get away from Carl's domineering presence, Jim appeared to take little notice. Jerome was good at organization, helpful at cooking school administration; and as long as travel arrangements went smoothly, Jim ignored the veiled reactions of friends.

Specifically, friends thought that Jerome wanted absolute control over Jim. They complained that Jim's lifelong enthusiasm for telephone contact with the outside world was deliberately being thwarted by Jerome. Beard's name had always been in the book, to be found by anyone who wanted to speak to him; but the pleasure Jim had had in picking up the phone with the chance to rescue a stranger in her faraway kitchen was gone—Jerome saw to it that he himself screened all calls. Not only was it more seldom that a frantic cook

received Jim's reassuring advice, his close friends often were required
to chat with Jerome before getting through to Jim.

In the Byzantine circle, Carl's effect on José Wilson kept her
away for days at a time, although she continued to shape the newspaper columns from tape-recorded discussions. Of them all, she had
known Jim the longest, back to the days before Gino even, when Jim
and Isabel Callvert had started doing articles for *House & Garden*. On
her good days José still reminded Jim of the English beauty she had
been when she had first worked as a magazine editor. She knew him
as a young sister knows a mulish sibling, and she could josh him,
"Come on, Jim—you don't mean that!" She was his writing partner,
and many of the good ideas were triggered by José. She helped to
organize his thinking on the big books to come, and she put together
his *Beard on Food,* ostensibly a mere catch-all of columns; but in the
hands of José, with editorial help from Knopf, the volume tempts
comparison with *Delights and Prejudices.* It is a circuitous journey
through the joys and predilections of his later years that is studded
with recipes, memories, and comments.

Here is James Beard, Greenwich Village householder, planning
how many guests he can squeeze in for a Christmas breakfast, or
asking a friend to come in advance, "sitting around my kitchen table,
shredding away and talking," to help make a pork rillette for the
holiday sideboard. Here's Jim with a dozen friends and with mag-

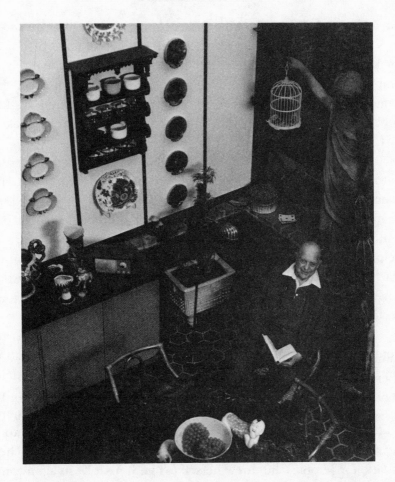

nums of champagne, remembering his father's hankering for both cream and Roquefort cheese as accents on a wedge of mincemeat pie. He describes a workday when Emily Gilder offered to run out at lunchtime and bring him a pumpernickel sandwich filled with smoked salmon, Russian dressing, red caviar, and onion—one of the best snacks he can remember. He gives glimpses of shopping at Balducci's and the Jefferson Market.

The household marketing, as well as that for the cooking classes, was the chore of Clay Triplette, and it made him the provisionary ambassador, the staff member whose diplomacy with butchers and grocers made life more comfortable. Clay was the household's butler when the occasion called for it, and his dimpled greeting of students and guests cheered the moody and the shy. He made newcomers to the school feel at ease, watching and encouraging their progress when they were cooking. It was he who kept a dozen pots of water boiling at the pasta party Knopf sponsored in the Beard kitchen for the publication of *Beard on Pasta.* Jim had insisted that every guest get the fettuccini or linguini or rotelle, whatever had been ordered, freshly cooked. (Clay made a hero of his employer, and women were as taken by Clay's charm as they were by Jim's.)

Carl Jerome had a calculated amiability to use when he chose, but his inclination was to dominate everyone in the household. His usurpation of José's work in promoting and managing the James Beard Cooking School failed to eliminate her entirely from participation in classes, and she was there when Richard Olney (in America to help his books' sales by giving demonstrations) was asked by Jim to teach in the school. Once more, Jim's health had interrupted work schedules, and his kitchen was being used for instruction by various protégés.

He described things to Marion Cunningham. As he listened from his bed he could hear that classes "are going great. Madhur Jaffrey has two evenings, John Clancy has two evenings, Julie Dannenbaum one morning and soon Richard Olney will have a week of morning and evening classes." When he arrived in Jim's tension-ridden forum, Olney was faced with José, who was drinking more heavily than usual because of the obvious friction. In response to her distaste for Jerome, she threw herself (while Jim sat by in agony and concern for her) at the wrong person.

For the rest of her life, Jim would be "concerned" about José, but there had been many in his career who had aroused his paternal regard, and there were intrigues more resonant than unrequited love. With the arrival of Burt Wolf after years abroad, Jim had become involved in another facet of the so-called food revolution that was now more than ever being talked about. Wolf had yet to be recognized by food people as a man to be watched. With wily charm, Wolf established his hold when Jim heard Burt's story of playing in his grandmother's cookware shop in much the way Jim had crawled around in Let's kitchen.

Beard was easily persuaded by Wolf's interest in importing high-quality kitchen knives to compete with the stainless-steel knives that unknowledgable Americans still preferred because they were easy to keep clean. Beard had a principal role in *House & Garden*'s book *The Art of Carving*. He was continuously pointing out that knives, next to hands, were a cook's most important tools, and he sent Wolf to consult with Elizabeth David, who was an expert on European manufacturers of cutlery. Ever since the literary critic Bernard De Voto had published an essay called "The Paring Knife at the Crossroads," Jim had been speaking up, to those who would listen, for better kitchen blades.*

It was Wolf's recent involvement in international investments, however, that was most important in the events that began to develop for Jim. When Wolf brought the designer Milton Glaser to lunch with Jim at Trattoria da Alfredo, one of Beard's favorite Village spots, the three were so beguiled by each other and by Wolf's assurances of financial backing for a new kind of venture into the United States food market that a corporation, "Beard-Glaser-Wolf," was formed, and their great success, *The Cook's Catalogue*, was soon on the drafting table.

It was a project timed for what Craig Claiborne termed "a beautiful revolution." No longer considered the most demanding of household chores, cooking was taking on glamour. The misnamed "gourmet cooking" of the midsixties had been transformed from hobby status to a "creative" activity for those who, status aside, found honest pleasure in the kitchen. There were opinion polls indicating that average citizens were planning to spend more on entertaining at home, with better cuts of meat, more interesting side dishes. Earle MacAusland, thirty years after the founding of *Gourmet*, told *Forbes* magazine that men deserved the credit for the new enthusiasm. Jim Beard looked around and found in the New York area alone more than a hundred cooking schools in competition with his—and the proportion of male students was close to 50 percent.

---

*De Voto's sharp-edged call to arms had reached the then unknown Julia Child in Paris, and she sent over a carbon steel knife to show her appreciation for the essay. A correspondence developed between De Voto's wife, Avis, and Mrs. Child, and the two became such friends that Mrs. De Voto was the person to finally find in Knopf a publisher willing to take on, as the first serious manual on French cookery, the manuscript that became *Mastering the Art of French Cooking*. The editor was Judith Jones, who had persuaded Beard to write the highly successful *Beard on Bread*. From that point on, he and Julia Child had the same editor.

With his forays into the hinterlands continuing, the signs that the catalogue could fill a need seemed undeniable, and the project did just that. The finished volume was a 500-page magazine-sized hardcover book, offering 4,000 retail items described by the jacket copy as "a selection of the best, the necessary, and the special in kitchen equipment and utensils." It included copperware of the kind Jim had had to buy in France in his youth, and every kind of device to tempt an earnest cook. The sales of the catalogue inspired new notions of power and fame, and Jim was lured into thinking of himself, after the early books he had done sans royalty, as a publisher instead of a contract player. He may have forgotten that he had rationalized his acceptance of a flat fee for *The Fireside Cook Book* on the basis of gaining more name recognition. Now a new dimension seemed to be added to his hard-won renown, and Jim was persuaded that Beard-Glaser-Wolf could lure the best-known food writers into its net. A sly letter went out over his signature to such authors as Madhur Jaffrey, who had just established herself as the leading authority on Indian cooking. She was offered the lure of a television series if she would commit her future books to B–G–W; a reasonable advance was suggested but no share in the royalties. Had Jim forgotten how bitter he felt when sales of *The Fireside Cook Book* soared, leaving him with no monetary share to augment his flat fee?

When Judith Jones, as his editor at Knopf, had confronted Jim with the letter, she reported that he had assured her he knew nothing about it: "When I answered, 'That's what Nixon keeps saying about Watergate,' he couldn't look at me, and I saw there were tears in his eyes."

The catalogue's editorial staff had been dominated by a woman, introduced to Jim by Wolf, who was to have a greater effect on him than anything else related to the misbegotten partnership. She was Barbara Poses Kafka, a magazine writer who may have known more at the time about courts of intrigue than she did about the world of food. Kafka and Beard erupted in sparks on first contact. Barbara, in characteristic style, according to Wolf's account, "went crazy defending things that were indefensible, and Jim, in a bitchy mood, stood fast, shooting her down." But Barbara Kafka was formidable (like his mother), and Jim saw at once that she was quick-minded and creative. And he admired her brassy confidence—she was the tough competitor that he sometimes thought he would like to be himself. "In my next life," he told Judith and me one day, "I'm going to be lean and mean."

He loved to see the wheels go around, and watched with submerged delight as contention flared up between staff members. He had recommended to Jane Montant that she send *Gourmet*'s neophyte editors to John Clancy's cooking classes, and he had suggested to Time-Life that Clancy be hired as chef of the book project's test kitchen. But as Clancy prospered Jim began to resent his friend's loss of modesty; his jealousy increased and he refused to go to the restaurant that a few years later gave Clancy's name a degree of fame. Whether or not he admitted it, Jim didn't want his courtiers to get too big.

Meanwhile his suggestion that Marion Cunningham brush up on Fannie Farmer had resulted in Knopf contracting with her to collaborate on *The Fannie Farmer Cookbook* for the twelfth revision of the classic which had always been Beard's favorite basic book. Unfortunately, during the forties and fifties it had increasingly become a conglomeration of quick and easy box-top recipes, so it was high time for a revised edition to bring the original Farmer standards up to date. With Jim as the gray eminence, and with Judith's support, Marion Cunningham worked hard to bring new life to Fannie, while also deeply involved in Beard's activities on the West Coast. She became, most poignantly, the colleague upon whom he depended as the indentured nurse who would change the bindings on his vascularly damaged legs.

Beard and Marion Cunningham shared the decade as teacher and pupil even though he frequently left her to deal with Barbara Kafka's sharp-tongued superiority. In spite of his misdemeanors both women were, each in her own way, devoted to him. Marion was his liaison with most of his California colleagues, and instrumental in the classes that were held for nine years in the Stanford Court Hotel. Cunningham and Chuck Williams were both important in registering students, and Nassikas provided Beard with a suite for weeks at a time;

in addition Nassikas turned over the daytime use of the Fournou's Ovens restaurant for the classroom installation of the Corning smooth-top cooking units Jim enthusiastically endorsed.

The friendship with James Nassikas echoes others Jim had with married men. Beard and Nassikas, like Beard and Baum, were bonded in the constant search for quality. Jim recognized Stanford Court as a hostelry that was admirably elegant and homelike, and he identified with it—contributed to its singular reputation as a hotel famous for its food. One example may suffice. "I picked up the phone in my office," Nassikas recalled, "and it was Jim asking me to come to his suite at once. He had a handful of fresh peas. 'Eat one,' he said. They'd been sent to him by Dr. Calvin Lamborn, the University of Idaho botanist. He was the progenitor of sugar snap peas. That night we served edible-pod peas at a large dinner party—first time they were ever served."

As Nassikas's guest, Beard helped to draw many patrons to Stanford Court, and among them was Nassikas's great movie-star companion, Danny Kaye, whose talents as a cook were known in the inner circle. Beard admired Kaye's mastery of Chinese cooking, although he didn't feel easy in repartee with the glib-tongued entertainer. Together with Nassikas, they met often at Johnny Kan's Grant Avenue restaurant, and here Jim Beard had the upper hand because he and Kan "treated each other like cousins." All of them came together in New York when Danny Kaye was the star of *Two by Two* on Broadway.

Beard and Nassikas traveled in Europe together. They visited restaurants like Giradet in Switzerland. Jim knew the best hotels on the Continent as he knew restaurants. He was a friend of Charles Ritz and had been his guest. He had taught American cooking in Venice's Gritti Palace, headed tours of British Isles inns and German spas.*

---

*Among friends who lived in Europe there seemed always to be many who provided welcome breaks in his schedule. After Marcella Hazan began her cooking school in Bologna, Jim looked forward to attending one of her classes and despite a serious operation in the late spring of '77, he showed up in June in her Bologna school kitchen in a new broadly striped red-and-white gondolier's shirt. He was under strict orders from his doctor not to eat salt so Marcella carefully cooked separate saltless dishes for him. But the day she brought forth her spicy fish soup, Jim spurned his unseasoned portion, grabbed the big bowl in the center of the table, and ate with such relish, Marcella recalled, that soon the soup was all over his red and white shirt. No one else, she added firmly, had "the

He loved to be in a high-powered automobile on a twisting European road, and he would urge on to maximum speed whatever friend might have been driving. "He kept elbowing me and crying, 'Faster! Faster! Pass that car!' " Marion Cunningham reports of a trip on the Italian Riviera when she was his chauffeur.

Among the pleasures of his friendship with the New York cooking school teacher Peter Kump was an invitation to bring Marion on a visit to a Tyrolian castle not far from Innsbruck. It had been constructed during the Middle Ages and overlooked two main roads between Rome and Germany. It was owned by Kump's father, an architect, and he had seen to it that modern amenities were installed; but the fact that the medieval kitchen remained unchanged fascinated Beard, and he noted that the great fireplace was huge enough to roast a whole ox. As a former California theater owner, Peter Kump was able to provide medieval costumes in which his guests dressed while listening in the great hall to a concert broadcast from nearby Salzburg. In baronial garb (his garment was too small to be fastened in back) and surrounded by the sounds of Mozart, Jim gave Marion the feeling that the ambiance was just about right.

Usually he was treated like a prince, as he expected to be, but when he and Marion Cunningham arrived at Michel Guérard's spa, Les Prés d'Eugénie, east of the Basque country, she found him unhappy, as she wrote in her diary, "because he had not received the attention a celebrity deserves. He is always measuring his success, never a static thing—struggle never ends." His damaged pride, however, was quickly assuaged when Jim and Marion were invited to the Guérard home for (as she noted) a "spectacular" lunch that included "pâté with a marmalade of onions."

In the last years he was as often on the way to an airport as he'd ever been. With a dozen food writers he made a flight to Australia and toured Hunter Valley vineyards, whose chardonnays, semillons, and cabernets were just beginning to be available in wine shops across the United States. In London one more time, he had Jerome as a

---

emotion, the abandon about food that Jim did." No doubt, what he learned about how cooks in northern Italy make and embellish their pasta enriched his own book on the subject, *Beard on Pasta* (Knopf, 1983). "But we're Americans," he told his readers. "We don't have to do things the classic way. We can do as we please."

companion, but Carl had become attracted to an Englishman. When they were back in the States, and when Jim was once more hospitalized, this time in San Francisco's Presbyterian, he got Carl's announcement that he was moving to London. Nobody had any certainty about his inner feelings—as much as anything, Jim knew now how tired he was.

Spells in hospitals had become almost commonplace in his life. In the hands of one doctor after another, he had been treated for heart disease, and had submitted to gastrectomy, as well as treatment of varicose veins. He had made himself a man of enormous willpower. As just one of those who witnessed his singular mixture of courage and stamina, Bettina McNulty wrote to me about seeing Jim once more when he was ensconced at the Childs' La Pitchoune. "Shortly after we arrived, Jim slipped in his bath and an awful, awesome hematose developed. He only *permitted* a doctor to come some days later, and by that time it was enormous, painful to a degree, and he was immobile. Henry and Nick [Lettunich] had to deal with his practical needs."

His doctor put him into New York Hospital as soon as he got home, and among his immediate visitors were Cecily Brownstone and her friend Lydie Marshall, who was working on a cookbook. "We went to bring him some cheer, and found him sitting up in bed surrounded by flowers," Lydie Marshall said later. "I thought how great to meet a great man—lunch had been sent by The Four Seasons, the phone rang constantly. It was—I don't know—like meeting a movie star. I said some-thing—it made him instantly laugh. Right away we hit it off, and a month later Cecily invited him to dinner with Gino and Richard [Nimmo], and us. Gino was impossible, and when I let him have it, Jim laughed and laughed. He didn't want you to know how sick he was."

His health had reached a stage in which he couldn't function without someone around to help when he was in trouble. And yet it was his ability to disguise his inner feelings that served him, even with some close friends. "He was always cheerful and glorious company," Bettina wrote. Others who had long periods of observing him every day emphasize the dark side. His depressions often closed in on him; the deafness that afflicted his seventies increased his irascibleness, and he took refuge in it when he didn't want to communicate.

The damage that he pushed aside at the departure of Carl

Jerome was somewhat obscured by the presence of Richard Nimmo. He was a graduate of Juilliard with a yen to cook and had been hired by Jim on the spur of the moment to augment the cooking school staff. With a private life of his own, Nimmo took on the role of professional factotum in New York, and he became Beard's equerry on the continuing travels.

While James Beard's *Theory & Practice of Good Cooking* was being pondered and put down on paper ("really José's book," Nimmo says), Beard persisted in his on-the-road life. With Richard he continued the periodic appearances at food contests of the kind for which he'd been acting as a judge since the early Pillsbury Bake-Offs and the Delmarva Chicken Fries on Chesapeake Bay that had attracted thousands of cooks from every state in the union. His San Francisco friend Chet Rhodes of the Fisherman's Wharf Association had lined him up as well to serve as arbiter—with his friend Philip Brown and others—of the National Crab Cooking Olympics that drew competitive chefs to San Francisco from places as far away as Honolulu, Anchorage, and Miami.

Beverly Allen, who handled the press for the Delmarva festivals, was one of Jim's friends who had been among the first to recognize his gifts as a judge of cooking. "Jim was very definite," Mrs. Allen recalled. "He looked for the way a thing was cooked—texture, appearance, originality. He was very gentle—unlike the self-important food people today, he wasn't pushy." He knew what a judge should know, could play the role without makeup. Not surprisingly, the word most often used by others who were judges too was "wonderful." "Fantastic palate," as Mimi Sheraton says, "when most true to himself."

Whatever it was that drove Jim, whether genie from a bottle or sheer escapism, he turned down few junkets. Mushrooms always attracted him, had since his Oregon youth; and the locus might be as affluent-suburban as a patch of woods near a Cincinnati friend's house, where he is remembered for the aromatically seasoned puffballs that he sautéed for exhilarated fungus-hunters. Or, as it happened in 1977, the mycological event of his life could take him back to the Willamette River Valley. He's famous around the Linn-Benton College campus as having been a headliner when mycologists from several nations gathered in Jim's home country for a symposium entitled "Mushrooms and Man." He was there for the mushrooms, of course. But he was also on hand as a local boy who had made good on a footing with scholars, despite having been denied a college education.

The event was significant enough for *House & Garden* to send Bettina McNulty to cover it on special assignment, and it was offbeat enough for him to bring along Richard Nelson, one of the Gearhart group who was beginning his own teaching career. They used up sixty pounds of freshly gathered regional mushrooms to show the range of gastronomic possibilities for the benefit of botanists and other scientists. There were recipes that included Alice Toklas mushroom sandwiches made to "taste like chicken," and one for stuffing mushroom caps with minced olives and garlic "as created by Albert Stockli at his lakeside house."

The "science" of food was too closely linked, in Beard's usual thinking, to what he called "home-eckery." However, his own health problems (plus the ability to get along on little sleep, which encouraged his voracious reading habits) stepped up his analytical interest in serious books on diets, most of which he found lacking. He had kind words for Michel Guérard's *Cuisine Minceur,* but in general he ignored the tomes on weight loss because he thought they brought readers a sense of being doomed to a future of self-denial and unpalatable eating.* In his seventies, in spite of lifelong tendencies to break even his own rules, he showed interest in the work of Dr. Keith Cohn, co-director of San Francisco's Pacific Medical Center, who was attending the cooking classes at Stanford Court. They discovered their mutual interest in Chinese cooking was reason enough for lunching together as Jim told stories of Portland's Chinatown and Johnny Kan, and Cohn shared with Jim his dedication to healthy eating.

When Cohn's *Coming Back: A Guide to Recovering from Heart Attack* was published in 1979, it gave no recipes, but Jim used it as a subject for a column because Cohn, as a part of his analyses of diet problems, had taken recipes from Beard's Stanford Court classes and cooked them again in his own kitchen, substituting low-cholesterol

---

*An exception is *Craig Claiborne's Gourmet Diet,* written in collaboration with Pierre Franey and Jane Brody. The basic premise is that the good life is killing us, and this, of course, came close to being Beard's biggest personal problem.

ingredients. Jim developed a personal, relaxed approach to dieting. ("Food was a center of gravity for him," Cohn told me.) Jim had a lifetime of respect for herbs and spices as seasonings, but now he began to use out-of-the-ordinary combinations of root vegetables, leaving out salt almost entirely. (He served the most magnificent Sunday luncheon dish for Gino, Julia and Paul Child, and ourselves, by stewing oxtail with seven underground vegetables, including parsley root.)

Cohn's view seemed to suggest that Jim was his own best diagnostician. He refused to deny life. He would follow medical instructions up to a point—when he believed himself to be devoted to a salt-free diet he might be caught eating saltine crackers. For a period he observed a wine-only regime, but occasionally sneaked a shot or two of Glenlivet, his favorite drink. On one of the last birthdays before the big eightieth bash at The Four Seasons in New York, eddies of friends swirled around him in his New York hospital room, balloons floating, bottles popping (at least for the guests), and Seppi Renggli, the gifted chef, arrived bearing a meal prepared as the result of his consultation with the hospital dietician.

Blessed with a natural gift that he had long ago labeled "taste memory," Jim was enough stimulated by his diet restrictions to urge guests and students alike to do more thinking about eating. Good food deserves to be tasted was his maxim, and he took note of a new awareness as Americans continued to show more curiosity and to seek out better food in public places as well as on their own tables. They had the word of scientists that taste nerves on the tongue and palate, and other parts of the mouth, send messages to the brain, and that tactile nerves sense texture, olfactory nerves detect odors, and optic nerves pick up appetizing appearance.

It was Jim's idea to add tasting classes to the school's curriculum.*

---

*Since his own early discovery of taste memory, he had occasionally pondered its physiological definitions, and once he and I discussed Henry T. Finck's *Food and Flavor,* because its author, a sometime music critic, had grown up in Oregon in much the same way as Beard. I thought Jim must have come across Finck's study of gastronomy, especially his analyses of taste as a part of understanding eating. Jim had read Finck, and he said to me: "That man had one terrific idea—he believed as I do, that it's not enough to teach children how to cook. We should take food seriously enough to teach everybody how to *eat,* how to savor what we eat."

He had told readers of his *Theory & Practice* that he discovered "all kinds of things about flavoring I never knew before" as a result of his no-salt, low-caloric diet, and so he wanted all those interested in food to find out for themselves how things really taste. "We finally thought up 'tasting' classes," he said, "as a route to real sharing." His students tasted thirty-two different vinegars at a sitting, compared nut oils with vegetable oils (even grape seed oil), and sampled many mus-tards as they learned the basics of tasting. In this challenging process they discovered more about their senses, more about what to do with flavors, good and bad. "If your horsy winter carrots seem a bit blah," the master pointed out, "don't automatically head for the spice shelf or the salt: try puréeing them with beets."

He was no vegetarian, but vegetables were increasingly on his mind as he grew older. In his column he pointed out that the skins of vegetables shouldn't be overcooked—nor should they just be thrown away. In fact, he'd come up with the then-novel idea of potato skins to be served crisp and crunchy as if they were the traditional potato chips. Cut the skins of baked potatoes in inch-wide strips, he said. Put them on a baking sheet, brush them with lots of melted butter, then sprinkle them with salt, freshly ground black pepper, a little Tabasco, and bake them in a 475 degree oven for four or five minutes. The idea soon went commercial and was a success in bars across the country.

In his final work, *The New James Beard,* he wrote, "I think I've provided here more, and more various, vegetable recipes than appear even in exclusively vegetarian cookbooks." And he taught his students to start learning about vegetable possibilities by tasting them raw, and to keep tasting at intervals during the cooking, as a means of informing themselves. "I wonder how many centuries it took," he wrote, taking notice of the new American appreciation, "for us to forget and then, only recently, to discover how good most vegetables are." Scathingly, he referred to the recent past, "when every restaurant in the country served forth a most boring combination of sliced carrots and fresh, frozen, or canned peas that was one of the most grim mixtures ever conceived."

Yet, admitting to an old prejudice about vegetarian restaurants, he went with an open mind when Marion Cunningham led him to "the place San Franciscans are talking about, and going to, called Greens." For some years he had been aware of the nearby Tassajara Monastery and its bread bakery, and he was interested in this youthful community whose philosophy urged the gathering and cooking of food as celebrations of life. His commitment to American history, and to food as a factor in it, raised the comparison between colonial New England austerity (and the denial of any pleasure to be found in eating) and a new generation's joyful appreciation of natural food.

He seldom expressed his inner sense of the serenity to be found in cooking, but many who speak of Jim today cite the fun he made obvious when he kneaded bread using only his right hand effortlessly or when he whipped egg whites so stiff and then raised them aloft showing how they wouldn't slide from a container held upside down. Vegetarian he was not, but he could be lyrical about a garden's yield. From Nantucket he had written to Helen Brown of "spectacular" peas produced in seashore soil, "as tender and melty as you ever find." He had cooked them, he said, with hardly a touch of salt because the salt air seemed to flavor vegetables beyond need for other seasonings.

Jim said José Wilson tracked down a Michigan farm where tiny vegetables could be provided as early as the 1960s, long before they came into vogue, and he shared with his friend Marion Cunningham his enthusiasm for the all-vegetable pizza that was served at San Francisco's Greens restaurant. In his frequent writing about restaurants he told his readers of his friend Alfredo Viazzi's trattoria, a small Village place where he habitually sat at a table next to the storefront window so that he could take in the passing scene, at the same time being hailed by strollers who recognized him. Alfredo, he wrote, was one of those responsible for introducing New Yorkers to pasta primavera, a dish much enthused over at the time by the cognoscenti.

It was simple enough—spaghettini or linguini tossed with the earliest vegetables from the garden—and *The New York Times* had taken note in calling it "by far the most talked-about creation of Italian origin" when it appeared on the menu of Le Cirque, a midtown luxury restaurant. Craig Claiborne had termed it "inspired," describing it as "the collaboration" of Le Cirque's chef and his partner, who had come to Claiborne's Long Island kitchen to demonstrate its mysteries. But according to the painter and amateur cook Ed Giobbi, the two restaurateurs, who were friends, had arrived in *his* kitchen several years earlier. In search of a new recipe, they had been shown by Giobbi how he learned from his Italian family to dress pasta every spring with the first tomatoes and basil fresh from the garden. It was a peasant dish, pasta primavera, and the authentic version, according to Giobbi, called for only tomatoes.

As Jim recognized, the thing that was really new about pasta primavera was that American diners were dazzled to discover that pasta need no longer be stodgy and drowned in sauce but could be transformed into a delicate dish when adorned with freshly picked, lightly cooked vegetables. He was particularly taken by Alfredo's combination, but the to-do over springtime pasta was chiefly interesting because it underscored his belief that there were no new recipes, there were simply variations, and that too often too much was made of changing fashions in food. Alfredo's dishes appealed to him because they were served unpretentiously.*

In articles, he chose almost invariably to review eating places about which he felt generally appreciative. He was more outspoken in conversation, and in dour moods, when his temper flared, he sometimes lashed out. "Pretty crappy," he scrawled on the opening page of a restaurant survey published in *Signature,* the magazine of the Diners Club.† Although the piece refers to Beard handsomely, he didn't resist

---

*There is evidence here of the way in which ethnic culinary ideas become thoroughly American. I'm unable to find any recipe, published in Italy, that is entitled pasta primavera. Giobbi's authority is based on what he learned in the kitchens of two grandmothers living in Italy. As an avid Westchester County gardener, his cooking is dominated by the seasons' produce, and he may be given credit for leading his restaurateur friends, and Claiborne as well, to develop the possibilities of dressing pasta with various combinations of freshly picked vegetables.

†It is interesting to remember that the Diners Club had been established a generation earlier, and that its founders changed life for everybody when it developed the first credit card system, an idea originally limited to the use of eating places.

adding to his pen-and-ink comment: "No one knows what they're saying." And through the paragraphs that followed, he wrote, "This is unadulterated *MERDE,*" and he dismissed a succeeding comment with the word "Bull."

A handful of restaurants—The Coach House, The Four Seasons, Lutèce, Gauloise on Sixth Avenue—could seemingly do no wrong, but Beard considered that part of his function was to speak out on the changing food scene. Surprising everybody by its sudden "discovery" was the American acceptance of the Oriental contributions.

Like John Kan, Jim's Portland "cousin," Cecilia Chiang had been ahead of the rapidly multiplying interest in Chinese food during the seventies and eighties, and she and Johnny were among the top of Jim's lists of priority visits whenever he flew into San Francisco. He had written the introduction to Kan's book, *Eight Immortal Flavors,* and frequently he and Kan joined in arranging Cantonese banquets that often included guests like Danny Kaye, Julia and Paul Child, Jim Nassikas, Chuck Williams, and others. Cecilia Chiang, who serves elegant northern Chinese dishes at her Mandarin Restaurant in Ghirardelli Square, in her close relationship with Jim, took him home for treats like red-cooked pork which she prepared for him in her own kitchen.

The memory of Cantonese Let turning out Occidental dishes in Elizabeth Beard's kitchen may have influenced him some, but in any event, Jim seldom cooked Chinese food for himself. He championed many cooks from Asia, along with the recently imported cooking styles of Hunan, Fukien, and Szechuan that became trendy after 1969. Beard's New York friend David Keh opened the first Szechuan dining room in the United States in 1968, and a decade later Keh laid out plans to conduct a tour of China for Beard, Claiborne, Danny Kaye, and Julia Child, but ran into road blocks when it became impossible to get everybody's schedules to jibe.

In this period, Jim came to hate the trend known as "American Nouvelle Cuisine." He wrote that "they are dreaming up food that is about as American as Peking Duck ... and everybody seems to have a different theory about what American cookery is now all about." Looking askance at what he described irascibly as the new age of cooking schools, he asserted "it appears that the average cook—man or woman—is expected to turn out slices of lobster pâté adrift in a sea of asparagus sauce (complete with a tomato rose), pheasant potpie with a dome of puff pastry and a mousse of watercress." He dismissed the fad that was hailed as "new" American cooking, and in an unrestrained moment, he called it ludicrous to single out restaurateurs or chefs—it seemed that the glamorizing of cooks had gone too far for a tired James Beard. "I have yet to meet any culinary vestal virgins, kings or queens of the food world." But in sum, he said that "we are now in a new epoch of gastronomical excellence," drawing upon the best of the American past and on technological advances as well.

Besides, he could point out that seemingly exotic combinations of flavors weren't something newly introduced, even by the so-called California cuisine. Maybe the combination of oranges and onions raised some eyebrows, but it was an idea made popular back in the thirties by his friend Helen Brown, whose tossing together of California navel oranges and sweet red Italian onions made a piquant salad. His own introduction of fish marinated in grapefruit juice had helped to popularize *seviches,* and one of his favorite vegetables at Trattoria da Alfredo was the lemon-saturated zucchini.

Alfredo, a former Italian actor, thought so much of his friend James Beard that he referred to Jim as *a fuori classe,* above classification. His unpretentious place could seat only about forty, and many who came, to Jim's delight, were such local stars as *New York* magazine critic Gael Greene, with whom Jim founded the highly successful Citymeals on Wheels, which still feeds hundreds of New York shut-ins. Alfredo's was for Jim very nearly a club.* All the regulars saluted him—such theater headliners as James Coco, the singer Bobby Short, the Metropolitan opera director James Levine. One birthday party for Jim at Alfredo's drew the presence of his old Hollywood friend Agnes de Mille.

Jim's admirers were apt to think as often of his passion for music as of his talent for eating prodigiously—one suggested the production

---

*Jim was decidedly not a joiner, and refused to be included in the professional association of cooking school teachers. When he was nominated for membership in the Century Club in New York by William North Jayme, Jim wrote apologizing that he had felt he had to refuse membership in the Players Club, as well as wine societies, because "there is something in my brain that tells me I just don't belong."

Renata Scotto serves up tagliatelli at Lang's party

Craig Claiborne, Jim, James Villas, Roger Yaseen;
(front from left) Marina Polvay and Barbara Kafka

of an opera based on the food establishment, in which Joan Sutherland might sing the role of Julia Child if it were arranged for Pavarotti to take the part of James Beard. In a more serious gambit, George Lang played host at an intimate party at which both Jim and Pavarotti were celebrated guests, and Lang put together a pasta dish bejeweled with caviar which he created in Jim's honor. Jim also applauded the *pennoni* that Pavarotti himself tossed with tuna, anchovies, onion, and tomatoes, and Lang lifted his glass to say, "Don't forget that music and food go together."

It was always a toss-up which rated higher. When we sat one evening in a midtown bar with James Villas, author of *American Taste* and other provocative books, Villas described their comradeship as one more closely bound to music than gastronomy. "Music was really his great love," Villas said. "It was something to go out to dinner with him—he might break out, humming something from an opera. Our last meal together, when I took him in, it was like the entrance of the Pope. The entire restaurant goes silent. Then a woman comes up and says, 'I know how to fry chicken better than you do,' and he just listens. When we get to the table Jim says the doctors are trying to kill him with this diet. 'Won't even let me have wine—will you get me a double malt whiskey?' More than once he talked about hearing Melba's last performance in London. Or how he'd just chatted with Callas the other night. Once he knew I'd just the day before seen *Parsival* and he broke out vocalizing—how Melchior had handled the phrasing after Kundry's kiss. He'd complain about the narrow seats at La Fenice in Venice."

The moods hung on in old age. He was never satisfied with what he'd been able to wring from life. In Bad Homburg, sitting in a park one dreary afternoon, he'd told Bill Fotiades, his photographer, how short of success he felt his life to be. He'd taken Marion Cunningham on long beach walks in Gearhart and talked of how as a child he'd practiced—in solitary strolls—what he would say to famous people when he himself was recognized. "I'm not famous enough," he said plaintively more than once to Marion and others.

He had wanted to be a leading singer in opera. What did he want most? "To be a star," he said. "Name above the title." He worked on, more and more in need of acolytes whose devotion was unimpeachable, but gaining less than he craved in his lifetime pursuit of recognition as a famous American.

Occasionally Jim's spirits were lifted willy-nilly by a pleasant surprise. The Culinary Institute of America, at Hyde Park on the Hudson, was in itself a recognition of Beard's years of urging Americans to take cooking more seriously, and when the CIA's American Bounty Restaurant was opened in 1982 there were chefs in the

graduating class who were soon to open restaurants on their own as disciples of Jim. He was the speaker at the American Bounty opening, and a bust of him was displayed prominently. Earlier Reed College's class of 1924 recognized the degree of fame that had come to him when he was invited to its fiftieth reunion. He still resented what Reed had done to him but he hungered to be recognized for his accomplishments. Yet he ignored the letter from Reed. In her office off the chapel, Florence Layman of the college alumni office said that on the appointed day "he just sauntered up the walk. We saw this great, distinguished gentleman using a cane. He came into the dining room saying something like, 'I'm go-

ing to eat my food.'" He knew why he was there, and he smiled when they gave him the ceremonial doctorate of humanities. But he told Marion Cunningham, "I hope some of *them* are here, so I can show them."

To see his photograph print-ed had become commonplace. To have his face on the cover of mag-azines was something to which he felt entitled—once *Travel & Leisure* put Jim in Santa Claus attire on its Christmas issue; the capricious editor of the monthly called *Cuisine* had the back of his shaved head photographed for the cover to show how indelible his image had become.* Jim Villas, as food editor of *Town & Country,* persuaded him to pose as a chestnut vendor with a sidewalk cart. "Changing clothes in front of the crew was what it might have been backstage at the *Opéra Comique,*" Villas says. "He was like a Wagnerian character—half naked, prancing like a warrior, he was getting so much fun out of it."

Something of the ham was in him whenever he sensed an audience and his friends loved him for those moments. Gael Greene saw him as "Big Daddy," Burgess Meredith told him one mellow evening that he wanted to produce a revival of *The Man Who Came to Dinner* if Jim would do the star turn as Sheridan Whiteside.† And Jim was pleased to be telling cronies that Woody Allen wanted to cast him in *Annie Hall.* He told himself, however, that he was too old to memorize the lines of any role.

A few weeks before his seventy-fifth birthday, he braced himself for an appearance that meant almost as much to him as an Oscar, had he spent his life as an actor. He took a cab uptown to Rockefeller Center, wearing a glen plaid jacket, a ribbon-striped shirt, and an orange bow tie, and rode the elevator to the French Consulate, where his friend Mary Lyons had gathered an admiring group that included his editor, José Wilson, Emily Gilder, Eleanor Lowenstein, Barbara Kafka, Alan Lewis, John Ferrone, and various media representatives. He was ceremonially presented with *Le Médaille d'Ordre du Mérite Agricole,* and as the gold star hanging from the watered silk ribbon was pinned on his lapel, Jim was cited for his World War II United Seamen's Service work in Marseille, his championing of wine on American tables, and his continuing encouragement of French standards in American kitchens. The tears that filled his eyes were dabbed away by Mary Lyons, as Barbara Kafka's small figure pressed against his large

---

*His thinning hair had almost vanished in Jim's fifties, and it had become one of Clay Triplette's duties to keep his boss's head clean shaven. The tonsorial distinction, as John Ferrone suggests, may well have been inspired by the success of Yul Brynner as a matinee idol in the title role of *The King and I.*

†"He could have *been* 'the man who came to dinner,'" Madhur Jaffrey said to me. "He played it all his life."

one in as much of a hug as her arms could manage around his girth. It seems unlikely that he could have been more touched by any other honor.

About this time Jim was deeply affected when a pug dog, to be known as Percival or Percy for short, arrived at 167 West Twelfth Street, and made it known that he'd come to be a member of the family. Percy formed immediate attachments with Clay and all the Beard regulars, and came close to turning Gino into a responsible household member. He was a gift from a Princeton friend, the restaurateur Steven Specter. Jim's way of life had never made it sensible to have a dependent pet, but Percy disregarded such limitations. He made himself comfortable on a stool of his own, one-third the height of his master's stool, as often as possible, and in the end won Jim's heart.

A short time later Jim was dismayed when a scandal broke at the publication of a book by Richard Nelson, whose whole career in food had been nurtured by Jim and, as it developed, the scandal had a questionable reflection on Jim himself. Nelson had been a student as well as an assistant in Jim's school at Seaside and had traveled as companion and aide. Jim had been asked by New American Library to write the introduction to *Richard Nelson's American Cooking*. But as soon as the book was published, there was an outcry accusing Nelson of flagrant plagiarism, and Suzanne Hamlin of the *Daily News* sought the reaction of other food writers.

In her piece, which led the newspaper's "Good Living" section, she pointed out that "Plagiarism and pilfering of recipes are subjects that have long rattled the larders of the food establishment." But no one had gone as far as Nelson in passing off as his own a total of fifty-six recipes, samples of which—in a searing indictment—were reproduced in photographs accompanying the article. Having tacitly given his endorsement of Nelson's work in the introduction, Jim was at a loss to explain.

Granted, most traditional cookbooks were put together with recipes gathered from printed sources, or from files of the author or his friends, in the belief that few if any recipes are original. "But when a good, honest cook," one editor said in reaction, "develops his own version of a dish, he is bound to change an ingredient or a flavoring, and he makes it in his own way in the way he puts it on paper. Recipes per se can't be copyrighted, but the recipe text—the instructions—are the author's own. The trouble in the Nelson case was that he copied verbatim and his chief victim was a highly talented cook and writer who had made a genuine and original contribution in his books."

Jim was quoted as responding, "Morally it is a major thing, although I can tell you that this kind of thing has been going on for years, and it is time something was done to stop it." It was an honest opinion, and although the case was settled out of court, it did establish some new precedents. The International Association of Cooking Professionals, of which Richard Nelson had been president, drew up new guidelines to be followed by the new wave of cookbook writers that had been spawned by the food revolution, and publishers have since, perhaps, questioned more closely an author's sources, or his credentials.

Saddened by the heavy flack that for weeks did not subside, Jim was equivocal. "Legally, there's nothing I can do about this," he told Hamlin, "but I can tell you I feel personally transgressed." It was suggested that there were also some Beard recipes in the Nelson book, picked up at his classes and only thinly disguised. But it was Jim's carelessness in having praised the book so readily, plus his sense of a friendship betrayed, that hurt him most deeply.

The year had been a bad one. Already he had lost his friends Helen McCully and Helen Evans Brown to cancer, and in 1980 after a long struggle with depression, which Jim and other friends had been helpless to alleviate, José Wilson committed suicide. Richard Nimmo called Jim from New York to find him in the company of John Carroll in Gearhart. José had flung herself into an abandoned quarry, and it was clear (when he received her matter-of-fact suicide letter) that no one could have easily deflected her from her intention. Jim slumped where he was sitting, and tears and sobs broke through his control. He was left profoundly depressed. Once he confessed to Marion Cunningham that he'd never been able to love. But inasmuch as he was able to give of himself, he had loved José.

In a farewell column to the readership they had shared, he wrote of the "staggering" loss. "We could laugh our way through almost any difficult situation," he wrote. "Whether we were working at the stove or at the typewriter or traveling. We shared an unforgettable culinary cruise on the *France,* cooked in the kitchen of Fredy Giradet's three-star restaurant in Switzerland, scouted for good food in England and Ireland." And he added, "One always needs a colleague who is caring and honest enough to set his thinking straight." The sorrow in Jim was pervasive.

It cast a pall over the new house on Twelfth Street and on Richard Nimmo, who had been José's confidant. In her demise, Jim reached out for someone to take over José's chore of helping him with the column, and he turned to his friend Jackie Mallorca, another Briton, who wrote Chuck Williams's highly admired catalogues. In New York, he rallied others to help him finish *The New James Beard* for October publication in 1981. It had become obvious that the changes in American food that he had helped evoke were radical enough to warrant reassessment in a summing up of his cooking and teaching career. His sense of taste had changed—as the palate does as one grows older. The reduction of salt intake, for instance, had heightened his awareness of subtler tastes—he was using more fresh herbs. For decades, like a winsome preening child, he had called himself "a butter boy," and now he was exercising a lighter hand with unctuous fats. "The new me had to write a new book," he said. The accumulated ideas, the results of the recent travels across the country, were topped off with Beard's encompassment of new trends.

"He's our Johnny Appleseed of culinary shifts," said Len Allison of Huberts, the New York restaurant that successfully fostered American cooking in its featuring of such classics as Country Captain. As one who loved all food passionately, Beard had never been content to ignore the old or to settle for only one way of preparing a particular dish. Sometimes at lunch, when he sat down with Richard and his secretary Caroline Stuart, who had moved up from being a student in the cooking classes, they would hold a brainstorming session about dishes they were eating. "He would take something like Tabasco—which he really *liked*—and add a bit at a time, seeing what it did to the taste. He was always experimenting with flavor," Caroline says. "Sometimes they became new recipes, sometimes he just liked the changing tastes. The result could be good, or, not acceptable."

The New James Beard, when it appeared, was full of new approaches. Its pages include recipes ranging from yogurt mayonnaise to a Seattle pudding with strawberries in which sour cream gives way to yogurt, or to Felipé Rojas-Lombardi's ribboned eggs. There are sausage-filled croissants for simplicity and surprise, and carrot blini to show off caviar; there are ginger pumpkin soup with slivers of Smithfield ham, and oyster sausages, a *nouvelle* notion but with roots in early New England fishing villages. Characteristic of Jim, he offers a sauce for pasta in which brains and fresh tomatoes are blended. (When a purist questioned Beard about his new free-wheeling attitudes, he repeated his maxim: "We're Americans—we can do as we please.")

This new and final book (profusely illustrated by the action sketches of Karl Stuecklen, whose work had equally enhanced *Beard on Bread* and *Beard on Pasta*) quickly topped the 100,000-copy mark and reviewers praised it. Nowhere was there more affectionate applause than in Oregon, where Jim was teaching when the advance copies arrived in July. He told Yvonne Rothert of the *Oregonian* in a Seaside interview that the new book "moves away from a lot of standard things that have been developed about food. I believe more and more that people should improvise—first, try a recipe as it is, then do it again and make it theirs." Certainly, his thoughts may have included the

Nelson incident, for he added, "We who write recipes are simply crutches—there is no completely original recipe any more, just adaptations of those we already have."

Edging eighty, he was sure that *The New James Beard* would be provocative. "People have no fear," he said. "I had a midnight phone call in New York, someone calling from Oklahoma to say they had reached an impasse in a recipe. I replied, 'If you had used the recipe for the same thing in my book, it would have told you what to do.' I also get calls—since I'm listed in the phone book—from people who say, 'I'm giving a dinner for twenty and I'd like to have you help me with a menu.'"

Menu planning was one of Jim's delights every day of his life. Long ago he had devoted almost four hundred pages to the subject in *Menus for Entertaining,* and he had passed on hints to Marion Cunningham. With his inspiration, she became consultant to the Union Hotel in an artists' colony north of San Francisco, designing a bill of fare to complement the restored Victorian hostelry. Beard had done much to encourage the rejuvenation of inns with architectural charm, and he was keen on menus that accented the American atmosphere—in this case he was keen on the selection of Judy Rogers, a talented young cook who had spent a year as an exchange student in the household of three-star chef Jean Troisgros. It symbolized for him the essence of his career. In his belief in French culinary technique, he'd had much to do with the frequent tours of the United States by France's best restaurateurs, urging that young Americans ground themselves as thoroughly in understanding food as their counterparts abroad were required to do. As he had shown in his sponsorship of Marion Cunningham, he was convinced that cooks in America had equal potential that could result in exemplary culinary style.

In aging, though, his characteristic optimism sometimes gave way to cantankerousness, even in public. In continuing to insist on accepting dates for public appearances, in judging especially, he became unpredictable. In one southern California event with Marion and Richard Nimmo as fellow judges in a fund-raising recipe contest, Jim had been drinking a lot. He announced emphatically that none of the entries was worthy of the prize. "In fact," Marion recalls, "they were all awful, according to Jim. We all tried to cajole him, saying that as judges—we were about five—we had to face up to picking someone's dish, in a charity event there had to be a winner to announce." But Jim dug in his heels even deeper, until there was one last entry. It was ice cream, with a sickly sweet, overwhelming mint-extract flavor. According to Marion, "Jim immediately proclaimed: 'Now this is original. This takes the prize.' No one agreed, but he wouldn't be crossed." With no more reason than the chance he saw, perhaps, to test his power, he insisted on his choice. In deference to his years and reputation, the other judges bit their tongues.

Another year, Nimmo was with him for a Beef Cook-Off in Texas, and Jim's annoyance with the way things went caused him to let off steam. He said there should be a "Society for the Prevention of Cruelty to Innocent Ingredients." He was angry about the dinner menu and the "unbelievable" fillet of beef Theodore; it consisted of fried eggplant shell with a layer of mushroom and tomato sauce, topped with a fillet of center-cut beef that had been stuffed with puréed sweetbreads and wrapped in spinach leaves.

Hurrah for creativity, of course, but. . . . Although he didn't want to discourage young chefs in pursuing the tenets and traditions of American cuisine, "I would counsel some common sense. Otherwise we're going to have some tough sledding to protect our wonderful natural bounty!"

Jim's health was worrying some of his friends, but he didn't let it affect his activity. Agents whose business was arranging endorsements of products were making overtures continually.* He was asked to lend his name and skills to product development, and frequently, Caroline Stuart recalls, "he'd get us all to play around with things like new ideas for salad dressings, and new pasta sauces. But he'd call off the experimenting before a deal got really serious. He seemed to have been not much interested in any of the possibilities—just doing it because it didn't interfere with more important stuff. He was restless all the time."

There had always been something magnetic that pulled Jim into

---

*As the result of having been quoted in an Art Buchwald column as praising a Portland breakfast restaurant, the establishment used his name in advertising. When Jim learned that he was being thus exploited, his lawyer persuaded the proprietor to refrain from using the approval that had been inferred.

orbit, going one way or another. But going. All his senses were aroused early in 1984 when he was asked to be a lecturer on something called a "Great Gourmet Getaway," a twelve-day Alaskan cruise on which he would be accompanied by Richard Nimmo. (Claiborne had agreed to appear also.) In spite of doctors' orders, Jim made up his mind to go, and he argued that he had more than once defied the odds, and he saw no reason why he should turn down the offer. The fact that one or two friends knew he had sworn never to let himself be hospitalized again aroused suspicions of suicidal thoughts. But others believed that it would be simply unlike Jim to reject a new adventure. (As M.F.K. Fisher said perceptively, "Jim always knows just what he's doing.")

Jim Nassikas and John Carroll met his plane in San Francisco, and they found him in a bad mood as Nimmo pushed his chair through the airport crowds. Aboard the *Pacific Princess,* about to sail, he said he didn't like the looks of the people with whom he was to share the cruise, and he and Richard both groused about the quarters they were assigned. To hell with it! Jim decided to make the most of the time that passed in boring surroundings of snow and ice. It was a last fling. Richard, whose own appetite for vodka was often talked about, says that Jim's drinking was out of control, his severe diet scornfully ignored, and he was eating enormous meals, overlooking no temptation in between.

Back in San Francisco, his condition worried all the friends he saw, but there had been so many times before when they had worried that they believed him almost indestructible. Jim *must* know what he's doing. In New York again, he settled back into the routine of his cooking school's fall-winter schedule. And he was lonely when he was left to himself on weekends. He would call Caroline Stuart in Connecticut, morose when she couldn't find time to take him for a country drive—which he loved as he had throughout his life in whatever country he might be in. On Christmas, when Caroline telephoned, he announced that he was spending the day in bed. What he didn't say was that Felipé had made for him an aromatically stuffed ballotine of piglet to eat all by himself.

Gino, still ensconced in the Beard house, was sometimes querulous, often gone-off in petulance. A nearby neighbor, his friend and fellow teacher Lydie Marshall, came to see him every Sunday that he was in town, and she was knitting him a sweater (waist sixty-six inches, she said). On the last Sunday in December, she was talking to him about coming over when the telephone went dead in the middle of a sentence.

Lydie and her husband, Wayne, ran to Jim's house and were let in by the upstairs tenant. "Wayne found him, with the phone dangling—he'd suddenly gone to sleep. But it didn't seem to bother him," Lydie says. "That night he went to The Coach House for dinner."

On the first weekend in January he was alone when he tripped on the cord of a desk lamp and fell to the floor. He called out to Gino, who was walking the dog in the garden. With help from neighbors, Gino got him to his feet, but in spite of a swelling that distorted his face and caused real pain, he refused hospitalization. In a couple of days his heart began to act up and he went across the street for an X-ray. Then, over his continued protests that he wouldn't be hospitalized ever again, he was forced by paramedics to accept an ambulance. In New York Hospital, when put to bed, he looked a little like Gulliver, his outsize body pinioned by captors who refused to heed. He couldn't talk because of the respirator. Friends who came felt helpless as he kept pawing, trying to free himself from tubes. Seppi Renggli, the chef at The Four Seasons who had so often cooked special meals, sent tempting food that the hospital approved; but Jim couldn't eat. Some who came for the brief visits he was allowed thought he had used up the energy to fight back.

He died in the night, on January 23, 1985, of a heart attack, a few weeks short of his eighty-second birthday. His name was not in lights, but his picture was on the front page of *The New York Times*. What he had wanted as much as anything was to go back to Gearhart—his ashes were scattered in the air over the beach where he had played as a child, and where he had learned much of what had kept him alive so long.

Index

Textual Acknowledgments

Photographic Acknowledgments

Photographs reproduced in this book were provided
with the permission of the following:

A NOTE ABOUT THE AUTHOR

Evan Jones was born and educated in Minnesota. His books and articles—in *Gourmet, Travel & Leisure, Americana, The New York Times, Food & Wine,* et cetera—reflect an interest both in the American past and in food. His book *American Food: The Gastronomic Story* was first published in 1975 and was republished in 1990. Other books on food include *The World of Cheese* and *A Food Lover's Companion.* Evan Jones is coauthor with his wife, Judith Jones, of *Knead It, Punch It, Bake It, The Book of Bread,* and *The L.L. Bean Book of New New England Cookery.* They live in New York City and in the Northeast kingdom of Vermont.